BUSINESS PROSPECTS in THAILAND

About the Author

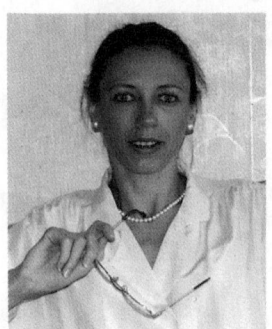

Denise Hall was trained in economics in France and in the United States. She obtained a doctorate in economics from Institut D'Etudes Politiques in Paris and an MA in economics from UCLA in the United States. In 1985, she moved to Hong Kong to teach economics at the University of Hong Kong for several years. Currently, she is involved in consulting work, specializing in Asian markets and advising on business opportunities in Asian markets.

BUSINESS PROSPECTS in THAILAND

Denise Hall

PRENTICE HALL
Singapore New York London Toronto Sydney Tokyo

First published 1996 by
Prentice Hall
Simon & Schuster (Asia) Pte Ltd
Alexandra Distripark
Block 4, #04-31
Pasir Panjang Road
Singapore 118491

 © 1996 by Denise Hall

All rights reserved. No part of this publication may be reproduced, stored in retrieval system or transmitted in any form, or by any means, electronic, mechanical, photocopying, recording or otherwise, without prior permission in writing from the publisher.

Cover illustration by Bertrand Martin

Printed in Singapore

1 2 3 4 5   99 98 97 96

ISBN 0-13-398165-7

Prentice Hall International (UK) Limited, *London*
Prentice Hall of Australia Pty. Limited, *Sydney*
Prentice Hall Canada Inc., *Toronto*
Prentice Hall Hispanoamericana, S.A., *Mexico*
Prentice Hall of India Private Limited, *New Delhi*
Prentice Hall of Japan, Inc., *Tokyo*
Editora Prentice Hall do Brasil, Ltda., *Rio de Janeiro*
Prentice Hall, Inc., *Upper Saddle River, New Jersey*

Contents

Preface _____ xi
Acknowledgments _____ xii
Abbreviations _____ xiii
Trademarks _____ xiii

Chapter 1 Introduction to Thailand _____ 1
  1.1 Thailand's place in Asia _____ 2
  1.2 Geography _____ 6
      1.2.1 Natural resources _____ 7
      1.2.2 Regions _____ 10
      1.2.3 Climate _____ 15
  1.3 The people _____ 16
      1.3.1 Language _____ 16
      1.3.2 Religion _____ 17
      1.3.3 Society _____ 18
  1.4 Political system _____ 20
  1.5 History _____ 21
      1.5.1 The Sukhothai era _____ 21
      1.5.2 The Ayutthayan era _____ 22
      1.5.3 The Bangkok period _____ 23
      1.5.4 Military rule _____ 25

Chapter 2 Life Styles _____ 29
  2.1 Demography _____ 30
      2.1.1 Structure of population _____ 30
      2.1.2 Regional distribution _____ 31
      2.1.3 Health _____ 36
  2.2 Purchasing power _____ 40
      2.2.1 Occupations _____ 41
      2.2.2 Incomes _____ 42
  2.3 Education _____ 48
      2.3.1 Educational attainment _____ 48
      2.3.2 Attendance _____ 50
      2.3.3 Vocational training _____ 52
      2.3.4 School system _____ 55
      2.3.5 Schools _____ 55
  2.4 Living quarters _____ 56

	2.4.1	Housing	57
	2.4.2	Household equipment	60
	2.4.3	Utilities	63
2.5	Recreation		66
	2.5.1	Festivities	67
	2.5.2	Gambling	69
	2.5.3	Sports	70
	2.5.4	Crafts	72
	2.5.5	Leisure activities	74
2.6	Religions		77
	2.6.1	Buddhism	78
	2.6.2	Islam	81
	2.6.3	Other beliefs	82

Chapter 3	Consumption and Distribution		87
3.1	Food		89
	3.1.1	Cereal products and staples	91
	3.1.2	Meat and poultry	92
	3.1.3	Fish and seafood	94
	3.1.4	Fruits and vegetables	96
	3.1.5	Eggs and dairy products	100
	3.1.6	Oils and fats	103
	3.1.7	Sugar and sweets	104
	3.1.8	Spices and seasonings	105
	3.1.9	Prepared meals	107
3.2	Beverages		109
3.3	Tobacco and betelnut		113
3.4	Clothing and footwear		116
	3.4.1	Clothing	117
	3.4.2	Footwear	121
3.5	Medical and personal care		125
	3.5.1	Medical care	125
	3.5.2	Personal care	129
3.6	Housing		132
	3.6.1	Home	133
	3.6.2	Utilities	134
	3.6.3	Furnishing and equipment	136
	3.6.4	Cleaning	141
3.7	Transportation and communications		142

		3.7.1	Public transportation	144
		3.7.2	Personal transportation	147
		3.7.3	Communications	148
	3.8	Recreation		149
		3.8.1	Religious activities and ceremonies	150
		3.8.2	Recreational and electronic equipment	152
		3.8.3	Admissions and reading material	154
	3.9	Distribution		156
		3.9.1	Department stores and shopping malls	156
		3.9.2	Supermarkets and convenience stores	157
		3.9.3	Direct selling	158

Chapter 4	Media and Advertising			161
	4.1	Television		162
		4.1.1	Broadcasting	162
		4.1.2	Audience	166
	4.2	Radio		172
		4.2.1	Broadcasting	172
		4.2.2	Audience	174
	4.3	Publishing		181
		4.3.1	Publications	182
		4.3.2	Readers	184
		4.3.3	Printing	191
	4.4	Cinema		192
		4.4.1	Producers	193
		4.4.2	Audience	193
	4.5	Advertising and public relations		195
		4.5.1	Media	195
		4.5.2	Advertising agencies	201
		4.5.3	Regulations	203

Chapter 5	Production and Trade			209
	5.1	Agriculture, fishery, forestry		211
		5.1.1	Crops	213
		5.1.2	Livestock products	220
		5.1.3	Fishery	223
		5.1.4	Forestry	225
	5.2	Extractive resources		226
		5.2.1	Oil and gas	226
		5.2.2	Lignite	229

	5.2.3	Tin	229
	5.2.4	Zinc	230
	5.2.5	Other minerals	230
5.3	Manufactured products		232
	5.3.1	Food processing	233
	5.3.2	Beverages and tobacco	236
	5.3.3	Textile, clothing, and footwear	238
	5.3.4	Oil and chemicals	240
	5.3.5	Electrical and electronic equipment	244
	5.3.6	Transportation equipment	244
	5.3.7	Gems and jewelry	248
5.4	Construction and building materials		250
	5.4.1	Construction	250
	5.4.2	Building materials	251
5.5	Electricity and water		254
	5.5.1	Electricity	254
	5.5.2	Water	256
5.6	Tourism		257
5.7	International trade		260

Chapter 6   Finance and Real Estate — 267

6.1	Bank of Thailand		267
	6.1.1	Monetary activities	268
	6.1.2	Financial reforms	270
6.2	Banks		272
	6.2.1	Commercial banks	272
	6.2.2	Special-purpose banks	275
6.3	Finance and credit institutions		277
	6.3.1	Finance and securities companies	277
	6.3.2	Real-estate-financing companies	279
	6.3.3	Industrial finance institutions	280
	6.3.4	Mutual fund management companies	281
	6.3.5	Factoring	281
	6.3.6	Cooperatives	282
	6.3.7	Pawnshops	282
6.4	Stock exchange		283
	6.4.1	Trading	284
	6.4.2	Supervision	286
	6.4.3	Getting listed	287
6.5	Raising capital		287

	6.5.1	Debt instruments	288
	6.5.2	Equities	289
	6.5.3	Financing joint ventures	289
6.6	Insurance		290
	6.6.1	Life insurance	291
	6.6.2	Non-life insurance	292
6.7	Real estate		295
	6.7.1	Investors	295
	6.7.2	Market	296

Chapter 7 Transportation and Communications — 300

- 7.1 Maritime transportation — 301
  - 7.1.1 Port of Bangkok–Klong Toey — 301
  - 7.1.2 Sattahip — 303
  - 7.1.3 Laem Chabang and Mab Ta Phud — 304
  - 7.1.4 Phuket, Songkhla, and Si Chang — 305
  - 7.1.5 Shipping lines — 305
- 7.2 Air transportation — 306
  - 7.2.1 Airports — 307
  - 7.2.2 Airlines — 308
- 7.3 Railroads, roads, and waterways — 309
  - 7.3.1 Railroads — 309
  - 7.3.2 Roads — 312
  - 7.3.3 Waterways — 313
- 7.4 Transportation in Bangkok — 314
  - 7.4.1 Roads — 314
  - 7.4.2 Mass transit — 316
- 7.5 Communications — 317
  - 7.5.1 Telephone, radio, paging — 317
  - 7.5.2 Satellite — 320
  - 7.5.3 Computers — 320
  - 7.5.4 Mail — 321

Chapter 8 Doing Business — 323

- 8.1 The business community — 324
  - 8.1.1 The Chinese — 324
  - 8.1.2 The military — 325
  - 8.1.3 The government — 326
  - 8.1.4 Foreign investors — 328
- 8.2 Business practices — 330

	8.2.1	Dealing with the administration	330
	8.2.2	Trading with Thailand	331
	8.2.3	Distributing and sourcing	333
	8.2.4	Thailand as a regional base	334
8.3	Labor		335
	8.3.1	Training	335
	8.3.2	Expatriates	336
	8.3.3	Social coverage	337
	8.3.4	Rights of workers	338
8.4	Regulation of business		339
	8.4.1	Business organizations	340
	8.4.2	Restrictions on foreign investment	340
	8.4.3	Taxation	341
	8.4.4	Price controls	343
	8.4.5	Protection of environment	344
8.5	Facilities for investors		348
	8.5.1	Promotion of investment	348
	8.5.2	Industrial estates	349
	8.5.3	Development zones	350
8.6	Protection of intellectual property		351
	8.6.1	Copyrights	352
	8.6.2	Patents	352
	8.6.3	Trademarks	353
8.7	Tips for business travelers		353
	8.7.1	Etiquette	353
	8.7.2	Business relations	354
	8.7.3	Practical information	355
	8.7.4	Sources of information	356

Appendix 1 — 361
Appendix 2 — 362
Appendix 3 — 363
Bibliography — 367
Further reading — 369
Index — 371

PREFACE

My first contact with Thailand was as a visitor. I wanted to see the kingdom's legendary scenery. I was thrilled by what I saw, but what impressed me most was the economic potential of the country. I found lush farmlands, bustling towns, modern business districts, well stocked shops, elegant boutiques, and open-minded and entrepreneurial people.

I had many more opportunities to appreciate this potential later. While consulting in Hong Kong, I spent much time evaluating the prospects of Asian markets and Thailand figured prominently. I also discovered that information was available, but that it was difficult to obtain and decipher.

Dealings with clients on these issues convinced me that there was a demand for a clear and detailed study of the Asian markets. This was, however, beyond the scope of a single book; I resolved to focus on Thailand. I set to the task with a view of drawing a profile of the country and its people. I inquired into the culture, living habits, consumption patterns, and business practices of the Thais and into the industries of Thailand.

I have relied on many different sources of information, especially surveys and statistical reports published by the Thai administration. This book reports my findings with the use of statistics, verbal descriptions, and anecdotes. Some 150 charts portray the patterns of life in Thailand. My goal is to offer an explanation to these findings, while providing readers with the elements for forming personal judgments about prospects for business in Thailand.

I have tried to record my sources carefully. Thai administrations, however, do not report years of publication consistently and the dates which appear in titles do not necessarily match the dates of publication. This leads to some apparent anomalies in the referencing, but interested readers may find these sources by following the notes in the references.

I have also made every effort to check the accuracy of my results. Mistakes and omissions, however, remain mine and I am solely responsible for the opinions expressed in this book.

Denise Hall

Acknowledgments

The author wishes to thank the following publishers for granting permission to use the sources listed:

Bangkok Post. Use of data on petrol stations published by BANGKOK POST/Thailand Department of Commercial Registration–July 9, 1993. Used by permission of the Editor.

Zenith Media Worldwide. Use of data on media and advertising published by Zenith Media Worldwide, *Asia Pacific Market and MediaFact*, various issues, London. Used by permission.

International Monetary Fund. Use of data on trade, population, exchange rate, and gross domestic product published by International Monetary Fund, *IFS*, various issues. Used by permission of the Copyright Office.

Abbreviations

IFS	International Financial Statistics
MAC	Ministry of Agriculture & Cooperatives
MPH	Ministry of Public Health
OPM	Office of the Prime Minister
SRT	State Railway of Thailand

Trademarks

Bangkok Post	The Post Publishing Public Company Limited.
The Nation	Nation Publishing Group Co Ltd.

1 INTRODUCTION TO THAILAND

Thailand's famed scenery and rich cultural heritage make it a popular tourist destination and a setting for Hollywood fantasies, but these attractions often overshadow the country's economic standing. For some time a world-leading supplier of agricultural and fishery products, Thailand embarked more recently on a bold program of development. Today, it is becoming an industrialized country and its purchasing power, already substantial, is increasing rapidly.

Doing business in Thailand is no longer the prerogative of adventurers, but it still holds many promises. The country's rapid economic growth, cheap labor force, and large consumer market offer potential for investors. In addition, Thailand's location at the heart of Southeast Asia makes it an ideal base for conducting regional business in this economically dynamic part of the world.

Business Prospects in Thailand explains how Thais make money, spend money, how they use their time, and how the economic and business conditions are evolving. This book touches on more aspects of Thai economic, political, and social life than most readers will care to know to evaluate their specific business prospects. However, the book is organized so that readers may skip between sections to extract information easily. It is designed as a reference book, a guide to participating in the expanding Thai economy.

Because it addresses both technical and human issues, this book combines information of various types. Data on economic and social activity assess the progress and potential of Thailand, but more anecdotal reports illustrate the unique features of Thais as consumers and as producers.

Part of this uniqueness results from the interaction between economics and culture. With its strong traditions and rapid development, Thailand is a land of contrasts. The capital, Bangkok, for instance, is a modern city whose shops, department stores, hotels, and restaurants rival those of major cities of the world. Bangkok has one of the best English-language newspapers in Asia and enough cars to make the Los Angeles traffic seem mundane by comparison. The city, however, retains a distinctive Thai flavor.

Everywhere in modern Bangkok, traditions are omnipresent. Temple spires emerge between modern buildings. Monks jostle with business people. Sarong-clad women make offerings to temple gods in the financial district. Luxurious condominiums look over river houseboats. Street vendors and food stalls sell their wares next to boutiques and elegant restaurants.

This continuity of Thai life owes a great debt to the country's exceptional history. Thailand escaped colonization, a rare fate in Asia. This is especially remarkable because all of Thailand's neighbors, Burma, Malaysia, Laos, and Cambodia, were less fortunate. Free from the trauma of colonization, Thais are open to Western ideas and technology, although they adapt them to fit local standards.

Thai politics also has its own pace. The country went from centuries of absolute monarchy to military dictatorship and recently turned democratic. The royalty survived these changes and Thais have maintained an unfaltering awe for their king.

This traditional kingdom is, nevertheless, an active business center. The following sections introduce Thailand from a marketing viewpoint, showing how its peculiarities affect business. They position the country within Asia, review its geography, introduce its people, and outline its political and historical background.

1.1 THAILAND'S PLACE IN ASIA

Investing in Thailand, once the preserve of multinational companies with diversified interests in Asia, is no longer a high-risk operation that requires large financial backing. Thailand is a rapidly developing country. It outperforms many of its Asian neighbors and attracts a steady flow of foreign capital. With its large and young population, increasing income, and expanding international trade, Thailand appeals to entrepreneurs looking for a cheap labor force and a large consumer market.

The Thai labor market offers good prospects. The demographic expansion of the past few decades combined with the high literacy rate guarantees an abundant supply of qualified labor. With about 29 percent of its people aged under 15,[1] Thailand has a younger population than leading Asian powers like Taiwan, Korea, Singapore, Hong Kong, and Japan. Only countries like Indonesia, Malaysia, and the Philippines have younger populations.

The consumer market is also attractive. Thailand's large population offers potential for mass consumption. In 1992, 57.8 million people lived in the kingdom. This is greater than the populations of Singapore, South Korea, and neighboring Malaysia and Burma, for example (see Figure 1.1).

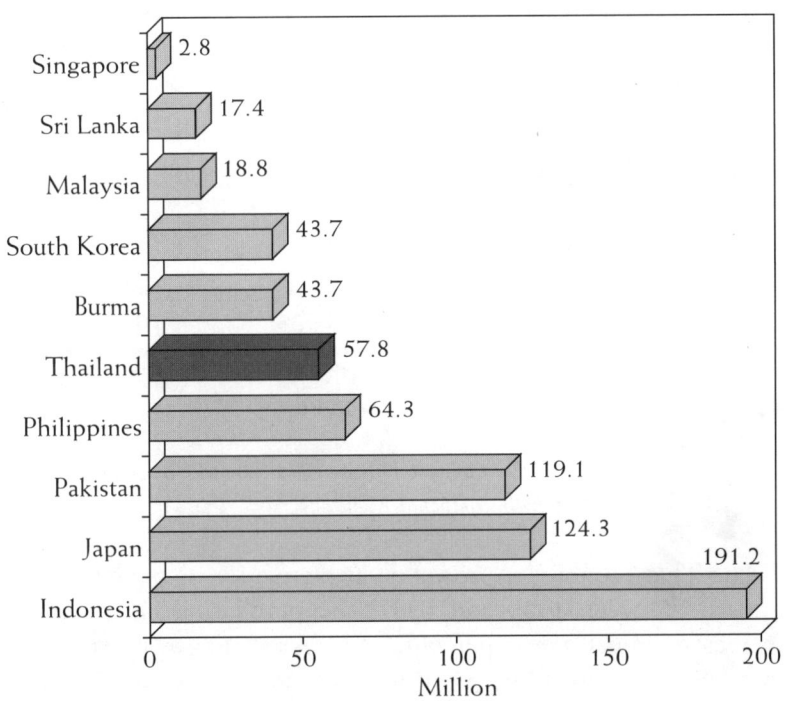

*Figure 1.1   Population of Asian Countries in 1992
(Source: Based on International Monetary Fund, IFS, April 1994.)*

Thailand is no longer a poor country, but it is not wealthy yet. With a per capita gross domestic product (GDP) of over US$1,800 in 1992, Thais are wealthier than the people of India, Pakistan, China, Indonesia, and the Philippines but poorer than the people of Malaysia, Singapore, and South Korea, for example (see Figure 1.2).

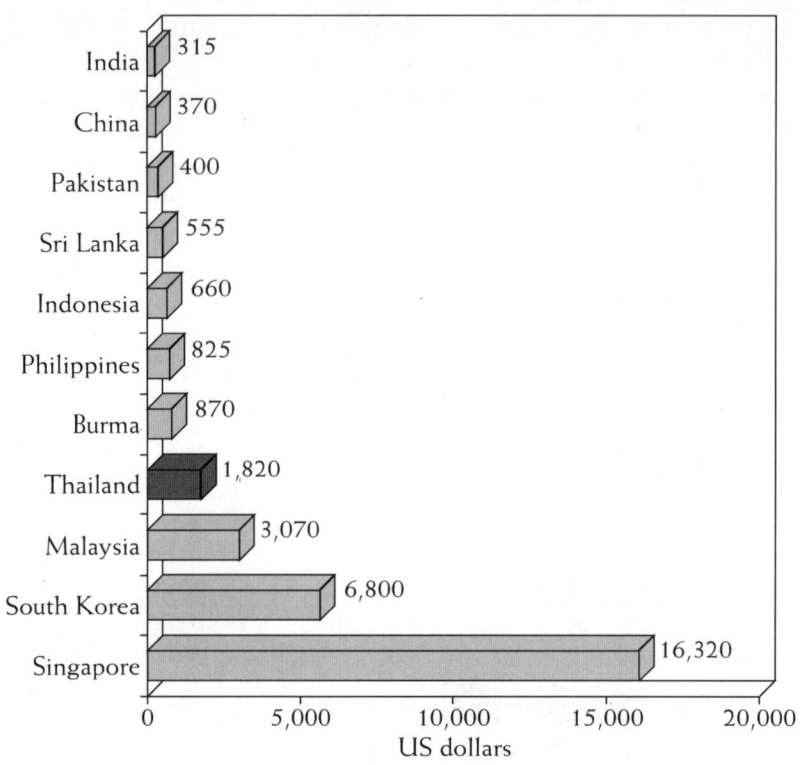

Figure 1.2   Per Capita GDP of Asian Countries in 1992
(Source: Based on International Monetary Fund, IFS, April 1994.)

The Thai economy is, however, attractive for its rapid and steady growth. Between 1980 and 1991, the purchasing power of Thais increased annually by 6 percent. Its growth rate was especially high between 1987 and 1990, when it exceeded 10 percent per year (see Table A.1.1 in Appendix 1). If maintained, such a progression will allow Thailand to catch up with other more-developed Asian countries. Except for Korea, which managed a sustained yearly income growth of over 10 percent during the past decade, the growth rates were much lower elsewhere. They stood at about 6 percent in Taiwan, Hong Kong, and Singapore 3 percent in Malaysia and Indonesia; and 2 percent in Australia and New Zealand.

This growing income is a boon for foreign products. Although consumption remains basic, the market is gradually opening to more sophisticated goods, many of which are not produced locally. Items that were once luxuries such as personal care products are becoming more common while new products and processes are readily accepted by these enthusiastic consumers.

International trade is responding to the economic changes by developing rapidly. Rising incomes fuel the demand for imported goods while growing industrialization increases export potential. Between 1987 and 1992, Thailand's total foreign trade increased by 24 percent per year in real terms, twice the growth rate of the GDP.

The expanding trade bodes well for foreign investors, but it still does not make Thailand a leading trader. Thai international trade remains moderate, especially when compared to the performances of world-leading trading centers like Hong Kong and Singapore. In 1992, with US$32 billion exports, Thailand stood well behind Hong Kong, Taiwan, South Korea, and Singapore (see Figure 1.3). As an importer, Thailand is not a leader either. With US$41 billion imports in 1992, it still ranked behind countries such as Singapore, Taiwan, South Korea, and Hong Kong[2] (see Figure 1.4).

The advertising industry is also feeling the effects of the economic growth. The Thai consumer market, until recently too narrow to justify much advertising, is now offering new opportunities. In 1992, the per capita advertising expenses stood at only US$14, compared to US$162 in Singapore and US$267 in Japan, but the advertising industry is developing rapidly (see Figure 1.5). Between 1980 and 1992, Thai per capita advertising expenses grew by 15 percent per year in real terms; this is over twice the growth rate of the purchasing power.

A sign of modern times, the booming economic activity stretches the limits of existing infrastructure. Congested ports and airports, traffic jams, and storage problems are but a few of the infrastructure headaches. Thai authorities, however, are responding by speeding up the development of additional facilities such as highways, railways, ports, airports, repacking warehouses, and inland container depots.

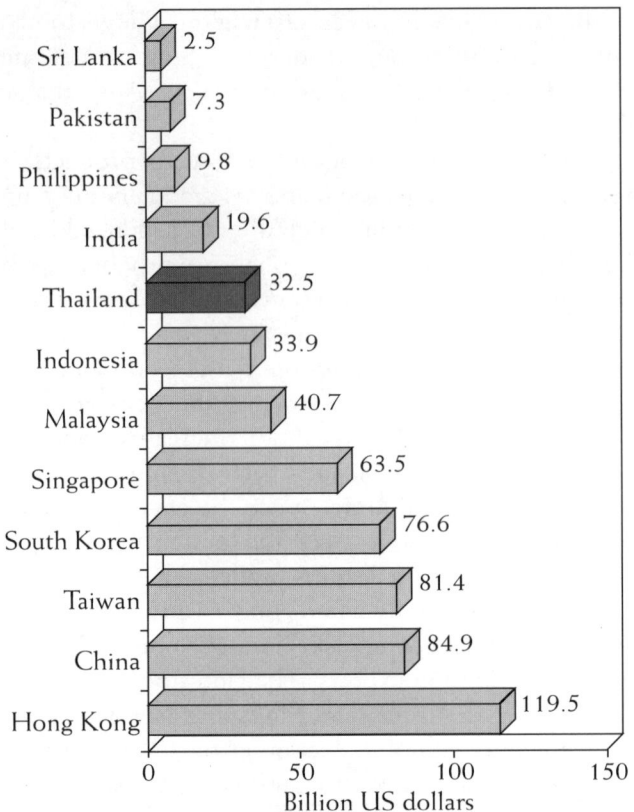

Figure 1.3 Exports of Asian Countries in 1992 (Source: Based on International Monetary Fund, IFS, April 1994, p. 64.)

1.2 GEOGRAPHY

Geographically, Thailand is in a strategic position to set up a regional office. It is located at the heart of Southeast Asia. It shares borders with Burma (now called Myanmar), Laos, Cambodia, and Malaysia and its less immediate neighbors include China, Vietnam, Singapore, and Indonesia. In addition, Thailand enjoys good access to the sea, a definite advantage for shipping. The country's sea coastal area stretches over 2,615 kilometers (1,625 miles), 70 percent of which is on the Gulf of Thailand and the rest on the Andaman Sea (near the Indian Ocean).

Thailand is also a sizeable country with varied resources and

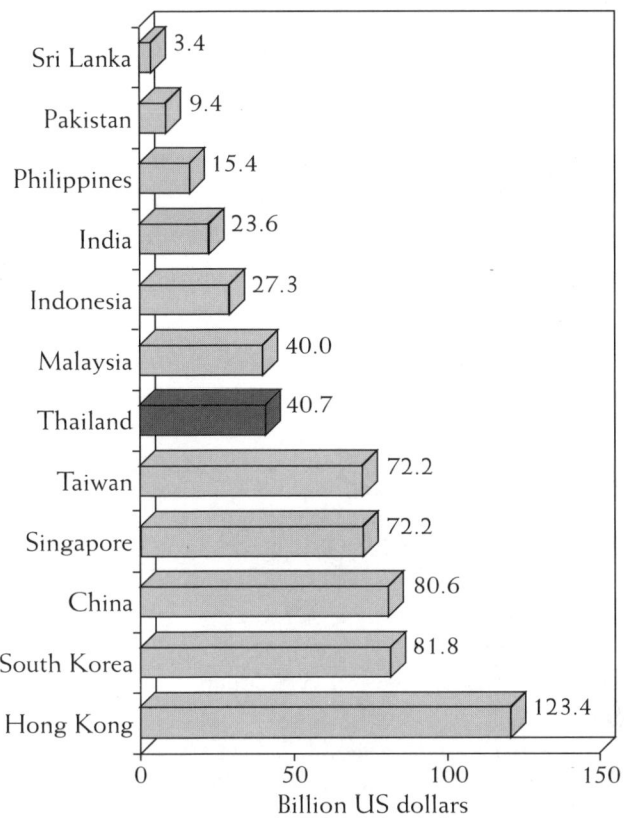

*Figure 1.4   Imports of Asian Countries in 1992
(Source: Based on International Monetary Fund, IFS, April 1994, p. 65.)*

topography. Its total area is about 513,000 square kilometers (198,000 square miles), almost the size of France. The country spreads from north to south over 1,650 kilometers (1,025 miles) and its greatest width is 780 kilometers (485 miles).

1.2.1 NATURAL RESOURCES

Thailand is rich in natural resources. Its fertile soil and warm weather are propitious for agriculture and forestry. Agricultural land and forests combined occupy two-thirds of the territory (see Figure 1.6). In addition, the country abounds with minerals and other extractive resources.

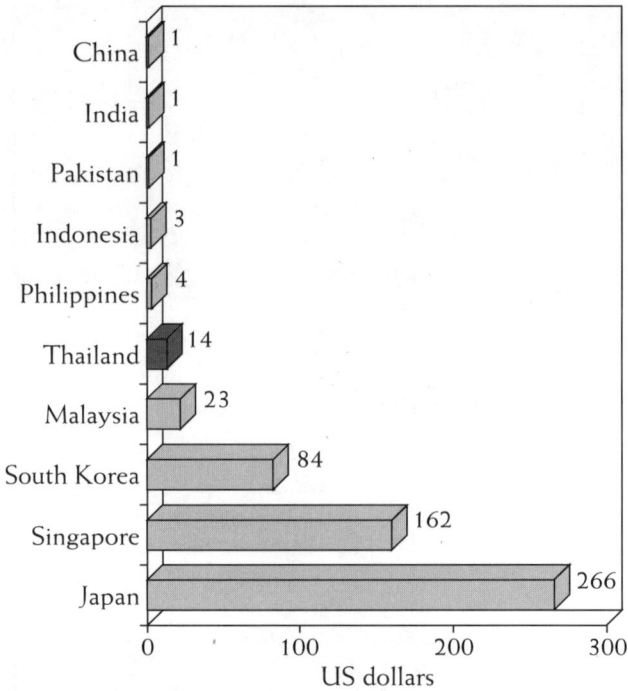

Figure 1.5 Per Capita Advertising Expenses in 1992 (Sources: Based on Zenith Media Worldwide, Asia Pacific Market and MediaFact 1993, London, 1993, p. 2, and International Monetary Fund, IFS, April 1994.)

With its varied natural resources, Thailand has a stable economy somewhat independent of world prices. It is, for example, a world-leading producer of rice, rubber, and tin, but it does not depend on these products to survive. Its economy is sufficiently diversified to absorb fluctuations in commodity prices easily.

Agriculture Agriculture is a large industry. In 1991, its output accounted for one-eighth of the Thai GDP.[3] Rice is the prime crop but Thai farmers grow many other products including cassava, rubber, sugar, maize, fruits, vegetables, chili peppers, soybeans, mung bean, palm beans, coffee beans, cotton, tobacco, and orchids. Many of these products, both fresh and processed, supply foreign markets. Together, they account for almost a third of Thailand's export earnings.

Chapter 1 Introduction to Thailand

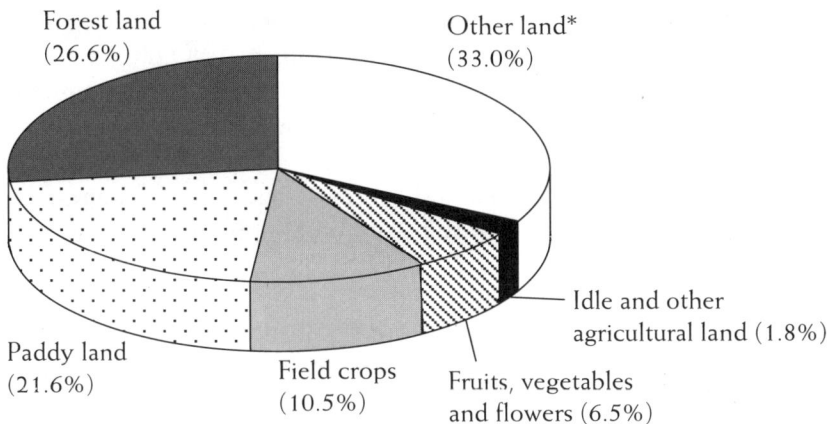

*Includes residential areas, railroads, highways, public areas, and swamps.

Figure 1.6   Land Use in 1991
(Source: Based on Center for Agricultural Statistics, Agricultural Statistics of Thailand, Crop Year 1991/1992, MAC, Bangkok, 1992, pp. 212–13.)

The economic weight of agriculture is, however, small compared to its social role. Farmers are the most numerous, but they are the poorest people in Thailand. In 1991, nearly two-thirds of Thais worked on farms, many living at or near subsistence level.[4]

This large farming population is a legacy of the past. Thais are farmers by tradition. For centuries, agriculture was Thailand's almost unique source of income and the sole occupation of nearly everyone. Rice, for many years the country's major crop, supplied both domestic and foreign markets. This earned Thailand the nickname of the "Rice Bowl of Asia." Well into the 1900s, it exported rice mostly. In 1921, for example, rice exports accounted for three-quarters of all Thai exports by value.[5]

The preeminence of agriculture, however, is eroding gradually. Agriculture is growing less rapidly than other sectors and since 1981, it has ceased to be the leading income earner in Thailand.

Forestry   Forestry is almost extinct. Thai forests, once famed for their abundance of teak wood and other hard woods, succumbed to extensive logging and encroaching. Forests used to cover most of Thailand, but they have shrunk gradually. Between 1950 and 1991, the size of the forest dropped from 62 percent of the territory to

27 percent.[6] To prevent further depletion, the Thai government imposed a nationwide logging ban in January 1989. It has also invited the private sector to participate in a reforestation program by developing commercial eucalyptus plantations.

Extractive resources Thailand is renowned for its numerous gemstones, especially the highly prized blue sapphires, but this is a small part of its extractive resources. Other valuable deposits include tin, lignite, zinc, limestone (for the cement industry), gypsum, feldspar, fluorite (of metallurgical grade), lead, shale, kaolin, glass sand, granite, marble, and dolomite. In addition, natural gas, recently discovered in the Gulf of Thailand, has become a major source of mining revenue.

1.2.2 REGIONS

With its dense jungles, cool hills, denuded plateaus, deep gorges, fertile plains, and white sandy beaches, Thailand has a varied geography. The Thai administration divides the country into four geographic regions: the North, the Northeast, the Central Region (occasionally subdivided into the Central, Eastern, and Western regions), and the South (see map on page 11).

This convenient division highlights the differences in population, topography, resources, and wealth in various parts of Thailand although it creates regions of unequal size. The North and the Northeast are the two largest regions; each covers one-third of the territory. The Central Region occupies 20 percent of the land while Southern Thailand, the smallest region, covers 14 percent of the territory.[7]

The North Northern Thailand, which stretches along the Burmese and Laotian borders, is better known for its opium cultivation and drug trade than for its other activities. The region's northernmost area, where the frontiers of Thailand, Burma, and Laos meet, is the lawless "Golden Triangle." For its greatest part, however, the North has a more licit economy. Its jungle-covered mountains, fertile valleys, and rich underground hold numerous resources (see Figure 1.7).

The mountains, chiefly composed of limestone overlaid with ferruginous sandstone, are covered with jungle where many varieties of wild orchids flourish (Thailand exports orchids). The North harbors about 77,000 square kilometers (30,000 square miles) of

Chapter 1 Introduction to Thailand

The Regions and Provinces of Thailand

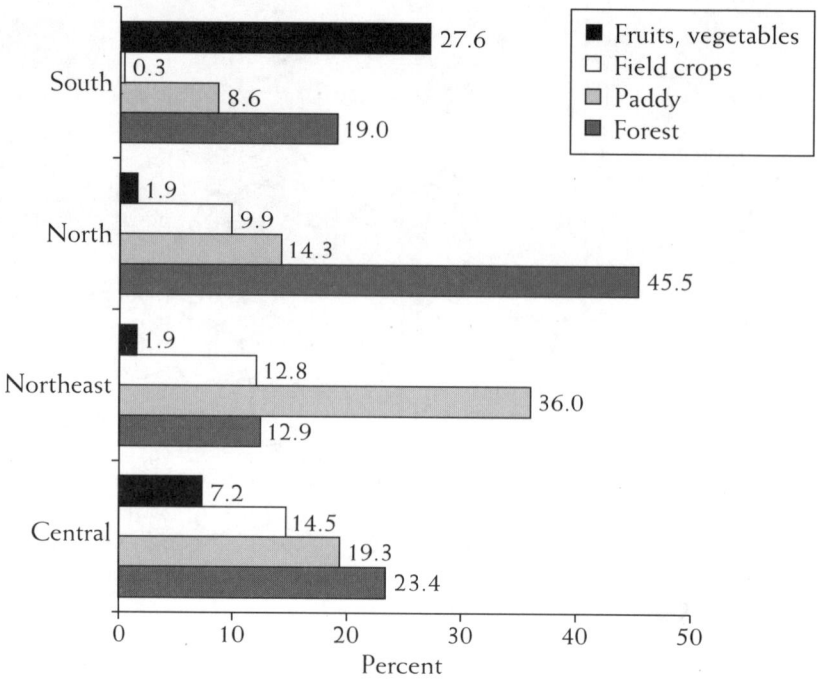

Figure 1.7 Land Use by Region in 1991
(Source: Based on Center for Agricultural Statistics, *Agricultural Statistics of Thailand, Crop Year 1991/1992*, MAC, Bangkok, 1992, pp. 212–13.)

forest, over half of the entire Thai forest.[8] Once a wild area where elephants, bears, and tigers roamed, the jungle is now much tamer.

Along with its wild life, the jungle has lost much of its productivity. It used to be a valuable source of teak wood for the logging industry and of firewood and building material for local residents. Decades of logging and encroaching have drained these resources. Today, logging is severely restricted and Thai authorities are promoting reforestation programs.

Between the jungle-covered mountain ranges are fertile river valleys. Three main rivers, the Ping, the Yom, and the Nan, drain the Northern Region north to south and they link to form the Chao Phraya River, Thailand's most important river. The broad valleys that these rivers irrigate are covered with rice fields and orchards.

Here, Northerners grow most of their crops. The North accounts for a large proportion of Thailand's agricultural output. The region produces over a quarter of the country's rice crop, about half of its maize, sorghum, and groundnuts, four-fifths of its soybeans and mung beans, and nearly all its lychees and longans.[9]

The North is also rich in mineral deposits. Its most valuable resources are gypsum, zinc, and lignite. The region is Thailand's leading producer of antimony, ball clay, calcite, diatomite, granite, kaolin, manganese, talc, and tungsten. In addition, the North has developed a marble quarrying and processing industry which supplies the domestic and foreign markets.

The Northeast The Northeast, in contrast, is Thailand's chronic problem. This region, bounded by Laos, is the driest and poorest area in Thailand. In prehistoric times, it was covered with jungles, but now it is a barren plateau plagued both by floods and droughts. The region's flat portion turns into a swamp during the rainy season and into a barren land the rest of the time while its elevated lands are often too salty to allow any vegetation to grow (see Figure 1.7).

The only fertile area lies around the region's sole river system, the Nam Mun River and its tributaries, which flow toward Laos into the Mekong River. The Northeast has about 55 percent of Thailand's entire paddy land, but it produces only 40 percent of the total rice crop.[10] Other products include kenaf, cassava, groundnuts, maize, sugarcane, and cotton.

The Northeast has few extractive resources. Its most valuable deposits are marble and barite. The region is also Thailand's sole producer of anthracite and, more importantly, of rock salt. It is believed to have some of the world's largest deposits of rock salt, with reserves estimated at several billion tons. Rock salt in itself is not a valuable material but it has many industrial uses.

The Central Region The Central Region, which stretches along the Gulf of Thailand and connects the North and the Northeast with the South, is the country's richest area. It is an expanse of fertile plains drained by the country's main river, the Chao Phraya River (see Figure 1.7).

The Chao Phraya River, which flows into the Gulf of Thailand at Bangkok, is to Thailand what the Nile is to Egypt. It irrigates surrounding fields and during the rainy season, it floods the flat central plains and deposits fertile silt.

Central Thailand owes its large farming industry to this river. The region occupies only one-fifth of the territory, but it produces about

30 percent of the country's rice and cassava, 60 percent of the sugarcane, and 25 percent of the maize.[11] In addition, its farmers raise livestock for domestic consumption and for export. They produce over half of Thailand's ducks, a third of its swine, and a quarter of its chickens.[12]

Extractive resources also abound. The Central Region is the kingdom's leading producer of gemstones, limestone, quartz, shale, pyrophyllite, glass sand, lead, and dolomite and it has sizeable deposits of feldspar, marble, phosphate, zircon, iron, and manganese.

More important, perhaps, are the region's trading and manufacturing activities. Central Thailand houses some of the country's biggest factories and almost all of its industrial estates. The Bangkok area is especially prominent, being Thailand's major business and shipping center.

The South The Southern Region, a long and narrow strip of land bordered by Burma to the northeast and by Malaysia to the south, differs in many ways from the rest of Thailand. This region remained isolated until the construction of the southern railroad line. It developed independently, relying on its own assets to prosper. The South has valuable and unique agricultural and mining resources, while its fishing industry is thriving. It is also legendary for its scenic beaches and limestone caves where small swifts build the bird's nests so highly prized in Chinese cooking.

The South has a prosperous and distinctive agriculture. Unlike other regions, Southern Thailand grows hardly any rice, but it is the kingdom's largest producer of coffee, fruits, and rubber (see Figure 1.7). Two-thirds of Thailand's fruit-growing areas and nearly all of its rubber and coffee plantations are located in the South.

The rubber industry, which started in 1900 with the introduction of rubber trees from Malaysia, is a leading export earner. Thailand is one of the world's largest producers of rubber. The kingdom is also a member of the International Natural Rubber Organization.

The South is renowned for its valuable extractive resources. It produces over 70 percent of Thailand's tin and two-thirds of its gypsum.[13] Tin is the region's most important mineral. Southern tin mines have been active for centuries and they have attracted a regular influx of Chinese migrants. Tin brought various fortunes, but it remains a substantial export earner. Thailand is a member of the

Association of Tin Producing Countries.

In addition, the South has a large fishing industry. This long peninsula is bounded on most of its length by the Gulf of Thailand to the west and the Andaman Sea to the east. It has some 1,600 kilometers (1,000 miles) of coast line. Fishing is the traditional activity in coastal villages. Most of the catch is marine fish, but fishermen also farm tiger prawns.

1.2.3 CLIMATE

Thailand is a tropical country which has a hot and humid weather. Its climate, which is dominated by the northeast monsoon in winter and by the southwest monsoon in summer, has three seasons: cold, hot, and rainy. During the cold season, from October to February, the northeast monsoon dominates and temperatures fall below 25°C (77°F). The hot season lasts from March to May with temperatures reaching 38°C (100°F). During the rainy season, from June to September, the southwest monsoon brings lower temperatures of about 30°C (86°F).

In most parts of the country, this tropical climate calls for light clothing preferably made of natural fibers. This applies especially to Central and Southern Thailand where the maritime influence produces mild temperatures throughout the year (see Table 1.1). The only exceptions are the hills of the North and the Northeast where cold air from mainland China may bring near-freezing temperatures occasionally in winter.

Table 1.1   Regional Climate

Region	Average temperature		Rain		Humidity
	Maximum °C (°F)	Minimum °C (°F)	Rainfall mm (in)	Rainy days	Percent humidity
Bangkok	33 (91)	24 (75)	1,610 (63)	126	73
North	33 (91)	22 (72)	1,200 (47)	114	71
Northeast	32 (90)	22 (72)	1,180 (46)	106	70
South	32 (90)	24 (75)	2,070 (81)	160	77

Source: Based on National Statistical Office, Statistical Yearbook Thailand 1989, OPM, Bangkok, pp. 9–11.

1.3 THE PEOPLE

Thailand is a melting pot of people. Besides ethnic Thais, the dominant people, there are Malay, Indians, Chinese, and many different hill-tribe people. The Chinese are, however, the biggest minority. Over centuries, Thailand has absorbed a constant stream of Chinese immigrants and in the late nineteenth and early twentieth century they arrived in large numbers. This immigration almost ceased after 1950, but the Chinese still form a sizeable community. Estimates claim that some 10 percent of Thais are ethnic Chinese, although it is difficult to know the exact number because many Chinese intermarry or assume Thai names.

Ethnic Thais are also a mixture of people of Indian and Chinese origin. Throughout history, four major migration waves, the first two from India and the following ones from Tibet and China, brought successively Austronesians, Mon-Khmers, Tibeto-Burmans, and finally Tais.

Tais are a Chinese ethnic group from Yünnan, a province of Southern China. They moved to what is now Thailand toward the end of the eighth century. Although they were not the first people to settle in Thailand, the Tais became the dominant power and they gave their name to the inhabitants of the country.

1.3.1 LANGUAGE

In this multiracial society, people use several languages, although most speak Thai, the official language. Foreign visitors, however, can get by with English in Bangkok and in major tourist areas. In these places, most businesses, administrations, hotels, and department stores have at least a few English-speaking employees. It is also possible to conduct simple transactions in English with large companies and high-ranking government officials. A local agent is, however, essential for complex negotiations.

Other languages are spoken by various minorities. The Chinese speak both Thai and their Chinese dialects (usually Teo Chiew), the hill tribes have their own languages, and the Muslims speak Yawi. English is the second language. It became the language of trade and diplomacy after the Bowring Treaty (with Great Britain) opened Thailand to Western merchants in 1855.

The Thai language has little in common with Western languages and may prove difficult to learn. Originally a tonal and monosyllabic language akin to Chinese, Thai later evolved to incorporate non-tonal polysyllabic words from other languages.

Speaking Thai does not guarantee good communication. The Thai language has many versions. It is really a family of languages spoken in Thailand, Laos, Burma, Northern Vietnam, and Southern China. Even within Thailand, people speak many different dialects which fall into four broad groups: Northern, Northeastern, Central, and Southern Thai. Standard Thai, the dialect of the Central Region, is the national language.

Written Thai is based on the Indian Devanagari system of writing. Initially, Thai was a spoken language only. The first attempt to develop a written language came from Buddhist scholars. These precursors used the Khmer alphabet to transcribe the Buddhist literature, which was written in the Pali language. Thai became a distinct written language only toward the end of the thirteenth century when Thai King Ramakamhaeng used the Indian Devanagari system of writing to design a Thai alphabet.

To the untrained eye, written Thai seems baffling. It stretches in long successions of characters that bear no resemblance to the Roman alphabet. The modern Thai alphabet has 32 basic vowels, 44 consonants, and 4 tone marks. In this system, vowels may be written before, after, below, or above the consonant they modify. There is no space between words so that a string of characters may cover several lines before a space is inserted. In a text, spaces indicate the end of clauses or of sentences and are equivalent to our periods and commas.

The construction of speech is equally foreign. The sentence is the unit of speech and any word is acceptable as a verb, an adjective, a noun, a pronoun, etc.

1.3.2 RELIGION

Thailand is a Buddhist country, but Buddhism is not the sole religious influence in its society. Some 95 percent of Thais describe themselves as Buddhists although they practice Buddhism jointly with other beliefs especially of Brahmanic and animistic origin. These beliefs, superstitious in essence, often relate to luck and eviction of evil spirits. Many Thais do not distinguish between their various religious practices and assume that they are all part of

Buddhism. Such is the intermingling that it is common to find altars for animistic spirits in Buddhist temples.

A few people practice other religions. About 4 percent of Thais are Muslim, and the rest have Christian or other religious affiliations.[14] These people often belong to ethnic minorities. Muslims are predominantly ethnic Malays living in the South near the Malaysian border—Malaysia is a Muslim country. Christians are usually Chinese, Vietnamese, or a few ethnic Thais that missionaries managed to convert.

Buddhism remains, nonetheless, the main religious influence on society. Over time, it has become an integral part of Thai life, a philosophy that dominates the arts, ethics, and traditions. Buddhist values pervade every aspect of life. Speech, mannerism, aspirations, and human relations, for instance, have some religious elements.

Centuries of Buddhist traditions have produced these deeply rooted values. Buddhism started in the third century B.C. when Indian emperor Ashoka dispatched missionaries to what would become Thailand. It became so successful that it spread to the various populations who came to Thailand later. Buddhism was the religion of the first Thai kingdom in the thirteenth century and it has maintained a strong foothold to this day.

1.3.3 SOCIETY

Thais are a pleasant and tolerant people. The first Thai settlers found a fertile land which provided a good living. This gentle life gave little incentive for development, but it enhanced cultural refinement. Early travelers often described Thais as respectful, mild-mannered, hospitable, and fun-loving people. Little has changed. Modern Thais are renowned for their restraint and for their relaxed, but subdued, behavior.

Dealing with Thais is often a nice experience. In all situations, Thais strive to keep even moods and they refrain from showing emotions. In this society, the smile is a communication device that conveys various messages. People smile, for example, to play down embarrassing situations or misfortune, to present a request, or to turn down a request.

These soft-spoken people dislike impulsiveness, impatience, high temper, and display of anger. Interactions must be amicable because verbal fights may damage relationships permanently. Embarrassing people with frank or challenging arguments is counterproductive. Discussions, when necessary, must remain strictly private and tactful.

Thais pay much attention to dress and behavior. Dress is neat and orderly. Behavior is respectful. Body movements and position of the head and feet, for example, conform to accepted norms. Although Thais do not expect foreigners to be fully aware of local customs, they appreciate deferential behavior.

Thais have a strong sense of hierarchy. The society is divided into flexible strata where ranks are meritorious. People say that ranks reward the moral and ethical excellence accumulated in previous lives. Inheritance, in contrast, has hardly any effect on people's position in society. Royal titles, for instance, degenerate and reach common status after five generations.

This concept of hierarchy bears heavily on human relations. Thais enjoy relaxed and informal exchanges, but they rarely show lack of respect. People have a great deference for ranks that they indicate by proper gesture and subdued behavior. A lower-ranking person, for instance, is expected to keep her head below that of a superior.

These behaviors are remnants of old court customs. In ancient times, Thais were required to crawl in front of their superiors. Although King Chulalongkorn abolished public crawling in 1874, Thais continue to crouch before a higher-ranking person. Officials kneel or squat during audiences with the king at the palace, keeping especially prostrated in difficult situations. In May 1992, for example, after the army fired on unarmed protesters, Thai television showed one of the generals held responsible for the killings crawling on all fours in front of the king.

Hierarchy also prevails in business. Decision-making rests exclusively with top officials and managers of administrations and companies. The traditional Thai enterprise has an autocratic and a paternalistic management. The company head does not expect initiatives and challenging ideas from his subordinates and he seldom delegates power.

In this hierarchical society, enjoying life is still the major goal of most people. Whatever is not fun is not worth doing. Work, study, or religion should have some element of fun to be undertaken. Monotonous jobs, hard work, and high-pressure tasks do not appeal to Thais.

1.4 POLITICAL SYSTEM

Thailand is a constitutional monarchy whose form is reminiscent of the British system. Since a military coup deprived the monarch of political power in 1932, the king reigns but does not rule. He is the head of the State, head of the armed forces, and the upholder of the Buddhist faith and of all religions in Thailand.

Although devoid of legal mandate, the king wields much power. The monarchy is the single strongest force that unites the people. Thais promptly forget their discords to rally behind their king whenever necessary and, in times of conflicts, they always turn to their king to seek advice and avoid bloodshed.

King Bhumipol Adulyadej, the ninth ruler of the Chakri dynasty, is widely respected both as a symbol of the monarchy and as a person. King Bhumipol acceded to the throne in 1946 and was officially crowned in 1950 after completing his engineering studies. He is acclaimed as a skillful non-obstructive player who often manages to diffuse crises. In rare occasions, the king abandons his neutral stance to restore peace. In 1973, for instance, when the military junta in power killed many protesters, King Bhumipol opened the palace gates to protect demonstrators.

Politics are left to the elected and appointed representatives. The executive power rests on a prime minister and his cabinet and the legislative power on a bicameral parliament. The latter comprises an elected House of Representatives, called the lower house, and an appointed House of Senate, called the upper house. In 1992, there were 360 representatives and 270 senators.

Since the end of absolute monarchy, Thailand has had many constitutions, none of which were successful. The first constitution, drafted in 1932, provided for a unicameral legislature, called Assembly of the People's Representatives. Subsequent constitutions experimented with unicameral and bicameral parliaments. In all of these, however, the drafters were careful to secure political control by appointing half of the legislature when it was unicameral or all the members of the Senate when the legislature was bicameral. This persistent concern for political control is probably what caused the failure of the constitutions.

The Thai administration is decentralized to some extent. The country comprises 73 provinces, called *changwats*, divided into 670 districts, called *amphoes*.[15] Each province is administered by a governor and each district by a district officer. Governors, who are appointed by the Ministry of Interior, report to the central government and carry out its policies. A governor, the highest-ranking authority in territorial administration, has wide powers. He allocates funds and makes recommendations for the placement and advancement of provincial officials.

1.5 HISTORY

The long-held belief that there was no civilization in Thailand until migrants settled there was refuted when recent findings showed traces of humanity dating from the stone age. Excavations in Ban Chiang, a village of the Northeast, indicate that an advanced civilization flourished there. By 2700 B.C., these people had developed bronze technology using sophisticated techniques such as alloying, bi-valve casting, lost-wax casting, cold working, and annealing. Little remains from these early inhabitants except for a few jewelry pieces and tools.

To understand the forces that drive politics and business in Thailand, however, it is not necessary to look that far back. The shaping of modern Thailand began several hundred years ago with the arrival of the Tais. These people started moving to what has become Burma, Cambodia, Laos, and Thailand toward the end of the eighth century. In 1238, the Tais established in Thailand took over the Khmer outpost of Sukhothai 430 kilometers (270 miles) north of Bangkok and there they founded the first Thai kingdom.

1.5.1 THE SUKHOTHAI ERA

The Sukhothai era was brief but decisive in the development of Thailand. During this period, Thailand became a separate entity with its own culture, written language, and administration. Modern Thais idealize these days of paternalistic and benevolent monarchies.

The original kingdom of Sukhothai was small, but it soon conquered more distant territories. Initially restricted to the capital, Sukhothai, and its surroundings, the kingdom later became a collection of small principalities with similar people, religion, and customs. These states traded with each other, but they did not form a political entity. Eventually, Sukhothai became vulnerable and by

21

1350, it had to acknowledge the suzerainty of former vassal city Ayutthaya, 80 kilometers (50 miles) north of Bangkok.

1.5.2 THE AYUTTHAYAN ERA

With the dominance of Ayutthaya came the centralized Khmer-influenced governments of Thailand. The Ayutthayan era saw the advent of absolute monarchy, an institution that lasted until 1932, and the consequent introduction of Brahmanic rituals. Thailand also owes to this period the expansion of its territory, and more importantly, its first trading experience with Western nations.

This was a period of despotism and isolation for the Thai monarchy. The rulers of Ayutthaya had inherited the concept of a god-king and the custom of elaborate court ceremonials from the Khmers. To support this new divine image, they introduced the Brahmanic rituals, which later became an integral part of the popular beliefs.

These powerful monarchs launched the many campaigns for territorial expansion that gave Thailand most of its current possessions. In the early years of Ayutthaya, the kings unified central Thailand and extended their control over the Malay Peninsula and lower Burma. Later, the government conducted campaigns against Cambodia, Chiang Mai, and Burma.

The Ayutthayan era was also a period of commercial expansion during which Thailand had its first contact with Western traders. In the early seventeenth century, these merchants set up some trading posts in the capital.

Trade soon fell under control of the royalty. The monarchy, seeing a valuable source of revenue, started a royal trade monopoly during this period, an institution that was to last two centuries. The king called on Chinese merchants to organize his trade. These people became the royal factors, warehouse men, accountants, captains, sailors, and customs officials. In short, they ran all aspects of the trade.

Thailand was willing to trade but it was also eager to maintain its autonomy. In 1688, when the Thai king perceived the military ambitions of the French, he expelled the European merchants and closed Thailand to Western trade. Commerce then focused on China. Luxury items for the court became the prime imports and rice and other local products, the exports. Trade catered exclusively to the royalty, but it remained a profitable enterprise.

The Ayutthayan era ended under Burmese fire. In 1767, the Burmese besieged and conquered Ayutthaya. Their control was brief but destructive. It lasted only six months, ending when Thai military commander Taksin drove the invaders away. By that time, Ayutthaya had been devastated and the now self-proclaimed King Taksin transferred the government headquarters to Thon Buri (next to Bangkok) where they remained until the end of his reign.

Thon Buri, however, was quickly given up. It had no natural protection against enemies and suffered constant erosion from the Chao Phraya River. When Rama I, the successor of Taksin and the founder of the Chakri dynasty, was enthroned in 1782, he established a new capital across the river from Thon Buri in Bangkok.

1.5.3 THE BANGKOK PERIOD

The Bangkok period brought more open and compromising governments. The royalty softened its despotic stance, renounced its trade monopoly, and reopened Thailand to Western merchants. Subsequently, the contacts with the West inspired the administrative and investment strategies that turned Thailand into a modern country.

This period is marked by the return to Buddhist values and the gradual decline, although not the abolition, of court ceremonials. The despotic god-kings of Ayutthaya, who called themselves the "lords of life," had little contact with their subjects. The kings of Bangkok were still revered as the lords of life, but they were more human and closer to their subjects.

These new kings were less powerful than their predecessors, especially in the early years of Bangkok, when Thailand was on the verge of bankruptcy. At that time, the traditional methods of tax collection were ineffective. Foreign ships did not call at Thai ports, and they could not contribute the measurement fees—a tax on mooring proportional to the space occupied by the ship. The state could not collect taxes on Thai subjects either because it did not have the resources to audit production.

Short of resources, the monarchy had to give up its trade monopoly. The kings attracted Chinese merchants and craftsmen to promote commerce. China trade resumed, although not as a state enterprise. In this new arrangement, the king remained a leading merchant, but he shared the commercial activities with officials, members of the royalty, and Chinese merchants.

Trade became a competitive industry gradually. As commerce grew, the Thai monarchs lost their tight control over it. The trade benefits to the royalty dwindled but the country prospered. When Rama III acceded to the throne in 1824, he finally abolished royal trading and several trade monopolies. Thailand opened to freer trade.

Free trade applied selectively but it benefited the population greatly. The Chinese merchants visited remote areas never exposed to commerce before. They secured regular supplies of merchandise by encouraging villagers to produce goods for exports. Thai labor became specialized and the economy monetized. Thais grew wealthier. Their time became valuable and they began commuting *corvée*, a specific labor tax, into cash payments.

This free trade policy did not extend to Westerners. The king claimed the exclusive right to trade with Western merchants and imposed high duties on them. It took years of negotiations and the cooperation of King Mongkut (Rama IV) to reach an agreement. In 1855 King Mongkut, trying to avoid a military confrontation with the West, ratified the Treaty of Friendship and Commerce, also known as the Bowring Treaty because it was negotiated by Sir John Bowring on behalf of Queen Victoria. Some historians claim that by agreeing to cooperate with the West, King Mongkut saved Thailand from colonization.

The Bowring Treaty was as far as Western powers ever came to infringing Thailand's autonomy. This treaty ended the last remnant of the Thai king's participation in overseas trade. It granted Britain a most-favored-nation status, lowered the taxes on Western traders, replaced the measurement fees by a 3 percent import tax, and prevented the Thai government from increasing the rates of internal tariffs and export taxes. The treaty allowed British subjects to trade at Thai ports and to reside permanently in Bangkok. It also established the system of ex-territoriality by which British subjects residing in Thailand were not subject to Thai tribunals, but to the British consular courts.

The Bowring Treaty, a strong reminder of Thailand's vulnerability, was to inspire a clever diplomacy. Thai governments could not keep Western powers out, but they tried to maintain a balance between them, playing them off against one another. Thai rulers were always careful not to antagonize any of these powers and they kept neutral during international conflicts, only siding with the sure winner at the last minute.

This diplomacy is best illustrated by Thailand's approach to World War I. At that time, Europeans were established in Bangkok. Thailand declared its neutrality, viewing the war as a European conflict. By 1917, however, when the United States entered the war, the odds turned against Germany. Thailand, seeing an opportunity to cancel its unfavorable treaties with Germany and Austria, declared war on Germany. The Thai government trained and despatched an army, which arrived on the battle fields only to witness the end of the conflict.

To avoid colonization, King Chulalongkorn (Rama V) embarked on an ambitious program of modernization. In addition to widely publicized social policies such as the abolition of public crawling, the king implemented fundamental political and economic changes. He enlarged the Thai administration, developed infrastructure, and organized a modern army along Western lines.

The king set up the administration to replace tax farmers. Since the days of Ayutthaya, Thai monarchs subcontracted tax collection to private individuals called tax farmers. These people, usually Chinese, bid for the right to collect taxes. Organizing tax collection, however, took time and tax farming survived King Chulalongkorn's reign.

King Chulalongkorn was also anxious to reinforce his military control, particularly in border areas. He organized the army as an elite group and promoted the development of strategic infrastructure like transportation and communications. In 1902, for example, the king allocated resources to the construction of railroads instead of investing in a dam and a network of irrigation canals for agriculture.

1.5.4 MILITARY RULE

The reforms of King Chulalongkorn helped Thailand resist colonization, but they also paved the way for the overthrow of the monarchy. By setting up a powerful administration and a modern army, the king had created a new elite which would later challenge the monarchy's power. The ensuing military rule started an era of dictatorship dominated by factional struggles. Between 1932 and 1991, Thailand experienced 17 coups, most of which were relatively peaceful. The military rule also brought new forces in the business community.

King Prachathipok (Rama VII), enthroned in 1925, was the last absolute monarch in Thailand. He found the treasury depleted and later faced further economic difficulties linked to the international crisis of 1929. His policy of cutting government salaries and increasing taxes proved unpopular. In 1932 the People's Party, a military and civilian group, staged a coup that toppled the government and ended the monarchy's absolute power. The king became a constitutional leader allowed to reign but not to rule.

For a while, the new regime governed along semidemocratic lines. It introduced direct popular suffrage and granted men and women the right to vote for representatives in the legislature. It increased the expenses on education and replaced the old unfavorable treaties with foreign powers by new reciprocal agreements. Thailand then recovered the right to impose customs duties and its courts gained unfettered jurisdiction over foreign nationals. The new rulers, however, proved less open to criticism and competition—they censored publications and radio speeches detrimental to public order and they prohibited the creation of new parties.

Semidemocracy gave way to full-scale dictatorship. After Luang Pibul became Prime Minister in 1939, nationalism intensified and autocracy surfaced. Pibul began calling himself the "Leader" and encouraged such propaganda. Sir Josiah Crosby, a British diplomat in Thailand at that time, reports that Pibul expected people to greet each other with the words "Hail Pibul" and to bow when his picture appeared on the screens of movie theaters.[16]

Despite these political changes, Thai diplomacy remained the same; Thai rulers were more interested in domestic matters than in foreign conflicts. During World War II, when Japan became threatening, Thailand tried to offset the Japanese influence by maintaining good relations with both Japan and the Western powers. The cooperation with Japan, however, turned into a forced alliance. In 1941, the Japanese invaded Thailand. Thai troops resisted briefly. On December 21, 1941, just two weeks after the beginning of the hostilities, Thais and Japanese ceased fire and signed a treaty of alliance. In January 1942, Thailand had to declare war on Britain and the United States.

For business, the situation was sometimes chaotic, especially in the early years of the military regime. From the start, the military sought to keep their hands on power. The government increased its control over the economy by introducing countless regulations, most of which proved ineffective or impracticable. Military officers secured appointments to top civilian posts in the administration and in public enterprises. Later, they extended their influence to the private sector, joining the board of private business firms and setting up their own businesses.

Despite the military grip over politics and the economy, democracy returned. In May 1992, following confrontations between demonstrators and the army, the non-elected military prime minister in power stepped down. Thais elected new representatives who formed a non-military government.

NOTES

1. Calculations based on National Statistical Office, *Statistical Yearbook Thailand 1992*, OPM, Bangkok, 1992, p. 27.
2. Re-exports, which account for a substantial proportion of international trade in Singapore and Hong Kong, inflate the import figures of these countries.
3. Calculations based on Office of the National Economic and Social Development Board, *National Income of Thailand, Rebase Series 1980–1991*, OPM, Bangkok, 1993, p. 11.
4. Calculations based on National Statistical Office, *Statistical Yearbook Thailand 1993*, OPM, Bangkok, 1993, p. 56.
5. Source: National Statistical Office, *Key Statistics of Thailand 1989*, OPM, Bangkok, 1989, p. 74.
6. Calculations based on National Statistical Office, *Statistical Yearbook Thailand*, OPM, Bangkok, various issues.
7. Supra 4, pp. 6–8.
8. Calculations based on Center for Agricultural Statistics, *Agricultural Statistics of Thailand, Crop Year 1991/92*, MAC, Bangkok, 1992, pp. 212–13.
9. Supra 8, pp. 10–63.
10. Supra 8, pp. 14–19.
11. Supra 8, pp. 10–39.
12. Calculations based on Department of Livestock Development, *Yearly Statistic Reports 1991*, MAC, Bangkok, pp. 49–51.
13. Calculations based on Department of Mineral Resources, *Mineral Statistics of Thailand 1986–1990*, Bangkok, pp. 29, 54.

14. Source: National Statistical Office, *Report of the Cultural Activity Participation and Time Use Survey*, OPM, Bangkok, various issues.
15. Source: National Statistical Office, *Statistical Yearbook Thailand 1989*, OPM, Bangkok, p. XXV.
16. Crosby, Sir Josiah, *Siam: The Crossroads*, Hollis & Carter Ltd., London, 1945. Reprinted by AMS Press Inc., New York, N.Y., 1973, p. 88.

2 LIFE STYLES

Thailand means "land of the free," but "land of diversity" might better capture the range of life styles found in this country. Feverish business districts, peaceful harbors, brash resort towns, ancestral hill-tribe settlements, and timeless farming villages tell of the many facets of Thai life.

Countless influences of ethnic, cultural, religious, and economic origin bear on life styles, although wealth is probably the single most important one. Money is the deciding factor on most family issues, from sending children to school to buying a television set and traveling; that is, people from different cultural backgrounds but with similar wealth spend money the same way. Since people are wealthier in cities than in villages, life styles fall into two broad types: urban and rural.

In many ways, Thailand is still a rural country. The vast majority of Thais live in villages, most of which are remote and traditional in character. Villages form small self-contained communities. Their isolation encourages superstitions. Villagers call on witch doctors to cure diseases and they ward off evil spirits with amulets, tattoos, and offerings on altars.

In contrast to this rural environment, the few large cities are modern, although they are surrounded by countryside. In Bangkok, for instance, a few miles away from the fashionable city center, life is traditional. Here, roads give way to canals. People move around in boats and they buy provisions at the floating markets, at the small shops that line the canals, and from the peddlers who float by.

The modern urban centers, however, attract the most educated, healthiest, and wealthiest Thais. Their life styles are sophisticated, especially in Bangkok, the kingdom's leading business center. Bangkok's luxurious shopping arcades, boutiques, upmarket night clubs and wine bars, numerous cultural and recreational facilities, and traffic congestion speak of the urbane living standards of its residents.

These urban life styles are indicators of future consumption trends for rural areas. Urbanites initiate changes in Thailand. New products sell in cities first and reach villages later. Radio and television, for example, once only available in cities, are now widespread throughout the country.

This chapter shows how the combination of the modern and the traditional affects consumption and production. It explains how people live and what influences their behavior in cities and villages. The topics include: demography, purchasing power, education, housing, recreation, and religion.

2.1 DEMOGRAPHY

Thailand has mixed demographic patterns. The age structure, regional distribution, and health of the Thai population integrate elements of the industrialized and of the developing world. Cities epitomize the modern side of Thailand. Urbanites have fewer children, better health, and longer life expectancies—they are wealthier. Villages are traditional and they develop more slowly.

2.1.1 STRUCTURE OF POPULATION

The Thai consumer is young, a result of decades of high birth rates and short life expectancies. In 1990, 39 percent of Thais were below 20 years old (see Figure 2.1), compared to 29 percent of Americans.[1] With the improvements in health care, the population has also grown rapidly. Between 1970 and 1992, it increased by 2.2 percent annually;[2] this is about twice the population growth rate of the United States.

Changes in demographic patterns are, however, bringing Thailand closer to its Western counterparts. Birth rates are declining and life expectancies are increasing. Between 1970 and 1990, the birth rate dropped from 3.1 percent to 1.7 percent.[3] Over the same period, life expectancy increased by about 2 years; Thais born in 1990 may expect to live for 66 years, compared to 60 years for those born in 1970.[4]

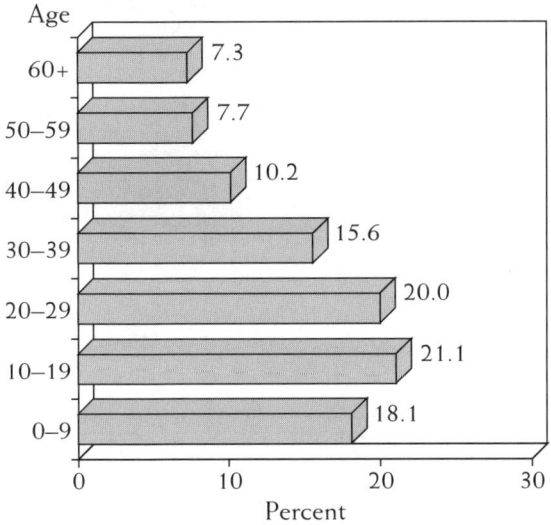

Figure 2.1 Population Distribution by Age in 1990 (Source: Based on National Statistical Office, Statistical Yearbook Thailand 1992, OPM, Bangkok, 1992, p. 27.)

These demographic changes are altering consumer profiles. The Thai population is ageing. Projections to year 2000 forecast more adults and fewer children (see Figure 2.2). Between 1990 and 2000 the population will increase by some eight million. There will be nine million more adults (15 years old and above) and one million fewer youngsters (below 15 years old). Adults aged between 25 and 54 will account for most of the growth with an increase of seven million. Since these people are also the greatest spenders, this may be the single most important demographic change for marketing in Thailand.

2.1.2 REGIONAL DISTRIBUTION

Thailand is sparsely, albeit unevenly, populated. In 1992, the kingdom had 113 inhabitants per square kilometer, a population density comparable to that of France and four times that of the United States. This density, however, varies greatly across regions, ranging from 69 people per square kilometer in the North to 3,550 in Bangkok Metropolis (see Figure 2.3).

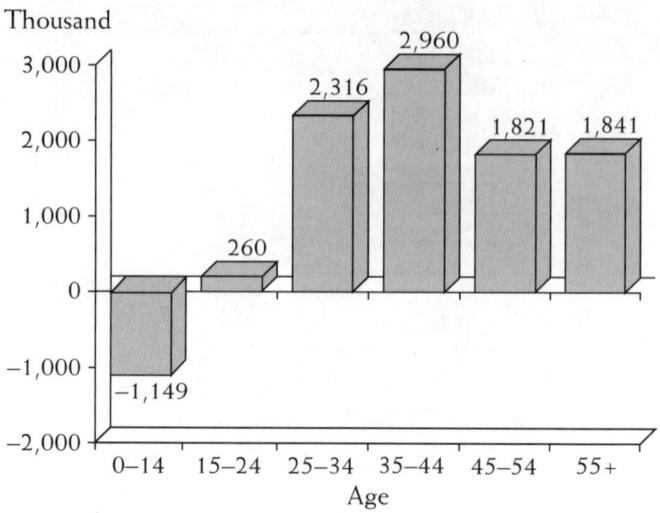

Figure 2.2 Projected Population Changes 1990–2000 (Source: Based on Office of the National Economic and Social Development Board, Population Projections for Thailand 1980–2015, OPM, Bangkok.)

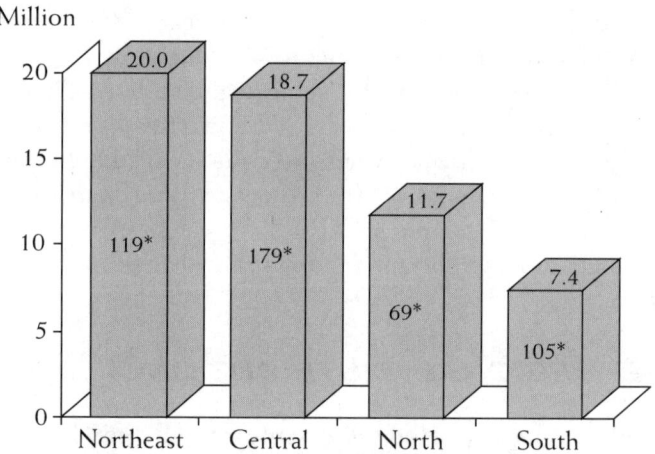

* People per square kilometer

Figure 2.3 Population and Population Density by Region in 1992 (Source: Based on National Statistical Office, Statistical Yearbook Thailand 1993, OPM, Bangkok, 1993, pp. 5–7, 28.)

There are few urban centers. Of the country's large cities, Bangkok is the largest by far. Over half of Thailand's urbanites live in Bangkok Metropolis. The next four largest cities are Nakhon Ratchasima and Khon Kaen in the Northeast, Chiang Mai in the North, and Hat Yai in the South. Although these are leading regional cities, their combined total population is smaller than Bangkok's.

For its greatest part, Thailand is a rural country. In 1992, over 80 percent of Thais lived in villages,[5] most of which are self-governing communities of less than a thousand inhabitants. Some of these villages are isolated. Their people have little contact with the outside world and the radio may be their sole communications device. Consumers in these parts can be difficult to reach.

The uneven distribution of the population has encouraged the development of many retailing methods. Thailand has almost every kind of retail outlet. The selection is greater in cities where retailers range from sophisticated shopping centers and specialty shops to peddlers. In villages, however, general stores and traveling sales people are the main suppliers.

The consumers that these various retailers cater to have different priorities. Urbanites are more demanding because they have access to a greater selection of goods. They pay attention to price and quality, and also to such attributes as packaging and design. Villagers, in contrast, look for products which are cheap, durable, utilitarian, and easy to use. They are less likely to buy goods that need servicing. Consumption in villages is also more basic. Rural outlets supply ordinary personal and household goods and traveling sales people carry such products as detergents, soaps, drugs, paper products, and inexpensive household items.

The North The North, Thailand's largest region, is sparsely populated. Northern Thailand spreads over a third of the territory, but it houses less than a fifth of Thais. With 69 inhabitants per square kilometer, it is the least densely populated area in Thailand. The North is also a rural region; some 92 percent of its people live in villages,[6] some of which are isolated.

Most Northerners are ethnic Thais, but the Northern Region is also the home of Thai hill tribes. There are about a dozen different tribal groups which fall into five major ethnic groups: Meo-Yao, Mon-Khmer, Tibeto-Burman, Tai, and Chinese. The size of the tribal population is not well known, but the 1985–1988 Survey of Hill Tribe Population recorded over half a million people.[7]

The hill tribes live in small settlements on remote and elevated lands along the Burmese border. Until recently, these people have been isolated and often inaccessible. They have perpetuated ancestral traditions dating from some several hundred years. Tribal groups have their own languages, cultures, and social organizations. They are especially distinctive because of their accouterment of fancy head dresses, colorful embroidery, and imposing silver ornaments.

Tribal people have, however, attracted much public attention lately because of their traditional farming practices. Some tribes, like the Hmong, Yao, Akha, Lisu, and Lahu, are still seminomadic agriculturists who slash and burn forests to cultivate hill fields for rice, corn, and occasionally, opium poppies. Producing opium, once encouraged by the Thai military, has now fallen out of favor, while the practice of clearing forests has become unpopular.

The Thai government is trying to ease the controversy by encouraging hill tribes to change their production patterns. Agencies promote crop substitution and they finance related infrastructure like roads and canneries. Their agricultural extension officers teach tribal groups to replant poppy fields with cabbages, potatoes, coffee, fruit trees, and flowers. In addition, the palace's Support Foundation encourages tribal groups to produce traditional handicrafts.

The publicity that surrounded these efforts has promoted the tourism industry in Northern Thailand and it has expanded the market for tribal crafts. Northern cities like Chiang Mai and Chiang Rai have become popular tourist destinations. The traditional crafts of tribal groups are now much sought after. Some have even become fashionable on foreign markets.

The Northeast The Northeast is a large and populated area. It is about as large as the North, but it harbors twice as many people. Over a third of Thais live here. The bulk of these people, some 93 percent, however, are villagers.[8]

This region is the poorest in Thailand and per capita consumption lags behind other regions. Poverty also drives away its workers, making the Northeast the biggest contributor to Thailand's internal migrations.[9] This region has become the kingdom's largest reservoir of unskilled workers. It supplies the bulk of the cheap labor force to Bangkok's manufacturers.

The South   The South stands out because of its small size and cultural diversity. This region is the smallest in Thailand and it has the smallest population. Only one-eighth of Thais live here. Culturally influenced by its Muslim neighbor, Malaysia, the South harbors the only large Islamic community in Thailand. These people account for a quarter of the southern population.[10] Most, however, live near the Malaysian border in the provinces of Yala, Narathiwat, Pattani, Satun, and Songkhla.

Muslims in the South differ from other Thais. They are ethnic Malay who speak Yawi, follow the Islamic dress code, and study in religious schools. They became Thai citizens because Thailand claimed some Malay territory but they resist integration.

Adding to the cultural diversity, the booming tourist industry brings in visitors of all nationalities year-round. Some coastal areas have gained international acclaim for their scenery and they have become major resorts. The busiest ones like Phuket and Hat Yai have even set up direct air connections with foreign countries; their airports are some of the few in Thailand to provide such services.

Central   Central Thailand, the kingdom's principal manufacturing area, is urban and populous. It is the second most-populated region after the Northeast and the most densely populated area in Thailand. In 1992, the Central Region housed one-third of Thais and it had 179 inhabitants per square kilometer. In Bangkok Metropolis, the region's most urban area, the population density reached 3,550 people per square kilometer.

Bangkok, the kingdom's capital, is a sprawling and cosmopolitan city. It has spilled beyond its boundaries and linked with surrounding towns to form a large urban area, called Bangkok Metropolis. In 1992, about one-tenth of Thais, some 5.5 million people, lived here.[11] Bangkok harbors a substantial expatriate community and an estimated two-thirds of its native population is of Chinese descent.

For centuries, Bangkok has been the hub for commerce and Thailand's principal port of entry. This is still true today. Bangkok is the kingdom's leading business center. Most foreign companies operating in Thailand set up their office in Bangkok and the bulk of Thai international trade transits in Bangkok.

In this wealthy and cosmopolitan city, consumption is greater and more diverse than in other parts of Thailand. Bangkok residents are trendsetters for the rest of their countrymen. New products sell in Bangkok before reaching distant provinces.

Internal migrations With its population expansion and economic development, Thailand is becoming more urban. Workers from the countryside move to cities, especially to the industrial towns near the Gulf ports. Between 1970 and 1992, the proportion of people living in cities grew by 50 percent, increasing from 13 to 18 percent.[12]

Bangkok draws many of these migrants. Some people come to study or to build a career, but the bulk of the newcomers are young farmers who show up between the planting and harvesting seasons. Over three-quarters of the migrants are aged between 10 and 29. About two-thirds of these turn up during slack agricultural periods (see Table A.2.1 in Appendix 2).

Although most migrants are young, Thais of all ages move to Bangkok. These people fall into three major groups: children, youths, and adults. About one-tenth of the migrants are children below 10 years old, three-quarters are youths aged between 10 and 29, and the remaining 15 percent are adults above 30 years old.

Children do not come by themselves; neither do they decide to migrate. The vast majority move to Bangkok with their families. About 6 percent of the children, however, come to study.

Youths, the principal migrants, include both workers and students, but most are workers. These workers are usually poor people with low skill levels looking for temporary jobs. Students, however, account for one in seven young migrants.

Adults arrive both for work and for family reasons. In this group, the distinction between males and females is pronounced. Females over 30 years old are often married and most move with their spouses. For males, career objectives dominate their motives, with four in five coming for work.

2.1.3 HEALTH

Health care is developing rapidly. Economic growth is raising the demand for hospitals, clinics, medical equipment, and medications.

Between 1970 and 1991, expenses on health care have increased annually by nearly 12 percent in real terms and their share of total consumption doubled, increasing from 4 to 8 percent.[13] Medical assistance is now well organized in Bangkok, but it is still poor in other parts of the country.

Health patterns combine characteristics of both the rich and the developing world. Like in many rich countries, heart failures, cancers, and accidents are the major causes of death in Thailand. Together, they account for about one-fourth of the deaths in the whole country and one-third of those in Bangkok (see Figure 2.4). Thailand, however, is also affected by the diseases common to tropical areas. Malaria, cholera, leprosy, dengue fever, intestinal diseases, and respiratory infections, for instance, are serious concerns.

In this mixed environment, Bangkok is the healthiest place. Bangkok residents enjoy better sanitation and medical facilities. They are less vulnerable to parasitic and infective diseases. That these people are more affected by illnesses linked to old age such as cancer and pneumonia and by diseases linked to consumption habits such as heart and cerebrovascular diseases (strokes) speaks of their longer and richer lives.

The main health problems occur in remote areas with poor sanitation and lack of medical assistance. In these places, preventable diseases recur frequently and claim many lives. While not always fatal, some of these diseases, such as malaria and diarrheal diseases, often become chronic and reduce the energy of their victims.

Malaria Malaria poses a quasi-permanent threat despite numerous efforts to thwart it. In 1990, it killed about 1,300 people.[14] For years, malaria was a chief cause of sickness and death in Thailand, especially in the hilly areas. Its incidence declined after the DDT spraying campaign of 1949. It receded further after the development of malaria clinics, the regular spraying of DDT and fenitrothion, and the introduction of larva-eating fish. In the past decade, however, multidrug-resistant and especially chloroquine-resistant parasites have appeared in border areas. They spread throughout Thailand because of interior migrations of infected people. Towns are usually free from malaria, but in villages, mosquito nets are almost mandatory.

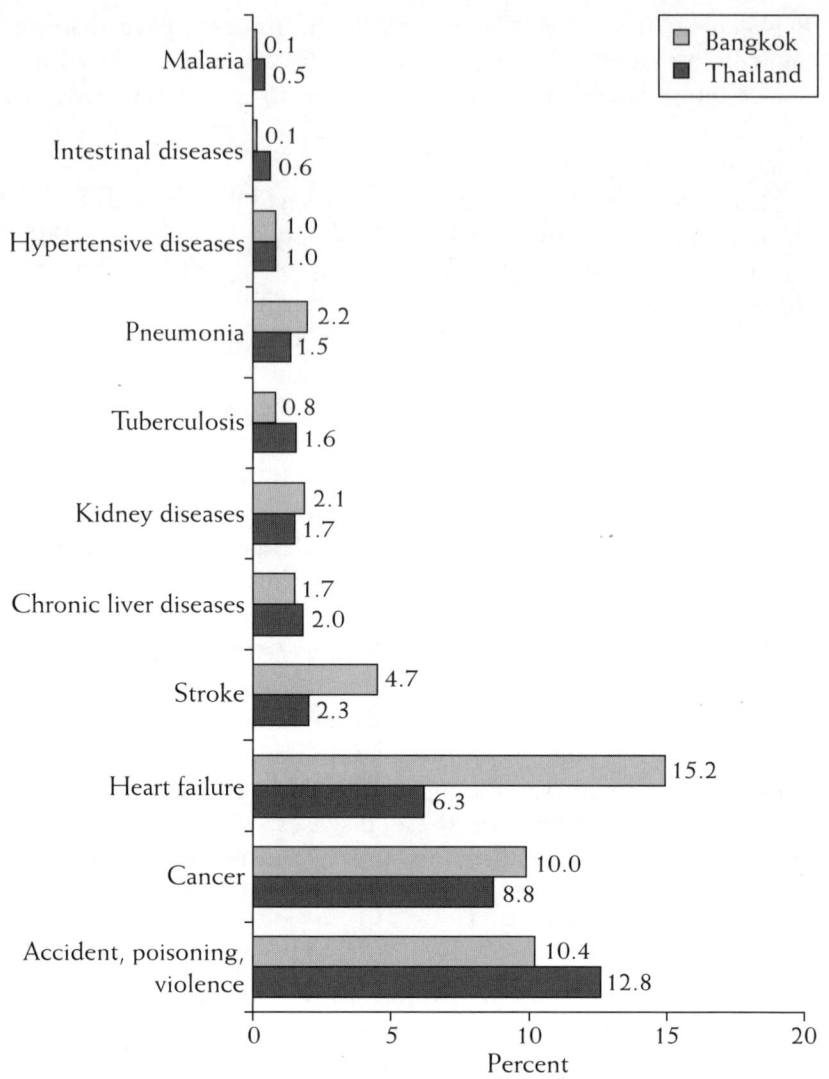

Figure 2.4 Major Causes of Death in 1990
(Sources: Based on Division of Health Statistics, Public Health Statistics A.D. 1990, MPH, Bangkok, 1992, pp. 77–207, and National Statistical Office, Quarterly Bulletin of Statistics, OPM, Bangkok, December 1991, p. 16.)

Diarrheal diseases Diarrheal diseases, although better controlled than in the past, remain widespread. In 1990, they caused over 1,500 deaths.[15] They are especially severe in rural areas where children under 5 years old suffer one or two episodes a year. In these places, medical teams try to improve public health education and they distribute rehydration salts.

Leprosy Leprosy is declining. In 1990, health institutions recorded only 10,500 cases, compared to 33,000 in 1985.[16] The leprosy control program started in 1953 in the Northeast, where the disease is endemic, and by 1976, it covered the whole country. The program emphasizes early detection and regular treatment of infected people. There are provincial leprosy units in all endemic areas, some leprosy training and research institutes, and a leprosarium.

Venereal diseases In this permissive society, venereal diseases are common, especially in Bangkok and in some provincial towns where prostitution is rife. The ubiquitous "VD clinic" signs in Bangkok speak of the situation. Since the spread of AIDS, the problem has become alarming. In May 1993, Thai health officials put the number of AIDS cases at about 4,300 and they estimated that an additional 400,000 people carried the HIV virus.[17]

Prostitutes, mainly young girls from the poor areas of Northern Thailand, Burma, and Southern China, are usually recruited against their will and are unaware of the dangers of their trade. Children as young as 10 years old are virtually enslaved; most are already infected when they are rescued.

For many years, prostitution has been a major attraction for the tourism industry, but AIDS is now taking its toll. Since tourism is the single largest source of foreign revenue, Thai officials are trying to change the image of their country. The Tourism Authority of Thailand, for instance, designated 1992 as "Women Visit Thailand Year" to attract visitors with different interests and spending patterns.

Tourists are not the sole people at risk. Prostitutes also cater to Thai males who have left their families to work in cities. While HIV infection is more acute in Bangkok and in a few other tourist destinations like Hat Yai and Songkhla, it is spreading to villages. Information campaigns are promoting the use of prophylactics. Although these are a novel concept for many Thais, their market potential is high.

Medical assistance Thais claim that Bangkok's medical facilities are the best in Southeast Asia. The city has enough physicians, nurses, and hospital beds per resident to rival such countries as Hong Kong and Singapore. Compared with the rest of Thailand, Bangkok has, by far, the best medical staff and equipment. In 1990, about half of the dentists and physicians, two-thirds of the pharmacists, a quarter of the nurses, half of private hospital beds, and a quarter of all hospital beds in Thailand were in Bangkok.[18]

Some of the medical personnel have been trained overseas, especially in Europe and in the United States. These people are used to working with high-quality Western equipment. They are more likely to buy their medical supplies from foreign producers.

Outside Bangkok, medical assistance is less organized. Many provinces lack qualified medical personnel and hospital beds. In these areas, people rely more on health workers, midwives, and nurses than on physicians. Repeated efforts to train medical personnel and set up clinics have failed to bring medical facilities in the provinces up to Bangkok standards.

Medications are also scarce. International agencies, missionaries, and the Thai government have joined forces to distribute medicines and organize specific disease control programs. Immunization campaigns began in the 1950s in the Bangkok area, but they reached the provinces only in 1977. That year, the Thai government launched a nationwide program to control such diseases as diphtheria, whooping cough, tetanus, polio, tuberculosis, and measles.

2.2 PURCHASING POWER

Decades of rapid economic growth have improved the purchasing power greatly, putting Thailand on the path to mass consumption. Between 1970 and 1991, incomes nearly tripled with the per capita gross domestic product increasing by 175 percent in real terms.[19] Products, like radios and televisions, once rare, became widespread. In the wealthiest parts of the country new shops appeared selling such luxuries as computers, electronic equipment, designer's clothes, and sports cars. In Bangkok, new upmarket clubs and wine bars cater to wealthy youths.

Throughout this period, the manufacturing sector led much of the economic expansion. Many foreign companies, especially Japanese, were relocating their production units in low-cost countries, bringing in capital and technology. In Thailand, these new ventures contributed significantly to industrialization and growth. Between 1970 and 1991, the manufacturing sector increased its output sevenfold and raised its contribution to the gross domestic product from 16 to 28 percent.[20]

Industrial centers, especially Bangkok, have been the major growth areas. In these places, the new manufacturers created both jobs and business opportunities. In the countryside, the benefits are less direct. Unskilled village workers willing to move to industrial areas find low-paid jobs. The vast majority of the people who stay in the villages, however, derive fewer advantages.

2.2.1 OCCUPATIONS

The effects of growing industrialization on the job market are slow to materialize. Rural areas supply the bulk of the cheap manufacturing labor, but this is a small fraction of their vast human resources. Most Thais, about 60 percent, are farmers (see Figure 2.5). Craftsmen and sales people together account for about a quarter of the labor force. The remaining 15 percent are managers, professionals, clerks, service workers, and transport workers.

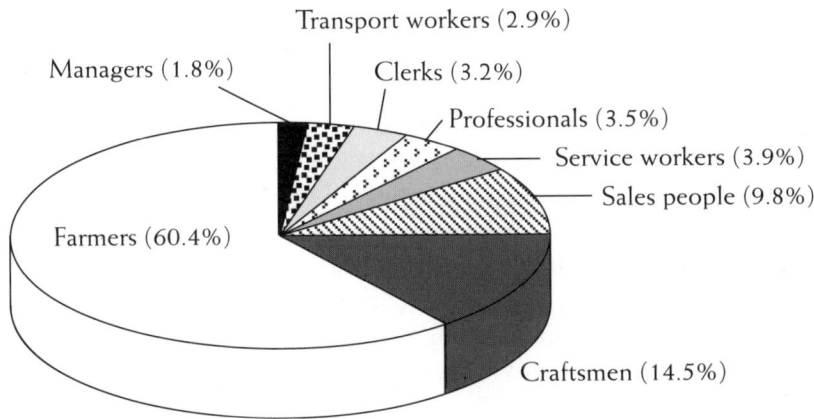

Figure 2.5 Occupations in 1991
(Source: Based on National Statistical Office, Statistical Yearbook Thailand 1993, OPM, Bangkok, 1993, p. 56.)

There are, however, significant seasonal changes in the labor force. Many farmers work at other jobs during slack agricultural periods. The farming population drops from about 19 million during the busy month of August to only 14 million in May, while craftsmen grow from 4 to 6 million.[21]

Most women join the labor force. In 1991, about 67 percent of the females worked in Thailand, compared to 57 percent in the United States. Far from being confined to low-paid jobs, Thai females are represented in most occupations, from farmers to company directors. As in other societies, however, Thai women avoid jobs which conflict with family life or are physically demanding. There are, therefore, slight discrepancies in the occupations of males and females. Fewer females work as managers, craftsmen, and transport workers, but more are sales and service workers (see Figure 2.6).

Some of the luckiest and most ambitious Thai females have risen to the top of their profession. Many hold prominent positions in enterprises. The kingdom has its share of women tycoons. They head a variety of concerns ranging from shopping mall chains to river ferry services and construction companies.

Youths also make up a substantial part of the work force. In poor families, children are an asset. Many end their studies early to become unpaid family workers or to get a job and send remittances home. Those who do not work help with the household chores. Such traditions are stronger in the villages. In 1987 the proportion of non-schooled youngsters working as unpaid family workers was twice as large in villages as in cities.[22]

Production is often informal, especially in villages. The household is the production unit and all members of working age contribute to its wealth. Thailand has a myriad of small family-owned companies that consist of a self-employed person aided by unpaid family workers. In 1991, 29 percent of Thai workers were self-employed and 38 percent were unpaid family workers (see Figure 2.7). In these enterprises, management is traditional and marketing strategy is nonexistent.

2.2.2 INCOMES

The average Thai consumer is poorer than his Western counterpart. In 1990, the average Thai household earned US$2,750 per annum.

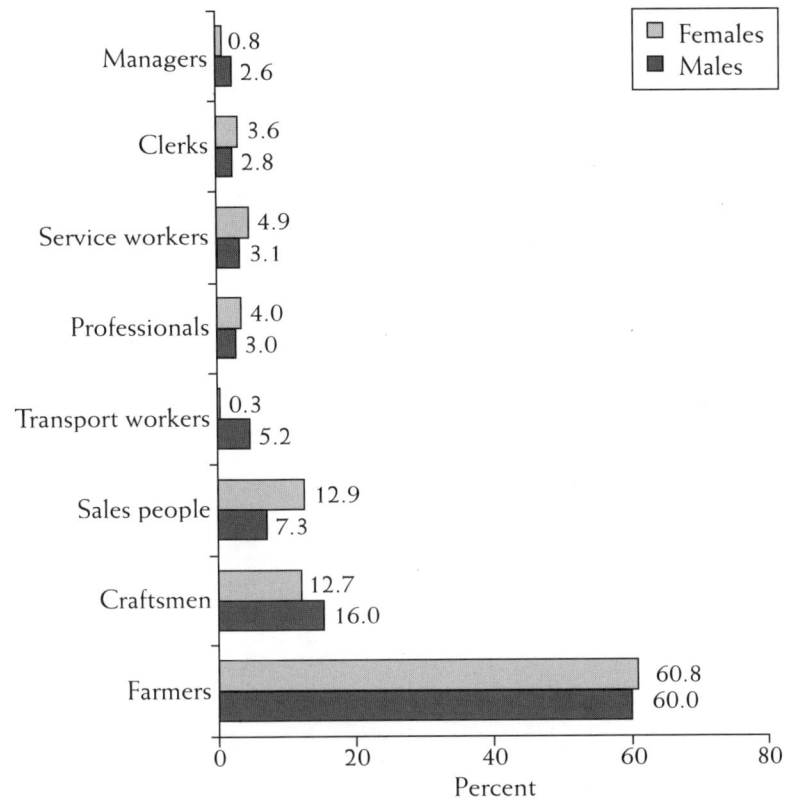

Figure 2.6 Occupations of Males and Females in 1991
(Source: Based on National Statistical Office, Statistical Yearbook Thailand 1993, OPM, Bangkok, 1993, p. 56.)

Incomes are higher in cities where there are better job opportunities, but they are still low by Western standards. In Bangkok, for instance, the average household earned US$5,300 per year in 1990, nearly twice the national average (see Figure 2.8).

These statistical records, however, understate the actual purchasing power. Many households, especially in villages, produce directly for the family's consumption. Thais build their own homes, raise cattle, grow vegetables, weave cloth, and make clothes. Such activities are not recorded in the household income accounts although they affect living conditions. In addition, the cost of living is much lower in Thailand than in Western countries.

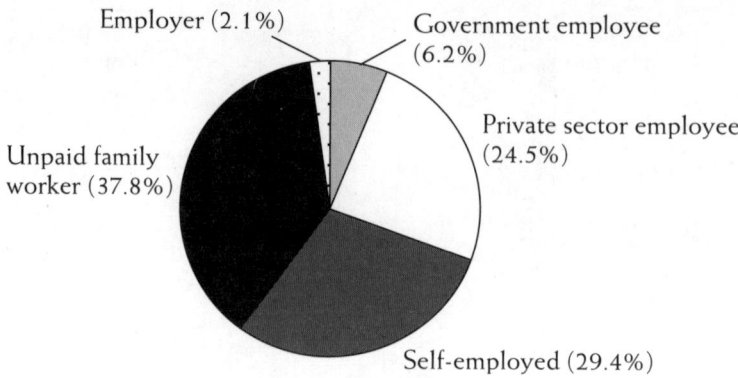

Figure 2.7   Working Status in 1991
(Source: Based on National Statistical Office, Statistical Yearbook Thailand 1993, OPM, Bangkok, 1993, pp. 58–9.)

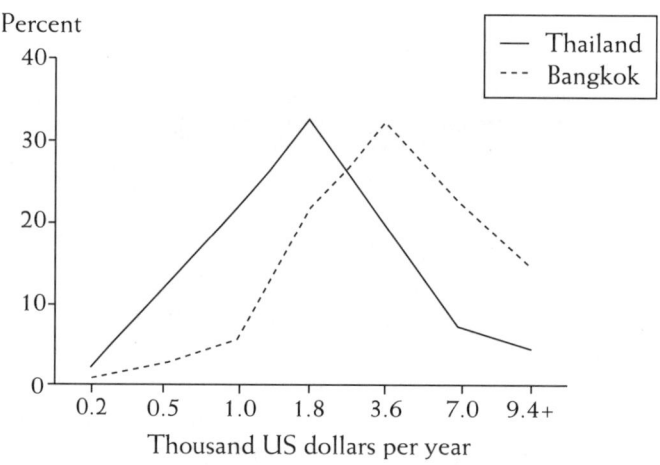

Figure 2.8   Household Income Distribution in 1990
(Source: Based on National Statistical Office, Report of the 1990 Household Socio-Economic Survey, Whole Kingdom, OPM, Bangkok, 1993, p. 111.)

Also biased but still revealing are the salary reports. In 1991, the average Thai worker earned US$950 per year and the average annual salaries ranged from US$390 for farmers to US$4,900 for managers. Workers fall into four income groups. Managers and professionals top the list with the highest salaries. Next are clerks and transport workers. The third group comprises sales people, craftsmen, and service workers. Farmers make up the last group and they earn the least.

Managers and professionals form a small group of better-paid people. In 1991, they numbered 1.6 million and the average salary was US$4,000 per annum for professionals and US$4,900 for managers (see Figure 2.9). These people are leading buyers of upmarket products.

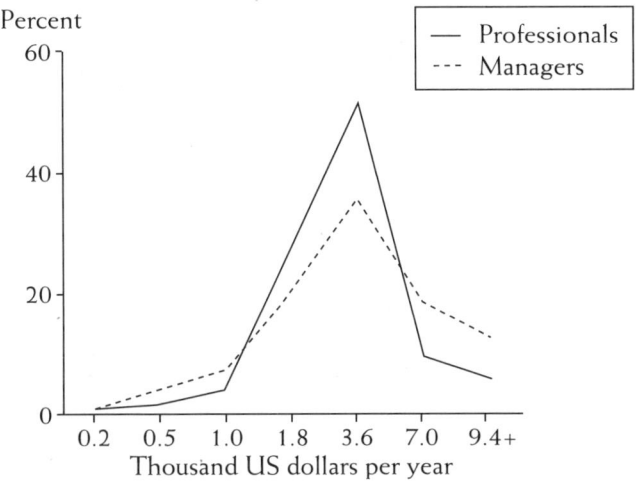

Figure 2.9 Distribution of Salaries of Managers and Professionals in 1991
(Source: Based on National Statistical Office, *Statistical Yearbook Thailand 1993*, OPM, Bangkok, 1993, pp. 64–5.)

Clerks and transport workers dominate the middle-class workers. In 1991, they numbered 1.9 million and the average annual salary was US$1,900 for transport workers and US$3,000 for clerks (see Figure 2.10).

Sales people, craftsmen, and service workers form a large group of lower-paid workers. In 1991, this category comprised 8.8 million people and the average annual salary ranged from US$1,300 for sales people to US$1,500 for service workers (see Figure 2.11).

Farmers constitute a separate group. This is the largest and poorest segment of the population. In 1991, there were 19 million

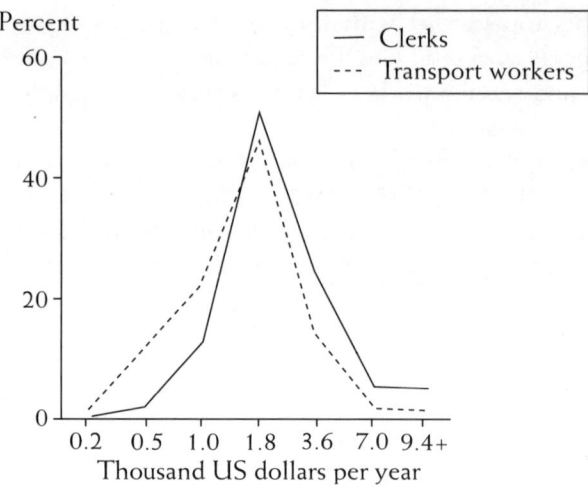

Figure 2.10   Distribution of Salaries of Clerks and Transport Workers in 1991
(Source: Based on National Statistical Office, Statistical Yearbook Thailand 1993, OPM, Bangkok, 1993, pp. 64–5.)

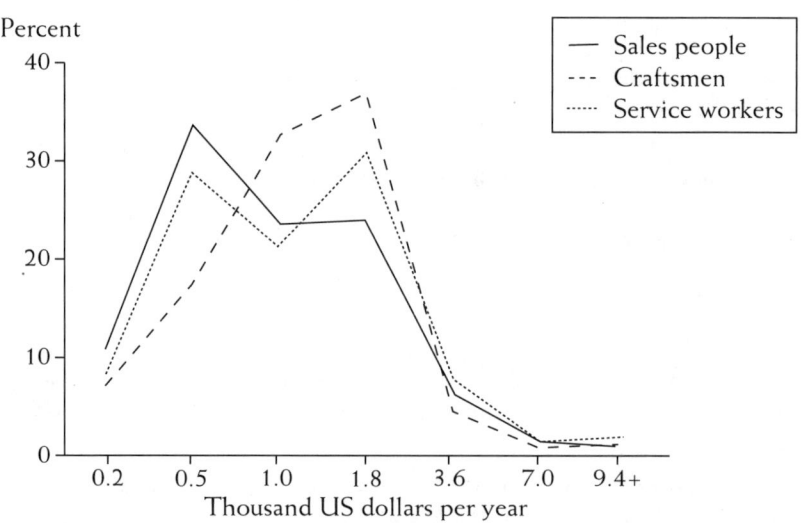

Figure 2.11   Distribution of Salaries of Sales People, Craftsmen, and Service Workers in 1991
(Source: Based on National Statistical Office, Statistical Yearbook Thailand 1993, OPM, Bangkok, 1993, pp. 64–5.)

farmers, 90 percent of whom earned less than US$700 per year. Their average annual salary was US$390 (see Figure 2.12).

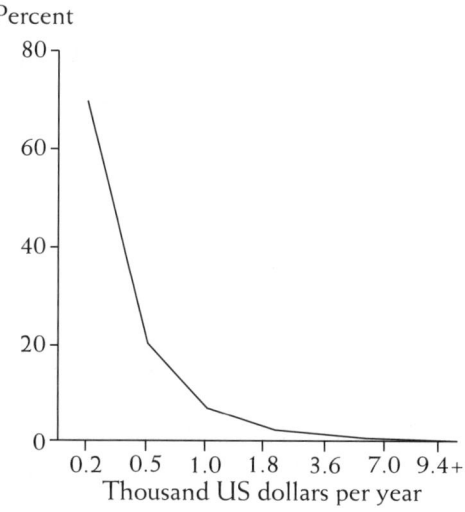

Figure 2.12 Distribution of Farmers' Salaries in 1991 (Source: Based on National Statistical Office, Statistical Yearbook Thailand 1993, OPM, Bangkok, 1993, pp. 64–5.)

Salaries understate actual earnings because many people work for no pay in family businesses. Such practices are especially common in the lower-paid groups. Many Thais, for example, work as sales people, craftsmen, and farmers with no recorded salaries. This pattern is shown clearly in Figure 2.12, Distribution of Farmers' Salaries in 1991, where there is a cluster of people with virtually no income.

Salary reports are, nonetheless, revealing. They highlight the major differences between various groups of workers, leading to similar conclusions as other less-biased indicators. Such measures as changes in income, for instance, also suggest that farmers are Thailand's poorest workers. These people have not benefited from the economic expansion as much as other Thais, although the returns to agriculture have increased. Between 1970 and 1991, the output of agriculture doubled in real terms, but production grew twice as fast in other industries.[23]

2.3 EDUCATION

Thailand produces highly skilled workers, although not in large numbers. Research institutes, active in many fields from medical and natural sciences to financial services, speak of the quality of the Thai elite. The Bangkok-based research center on snakes, Red Cross Snake Farm, for example, distributes its snake venom serums worldwide. Thailand also has excellent craftsmen of international standing. Thai jewelry designers, for instance, have won numerous awards including the prestigious De Beers's Diamonds International Award. The vast majority of Thais, however, have little training and they work at simple repetitive jobs.

2.3.1 EDUCATIONAL ATTAINMENT

The typical Thai worker compares favorably with other Asian workers. He is highly literate, although poorly educated. The 1985 survey of literacy estimated that over 90 percent of Thai adults were literate, one of the highest literacy rates in Asia.[24] Many people, however, do not study beyond the compulsory six-year primary cycle. In 1991, 81 percent of the working population had primary education only or no schooling.

This abundance of cheap labor attracts foreign investment. Companies trying to reduce production costs transfer their labor-intensive plants to Thailand. A survey conducted in November 1992 by the ASEAN Promotion Center on Trade, Investment and Tourism,[25] for example, indicates that a third of the Japanese companies planning to invest overseas consider investing in Thailand. Of these, nearly 60 percent are attracted by the low labor costs.

While cheap labor abounds, high-quality staff is scarce. To counter the chronic shortage of managers, foreign companies dispatch executives from their head office and they hire Thai workers in operational positions. Most investors set up simple assembly lines, at which Thai laborers are efficient when closely monitored for consistency. Some companies, however, train their staff for more sophisticated processes. Some assembly plants, for instance, have upgraded their output from simple products like electric fans and black-and-white television sets to more complicated equipment like telephones, color television sets, and electronic appliances.

The quality of the labor force is, however, improving steadily. The illiteracy rate keeps declining. Today, almost all youngsters are literate and since younger generations are more numerous, illiteracy is now common only in older age groups (see Figure 2.13). In 1985, 70 percent of illiterates were above 40 years old.

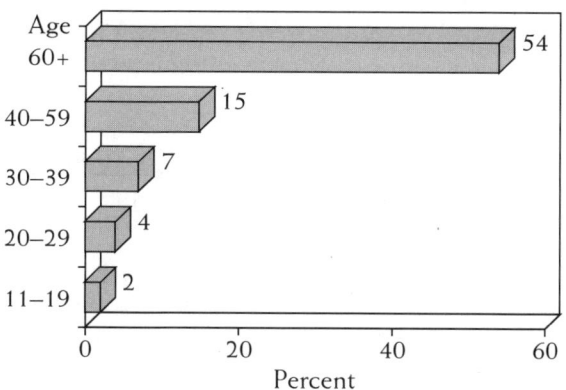

Figure 2.13 Illiteracy Rate by Age in 1985 (Source: Based on National Statistical Office, Statistical Handbook of Thailand 1989, OPM, Bangkok, pp. 34–5.)

The growing demand for managers also encourages more Thais to go to high school and college. Some local companies even finance the studies of people who promise to work for them later. Between 1980 and 1991, the proportion of high school graduates doubled, increasing from 9 to 19 percent (see Figure 2.14).

Thais owe their high literacy rate to a long history of compulsory education. The first compulsory education act dates back to 1921. It required children between 7 and 14 years old to attend primary school until completion of grade five. Subsequent governments extended the coverage of the law and lengthened the compulsory cycle. Children must now start elementary school between the age of 6 and 8 and complete the six-year primary cycle. Again, this is about to change. The Thai authorities have launched a new program that will increase compulsory schooling from six to nine years by 1996.

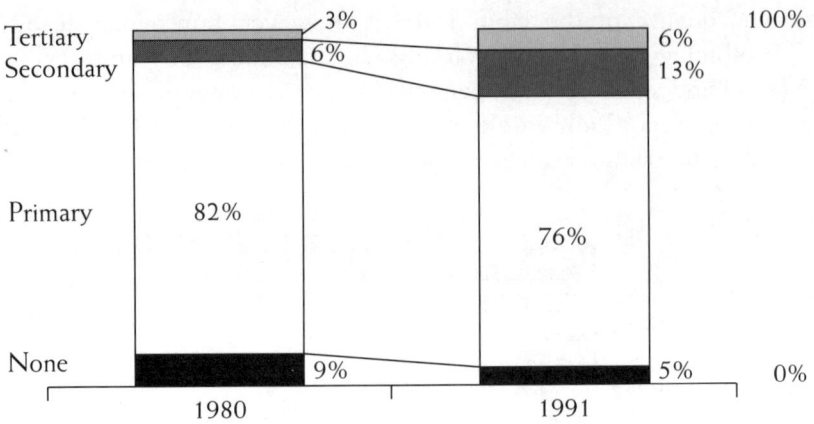

Figure 2.14 Educational Level of Workers in 1980 and 1991 (Source: Based on National Statistical Office, Report of the Labor Force Survey, Whole Kingdom, OPM, Bangkok, various issues.)

2.3.2 ATTENDANCE

Efforts to improve educational standards have been less successful in rural areas. Village children spend little time studying (see Figure 2.15). They stay under family care until they can enroll in primary school. Most quit school and start working after completing the compulsory cycle. The Labor Force Survey indicates that in 1991, only one-fifth of the villagers aged between 15 and 19 kept studying, compared to over half of the urbanites.[26]

Females are less educated than males. Thai families invest selectively in child education, spending more on their male offspring. Most males and females go to primary school because it is compulsory, but more males get secondary education. In the working population, for instance, the proportion of high school graduates is 30 percent greater for males (see Figure 2.16). This may explain the large proportion of females among low-skilled workers in Bangkok's manufacturing industries.

Poverty seems to be the principal hindrance to education. Most Thai children, over two-thirds, end their studies for financial reasons, claiming lack of financial support or the need to make a living as their principal motives (see Figure 2.17). That villagers are less educated only reflects their lower living standards.

Chapter 2 Life Styles

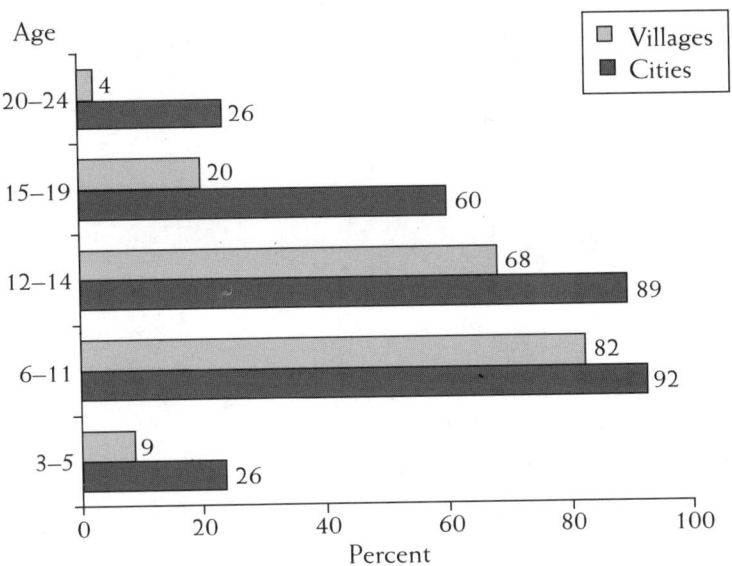

Figure 2.15 School Attendance by Age in 1987
(Source: Based on National Statistical Office, Report of the Children and Youth Survey 1987, OPM, Bangkok, p. 24.)

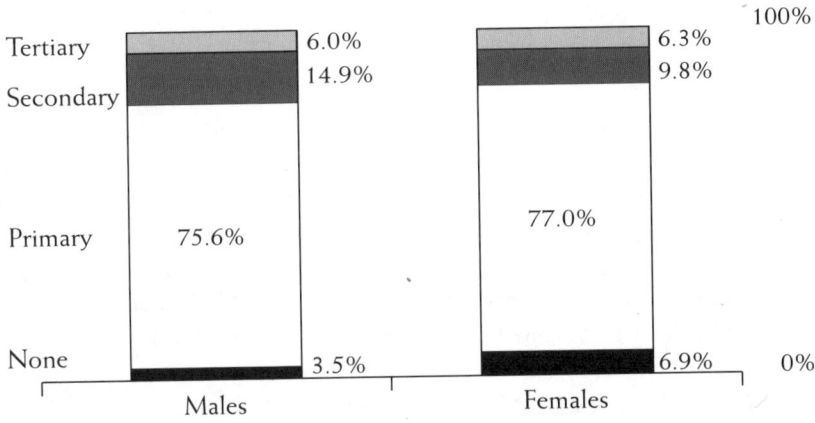

Figure 2.16 Educational Level of Workers by Sex in 1991
(Source: Based on National Statistical Office, Report of the Labor Force Survey, Whole Kingdom, May 1991, OPM, Bangkok, pp. 14–7.)

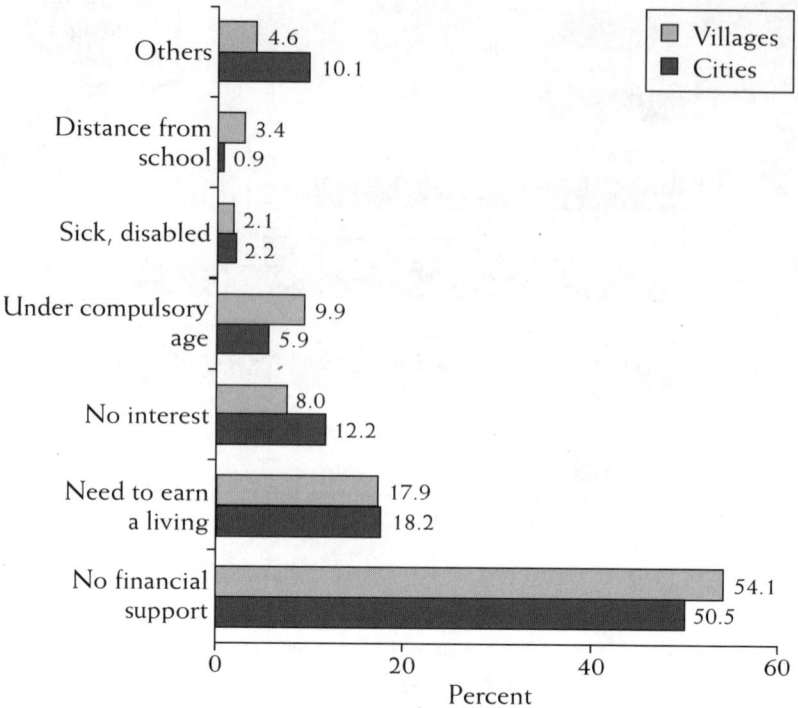

Figure 2.17 Reasons for Not Attending School in 1987
(Source: Based on National Statistical Office, Report of the Children and Youth Survey 1987, OPM, Bangkok, pp. 26–7.)

Going to school is expensive. Students must pay for tuition, books, school supplies, uniforms, and personal expenses such as food and transportation. In 1987, the average public school student spent about US$45 per year for elementary education, one-and-a-half month's salary for a typical farmer.[27] In addition, children who go to school do not contribute to the household income: in rural areas, children may find regular employment on the family farm.

2.3.3 VOCATIONAL TRAINING

In this society where many people quit school early, vocational training is valuable. Thai authorities are intent on developing such programs, but they lack funds and qualified instructors. Companies willing to train their staff may have to set up their own training program.

More Thais train to improve their income than for the sake of interest or as a hobby. Respondents give two principal and similar reasons for training: improving knowledge (that is, skills) and making a living. These account for 87 percent of the motives for training (see Figure 2.18). Successful training programs focus on marketable skills. Villagers study agriculture, cooking, handicrafts, and cattle raising and urbanites accounting, electronics, beauty therapy, and tailoring (see Figure 2.19). Adult education also fares better in cities, where more people work in offices and seek general training.

Seminars and short training courses have become popular in business circles. Consulting companies organize training sessions for managers, while foreign academics and business people give seminars during visits to Thailand. Topics are diverse, with speakers addressing either people working in specific industries or mixed audiences.

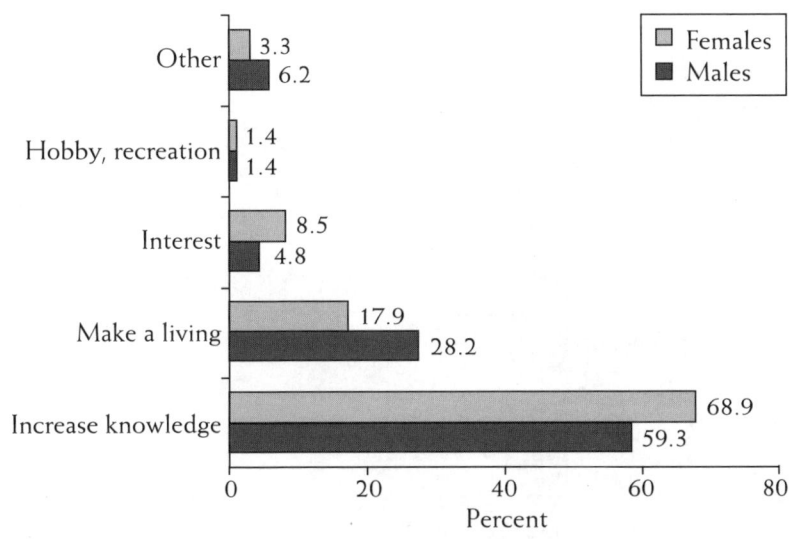

Figure 2.18 *Reasons for Training in 1985*
(Source: Based on National Statistical Office, Report of the Cultural Activity Participation and Time Use Survey 1985, OPM, Bangkok, p. 61.)

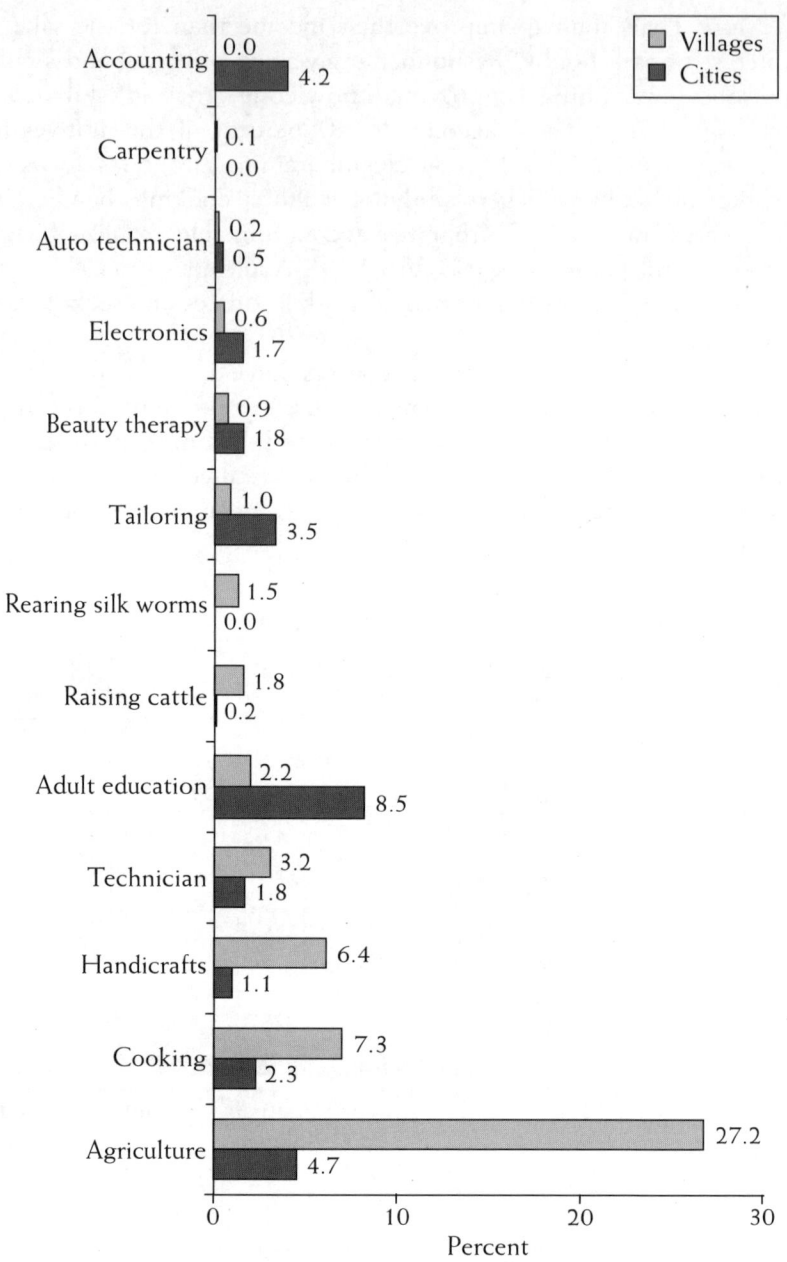

Figure 2.19 Vocational Training by Type in 1985
(Source: Based on National Statistical Office, *Report of the Cultural Activity Participation and Time Use Survey 1985*, OPM, Bangkok, pp. 59–60.)

2.3.4 SCHOOL SYSTEM

The Thai school system is designed on the Western model. It uses the standard four levels of education: kindergarten (or pre-primary), elementary (or primary), secondary, and tertiary. Kindergarten is for three years. Elementary school lasts six years and is compulsory. Secondary education lasts another six years and leads to tertiary education.

The curriculum also follows the Western pattern. Kindergartens prepare children for primary school, teaching the basics of reading and writing. Primary schools emphasize reading, writing, and arithmetic and provide general knowledge in history, geography, and the natural sciences. Secondary training comprises two levels, lower and upper; and three streams, academic, technical, and teacher training. The academic stream prepares students for college.

This similarity between Thai and Western school systems stems from the tradition of hiring international advisory teams. Since the Bowring Treaty with Great Britain opened Thailand to Western trade, Thai authorities have appointed foreign consultants for many public projects like canals, railroads, ports, and airports. Education was no exception. At the turn of the century, when the king set up public education, he called on British advisers.

2.3.5 SCHOOLS

Public and private schools share the market for education. The Thai government runs the public schools while various other concerns run the private schools, some of which are renowned for their quality. Among the many different private schools are Christian, Muslim, Chinese, Buddhist, and non-affiliated profit-making private schools.

Thai governments have a long tradition of working on public projects with the private sector. Since the days of Ayutthaya, Thai kings have subcontracted tasks that were beyond the means of the treasury to private parties. Even tax collection was handled by private entrepreneurs for many years. Education followed the same course.

In their urge to modernize their country, Thai kings promoted national education, but they lacked resources. In 1921, when education became compulsory, there were only some 4,000 public schools, not enough to accommodate all students. Soon, the authorities faced the difficulty of providing qualified instructors and of financing schools. Being short of both teachers and funds, the authorities focused on primary education and they encouraged the private sector to join in. They were not particular about the affiliation of private schools, which accounts for their diversity.

Successive governments invested in additional facilities, catching up gradually with the population growth. They set up schools in villages, using the temples for school buildings when necessary, and they called on the Border Patrol Police to organize education in remote places. In 1991, this police corps still supervised 168 schools staffed with 923 teachers.[28] The prime objective was to ensure elementary education for all children. Later, the government turned to less pressing issues such as developing kindergartens. In the interim, private schools filled the gap, at least for people who could afford them.

Private schools train students from kindergarten to university level. In 1990, they enrolled one in seven Thai students, 45 percent of whom were in the primary cycle. Private institutions, however, capture only a small part, some 10 percent, of the vast market for primary education. They are more prominent at the kindergarten and college levels where their market share reaches 30 percent.[29]

Most private schools are in cities. As they charge higher tuition fees, these institutions cater to wealthier students. About two-thirds of Thailand's private schools are in cities and over a third of the urbanites get private education, compared to only 6 percent of the villagers.[30]

Temples run the only free private schools, but these are reserved for boys. Before education became compulsory and public schools widespread, temples were the principal providers of education. Today, Buddhist priests still teach reading, writing, arithmetic, and religious precepts to young boys who serve the temple as novices or as temple boys. Good students may study in free monk's universities, which deliver certificates equivalent to bachelor's degrees. Later the young graduates may quit the robe and work as laymen.

2.4 LIVING QUARTERS

Living quarters are often basic. The vast majority of Thai houses are

Chapter 2 Life Styles

simple structures. They have little equipment and their utilities seldom meet Western standards, although homes are better equipped in urban areas. Electrical appliances, furniture, and utilities are still considered luxuries in parts of Thailand.

Consumption is, however, growing. Thais improve their living environment as they get richer. Between 1970 and 1991, expenses on household goods have increased annually by 12 percent in real terms and their share of total consumption nearly tripled.[31] With a market of nearly 13 million homes,[32] this trend is encouraging.

2.4.1 HOUSING

Housing is still traditional. The vast majority of Thais, some 94 percent, live in small individual dwellings (see Figure 2.20). High-rise structures are usually office buildings so that even in Bangkok, most people live in houses. Here, the luxurious high-rise condominiums which have appeared recently cater to expatriates and upper-income Thais.

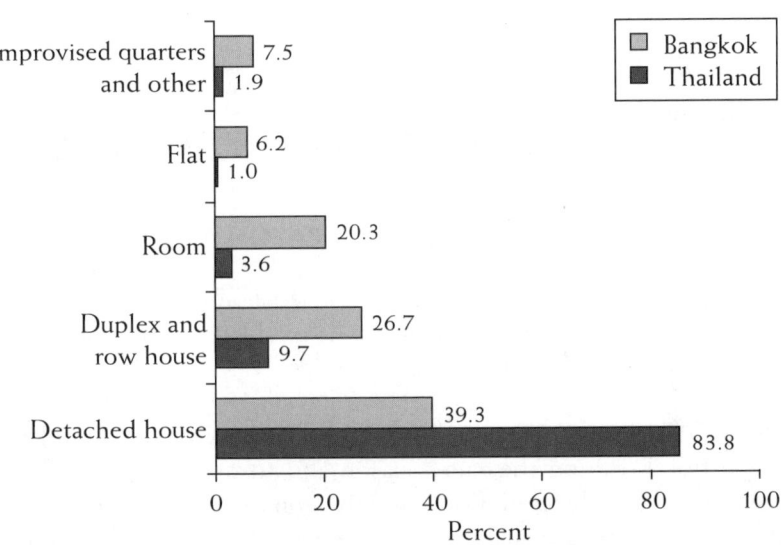

Figure 2.20 Accommodations by Type in 1990
(Source: Based on National Statistical Office, Report of the 1990 Household Socio-Economic Survey, Whole Kingdom, OPM, Bangkok, 1993, pp. 107–8.)

Because Thai cities tend to spread out, real-estate prices are lower than in other Asian cities. Bangkok, although swarming by Thai standards, is still much less crowded than most other Asian cities and Bangkok properties are some of the cheapest. In 1990, for instance, the rental price of office space in Bangkok was about one-tenth that of Tokyo and one-fifth that of Hong Kong.

Low real estate prices encourage home ownership. Over three-quarters of Thai households own the dwelling and the land they live on. Even in Bangkok, many people own their homes. Some 35 percent of Bangkok households own both dwelling and land and an additional 11 percent own a home on a rented land (see Figure 2.21).

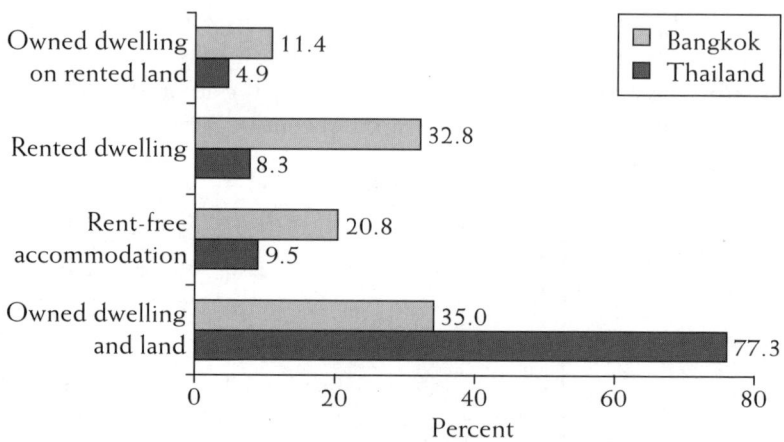

Figure 2.21 Ownership Status of Dwellings in 1990
(Source: Based on National Statistical Office, Report of the 1990 Household Socio-Economic Survey, Whole Kingdom, OPM, Bangkok, 1993, p. 107.)

Most Thai homes, however, are simple. They are built on piles to escape floods during the rainy season and to prevent animals from intruding. The elevated floor usually comprises a main room, a kitchen, a sleeping quarter, and a veranda. Under the living area, people store tools and firewood, and they leave some space to shelter buffaloes, pigs, and cattle.

Houses are often built near rivers and canals. This is a legacy of the past. When jungles covered Thailand, people lived on river banks and seashores and they traveled by boats. Rivers and canals were then the sole highways. Roads are more numerous now, but they do not reach all communities. In some places rivers remain the only access.

Construction is basic. Most homes are wooden structures with corrugated steel roof and in small villages they may be simple bamboo huts with thatched roof. In 1990, nearly three-quarters of Thais lived in wooden homes (see Figure 2.22). These are especially common in upper Thailand. In other regions where forests are depleted, people are turning to cement, bricks, and stone, a trend that will soon affect many provinces. Cheap prefabricated cement houses, for instance, are becoming successful throughout the country.

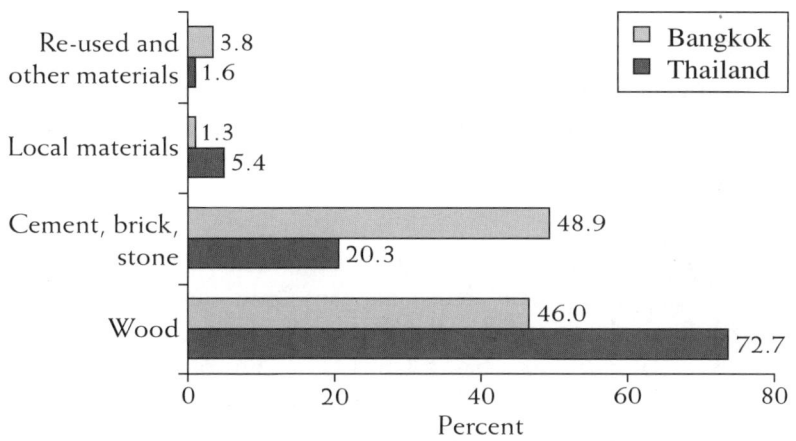

Figure 2.22 Building Materials of Dwellings in 1990
(Source: Based on National Statistical Office, Report of the 1990 Household Socio-Economic Survey, Whole Kingdom, OPM, Bangkok, 1993, p. 108.)

Fires are common in these wooden homes and bamboo huts. They are destructive because houses are usually clustered. In 1990, there were over 2,000 fires, this is about five per day, and they caused US$54 million in damages.[33] Thais often buy coverage against this hazard. For many years, fire insurance has been the most common non-life policy in Thailand.

Refined Thai-style houses contrast sharply with the ordinary homes. With their panelled walls slightly leaning inwards, steep roofs with pointed ends, ornate gables, and glassless windows, these elegant houses are the privilege of the wealthy Thais. They make durable homes because they are built of teak, whose dense and oily texture resists rot and insects. They are also movable: their panels can be disassembled and reerected elsewhere. Some of the finest old houses from upper Thailand, much sought after for their exquisite carving and craftsmanship, find a secondhand market in Bangkok.

2.4.2 HOUSEHOLD EQUIPMENT

Household equipment is still limited. The typical Thai home has almost no furniture. There is little use for tables, chairs, and beds; people sleep on a mat that they roll up in the morning; they cook on a clay stove; and they serve food on a cloth spread on the floor or on a low table. Except for a few altars to spirits, other household items are restricted to the bare necessities.

Growing incomes are, however, raising the demand for household equipment. Basic products like small electrical appliances, wiring, plumbing equipment, and sanitary ware have good potential, especially in villages where they are scarce.

Appliances and furniture   Western equipment is becoming more common. Small electrical items like fans, pots, and irons are the most common. In this tropical country, fans are favorites. In 1990, some two-thirds of Thais had a fan. Ownership of more expensive equipment, however, progresses slowly. Well-off households have a bed and a refrigerator, occasionally a sofa and a sewing machine, but rarely a washing machine or an air conditioner (see Figure 2.23).

Bangkok households are better equipped, mainly because they are wealthier. The vast majority, some 80 percent, have small electrical items and about half also have beds and refrigerators. Expensive goods like air conditioners are also more common in Bangkok, although they are not widespread.

Price affects purchases, but it is not the sole influence. Some Western goods are impractical. Washing machines, for instance, need both electricity and running water, a requirement seldom met in villages; besides, they are time-saving devices unlikely to be valued by poor people with low time cost. Sewing machines, in contrast, fare better because they are cost-saving home-production devices which may be foot-powered. People also use them to produce garments for shops and factories.

Chapter 2 Life Styles

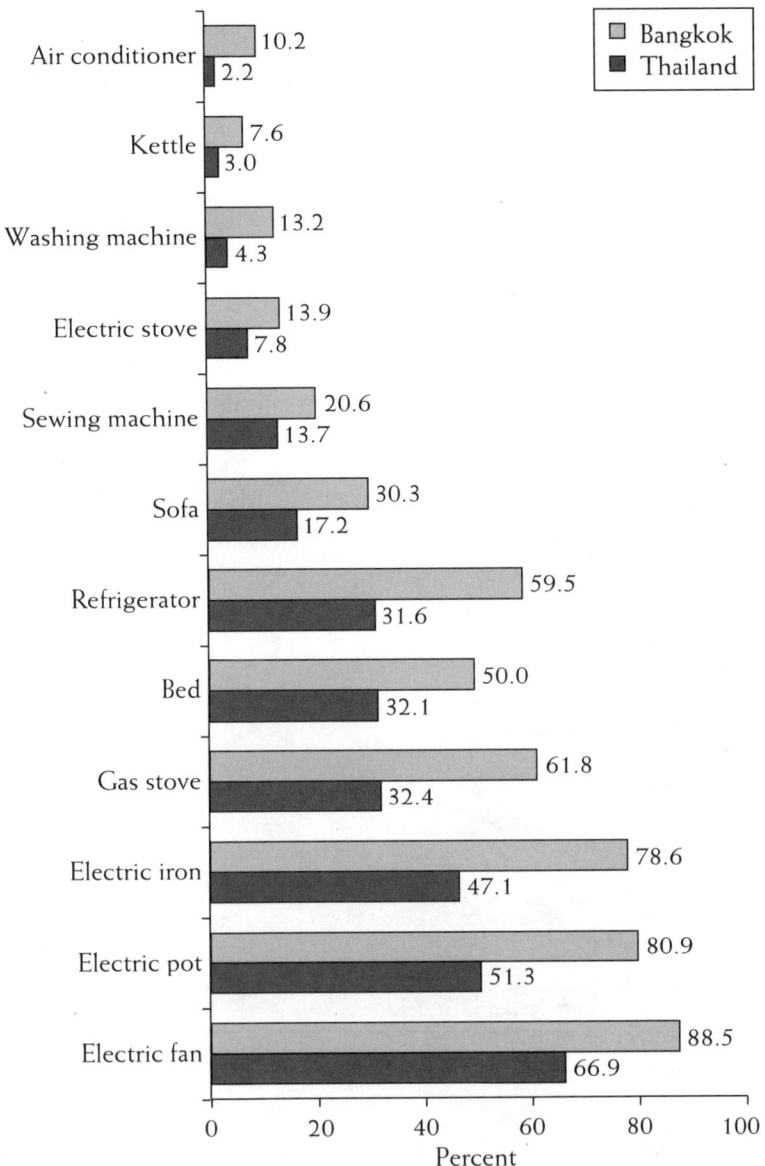

Figure 2.23 Ownership of Household Items in 1990
(Source: Based on National Statistical Office, Report of the 1990 Household Socio-Economic Survey, Whole Kingdom, OPM, Bangkok, 1993, p. 121.)

In this tropical country, refrigerators have good potential, but they need a constant supply of electricity. They are more successful in cities, although they are beginning to sell well in villages. Incidentally, the lack of refrigeration prevents storage of perishable goods and calls for frequent shopping. It also affects packaging. Products such as ice cream and yogurt, for instance, sell better as snacks consumed away from home.

Radio, television, and video Radio and television probably come first on the purchase list of many families. Thai households are more likely to have a television set and a radio than a bed or a refrigerator. In 1990, 73 percent of Thai homes had a radio and 60 percent a television (see Figure 2.24). Recently, videocassette recorders have also become more common, although they are still a luxury. In 1990, 7.4 percent of the households had one, up from 2.3 percent in 1984. Videocassette recorders are especially popular in the Bangkok area where ownership exceeds 24 percent, compared to 2 percent in the Northeast.

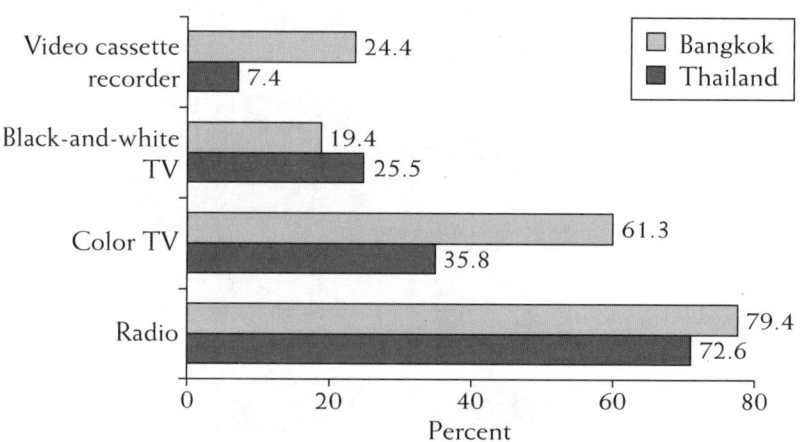

Figure 2.24 Ownership of Radio, Television, and VCR in 1990 (Source: Based on National Statistical Office, Report of the 1990 Household Socio-Economic Survey, Whole Kingdom, OPM, Bangkok, 1993, p. 121.)

Radios have been fairly widespread for some time, but television sets became common only recently. Until the 1980s, only people living in cities and in small towns could afford a television. Recent economic growth, however, brought television sets within the reach of many more Thais. Between 1984 and 1988, for instance, the penetration of television in small villages doubled, growing from 20 to 41 percent.[34]

The quality of equipment is also improving gradually. The color TV dominates, especially in Bangkok where it accounts for three-quarters of the sets. In poorer areas, however, people buy more black-and-white sets. In the Northeast, for instance, these capture 58 percent of the market for television.[35]

Vehicles Few budgets allow for the purchase of expensive vehicles like automobiles and pickup trucks. In most places, bicycles and motorcycles are more common than cars (see Figure 2.25). In 1990, about one-eighth of Thai households had a car or a truck, over a third a motorcycle, and one-half a bicycle. To many youngsters, a motorcycle is a coveted luxury. It is, for instance, the first buy of a Northeastern boxer who starts making good money.

The situation is, however, different in Bangkok where traffic congestion is legendary. In this sprawling city, buses are the only means of public transportation aside from taxis. People often spend a large proportion of their income on cars. Bangkok residents have fewer bicycles and motorcycles than other Thais, but many more cars.

2.4.3 UTILITIES

Thailand is renowned for its poor utilities. Running water, sewers, gas, and electricity are scarce. These utilities exist in urban areas where they are more economical to provide, but elsewhere they are in short supply.

Water Running water is still a luxury in most parts of the country. In 1990, less than a third of Thai households had indoor plumbing. Only Bangkok residents enjoy good amenities. Nearly 90 percent have running water, although a third share the piping facilities (see Figure 2.26). In the provinces, in contrast, only 14 to 29 percent of the households have running water.

People who do not have running water usually rely on public taps although in the well-irrigated Central Region, they also use the water from rivers and streams. This tradition even persists in parts of Bangkok where people living by the Chao Phraya River bathe and wash clothes and dishes in the river.

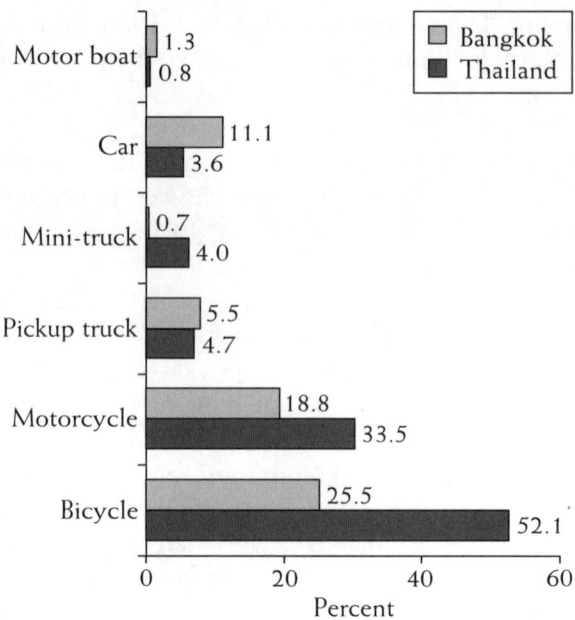

Figure 2.25 Ownership of Vehicles in 1990 (Source: Based on National Statistical Office, Report of the 1990 Household Socio-Economic Survey, Whole Kingdom, OPM, Bangkok, 1993, p. 121.)

Drinking water Thais select their drinking water carefully. By tradition, they avoid drinking river water. In the past, rivers were often contaminated and during epidemics their waters were fatal. Only poor people who could not afford a rainwater tank drank river water. Epidemics are better controlled now, but sewage and industrial waste pollute many rivers.

People get drinking water from three main sources: public taps, rainwater tanks, and home taps (see Figure 2.27). Their supply, however, differs across regions. In Bangkok, most people drink running water because they have indoor plumbing, although 15 percent drink rainwater. In the provinces, people rely more on public taps and rainwater tanks, the latter being especially prominent in Central and Northeastern Thailand.

Toilets In most places, Thais have some form of sewage system and many homes have a flush toilet. In 1990, over 80 percent of the

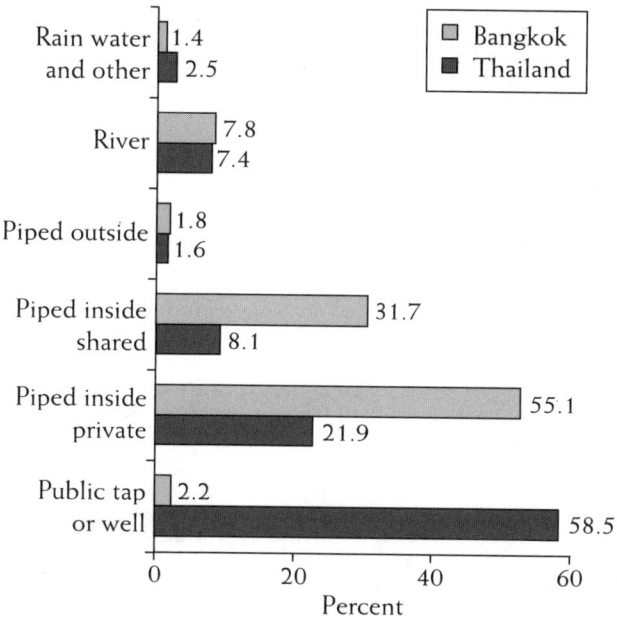

Figure 2.26 Sources of Non-Drinking Water in 1990 (Source: Based on National Statistical Office, Report of the 1990 Household Socio-Economic Survey, Whole Kingdom, OPM, Bangkok, 1993, p. 108.)

households had access to a flush toilet, whether private or shared (see Figure 2.28).

Sanitation, however, varies substantially across regions. In Bangkok, nearly everyone has access to a flush toilet, but in poor and remote areas, many people do not. The situation is especially severe in the Northeast and the South where up to a third of the households have no toilet. In these regions, plumbing equipment and sanitary ware have potential.

Cooking fuels Charcoal and wood are leading cooking fuels, but gas is becoming more popular. Thais traditionally cooked on small clay stoves fueled by charcoal or wood. Many, some two-thirds, still do (see Figure 2.29). More people, however, are using gas stoves. For the past decade, gas has been extracted in the Gulf of Thailand and it has become a popular cooking fuel in the nearby Central and Southern regions. Gas consumption peaks in Bangkok, where charcoal and wood are difficult to deliver and expensive to store.

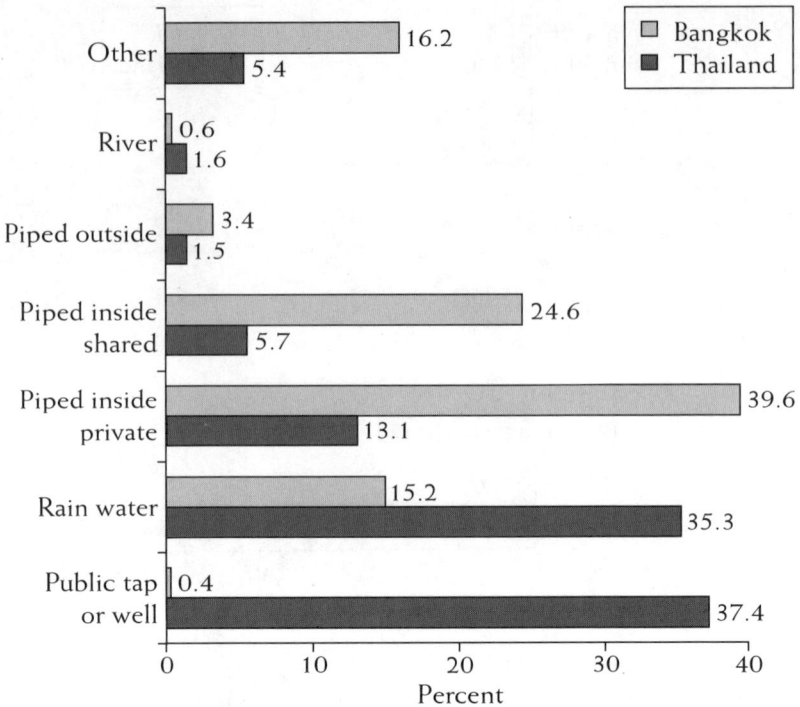

Figure 2.27 Sources of Drinking Water in 1990
(Source: Based on National Statistical Office, Report of the 1990 Household Socio-Economic Survey, Whole Kingdom, OPM, Bangkok, 1993, pp. 108–9.)

2.5 RECREATION

Talking about recreation in Thailand may be an endless task. Early travelers claimed that Thais never missed an opportunity of having a good time and worked harder at preparing festivities than at ordinary work. They also described Thai people as passionate gamblers who bet on anything from kite-flying contests to cockfights and card games. This remains true today. Modern life does not alter the quest for amusement, although it brings new forms of entertainment.

Like their Western counterparts, Thais use their leisure time to relax. They meet friends, watch television, listen to the radio, go to the movies, attend festivals and ceremonies, play sports, watch sports games, read, and make handicrafts. In short, recreation is diverse.

Chapter 2 Life Styles

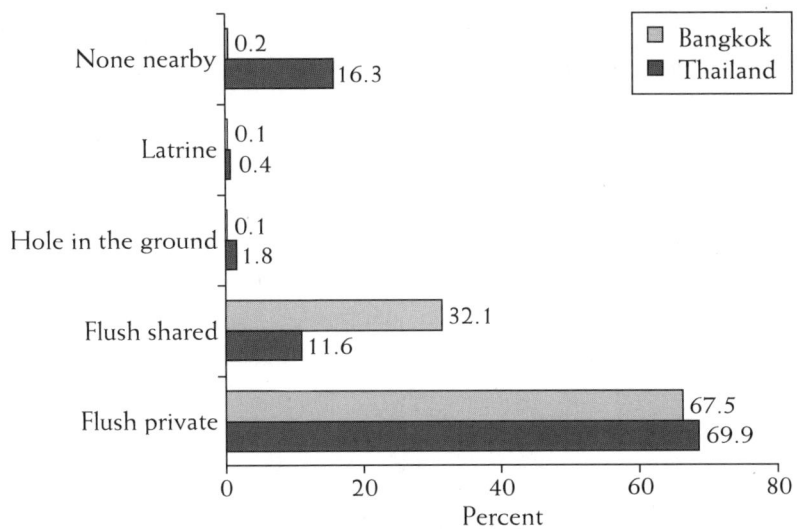

Figure 2.28   Toilets by Type in 1990
(Source: Based on National Statistical Office, Report of the 1990 Household Socio-Economic Survey, Whole Kingdom, OPM, Bangkok, 1993, p. 109.)

2.5.1 FESTIVITIES

Thailand has countless festivals, fairs, and other celebrations of various origin. There are Buddhist, Brahmanic, and animistic festivals and many different regional festivities. Buddhist celebrations are times for temple ceremonies, religious deeds, and processions. Brahmanic and animistic festivals highlight parades and outdoor entertainment. Regional fairs like the fruit, flower, umbrella, handicraft, and silk fairs promote local specialties, while some regional festivities like boat races and buffalo races are for pure fun.

Even religious celebrations are opportunities for fun. Festivals are noisy street parties with singing, drum beating, parades, and occasional beauty contests. Buddhist festivals are no exception; they combine formal rituals and fun. After the religious ceremony at the temple, Buddhist celebrations turn into merry festivities. Thais are also quick to cash in on foreign celebrations. If the French expatriate community were to celebrate Bastille day in Bangkok, Thais would invariably join in to share the fun.

Thais treat the important festivals as holiday periods, whether official or not, and these vary across provinces. Each locality has at

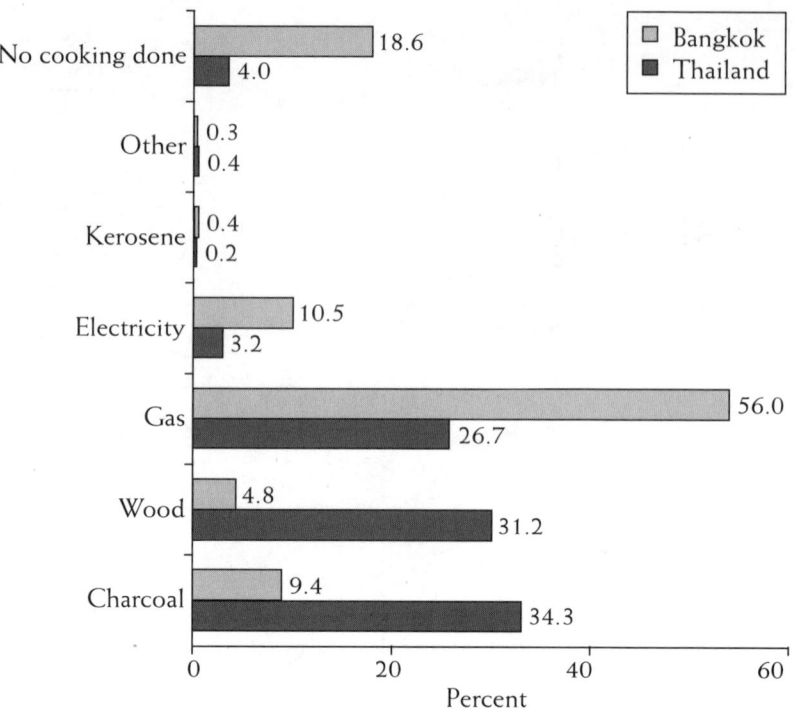

Figure 2.29 Cooking Fuels by Type in 1990
(Source: Based on National Statistical Office, Report of the 1990 Household Socio-Economic Survey, Whole Kingdom, OPM, Bangkok, 1993, p. 109.)

least one major festival per year. In the Northeast, for instance, the sky rocket festival, a rite that honors a mythological rain god to ensure a good rainy season, is the principal event. The festivities start with parades, dances, banquets, and they culminate with the launch of a rocket. For this occasion, Northeastern Thais who work in cities take some time off and return to their native village.

Nationwide, the principal events are the New Year festivities. Thais celebrate no less than three New Years, all of which are best avoided if on a business trip. The Western, Thai, and Chinese New Years are periods of traffic congestion, business interruption, and high hotel occupancies.

The Western New Year, although a recent introduction, is much celebrated. It became a public holiday in 1941 following the adoption of the Western calendar. It was then foreign to most Thais, but they caught on quickly; welcoming an extra opportunity to have fun. December 31 and January 1 are public holidays. People celebrate them with parades and public gatherings, and major hotels offer Western-style entertainment.

Thais, nevertheless, kept Songkran, their old new year. The Songkran, which lasts from April 13 to 15, is a time for vacation and travel. Many factories take their annual holiday during this period and people either visit relatives or travel. Airlines even schedule extra flights to accommodate the traffic.

The festivities of Songkran are a mixture of religious rituals and merrymaking. In many places, the celebrations start with a parade of Buddha images that crowds sprinkle respectfully with scented water. Soon after the religious ceremony, the spirit of fun takes over, especially in the provinces. The traditional water sprinkling then turns into street parties where youngsters armed with buckets of water drench all passersby copiously. Sprinkling may also be hard work, and some people seek help. In 1994, an enterprising monk from Northeastern Thailand borrowed a fire engine to spray holy water on crowds of followers to bless them.[36]

The Chinese New Year, although not an official holiday, is a slow period for business. It falls on the first day of the Chinese lunar year, which may be any time between late January and early March. As this New Year is much celebrated in Chinese circles, it affects many companies. Chinese shops and businesses, which are especially numerous in Bangkok, close for three to four days and many Chinese take an extended vacation. Unlike the Western and Thai New Years, Chinese New Year is a quiet family-oriented celebration during which Chinese visit relatives and exchange good luck red envelopes containing money.

2.5.2 GAMBLING

Gambling is another national pastime. Almost any contest qualifies for betting. Although the Thai government confines legal gambling to state lottery and horse racing, actual gambling is much more diverse. Thais place illegal wagers on foreign lotteries, boxing, and semiprofessional league soccer matches. They also bet informally on many other contests. Illegal gambling is the single most common offence in Thailand, with about 96,000 cases recorded in 1991.[37]

Fun, more than money, animates gamblers. How much Thais gamble illegally is anyone's guess, but the legal betting expenses are moderate. In 1990, Thais spent US$3 per person per year in legal bets,[38] a modest achievement compared to about 500 times as much in Hong Kong.

Lottery, a game that many people can afford, is the most common form of gambling. It accounts for almost all legal bets. The State Lottery Bureau, which runs the national lottery, organizes two draws per month, with a ticket output of 28 million per draw. In addition, foreign lotteries, known as *lotto*, although illegal under the Thai anti-gambling law, are also popular because of their greater prizes. In 1990, Thais spent US$5 per person per year on number games.[39]

Playing the domestic lottery is an institution. It was already popular in the days of Ayutthaya, when Thais kings auctioned off the right to run the lottery monopoly. Today, guessing the winning lottery number is still a social event that involves numerous prayers and rituals.

Horse racing is less popular. Only Bangkok's two race tracks are of some importance. These get most of the bets. By Asian standards, the betting volume on Thai horse races is, however, low. In 1991, it was forty times smaller than in Hong Kong.[40]

Informal betting is common. In rural areas, cock and other animal fights are popular betting events. People also gamble on such traditional games as kite-flying contests. These contests, which take place throughout Asia, pit a "male" kite against a "female" kite. In the Thai version, a large and powerful male kite tries to tangle and bring down a small, but agile, female kite. Even in Bangkok crowds gather between February and April, when the afternoon wind blows steadily, to watch and bid on kite-flying contests.

2.5.3 SPORTS

The sports industry is still in its infancy, but it has good potential, especially with Thai youths. Sports provide much entertainment, although people spend more time watching than playing them. Adults dislike physically exerting games, leaving these strenuous activities to youngsters and professionals. For the sports aficionado, however, Thailand offers many opportunities to practice Western and Thai sports (see Figure 2.30).

Thai sports Traditional Thai sports have much visual appeal. They are both athletic and aesthetic performances that enhance the

Chapter 2 Life Styles

elegance of body movements. *Takraw* and Thai boxing, Thailand's most renowned and popular sports, are no exceptions.

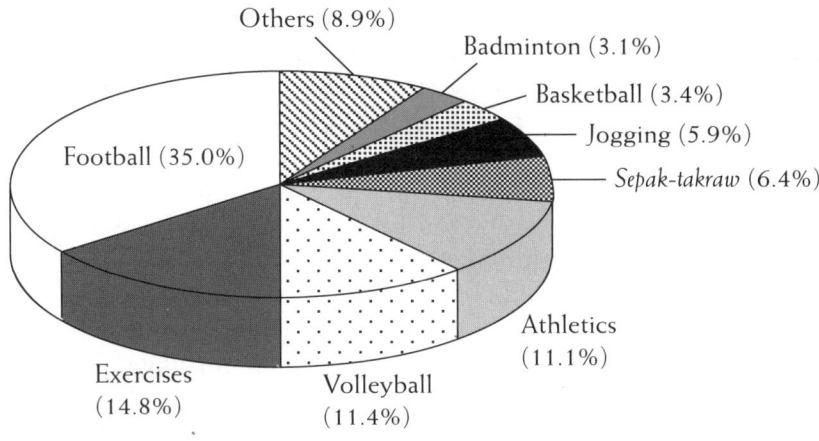

Figure 2.30   Sports Played by Thai Youths in 1987
(Source: Based on National Statistical Office, Report of the Children and Youth Survey 1987, OPM, Bangkok, p. 36.)

Takraw is the national pastime that people play from their teens onwards. It is an elegant game where players stand in a circle and try to keep a hollow rattan ball aloft by knocking it with any part of the body but the hands. Young males often gather for an informal game of *takraw* during work or school breaks. In a modern version of this game, players pass the rattan ball back and forth across a net like in a volleyball game. Each version of this sport has its professional teams, and the modern version is more common in international competitions.

The more aggressive, but equally graceful, Thai boxing is popular both as a martial art and as an opportunity to gamble. Thai boxing, also called kick boxing because it uses both hands and kicks, is the Thai art of self-defense that goes back to the days of Ayutthaya. In this game, boxers wear gloves but no shoes. Almost any part of the body is both a weapon and a target, a technique that makes Thai boxing more effective than most other martial arts. For many people, however, boxing provides them with an opportunity to gamble. There is no record of the bets wagered because they are illegal, but they are said to be considerable.

Boxing has its stars. Pugilists often come from the poor Northeast, where hardship and poverty seem to enhance fighting skills. The best boxers become celebrities. They fight major bouts, drawing large crowds and securing high prize money. A boxing career is, however, brief because this physically demanding sport wears down fighters rapidly. The average Thai boxer reaches the top of his form in his early twenties and retires in his late twenties.

Western sports A few Western sports also command an enthusiastic following. Soccer is probably the most popular one. Introduced in the 1930s, it soon became a favorite game in Thai schools. Youngsters learn to play soccer in their teens and they keep up with it until their mid-twenties. Adults rarely play soccer, but they enjoy watching it. Live broadcasts of international soccer matches secure large audiences. Some even manage to clear Bangkok's traffic.

While Thai adults like watching sports, they spend little time playing them. People above 20 years old prefer quiet outdoor activities to strenuous games. It is probably this interest in mild exercise that spurred the development of golf.

Golf has become a favorite game among the middle- and upper-income Thais. It was initially the preserve of Japanese businessmen, but it has grown fashionable in local business circles. Golf draws many new participants from the expanding Thai middle class. Estimates of the number of regular players vary widely but they suggest that between 1987 and 1993, membership grew tenfold. In 1993, there were about 100 golf courses in Thailand, a third of which were in the Bangkok area, and some 100 more projects were under way.

The growing interest in golf has created business opportunities. Developers call on famous international players to design new upmarket courses. Gardening companies import grass suitable for humid climates. Specialized shops cater to golfers, while brokers trade golf course debentures.

2.5.4 CRAFTS

Thais have a long tradition of making handicrafts both for leisure and for work. Many of these were once domestic items. Their production started as a cottage industry. Until the last century, wealthy families maintained in-house artisans to produce household goods while most other households bought their wares from the local craftsmen. For centuries, these workers were the sole producers of domestic items like fish traps, coconut graters, rice baskets, jars, bowls, mats, cloths, and floral decorations.

Whether made by artists or artisans, these household items were graceful objects. A simple coconut grater, for instance, would become a stool finely carved in the shape of an animal with a scraper inserted in the mouth. Much of this tradition is still alive. Stalls near temples sell elaborate floral decorations while handicraft shops display fine pieces.

A recent surge of interest for Thai crafts brought many of these traditional products in the foreign markets. In the process, some like silk gained international notoriety while others like wood carvings became collectors' items.

Many handicrafts are made of bamboo, which grows in most parts of the country. The resourceful Thais shape bamboo into countless structures like baskets, fish traps, storage boxes, chicken houses, and silkworm trays. Baskets are especially diverse, coming in different shapes and sizes to fit specific purposes. They are made to carry anything from rice and coconuts to pigs.

More renowned, perhaps, are the northeastern silks prized for their luster and bright colors. In the Northeast, where mulberry trees grow well, silk weaving is a traditional way of earning extra income between harvests. People in this region produce both regular silk cloth and *ikats*. The latter are decorative cloths whose threads are tied and dyed by segments in different colors before being woven into subtle patterns.

Each area has its specialties, but the greatest concentration of handicrafts is in the North. This region, which abounds with natural resources and remained isolated until the development of railroads, has developed numerous crafts. Its productions include wood carvings, celadon porcelain, lacquer, silverware, cloth, and some exclusive specialties like paper umbrellas.

Wood carving is probably the most celebrated northern craft. To its skilled artisans, the North owes the elaborate carvings in its temples. These craftsmen have built a reputation that reaches distant provinces. Thais throughout the country still call on Chiang Mai artisans to carve fine structures.

The North is also renowned for the crafts of its hill tribe people. The movable possessions, like the ornate accouterment, which nomadic life compelled tribal people to invest in, have become much sought-after. Especially popular are the colorful embroideries and the silver ornaments like belts, bangles, and necklaces.

2.5.5 LEISURE ACTIVITIES

Leisure activities differ across individuals. Income, age, and sex bear on the choice of amusement. Poorer people seek cheaper forms of entertainment. Young people enjoy outings and greater physical activity. Females spend more time indoors reading and making handicrafts. Males go out more often to meet friends, play sports, and watch movies (see Figure 2.31).

Villages In rural areas, recreation is traditional. Villagers, who have little access to the facilities of modern life, derive most of their entertainment from social gatherings. Their care at preparing ceremonies is legendary. Villagers also rely on cinema, radio, television if they have it, and whatever publication comes along. Flexible schedules encourage hobbies. Villagers train pets, do some gardening, produce handicrafts, and weave cloth. Weaving, a time-consuming activity, takes place almost exclusively in villages (see Figure 2.32).

Cities In cities the leisure industry is developing rapidly. Urbanites, who are busy, try to make the most of their scarce leisure time. They rely on modern equipment to get instant amusement and they curtail lengthy social gathering and time-consuming hobbies. Urbanites often watch television and videos and they listen to tapes. Better access to reading material gives them more chances to read books, magazines, and newspapers. These people also have fewer opportunities to exercise than villagers; they compensate by walking and playing sports more often.

Children Children below 10 years old have limited interests. They enjoy watching television mainly. Some also listen to the radio and go to the movies. They rarely have a hobby; only a few children like training pets and gardening. Their cultural activities are especially restricted; they seldom read books and magazines, probably because many are still illiterate.

Chapter 2 Life Styles

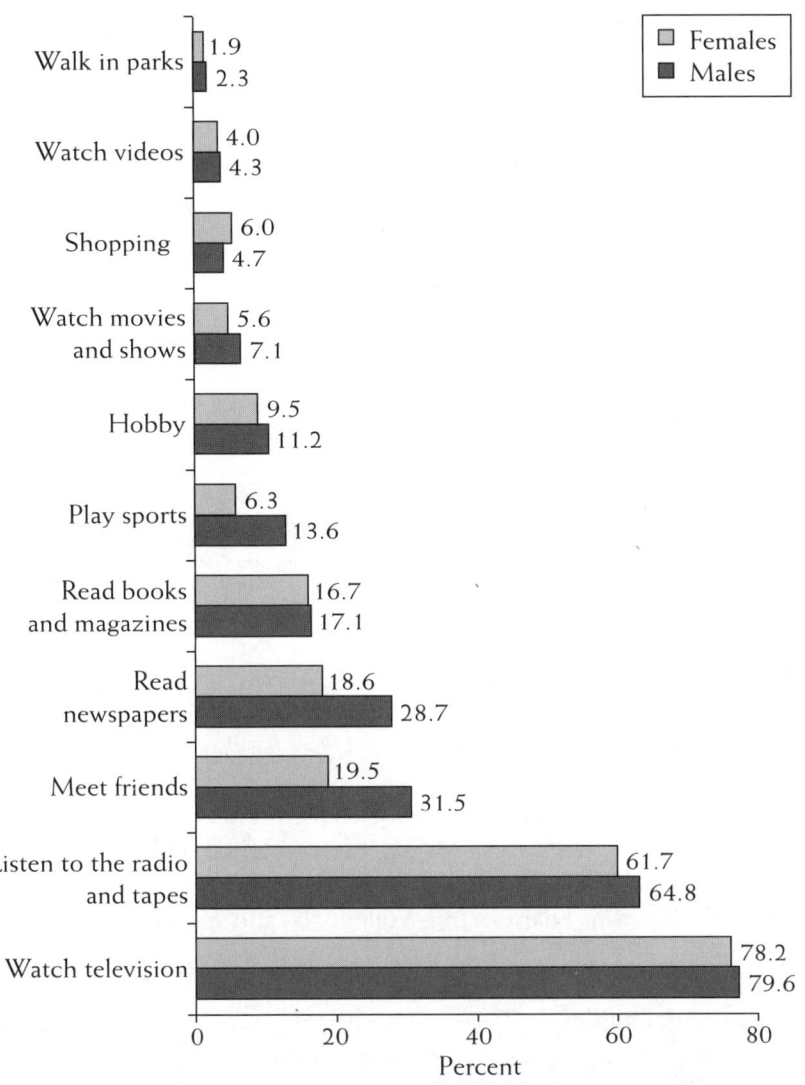

Figure 2.31   Participation in Selected Activities in 1990
(*Source:* Based on National Statistical Office, *Report of the Cultural Activity Participation and Time Use Survey 1990*, OPM, Bangkok, 1992, Statistical Tables, pp. 46–7.)

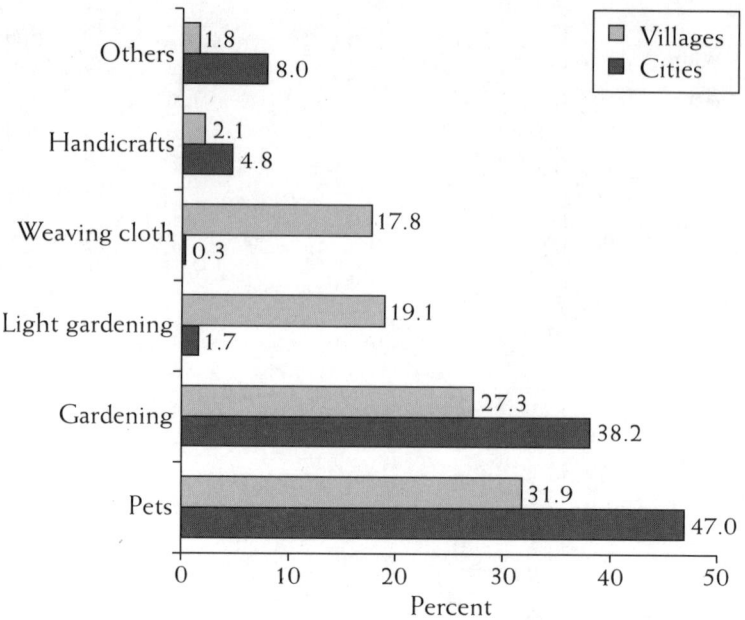

Figure 2.32 Hobbies in 1985
(Source: Based on National Statistical Office, Report of the Cultural Activity Participation and Time Use Survey 1985, OPM, Bangkok, pp. 53–4.)

Children, however, play sports frequently. Their training concentrates on exercises, soccer, and athletics and it includes a little jogging and volleyball. They also enjoy watching sports, especially soccer, Thai boxing, volleyball, and athletics.

Teenagers Teenagers aged between 11 and 14 have broader interests than children. They are both active and sociable. They pay more attention to media than children and they spend time meeting friends. Teenagers watch television, read books and magazines, and play sports more than any other generation. Few, however, have hobbies and these focus on pets and gardening.

Teenagers prefer team games to individual sports like athletics, exercises, and jogging. Sports players in this age group specialize in ball games, with over 40 percent playing soccer and 17 percent volleyball. Like children, however, teenagers enjoy watching soccer, Thai boxing, volleyball, and athletics.

Young adults Young adults aged between 15 and 24 are probably the most active Thais. They listen to the radio, play tapes, and go to the movies more than any other generation. Like teenagers, young adults often read books and magazines, but they also like reading newspapers. They are sociable people who enjoy meeting friends. Their interests are well defined and their hobbies are more numerous. Young adults train pets, do some gardening, weave, and make other handicrafts.

People in this age group drop exerting physical activities gradually. They still play much soccer, but they seldom play volleyball and they give up exercises and athletics. Instead, they are interested in *sepak-takraw*, *takraw*, and jogging. Young adults are also more selective than teenagers, watching soccer and Thai boxing games almost exclusively.

Adults Adults aged between 25 and 39 have often settled in a career and a family. They are wealthier than their younger peers but are constrained by family life. These people are prime users of television, radio, tapes, and videos. They meet friends and read newspapers more than other Thais. Well-off people in this age group also play golf. Adults, otherwise, read fewer books and magazines than younger Thais and they go to the movies and play sports less often.

People above 40 years old lead more sedentary lives. They listen to the radio, watch television, read newspapers, and meet friends. These adults also allocate more time to their hobbies and they keep up with golf if they can afford it.

2.6 RELIGIONS

Thailand is a Buddhist country. Over 95 percent of its people are Buddhist, 4 percent are Muslim, and less than 1 percent are Christian.[41]

Thais are also a mystic people who worship many gods and spirits. They add numerous rituals of various origins to their religious practices. Ethnic Thais hold Brahmanic and animistic beliefs, ethnic Malay practice Shamanistic rituals, and the Chinese community reveres its own gods.

2.6.1 BUDDHISM

Buddhism is not only the predominant religion, it is also the greatest influence on Thai society. Buddhist values pervade every aspect of life. Speech, gesture, behavior, and social activities hold some religious element. People, for instance, follow the Buddhist teachings when they say "never mind," when they lower their head respectfully in front of a superior, when they refrain from showing emotion, and when they do social work. Less obvious, perhaps, are influences on such issues as the choice of a profession. Since Buddhism discourages killing, Thais dislike jobs as butchers and they often leave these occupations to the Chinese.

Thais practice Theravada Buddhism, one of the two major branches of Buddhism. Mahayana Buddhism, the other branch, uses different scriptures.[42] Theravada Buddhism prevails in Sri Lanka, Laos, Burma, and Cambodia and Mahayana Buddhism in Tibet, China, Mongolia, Japan, and Vietnam.

Nowhere, however, is Buddhism as colorful and mystic as it is in Thailand. Here, it has absorbed numerous external influences like the Khmer decoration of the temples, the Chinese custom of food offerings, and some animistic and Brahmanic rituals.

Buddhist activities Buddhism inspires many religious and charitable activities. Praying, visiting the temple, offering food, getting ordained, doing social work, and making financial donations are common practices. People gain merit for these deeds, thereby improving their chances of being reincarnated in a higher-ranking position. Some acts are especially meritorious. Joining the monkhood and being generous to the temple, for instance, brings considerable merit.

Making merit is a powerful force in the development of the kingdom because everyone contributes to temple-initiated projects. Poor people donate their labor and rich people, their money. The drive to make merit has, in the past, given Thailand its elaborate temples and today, the same drive lies behind the construction of many schools, hospitals, and other public establishments.

Even business people make merit. They sponsor projects and donate to charities. Since the press covers such events, both merit and publicity are rewards for their benevolence.

Making merit is also an important factor in the continuity of religion. Almost all Thai males join the monkhood at least once in their lives for the sake of merit. They spend two weeks to six months as monks learning Buddhist precepts. Becoming a monk carries much prestige in Thai society, where it is said to "ripen" a man.

Shaven monks with their saffron robes and alms bowls are common sights although their number varies considerably throughout the year. The size of the monkhood peaks during the Buddhist Lent, from July to October. This is the most prestigious time to serve the temple. People take leave from their jobs to spend Lent as a monk.

Regional differences   The practice of Buddhism is more visible in villages where the temple is the heart of the community life and the monk is the learned one. The village temple serves as school, medical center, hospital, employment agency, news agency, recreation center, warehouse, hotel, etc. Monks carry much authority. They treat diseases and officiate at family events like birth, marriage, and cremation. Senior monks also arbitrate in disputes and they organize festivals and other community events.

The village temple is instrumental in rallying labor and financial support for public projects. The abbot of the temple organizes villagers, especially males, into groups of activities to do social work in their community. This covers many different tasks ranging from health and social services to scouting, national security work, and maintenance of public places and facilities. The bulk of it, however, consists in the upkeep and development of public places (see Figure 2.33).

Buddhism is less visible in cities. Urbanites, although faithful Buddhists, are often too busy to indulge in time-consuming rites. Urban Thais seldom listen to sermons and they organize fewer festivals. They, however, offer food to monks, pray, and make numerous contributions to charities. These people do social work, but they are more likely to donate money than time.

Religious education   Many institutions contribute to the religious education. Families and schools instill the basic Buddhist values and temples teach the Buddhist philosophy. The Thai male who joins

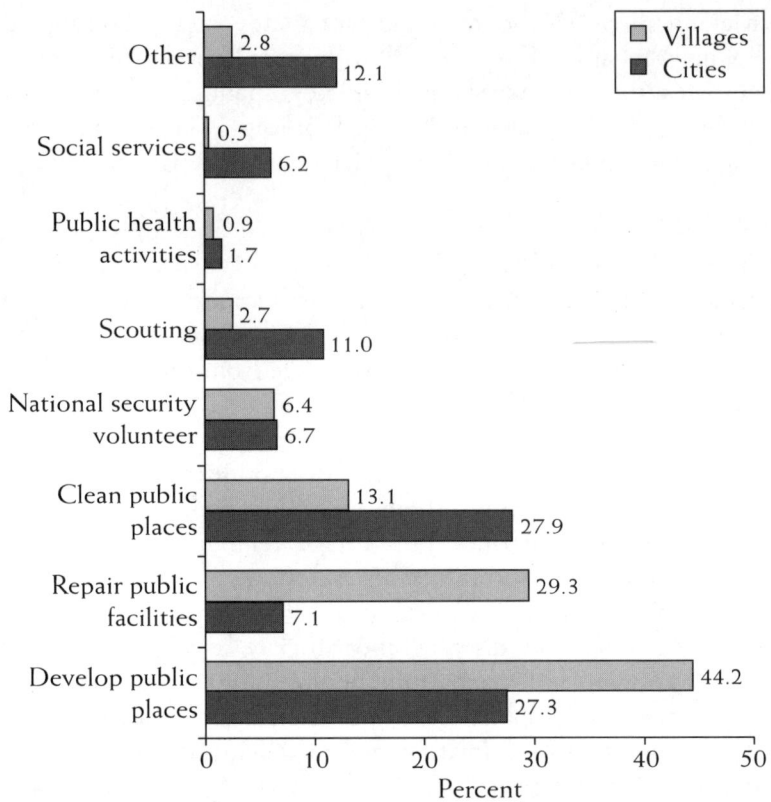

Figure 2.33   Social Work Activities in 1985
(Source: Based on National Statistical Office, Report of the Cultural Activity Participation and Time Use Survey 1985, OPM, Bangkok, pp. 65–6.)

the monkhood, for instance, must learn to live without material possessions, receiving his meals from benevolent laymen. The monk also learns meditation and many rules of behavior, some say over 200.

This Buddhist education enhances the natural serenity of Thais. The young child, for instance, learns that he should not kill, lie, steal, or become intoxicated. Older children get a wider exposure to Buddhist rituals and they learn to meditate. This training produces peaceful people. Strikes and demonstrations seldom turn riotous, and if they do peace is quickly restored.

Buddhist philosophy   Siddhartha Gautama, who founded Buddhism in the sixth century B.C. and later became known as the

Lord Buddha, reflected on the destiny of man. Gautama taught that people are victims of their desires. They have unlimited wants that their limited resources cannot fully satisfy, which makes them unhappy.

As an alternative to pain and sorrow, Buddhism offers Nivarna, an ultimate state where people abandon all desire and find permanent happiness. Man must suppress desire, the cause of suffering, to reach Nivarna. He may do so by following the Eightfold Path, a code of conduct that advocates a right approach to mindfulness, views, intentions, speech, livelihood, concentration, effort, and conduct.

People who do not follow the Eightfold Path to Nivarna are reincarnated in a form that depends on their karma, the balance of evil and merit accumulated in previous lives. People with poor karma risk reincarnation in an inferior form of life, but a good karma promises riches in a future life. Few Thais are familiar with the intellectual complexities of Nivarna, but they are content to be reincarnated. They make merit to improve their karma and secure a good position in their next life.

2.6.2 ISLAM

Thai Muslims are not numerous, but they form a tight-knit community. Most live in the South near the Malaysian border, with a few more in the Bangkok area. Southern Muslims are ethnic Malays who have a distinct religion, language, and culture. They resist integration. Bangkok Muslims, in contrast, are mainly descendants of slaves and prisoners of war resettled outside the Malay peninsula. These people are well integrated, differing from the rest of their countrymen only in religion.

Thai Muslims are Sunnites, one of the two major groups of Islam. Shiites form the other group. Sunnites and Shiites disagree on theological issues such as the legitimate successors to the Prophet Muhammad, the status of the *Imam*, and the interpretation of some verses of the Koran. Sunnites, for instance, say that Shiites confer the *Imam* (the religious leader) too many superhuman qualities.

Muslims are active worshippers who go to the mosque frequently. About 80 percent worship regularly and 40 percent go to the mosque on Fridays.[43] Festivals are, however, the busiest times. On *Idil Fitri* day, which marks the end of Ramadan, and on *Idil Adha* day, about three-quarters of the Muslims congregate at the mosque.

Muslims, unlike Buddhists, do not get so involved in religion at early ages. Few children below 10 years old are religious. Worship, however, spreads quickly among teenagers because religious education is compulsory for all Muslims. Past 15 years old, over 90 percent of Muslims worship regularly.[44]

2.6.3 OTHER BELIEFS

Buddhism and Islam are only part of the many beliefs of the Thais. People add numerous rites of various origins to their religious observances. They indulge in Brahmanic and animistic rituals, and in untold other superstitious practices.

Brahmanism is the religious system of the Brahmans of India. It was introduced in the days of Ayutthaya and it has become deeply ingrained in Thai culture. People worship Brahmanic deities and they call on Brahman priests to officiate at family ceremonies like birth, marriage, and cremation. Many festivals and rituals have a Brahmanic origin. The First Plowing Ceremony, which marks the start of the planting season, for instance, is Brahmanic. So is the marriage ritual of pouring lustral water from a conch shell on the hands of the bride and groom.

Animism, the belief that spirits inhabit objects, predates Buddhism. It belongs to the aborigine cultures of Thailand. Animistic practices have survived centuries of Buddhism and are all-powerful. They prevail in times of crisis, when Thais rely more on spirits than on merit.

There are countless animistic spirits that fall into two categories: benevolent and malevolent. Spirits are the souls of departed ones and they may cause trouble unless properly supplicated with offerings and prayers. People build altars to spirits in fields, homes, and Buddhist temples.

Thais ascribe almost all events to the will of spirits. Mischievous spirits, for instance, are said to cause sickness, sorrow, and pain—they make people lose their way, fall out of love, and cause virtually any problem in life. Any odd event may be interpreted as a sign from the spirits. In June 1993, for instance, people from the Phetchabun province, 300 kilometers (200 miles) north of Bangkok, turned a soccer ball-sized meteorite that had landed there into an instant object of worship. They said that it could tell the winning lottery numbers.[45]

Magic amulets ward off nefarious influences. They may carry much power. Some make the wearer invincible; others, more modestly, protect him from ghosts and demons. There are also the ones which, when carried in a hand bag, discourage pickpockets. Buddhist monks often recommend the kind of amulet victims should use and the most enterprising monks produce their own brands of amulets.

Magic tattoos also protect against evil forces. Once widespread, they are now popular only in the countryside. Thai tattoos are intricate and colorful designs of leaping tigers, fierce dragons, flying angels, astrological maps, etc., whose protective powers are rarely questioned. They are more popular with people employed in dangerous occupations. Policemen, soldiers, gangsters, fishermen, and taxi drivers seldom risk their lives without the protection of a tattoo.

Other superstitions focus on good luck and bad luck. Days, months, numbers, trees, flowers, may be lucky or unlucky. These superstitions affect business. Some days and some months, for instance, are more auspicious to start construction work or to get married. Many hairdressers close on Wednesdays because it is unlucky to have a haircut on that day of the week. Contractors organize ground-breaking ceremonies to ensure the good fortune of their construction projects.

Managers of foreign companies may ignore these issues, but their staff seldom does. Writer and Thai resident Denis Segaller reports that after a series of misfortunes plagued the construction of the prestigious Erawan hotel in Bangkok,[46] construction workers decided that evil spirits caused the trouble and they demanded that something be done. Upon consultation with a Brahman expert, the hotel management built the Erawan shrine next to the hotel. This shrine has since become a leading place of worship and a tourist attraction. It teems with crowds of worshippers who make offerings of flowers, food, small carved wooden elephants, joss sticks, and money.

Building a shrine is probably as far as most companies would ever go to appease superstitious beliefs. In most cases, however, requests are modest and putting up with them is easier and more productive than opposing them.

NOTES

1. Calculations based on US Bureau of the Census, *Statistical Abstract of the United States: 1992*, 112th ed., Washington, D.C., 1992, p. 8.
2. Calculations based on National Statistical Office, *Statistical Yearbook Thailand 1993*, OPM, Bangkok, 1993, p. 27.
3. Source: Division of Health Statistics, *Public Health Statistics A.D. 1990*, MPH, Bangkok, 1992, p. 33.
4. Calculations based on Division of Health Statistics, *Public Health Statistics A.D. 1990*, MPH, Bangkok, 1992, pp. 18–19.
5. Supra 2, p. 29.
6. Supra 2, p. 35.
7. Calculations based on National Statistical Office, *Key Statistics of Thailand 1989*, OPM, Bangkok, 1989, pp. 10–11, and National Statistical Office, *Key Statistics of Thailand 1991*, OPM, Bangkok, pp. 6–7.
8. Supra 2, p. 36.
9. See National Statistical Office, *Key Statistics of Thailand 1991*, OPM, Bangkok, p. 13.
10. Source: National Statistical Office, *Report of the Cultural Activity Participation and Time Use Survey 1990*, OPM, Bangkok, 1992, p. 14.
11. This number increases to 8.7 million for Bangkok Metropolitan and vicinity, a figure often quoted in the press. See supra 2, p. 29.
12. Calculations based on National Statistical Office, *Statistical Yearbook Thailand*, OPM, Bangkok, various issues.
13. Calculations based on Office of the National Economic and Social Development Board, *National Income of Thailand*, OPM, Bangkok, various issues.
14. Supra 3, p. 184.
15. Supra 3, p. 201.
16. Supra 4, pp. 241–2.
17. Agence France Presse, "Thais draw up new laws to combat rising prostitution," *Bangkok Post*, 14 July 1993.
18. Supra 4, pp. 12, 233–4.
19. Calculations based on Office of the National Economic and Social Development Board, *National Income of Thailand*, OPM, Bangkok, various issues, and National Statistical Office, *Statistical Yearbook Thailand 1993*, OPM, Bangkok, 1993, p. 27.

20. Supra 13.
21. Source: National Statistical Office, *Report of the Labor Force Survey, Whole Kingdom*, OPM, Bangkok, various issues.
22. Calculations based on National Statistical Office, *Report of the Children and Youth Survey 1987*, OPM, Bangkok, Appendix, pp. 28–9.
23. Supra 13.
24. See National Statistical Office, *Statistical Handbook of Thailand 1989*, OPM, Bangkok, pp. 34–5.
25. "Japanese investors focus on Indonesia, Thailand in ASEAN," *Bangkok Post*, 17 May 1993, Business Post section, p. 20.
26. Calculations based on National Statistical Office, *Report of the Labor Force Survey, Whole Kingdom, May 1991*, OPM, Bangkok, Appendix, pp. 5–6.
27. Supra 22, Appendix, pp. 12–13.
28. Source: National Statistical Office, *Statistical Yearbook Thailand 1993*, OPM, Bangkok, 1993, p. 133.
29. Calculations based on National Statistical Office, *Statistical Yearbook Thailand 1992*, OPM, Bangkok, 1992, pp. 126–7.
30. Source: National Statistical Office, *Report of the Children and Youth Survey 1987*, OPM, Bangkok, p. 20.
31. Supra 13.
32. Supra 28, p. 40.
33. Calculations based on National Statistical Office, *Statistical Handbook of Thailand 1991*, OPM, Bangkok.
34. Source: National Statistical Office, *Statistical Handbook of Thailand 1989*, OPM, Bangkok, p. 61.
35. Calculations based on National Statistical Office, *Report of the 1990 Household Socio-Economic Survey, Whole Kingdom*, OPM, Bangkok, 1993, p. 121.
36. Reuter, "'Holy' sprinkler," *Bangkok Post*, 3 January 1994.
37. Supra 28, p. 151.
38. Supra 35, p. 13.
39. Supra 35, p. 13.
40. Moy, Joyce, "Living on luck," *Asia Magazine*, 4 December 1992, pp. 10–16.
41. Supra 10, p. 14.
42. The Thevarada scriptures are in the Pali language and the Mahayana scriptures in the Sanskrit language.
43. Supra 10, p. 21.

44. Supra 10, Statistical Tables, p. 26.
45. Reuter, "Experts rule on meteorite," *South China Morning Post*, 27 July 1993.
46. Segaller, Denis, *Thai Ways*, Asia Books, Bangkok, 1989, p. 88.

3 CONSUMPTION AND DISTRIBUTION

Decades of rapid economic growth have changed the consumer market dramatically. Between 1970 and 1991, total expenditures more than tripled in real terms, while per capita spending doubled. A middle class has emerged, buying an expanding array of goods.

People upgrade their life style as their incomes increase. They make their homes more comfortable and they pay greater attention to their health (see Figure 3.1). They also become more discerning, spending more on quality goods and services.

Changes are more noticeable in wealthier areas. Bangkok households, for instance, buy modern equipment like video cameras, computers, mobile telephones, and laser disk players. They eat in fine restaurants, shop at boutiques and upmarket department stores, and have an active cultural life.

In the provinces, consumption is also increasing, although not as rapidly as in Bangkok. Refrigerators and fans, for example, have become fast-selling items throughout the country. More expensive products, however, have a smaller market. The average Thai household is still poor. In 1990, it spent most of its US$2,300 annual consumption budget on food and housing (see Figure 3.2).

Increasing wealth and changing consumption habits have modified distribution channels and distribution concepts. Luxurious modern shopping centers are developing in large cities. Fashion designers open boutiques in elegant shopping arcades; department stores upgrade their product lines and improve their display; while

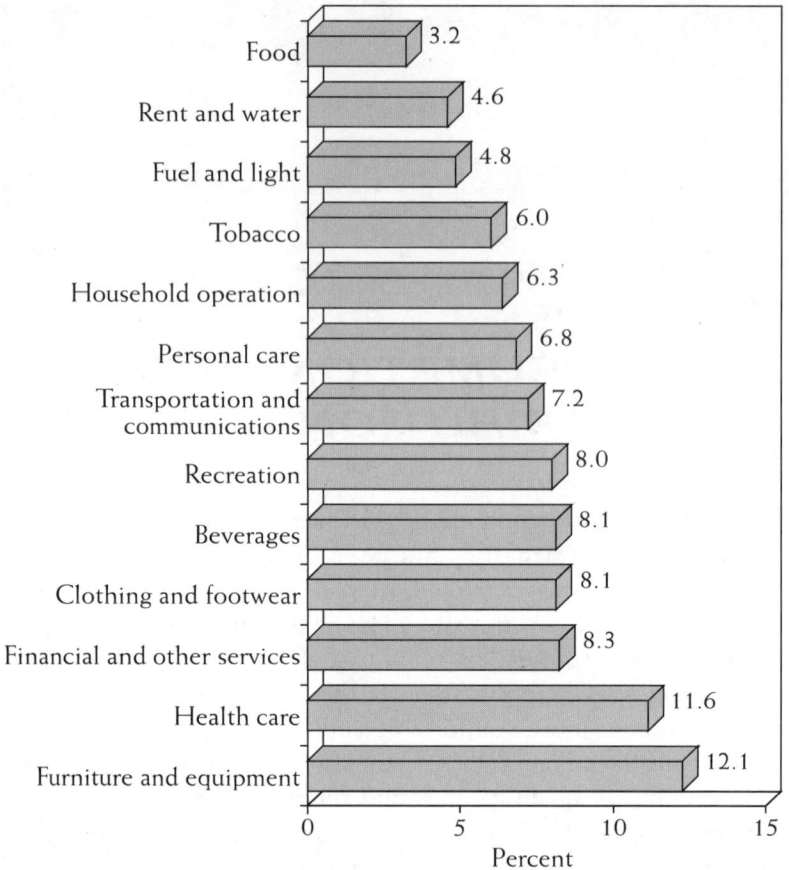

Figure 3.1 Average Annual Growth Rate of Consumption 1970–1991 (Source: Based on Office of the National Economic and Social Development Board, National Income of Thailand, OPM, various issues.)

convenience stores are gradually replacing the traditional corner stores.

The growing demand for quality goods and services is creating business opportunities. Shops throughout the country sell a greater variety of imported products, while companies hire foreign consulting and management teams to improve services. The following sections review these consumption and distribution trends and highlight their marketing implications.

Chapter 3 Consumption and Distribution

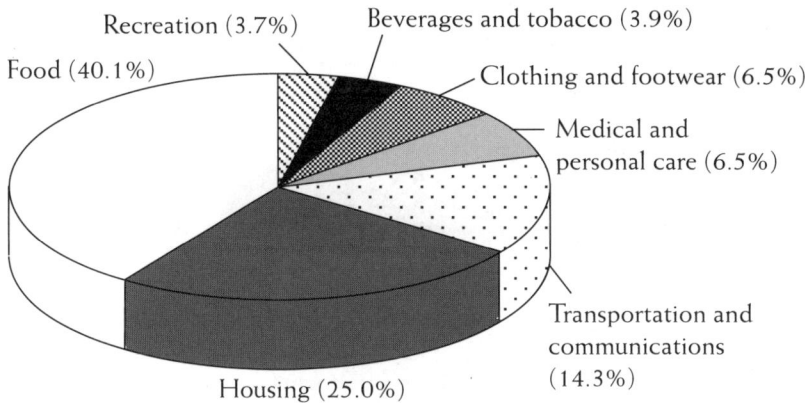

Figure 3.2 Consumption Pattern in 1990
(Source: Based on National Statistical Office, Report of the 1990 Household Socio-Economic Survey, Whole Kingdom, OPM, Bangkok, 1993, pp. 1–21.)

3.1 FOOD

Food is an important part of consumption. It is the single largest expenditure of Thais. In 1990, the average household spent US$918, some 40 percent of its consumption, on food.[1] This proportion is, however, declining gradually although food purchases are still growing.

Eating habits are changing. People consume richer and more diverse foods although rice remains the staple. Meat, fish, dairy products, fruits, vegetables, fats, and spices together account for over half of the food budget (see Figure 3.3). Eating out is also becoming more common, especially in wealthier areas. In Bangkok, for instance, people spend over half of their food budget at restaurants and stalls, compared to only 12 percent in the Northeast.

In poorer areas, however, meals are less varied. People eat mainly rice. Villagers who cannot afford to buy food at the market rely on homegrown fruits and vegetables, and on fishing and hunting. Their diet often lacks vitamin A, iron, and iodine. Such problems are common in the Northeast. In 1990, a survey conducted by Ubon's Public Health Office found that about a quarter of northeastern preschool children suffered from malnutrition.[2]

Thai cuisine is internationally renowned for its hot and subtle flavors and for its diversity. Cooks combine spices, herbs, and seasonings in varying proportions to produce countless dishes.

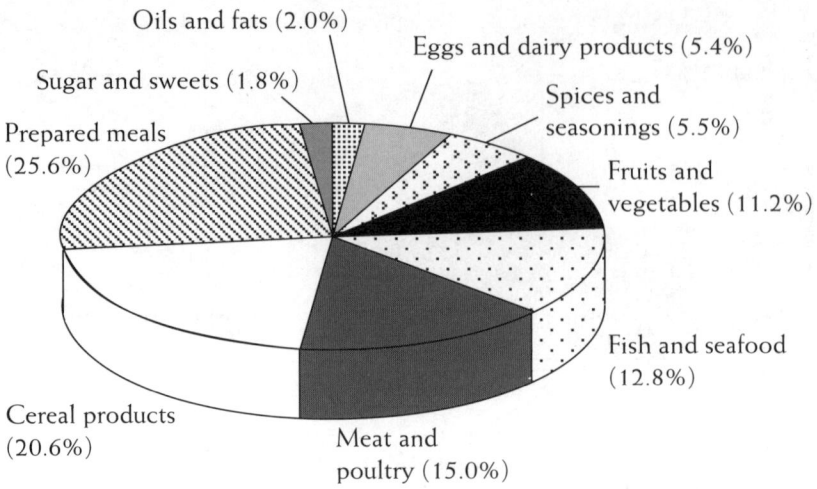

*Figure 3.3 Composition of Food Consumption in 1990
(Source: Based on National Statistical Office, Report of the 1990 Household Socio-Economic Survey, Whole Kingdom, OPM, Bangkok, 1993, pp. 1–21.)*

Curries are, perhaps, better known, but they are only a small part of the cuisine. Soups, salads, and dips add to the many meat, fish, and vegetable preparations.

Thais treat cooking as an art. Each region has its culinary specialties, usually based on local ingredients. Fish and seafood dishes, for instance, are more common in coastal areas, while the famed green chicken curry comes from Central Thailand, a chicken-raising area. Regional cuisines also reflect cultural influences; southern curries have Indian flavors and northern food is more Chinese.

Although unique in flavor, Thai cuisine is Asian in composition. A typical Thai meal consists of spiced meats and vegetables served with a large quantity of rice. Cooks prepare dishes which mix easily with rice. They chop meats and vegetables and pound spices. There is little use for knives. Most people eat with forks and spoons.

Cooking processes are as diverse in Thailand as elsewhere. People barbecue, broil, steam, boil, fry, and bake food. They, however, cook mainly on stoves; baking creates too much heat. Thais are more likely to buy mixes and other food preparations made for stove cooking rather than for baking. Preparations like instant noodles, which can be reheated in microwave ovens, also have potential.

Chapter 3 Consumption and Distribution

3.1.1 CEREAL PRODUCTS AND STAPLES

Cereals are leading purchases because they include rice. In 1990, the average household spent US$189 on cereal products; the bulk of it, some 87 percent, on rice (see Figure 3.4). Pastries, noodles, bean curd, bread, and flour, which account for the remaining 13 percent, are marginal by comparison.

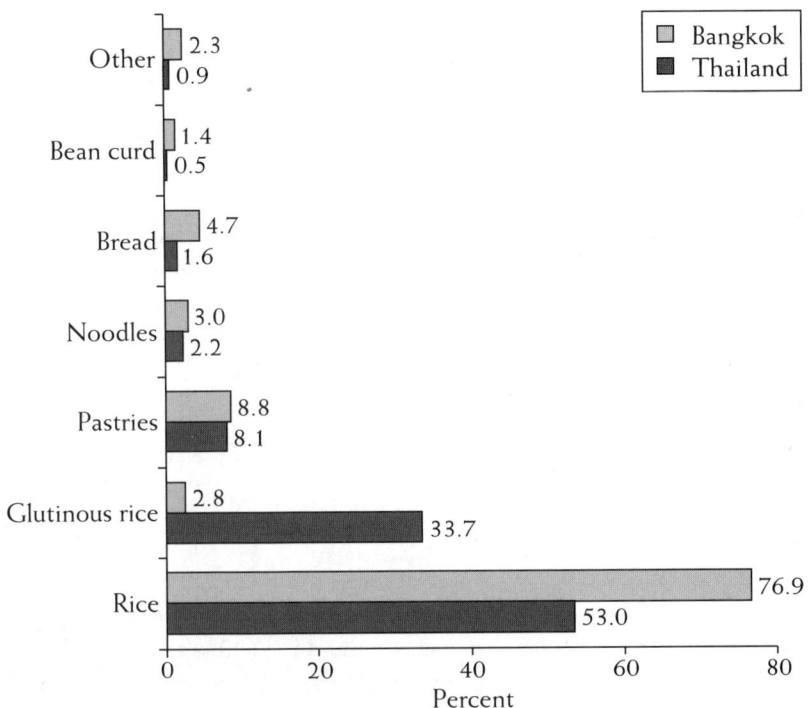

Figure 3.4 Composition of Cereal Product and Staple Consumption in 1990 (Source: Based on National Statistical Office, Report of the 1990 Household Socio-Economic Survey, Whole Kingdom, OPM, Bangkok, 1993, pp. 1–21.)

Rice Rice is the staple. This traditional nutriment accounts for nearly one-fifth of the food budget, a prominence that goes far back in history. Until recently, rice was the sole food for almost everyone, feeding noblemen, peasants, horses, and cattle alike. It was also used to produce beer and spirits and its husks fueled furnaces.

Modern Thais eat both regular and glutinous rice. In the North and the Northeast, people split their consumption almost equally between these two varieties. In Central and Southern Thailand, in contrast, people consume mainly regular rice and they reserve glutinous rice for desserts.

Bread and pastries Bread and pastries are recent introductions from the West. They are more common in tourist areas especially in the South, where people allocate 15 percent of their expenses on cereal products to bread and pastries, compared to less than 1 percent in the Northeast.

International hotels are leading producers. They bake bread and pastries for their guests and they often set up a bakery shop for take-away sales. These bakeries usually buy their ingredients and their kitchen equipment from foreign suppliers.

Noodles and bean curd Thais seldom cook noodles at home. Raw noodles, which include wheat, rice, and mung bean flour noodles, account for only 2 percent of the expenses on cereal products. Noodles are, however, popular. Countless stalls, peddlers, and noodle shops sell cheap and tasty food. Most Thais buy ready-made noodle dishes from these places.

Bean curd, in contrast, appeals to fewer people. It is popular only in Bangkok because of the Chinese community.

3.1.2 MEAT AND POULTRY

Thais use meat sparingly although consumption is increasing. In 1990, the average household spent only US$138 on meat;[3] this is less than the expense on rice. In Thailand, as in most parts of Asia, pasture land is scarce and breeding livestock is expensive. Until recently, few people could afford meat in large quantities. This has affected culinary practices. People are now richer, but Thai cuisine still uses small amounts of finely chopped meat.

Shops sell both fresh and prepared meat. Consumers, however, buy the bulk of it, some 90 percent, fresh.

Fresh meat Meat is less diverse in Thailand than in the West. Pork and chicken are, by far, the most common. Pork alone captures over half of the expenses on fresh meat and chicken, one-fifth (see Figure 3.5). Beef is becoming more popular, but good cuts are still expensive. These sell in supermarkets which cater to Westerners and

Chapter 3 Consumption and Distribution

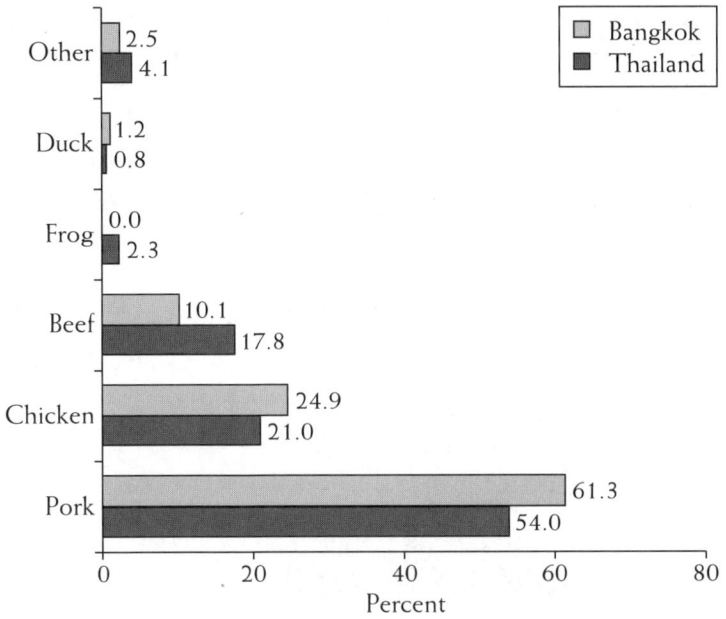

*Figure 3.5   Composition of Fresh Meat Consumption in 1990
(Source: Based on National Statistical Office, Report of the 1990 Household Socio-Economic Survey, Whole Kingdom, OPM, Bangkok, 1993, pp. 1–21.)*

wealthy Thais. High-quality beef dishes are also available in upmarket hotels and restaurants. Ducks, frogs, and game also appeal to many people. Mutton and veal, in contrast, are rare and not liked.

Cultural factors and resources, however, affect consumption. Beef dishes, for instance, are more common in the South, home of the large Muslim community, and in the cattle-raising areas of the North and the Northeast. Ducks and frogs sell better in the Northeast. Game is popular in rural areas, especially during the dry season when rivers run low and fish is scarce.

Northeastern consumption is especially distinctive. Cooks in this region must be inventive to make the best of poor resources. They use less-conventional meats. Northeasterners are, for instance, the biggest consumers of frogs in Thailand, spending 6 percent of their fresh meat budget on them. Frog curry is a local delicacy. More exotic, perhaps, are the field-crab dishes. These are common in farming villages because crabs live in rice fields. Roasted grasshoppers, fried bees, and raw ant eggs also make popular snacks.

Prepared meat Stalls sell a variety of prepared meats. Usual fares are roasted pork, dried beef, barbecued sausages, and sticks of chicken satay. Because chicken is cheap and makes a convenient snack, it is the most common stall food. Cooked chicken (prepared fowl) captures about one-third of the market for prepared meat (see Figure 3.6).

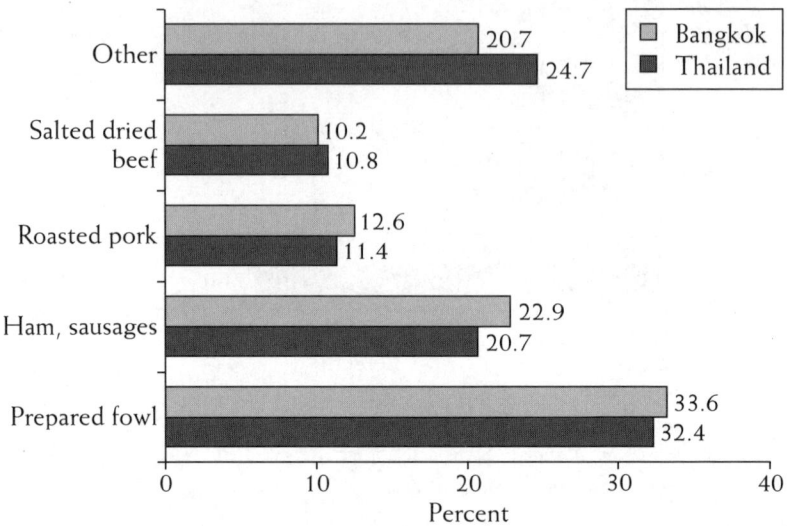

Figure 3.6 Composition of Prepared Meat Consumption in 1990 (Source: Based on National Statistical Office, Report of the 1990 Household Socio-Economic Survey, Whole Kingdom, OPM, Bangkok, 1993, pp. 1–21.)

Some preparations are regional specialties. Sausages, for instance, are more common in the North and the Northeast, while roasted pork sells better in the North. Bangkok is the only place where all these products are widely available.

Less traditional are the Western-style prepared meats that have recently appeared in supermarkets. Foreign meat packers have set up joint ventures with local companies to distribute products like ham, sausages, and bacon, which are targeted at middle-class Thais.

3.1.3 FISH AND SEAFOOD

Fish features prominently in Thai cuisine. In the past, it was an integral part of the diet and people used to eat it at almost every meal. Modern Thais have more varied eating habits, but they still consume much fish. People buy fish both fresh and prepared. Fresh products, however, dominate. They capture over two-thirds of the purchases while prepared fish accounts for the rest.

Fresh fish   People buy fresh fish caught locally. They eat saltwater fish and other seafood in sea coastal areas and freshwater fish inland (see Figure 3.7). Consumption, however, differs in each region.

In the Northeast, fish is the poor man's dish and a leading source of protein. Villagers catch fish in the local streams and they only buy meat during the dry season.

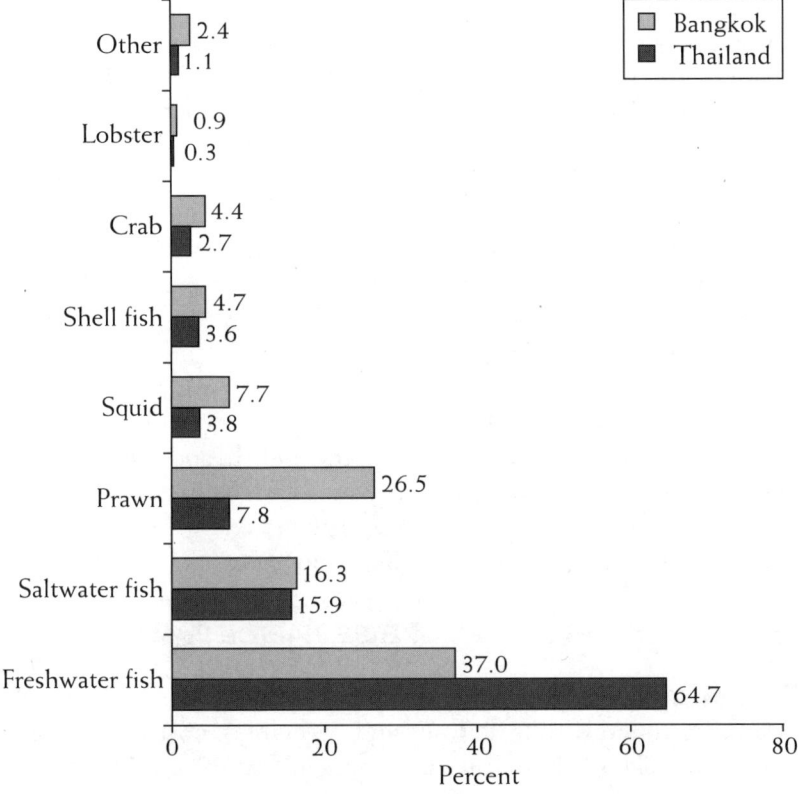

Figure 3.7   Composition of Fresh Fish and Seafood Consumption in 1990 (Source: Based on National Statistical Office, Report of the 1990 Household Socio-Economic Survey, Whole Kingdom, OPM, Bangkok, 1993, pp. 1–21.)

In the North, consumption is lower. The rivers of this region are too shallow during the dry season and their powerful currents during the rainy season prevent much animal life from flourishing.

In the South, people eat mainly saltwater fish and seafood. This region has the largest sea coastal area in Thailand and its fisheries are some of the world's biggest. Here, people eat fish often, spending 45 percent more on it than other Thais.[4]

In Central Thailand, consumption is mixed. This region has many rivers and good access to the sea. People eat both freshwater and saltwater fish and other seafood. Bangkok markets are especially well stocked, selling such seafood products as lobsters, squids, shellfish, crabs, and prawns as well as freshwater and saltwater fish.

Prepared fish Prepared fish is common throughout Thailand. Its share of the total fish budget ranges from one-fifth in the South to one-third in Central and Northern Thailand. Prepared fish includes two important categories: cooked and preserved.

Cooked fish is often stall food. Thai peddlers have a long history of selling it. In the past century, travelers to Thailand described food vendors selling fish on rice from their portable kitchens. This is still common today. People spend over a quarter of their prepared fish products budget on steamed fish (see Figure 3.8).

Preserved fish is also an integral part of the diet. Centuries of fishing traditions have produced many ways of preserving fish. Principal processes are fermenting, drying, and salting. Fermented fish is, however, common only in the North and the Northeast, where people often add it to local dishes. In sea coastal areas, people eat mainly dried and salted fish. Fish balls and salted shrimps are Chinese products and they sell better in Bangkok.

3.1.4 FRUITS AND VEGETABLES

Thais rightly describe their country as a fruit and vegetable paradise. Markets abound with fresh fruits and vegetables, neatly assembled in colorful displays. These feature prominently in the diet. In 1990, the average household spent US$103 on fruits and vegetables;[5] this is about one-eighth of the food budget.

The high quality of these products undoubtedly influenced culinary traditions, especially presentation. Cooks enhance the visual appeal of their preparations by carving fruits and vegetables

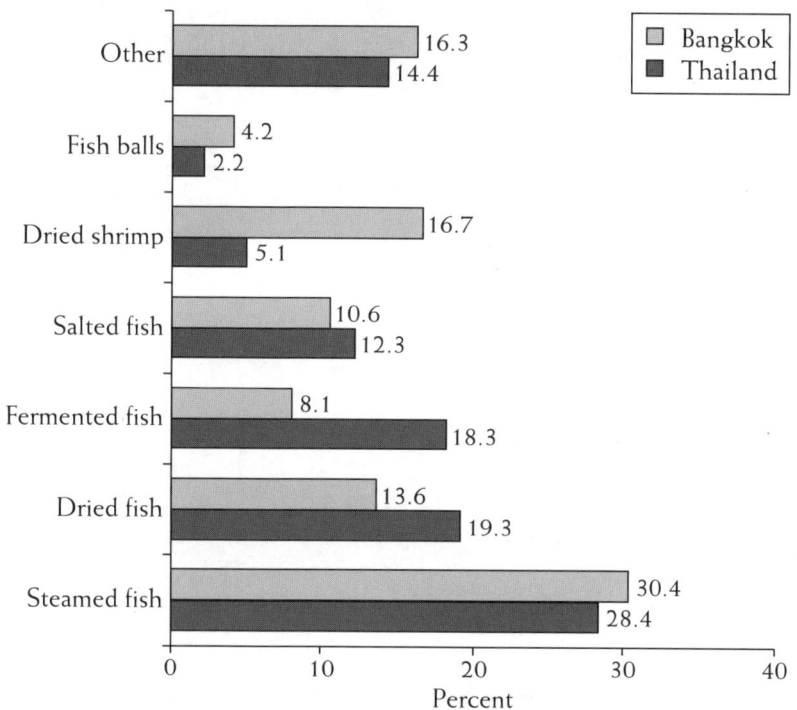

Figure 3.8 Composition of Prepared Fish Product Consumption in 1990 (Source: Based on National Statistical Office, Report of the 1990 Household Socio-Economic Survey, Whole Kingdom, OPM, Bangkok, 1993, pp. 1–21.)

into intricate designs. This is an art that Thais learn at a young age. Skilled people even take part in carving competitions.

Growing fruits and vegetables in this fertile country is a prosperous business. Cultivation area keeps expanding and in 1991, it accounted for 16 percent of farmland;[6] this is one-third the size of the paddy area. Fruits grow primarily in the Central Region and in the South while vegetables come from Central, Northern, and Northeastern Thailand.

Fruits Many different tropical fruits grow in Thailand. The principal ones include oranges, bananas, melons, coconuts, rambutans, mangoes, papayas, durians, and pineapples (see Figure 3.9). More exotic, perhaps, are such fruits as mangosteens, longans, pomelos, jujubes, custard apples, sapodillas, guavas, lichees, and langsats. Fruits also come in many varieties. There are, for

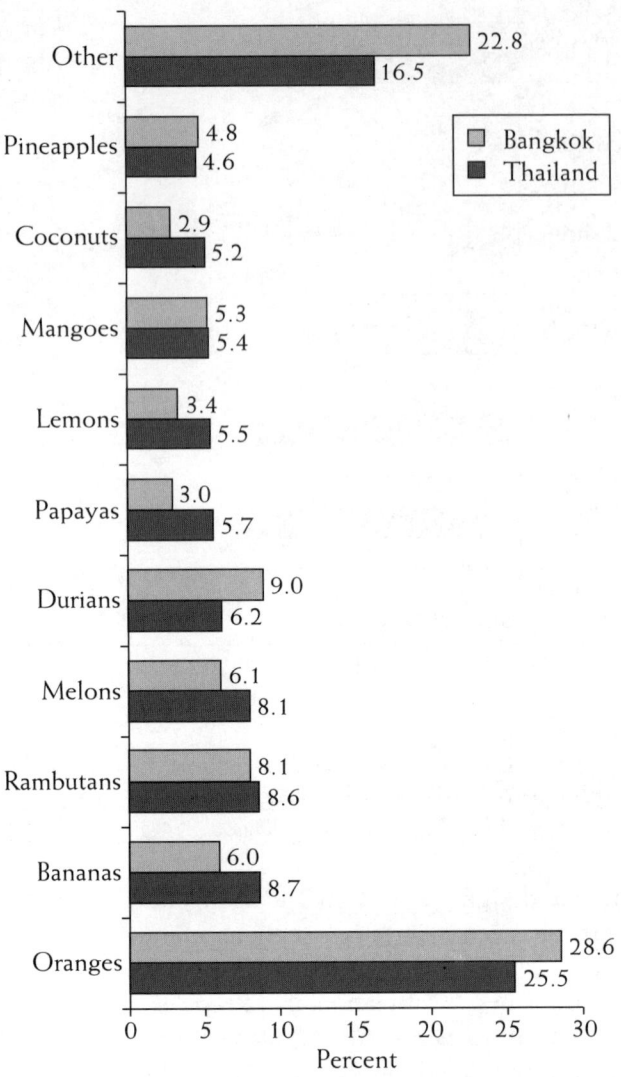

Figure 3.9 Composition of Fresh Fruit Consumption in 1990 (Source: Based on National Statistical Office, Report of the 1990 Household Socio-Economic Survey, Whole Kingdom, OPM, Bangkok, 1993, pp. 1–21.)

instance, a dozen varieties of mangoes, twenty different types of bananas, and several dozen kinds of durians.

This abundance of fruits makes for a large consumption. The average household spends 5 percent of its food budget on fruits and expenditures are greater in Central and Southern Thailand,[7] the two main fruit-growing areas. In these regions, people spend twice as much on fruits than other Thais. In all provinces, however, people eat high-quality fresh fruits year-round. They rarely buy canned fruits. Canneries are expanding rapidly, but they produce mainly for foreign markets.

Consumption is also diverse. No fruit dominates the purchases, although oranges sell very well, capturing about one-fifth of the market. Thai oranges have a greenish peel and a bright yellow flesh. They are sweet, juicy, and tangy. People use them mainly for making juices. Fresh orange juice is a common drink in restaurants and cafeterias. This suggests that juicers have potential.

Some fruits, especially papayas and durians, sell better locally. The controversial durian, famous for its fetid smell, grows in the South. It is highly regarded by the inhabitants of this region and it is also popular in Bangkok. Papayas grow well in the Northeast. Here, people serve them ripe as desserts and unripe as salads. The northeastern specialty, *som tam*, for instance, is a dish of unripe papayas, tomatoes, and dried shrimps.

Thais have countless uses for their fruits although they often consume them fresh and in juices. Some fruits are especially versatile. Mangoes, for instance, can be made into jams, chutneys, desserts, pickles, salads, snacks, and condiments. Mango and glutinous rice is a common Thai dessert. Coconut also has many functions, flavoring curries, custards, and other desserts.

Fresh vegetables The diversity of vegetables matches that of fruits. Thais grow many greens like kale, lettuce, cabbage, and morning glory. They also produce other vegetables like tomatoes, potatoes, eggplants, peas, string beans, bamboo shoots, chayotes, okras, squashes, and gourds. Some of these vegetables come in many varieties. Eggplants, for instance, can be long or egg-shaped and they come in purple, yellow, green, and white colors. They also differ widely in size. The biggest Thai eggplants are similar to the Western varieties and the smallest are about the size of a marble.

Although most vegetables grow up-country, markets are well stocked everywhere. People eat many different kinds of vegetables (see Figure 3.10). Consumption patterns are similar in all regions although bamboo shoots are more common in the North and the Northeast.

Vegetables grow year-round and Thais buy them mainly fresh. They eat vegetables raw in salads and slightly cooked in soups, curries, and other dishes. People usually add vegetables toward the end of the cooking to keep them crisp. They have little use for canned and frozen products. Locally canned vegetables supply foreign markets.

Pickles Pickles are common, but they differ from Western versions. Thai pickles are vegetables and unripe fruits marinated in brine with a few herbs. They are traditional snacks; in the fourteenth century, citrons and mangoes packed in salt were already famed delicacies in Asia. Modern Thais pickle many different products including garlic, bamboo shoot, and mustard green. Shops sell them by the jar and by the piece.

Dried vegetables There are few dried vegetables, and Thais spend little on these. Beans, seeds, and mushrooms account for most purchases. Dried mushrooms are of the shiitake variety. Thai farmers are trying to grow them, but so far, the bulk of these mushrooms are imported. Since dried mushrooms are prized ingredients in Chinese cooking, they sell mainly in upper Thailand.

3.1.5 EGGS AND DAIRY PRODUCTS

Eggs and dairy products play a minor role in Thai diet. In 1990, the average household spent only 5 percent of its food budget, some US$49, on these. Eggs and milk are the principal products together capturing 93 percent of the market (see Figure 3.11). Other dairy products like ice cream, yogurt, and cheese account for the rest.

Dairy products are new to Thai consumers. Until recently, milk was a luxury; people used it only to feed babies. The poorly fed older generations did not develop the enzyme required to digest milk and its by-products. Recent improvements in living standards, however, have produced more milk-fed youngsters. Their greater exposure to milk encouraged companies to introduce new dairy

Chapter 3 Consumption and Distribution

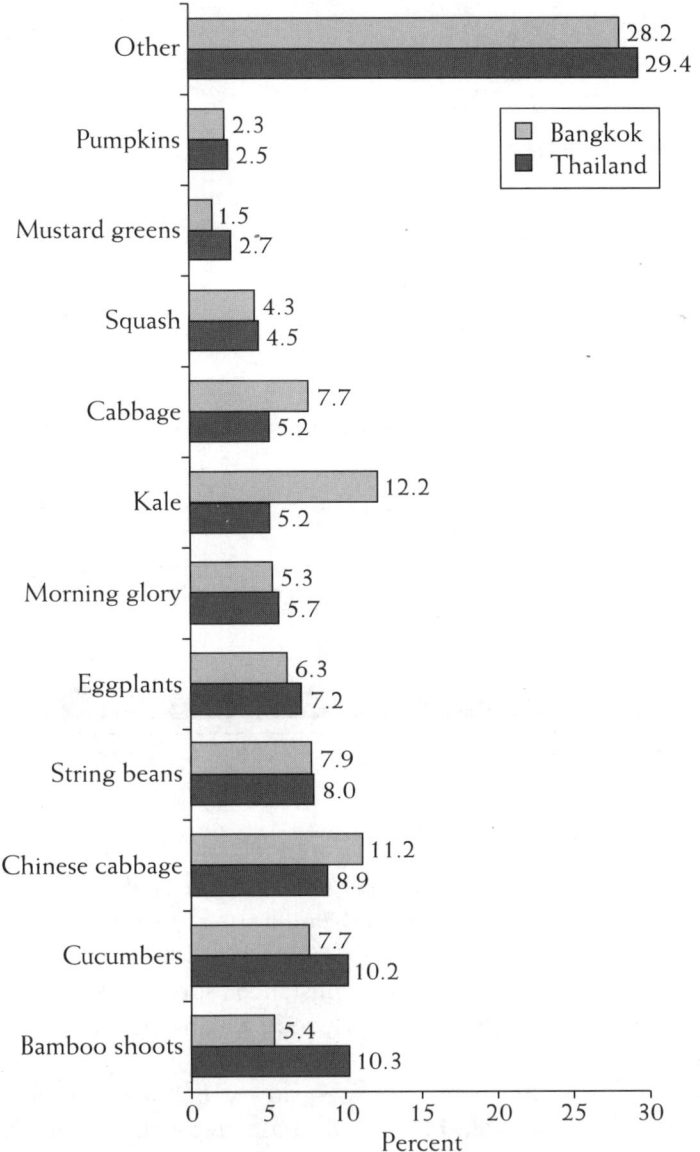

Figure 3.10 Composition of Fresh Vegetable Consumption in 1990 (Source: Based on National Statistical Office, Report of the 1990 Household Socio-Economic Survey, Whole Kingdom, OPM, Bangkok, 1993, pp. 1–21.)

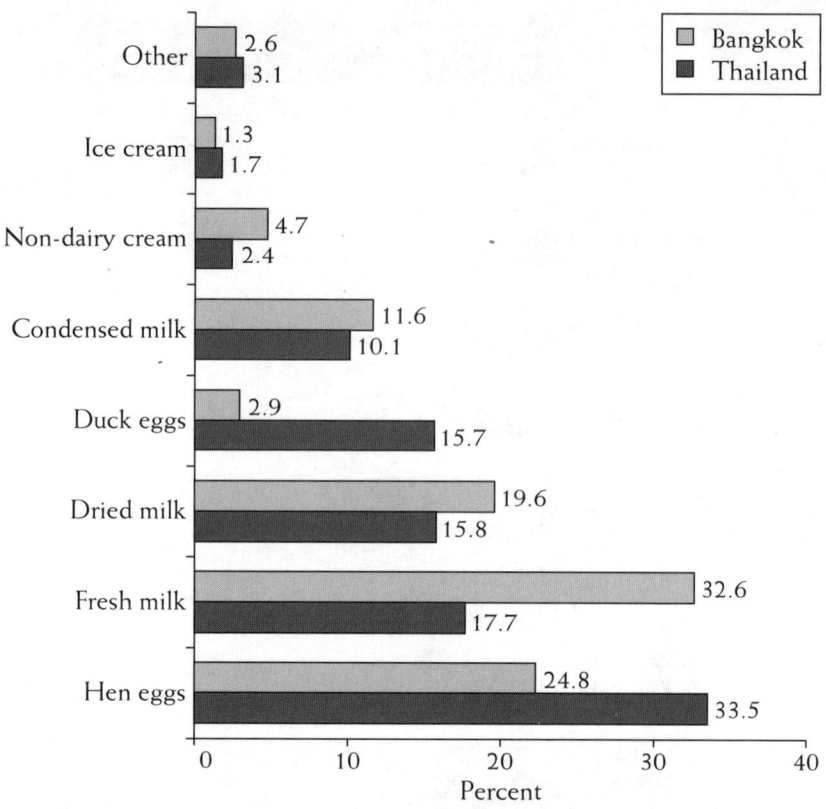

Figure 3.11 Composition of Egg and Dairy Product Consumption in 1990 (Source: Based on National Statistical Office, Report of the 1990 Household Socio-Economic Survey, Whole Kingdom, OPM, Bangkok, 1993, pp. 1–21.)

products. In wealthier areas, for instance, supermarkets distribute cheese and yogurt drinks and fast-food chains sell ice cream and frozen yogurt.

Consumption, however, increases slowly because poorer people still spend little on milk. In 1992, an estimated half million children under 5 years old, which is one in ten children in this age group, suffered from malnutrition.[8] People who have less exposure to milk make better targets for non-dairy substitutes like soy milk and non-dairy cream.

Storage costs are another hurdle. Few homes have refrigerators. This affects consumption of perishables. In rural areas, for example, people buy dried or condensed milk. In cities, however, fresh milk

Chapter 3 Consumption and Distribution

sells better because more households have refrigerators. Heat also impairs the importation of sensitive products. Processed and pasteurized cheeses, for example, have better chances of arriving unspoiled than regular cheeses.

3.1.6 OILS AND FATS

The consumption of oils and fats is growing with incomes. While the traditional Thai diet was lean, and still is, this is changing. In 1990, the average household spent US$19 on oils and fats, but consumption ranged from US$27 in wealthier areas like the Central Region to only US$11 in the poor Northeast.[9]

Thais cook mainly with lard and vegetable oil. They rarely use butter or margarine. Vegetable oil accounts for about two-thirds of the consumption and lard for one-third (see Figure 3.12). These two products have distinct markets. Oil is more popular in Bangkok and in the South where it captures 81 and 88 percent respectively of the market. Elsewhere, people split consumption almost equally between lard and oil.

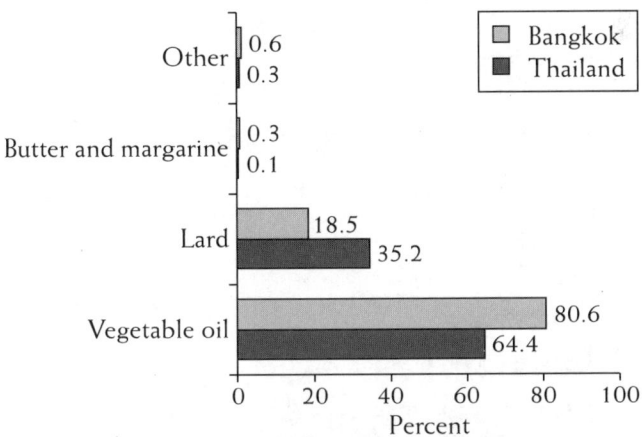

Figure 3.12 Composition of Oil and Fat Consumption in 1990 (Source: Based on National Statistical Office, Report of the 1990 Household Socio-Economic Survey, Whole Kingdom, OPM, Bangkok, 1993, pp. 1–21.)

103

Palm oil is the principal vegetable oil, but people also use some of the local soybean, coconut, groundnut, castor, and sesame oils. Palm oil is produced in the South and some is imported (or smuggled in) from Malaysia. Incidentally, both palm oil and lard have a high proportion of saturated fat. Health-conscious Thais are now looking for alternative products.

3.1.7 SUGAR AND SWEETS

Thais use sugar generously. In 1991, local mills set aside one million tons of sugar for domestic consumption; this is about 20 kilograms (44 pounds) per person per year. Part of it supplies companies like soft drink manufacturers. The rest is sold to consumers directly. In 1990, the average household spent US$17 on sugars and candies; this is 2 percent of the food budget.[10]

Sugars come in various colors and textures and they have different flavors and functions. Principal products are cane, coconut, and palm sugar. Cane sugar is especially important, capturing about half of the market (see Figure 3.13). Raw cane sugar makes molasses, while the refined version is white and crystalline. Coconut sugar is thick and brown. Palm sugar, made from the sap of the palmyra palm, is a heavy brown paste.

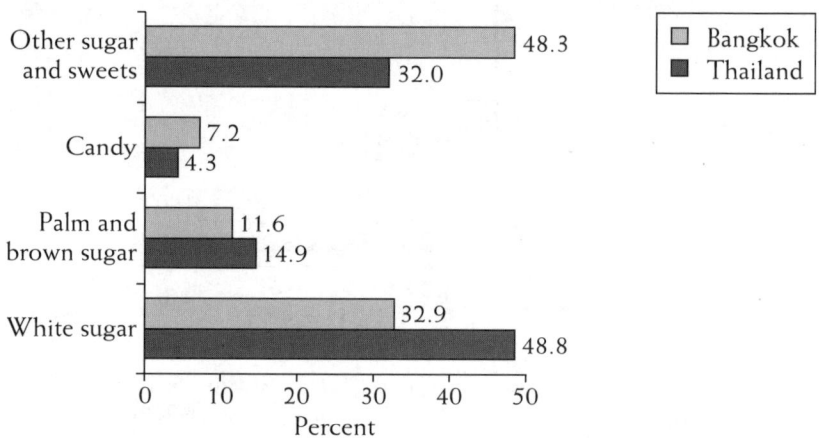

Figure 3.13 Composition of Sugar and Sweet Consumption in 1990 (Source: Based on National Statistical Office, Report of the 1990 Household Socio-Economic Survey, Whole Kingdom, OPM, Bangkok, 1993, pp. 1–21.)

Sweets abound but they have little in common with Western-style candies. Thai sweets are usually small, jellylike, brightly colored pieces shaped as fruits and flowers. These are made with rice flour and cane sugar. People also make various coconut-flavored sweets. *Kalamae*, for instance, is a taffy made with coconut milk, coconut sugar, and glutinous rice flour. In addition, people also candy vegetables such as pumpkins and beans.

3.1.8 SPICES AND SEASONINGS

Thai food is spicy. In 1990, the average household spent US$50 on spices and seasonings, a quarter of which was on dried and fresh chilies (see Figure 3.14). Over forty different species of chili peppers grow in Thailand, ranging from exceedingly hot to mild. People use about ten varieties of these regularly, especially the smallest but hottest ones. Even Western food has chili pepper to suit local tastes.

The more familiar garlic, onion, green onion, basil, and mint are also standard ingredients. Several varieties of garlic, including the common and the giant, grow locally. Common garlic is small and pungent. Thais use it both by the clove and by the bulb. The giant garlic is similar to the Western varieties.

Thai cuisine, however, derives its distinct taste from a unique blend of fragrant herbs and seasonings. It combines the lemony flavors of lemon grass, galengale (a root related to ginger), lime juice, lime leaves, and coriander with the pungent tastes of shrimp paste and fish sauce (a mixture of fish brew and salt). Lime juice and fish sauce combined, for instance, is a common salad seasoning; Thais do not add oil to their salads.

Fish sauce is probably the most basic flavor enhancer. It is to Thais what salt is to Westerners. People use it in many food preparations and they place it on the table as a condiment. Other seasonings include salt, soy sauce, and monosodium glutamate (MSG). People often use soy sauce in vegetable dishes, especially in Bangkok because of the large Chinese community.

Western sauces and spices, in contrast, have a smaller market. They are common only in cosmopolitan areas. In Bangkok, for instance, vinegar, chili sauce (prepared in various degrees of hotness), and tomato sauce together account for nearly 8 percent of the purchases, compared to less than 1 percent in the Northeast.

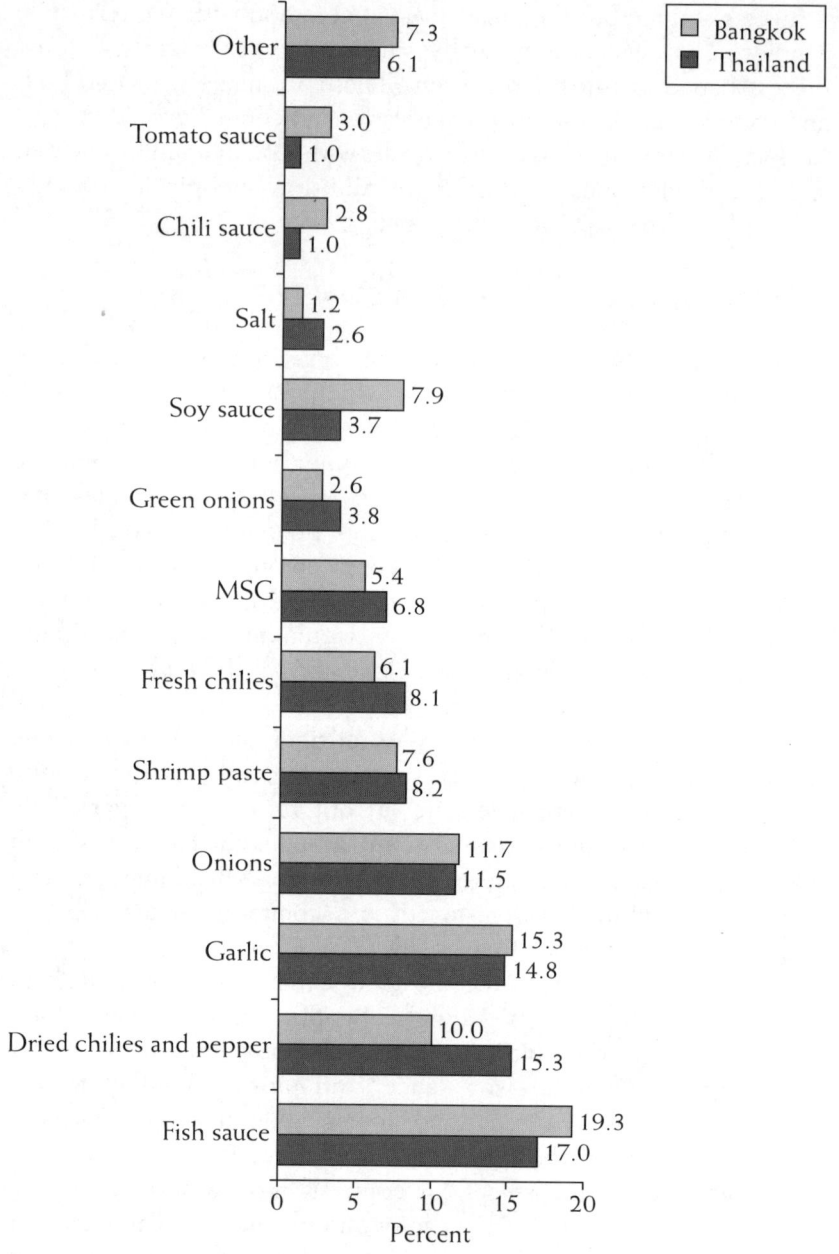

Figure 3.14 Composition of Spice and Seasoning Consumption in 1990 (Source: Based on National Statistical Office, Report of the 1990 Household Socio-Economic Survey, Whole Kingdom, OPM, Bangkok, 1993, pp. 1–21.)

3.1.9 PREPARED MEALS

Eating out is a leading recreation, especially in wealthier areas. In 1990, the average household spent US$235 on prepared meals, while in Bangkok, expenses reached US$760.[11] Thailand has many different eating places that range from portable kitchens to world-class restaurants. Most food places, however, are basic.

Typical Thai restaurants are informal. They are large open-air places. Prices are low and the fare is excellent. Friends and relatives often meet there at night. They order collectively and they share small but numerous dishes. Diners come in larger groups to sample more dishes, and most tables in these restaurants accommodate six to eight people.

Smaller, but also popular, are the noodle shops. There are many hundreds of such places in Bangkok. Thais have a well-developed taste for noodles. They may drive several miles to eat at their favorite shop and they exchange tips on good dining places. Reputable shops have waiting lines at lunchtime and they get reviewed by the press.

Foreign restaurants are often upmarket. They are more common in Bangkok and in tourist areas. Almost any foreign food is available in Bangkok. Major hotels usually have several specialized restaurants producing such cuisine as French, Swiss, Italian, Russian, and Japanese. Some of these restaurants are exclusive. They cater to hotel guests, expatriates, and wealthy local business people.

Cheaper foreign cuisine is available at the new fast-food outlets and cafeterias. In the early 1970s, only major hotels had coffee shops, but these have since multiplied. Cafeterias are now sprouting and leading American food chains have opened outlets in Bangkok and in large provincial cities. Food parks selling many varieties of Asian foods are also spreading rapidly in shopping arcades.

These fast-food places are successful more for their setting than for their dishes. They are quiet, clean, and air-conditioned. Thais, especially young people, use them for meeting friends. Patrons often linger over their food or drink, talking and relaxing. Some students even go there to do their homework. This popularity bodes well for sales of modern commercial equipment.

Cafeterias, however, have failed to replace the traditional food stalls. These are an institution. Street vendors do business throughout Thailand. In Bangkok, they line the sidewalks. They cluster near schools, offices, and bus stops, catering to students and workers. Most are makeshift counters with a charcoal burner and a glass case of ingredients. They sell snacks and light meals. These places are inexpensive and often serve good food.

Stalls are convenient sources of take-away meals, and Thais take away about one-third of the prepared meals they buy. The bulk of these, some 90 percent, are curry on rice and noddle dishes. Takeaway food is especially common in cities where seasonal workers live in rooms with no cooking facilities. In Bangkok, for instance, about 19 percent of the residents do not cook.[12]

Lunchtime is probably the busiest period for food vendors. Some two-thirds of the meals that Thais eat out are lunches (see Figure 3.15). These are usually light and speedy. Lunch favorites include noodles with meat or vegetables and curry on rice. When eaten out, breakfasts also come mainly from stalls. Only the most Westernized Thais have bread and coffee in a cafeteria.

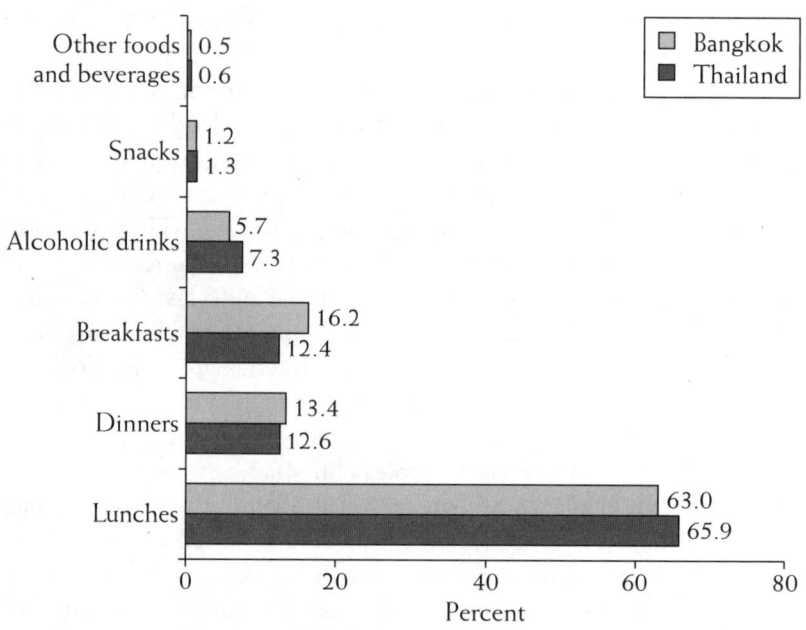

Figure 3.15 Composition of Expenses on Prepared Meals and Drinks in 1990 (Source: Based on National Statistical Office, Report of the 1990 Household Socio-Economic Survey, Whole Kingdom, OPM, Bangkok, 1993, pp. 1–21.)

Thais seem to be eating all the time. They stop at any time of the day for a bowl of noodles, a skewer of satay, some fried bananas, or any other treat selling at the nearby stall. This persistent habit of snacking has created a market for packaged food. Local brands sell standard Thai snacks and some Thai versions of Western products like chips and cocktail sausages. These usually differ from the original by the addition of chili pepper.

3.2 BEVERAGES

The beverage market is growing rapidly especially in wealthier areas. Between 1970 and 1991, it increased by over 400 percent in real terms.[13] In 1990, the average household spent US$50 on beverages, but consumption ranged from only US$24 in the Northeast to US$110 in the Bangkok area.[14]

In all regions alcoholic beverages are the leading purchase. They capture between half and two-thirds of the beverage budget. Non-alcoholic beverages and ingredients for beverages account for the rest.

Ingredients for beverages Ingredients for beverages have a small but growing market. In 1990, the average household spent US$8 on these and expenses ranged from US$21 in Bangkok to only US$3 in the Northeast. The consumption pattern is, however, similar throughout the country. In all provinces, coffee and chocolate drinks combined account for the bulk, some 90 percent, of the purchases (see Figure 3.16).

Coffee is popular. Grocery stores carry a variety of coffee beans, instant coffees, and dairy creamers. Most cafeterias serve coffee. They also advertise espresso, although this usually refers to coffee made in a percolator. (So far, only the most sophisticated coffee shops have espresso machines.) This distribution suggests that products like pots, electric coffee makers, office coffee machines, and espresso machines have potential.

Non-alcoholic beverages Non-alcoholic beverages are in growing demand, although their market is still small. In 1990, the average household spent US$16 on non-alcoholic beverages. High temperatures year-round, however, encourage consumption and in wealthier areas, demand is greater. It peaks at US$39 in Bangkok.[15]

109

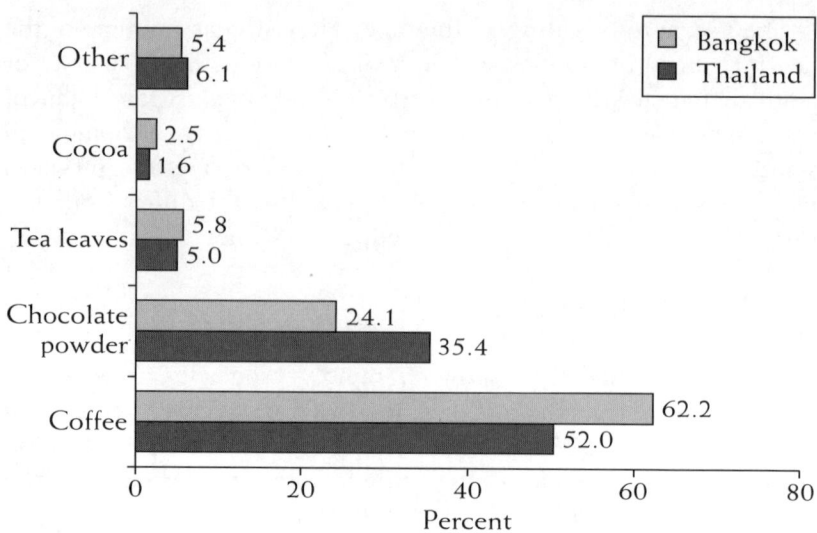

Figure 3.16 Composition of Expenses on Ingredients for Beverages in 1990 (Source: Based on National Statistical Office, Report of the 1990 Household Socio-Economic Survey, Whole Kingdom, OPM, Bangkok, 1993, pp. 1–21.)

Non-alcoholic beverages are new to Thailand, but they are rapidly becoming popular. Until recently, most people drank water. In villages, for instance, people used to leave a jar of water outside their homes for passing strangers to quench their thirst. Thais now have a wide range of beverages to choose from. There are mineral and soda water, fruit juices, iced coffee, iced tea, soft drinks, and some caffeine-based products called "energy drinks."

Soft drinks are popular. They account for 45 percent of the purchases (see Figure 3.17). Many international and local brands share the market. There are cola drinks, tonics, root beers, lemonades, and other flavored carbonated drinks.

Energy drinks are, perhaps, more peculiarly Thai. They are tonic drinks mixed with caffeine. Their stimulating properties appeal to people who work at hard manual jobs like truck drivers and factory workers. Energy drinks account for one-fifth of the expenses on non-alcoholic beverages. Their market share is greater in poorer areas, reaching 30 percent in the North, compared to 17 percent in Bangkok.

Mineral and soda water are widely available. Almost every stall sells bottles or plastic bags of water. Supermarkets carry both local

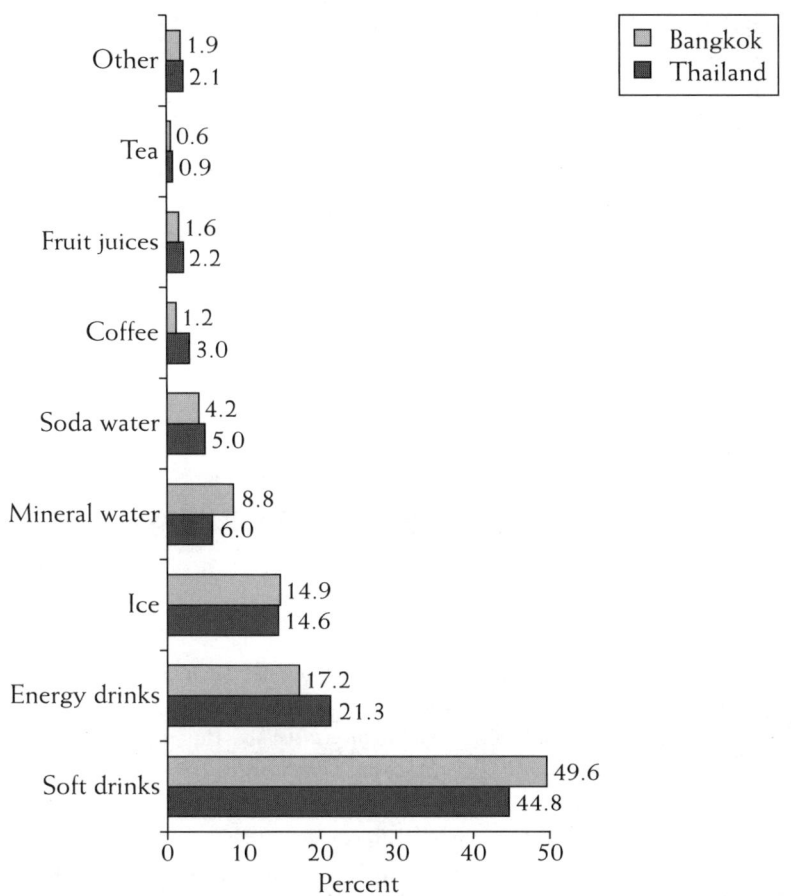

Figure 3.17 Composition of Non-Alcoholic Beverage Consumption in 1990 (Source: Based on National Statistical Office, Report of the 1990 Household Socio-Economic Survey, Whole Kingdom, OPM, Bangkok, 1993, pp. 1–21.)

and imported products. Foreign brands, however, target mainly expatriates and wealthier Thais.

Packaged coffee and tea drinks have a smaller market. Together, they account for about 4 percent of the purchases of non-alcoholic beverages. Both are, however, more popular in the South where they capture about 14 percent of the market. Southern Thailand is the country's major producer of coffee.

Alcoholic beverages Alcoholic drinks top the purchases of beverages, but they are the least diverse. They consist mainly of whiskey and beer. In 1990, the average Thai household spent US$26 on alcoholic beverages, 86 percent of which was on whiskey and 10 percent on beer (see Figure 3.18). Wines and other beverages accounted for the rest.

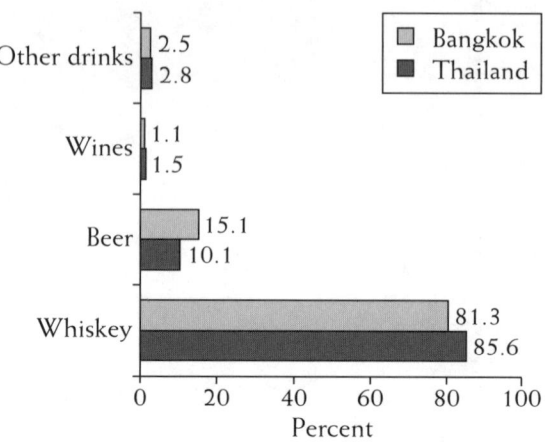

Figure 3.18 Composition of Alcoholic Beverage Consumption in 1990
(Source: Based on National Statistical Office, Report of the 1990 Household Socio-Economic Survey, Whole Kingdom, OPM, Bangkok, 1993, pp. 1–21.)

Whiskey is made from rice and it is the poor man's drink. It accompanies dinners and snacks. In the provinces, it is almost the sole alcoholic beverage. In Bangkok, consumption is more varied but whiskey remains the leading purchase.

Beer is in growing demand although it is expensive. It is heavily taxed, and only wealthier Thais drink it. In Bangkok, for instance, beer accounts for 15 percent of the purchases of alcoholic beverages, compared to only 5 percent in the Northeast. Until the late 1980s, local brands dominated the market. Increasing demand has, however, encouraged foreign manufacturers to set up breweries.

Brandy has a small market. In Thailand as in other Asian countries, it appeals mainly to the Chinese and marketing efforts focus on these people. Distributors, for instance, advertise their brands during Chinese New Year, a gift-giving period for the Chinese community.

Western wines have become fashionable lately. Supermarkets,

hotels, and wine bars carry quality wines from around the world. Leading hotels train their butlers to taste and serve wine and to match it with food. Wine traders organize tasting events to promote their products, especially to expatriates and wealthier Thais. This trend suggests that accessories for the storage and consumption of wine have potential.

Local wines are also available. Research teams at Kasetsat University have developed varieties of grapes suited for tropical climates. Both green and black grapes grow year-round. Although Thai wines are often too sweet for the Western palate, they are promising.

3.3 TOBACCO AND BETELNUT

Demand for tobacco products and betelnut is substantial. In 1990, the average household spent US$39 on these. Cigarettes are successful, capturing the bulk, some 80 percent, of the purchases (see Figure 3.19). Betelnut, cigars, and tobacco, in contrast, have less appeal.

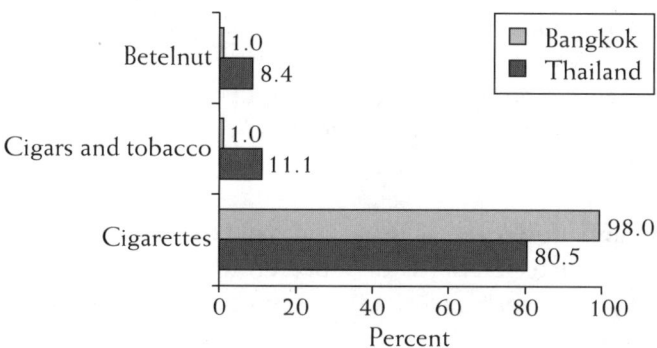

Figure 3.19 Composition of Tobacco Product Consumption in 1990 (Source: Based on National Statistical Office, Report of the 1990 Household Socio-Economic Survey, Whole Kingdom, OPM, Bangkok, 1993, pp. 1–21.)

Betelnut The consumption of betelnut is declining. It is now common only in poor and remote areas. In the Northeast, for instance, betelnut accounts for 16 percent of the purchases, compared to only 1 percent in Bangkok.

Betelnut is a traditional stimulant in Asia. In the mid-nineteenth century, everyone from slaves to kings chewed it. In Sarawak (northern Borneo), for instance, masters supplied their slaves with tobacco and betelnut and rajahs chewed the nuts during meetings with British navy officers. There was also an international trade of betelnut, and British merchants took part in it.

At the turn of this century, Thais still consumed a lot of betelnut. They chewed the nuts with a mixture of tobacco, seri leaves, turmeric, and lime. Betelnut palms grew in gardens all over the country. Their production barely sufficed to meet the domestic demand.

Betelnut was then a crucial part of social life. People stored the nuts and their ingredients in ornate boxes and they always offered them to guests. Regular chewing colored lips and gums red. It also turned teeth shiny black and made them protrude at an old age. Black teeth were then fashionable. Dentists kept complete sets of black false teeth.

Betelnut chewing, however, turned from a social custom to an illegal activity. A little before World War II, nationalistic ruler Luang Pibul outlawed the consumption of betelnut. This regulation, like many others passed at that time, was difficult to enforce. Thais ignored it. As they grew wealthier, however, people switched to more expensive products like cigarettes. The color and decoration of streets must have also changed with this switch, as betelnut chewers spit the dark red juice frequently.

Cigars and tobacco Cigars and raw tobacco are also on the decline. They have almost disappeared in Bangkok, although they still sell in the provinces. In the Northeast, their market share reaches 26 percent, but in other regions, it ranges from 8 to 12 percent. Part of the consumption of raw tobacco is linked with betelnut because people chew these together. Cigars are often homemade cheroots. They are more popular with elders.

Cigarettes Cigarettes are the upmarket substitute to raw tobacco and betelnut. Their demand peaks in wealthier areas. In Bangkok, for instance, cigarettes account for 98 percent of the purchases, compared to only 58 percent in the Northeast.

Both local and imported cigarettes sell in Thailand. Local brands dominate the market. Foreign cigarettes, while prized for their quality, are expensive. Until 1990, the government banned their importation, and smugglers brought them in at dear prices. Foreign brands now sell legally, but they are heavily taxed.

Typical smokers are adult males. In 1988, there were over ten million regular cigarette smokers in Thailand and the bulk of them, some 93 percent, were males. Smoking starts only in early adult life, but the habit spreads quickly (see Figure 3.20). Over half of males above 20 years old smoke.

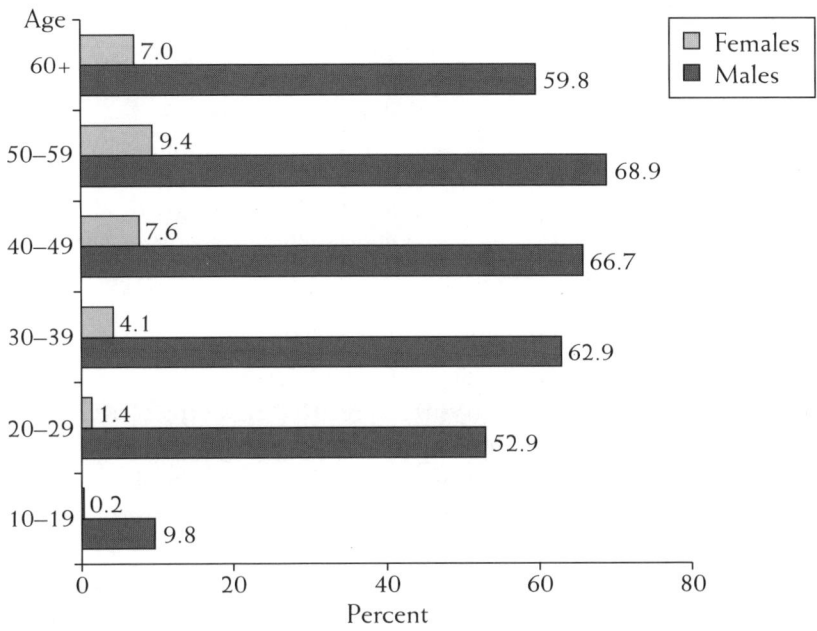

Figure 3.20   Smoking by Age and Sex in 1988
(Source: Based on National Statistical Office, Statistical Handbook of Thailand 1990, OPM, Bangkok, p. 23.)

This consumption pattern bears on marketing. Cigarette packages that fit in the shirt pocket, for instance, have better potential because Thai males rarely wear jackets. This also creates a market for a line of smoking accessories for men.

The incidence of smoking is, however, declining. Between 1981 and 1988, the proportion of male smokers dropped from 51 to 45 percent (see Figure 3.21). Lobby groups campaign to curb smoking. They get support from local businesses. In August 1991,

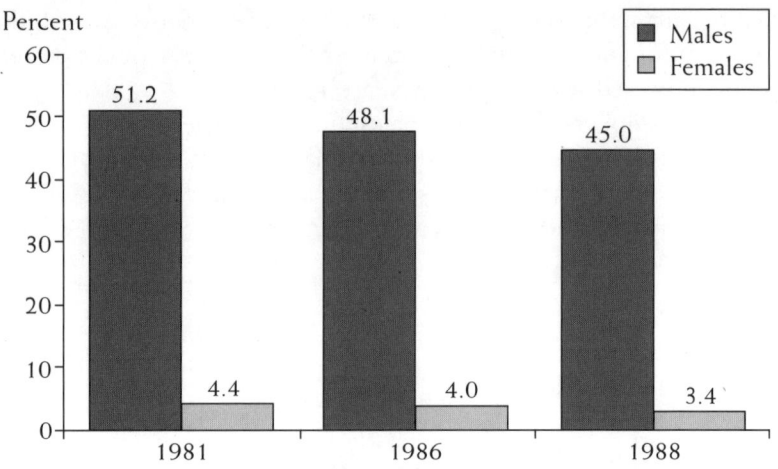

Figure 3.21   Evolution of Smoking, 1981, 1986, 1988
(Source: Based on National Statistical Office, *Statistical Handbook of Thailand*, OPM, Bangkok, various issues.)

for example, one of Thailand's largest department store chains announced that it would stop selling cigarettes.

The government is also trying to restrict cigarette consumption. Laws passed in 1992 require owners and operators of public places and vehicles to arrange for non-smoking sections and to provide proper ventilation in smoking areas. They prohibit cigarette vending machines and sales to people under 18 years old and they ban all types of advertising and marketing promotions. The laws also introduced new standards on tar and nicotine content. In addition, since September 1993, warnings on cigarette packages must be printed in black and white and occupy at least 25 percent of the packet's surface.

These restrictions are novel concepts in Thailand, but people are catching up. Progress is more noticeable in Bangkok where a growing number of businesses are complying to the regulations. This trend suggests that "No Smoking" signs and ventilation equipment have potential.

3.4 CLOTHING AND FOOTWEAR

Expenses on clothing and footwear are growing rapidly. Between 1970 and 1991, they increased by 400 percent in real terms. Thais, however, remain frugal. In 1990, the average household spent about US$150 on its wardrobe, most of it, some 84 percent, on clothes and the rest on shoes (see Figure 3.22).

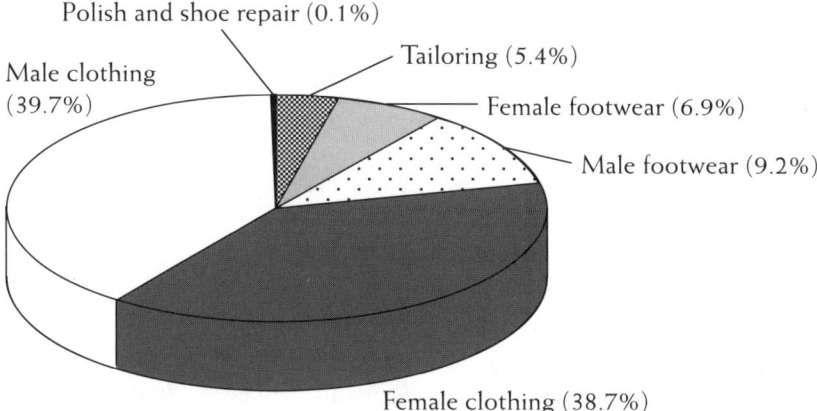

Figure 3.22 Composition of Expenses on Clothing and Footwear in 1990 (Source: Based on National Statistical Office, Report of the 1990 Household Socio-Economic Survey, Whole Kingdom, OPM, Bangkok, 1993, pp. 1–21.)

Western-style clothes have been selling for some time. Thais have had a long exposure to Western communities and they are open to changes. Thai authorities have also promoted Western concepts at various times. In 1941, the military government even decreed that people should wear hats and shoes outside their homes.

This attempt to change outfits was then unsuccessful, but time took care of it. Western clothing is now widespread, especially among males. In Thailand, as in other societies, males go out often and they adopt Western apparel before females.

Thais are also fashion-conscious. Trendy clothes and shoes sell in department stores and boutiques. They are however, smaller than in the West. Female sizes, for instance, seldom exceed eight for shoes and fourteen for garments (American measures). Larger sizes are available only in tourist areas.

3.4.1 CLOTHING

Thais wear light clothes most of the year. They often select loose cotton outfits that stand the occasional downpour and dry quickly.

Even during the cool season, from October to February, temperatures remain around 23°C (73°F) in most places. People rarely wear warm clothes except in the hilly areas of the North and the Northeast where sweaters do sell.

Despite the heat and humidity, people dress neatly. They wear standard office clothes in business circles and more casual but elegant outfits otherwise. Thais pay much attention to clothing. Well-dressed business visitors inspire greater respect.

Fashionable outfits are plentiful, and Thais usually buy their clothes ready-made. Although tailoring is becoming more common in wealthier areas, ready-made garments capture the bulk, some 94 percent, of the clothing market. Many of these clothes are manufactured locally. The kingdom's large garment industry produces for domestic consumption and for export.

Expenses on clothes vary with professional activity. In cities, they are greater because more people work in offices. In Bangkok, well-off residents even shop for designer's clothes. This trend will intensify because more Thais, especially females, are working outside the home.

Male clothing The vast majority of males wear Western clothes. Pants, shirts, and T-shirts together capture almost three-quarters of their expenses on clothing (see Figure 3.23). Businessmen wear suits and ties or short-sleeved safari suits during the day. After work, however, most males dress casually. They go out in slacks and open short-sleeved shirts. Only a few upmarket restaurants require a jacket and a tie.

Dress is more formal in Bangkok because of business activity. This affects the purchases of both outer garments and underwear. Bangkok males, for instance, buy more socks and undershirts because they wear more office clothes.

The sarong, the ethnic costume, is now common only in the South. Muslims in this region conform to the Islamic dress code and they wear sarongs. Southern males allocate about 5 percent of their clothing budget to sarongs, compared to 1 percent for other Thais.

Female clothing Many females have adopted Western outfits, especially in cities. Blouses, slacks, skirts, and dresses together account for half of their clothing budget (see Figure 3.24). Dress, however, is conservative. Women cover shoulders and upper legs.

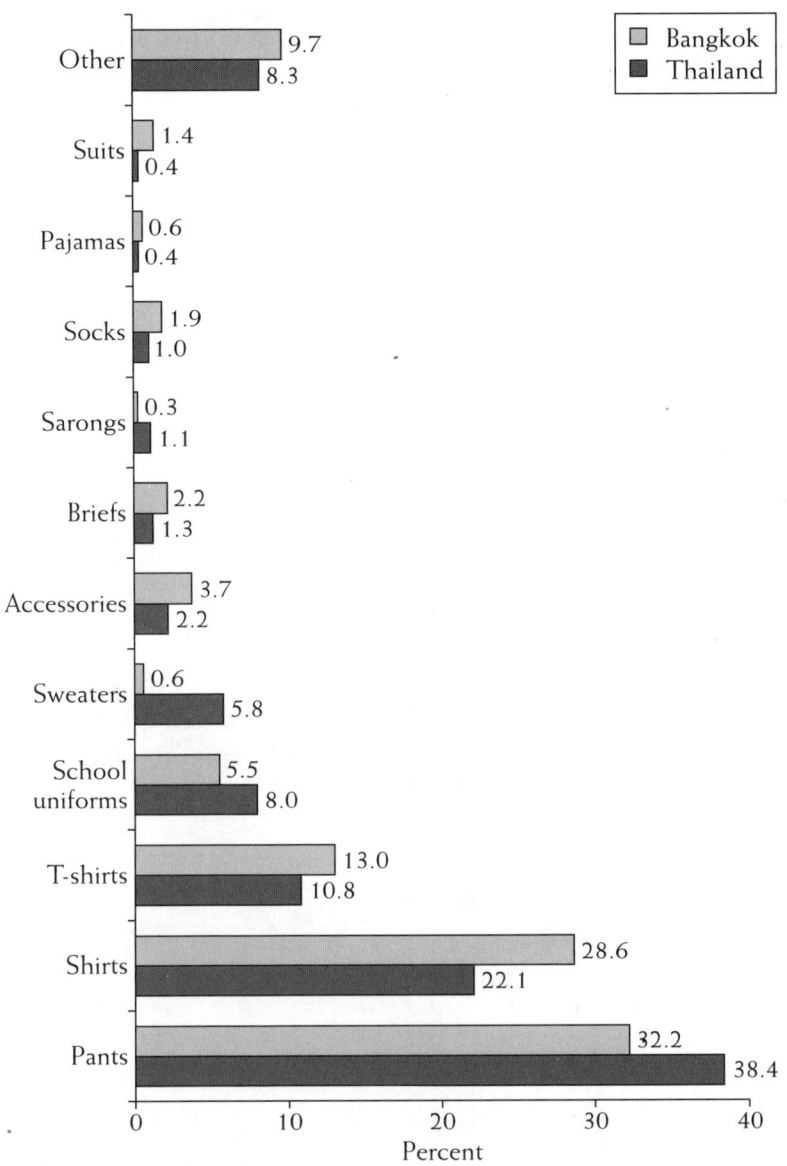

Figure 3.23 Composition of Expenses on Male Clothing in 1990 (Source: Based on National Statistical Office, Report of the 1990 Household Socio-Economic Survey, Whole Kingdom, OPM, Bangkok, 1993, pp. 1–21.)

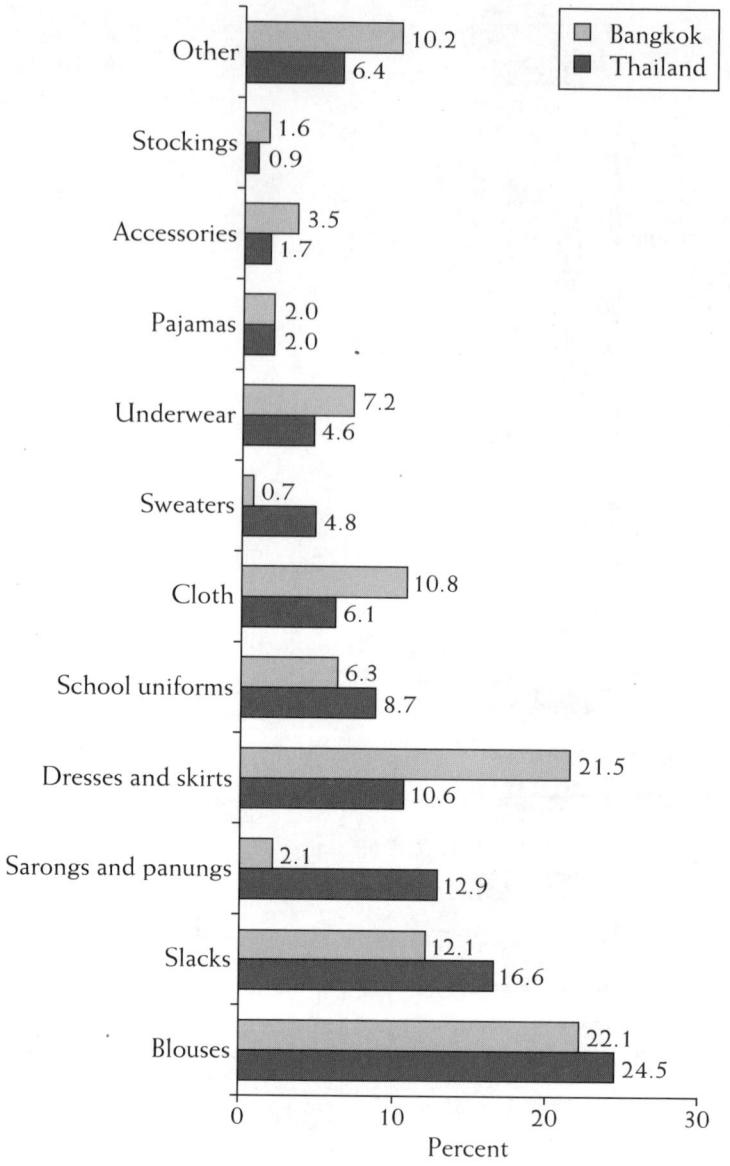

Figure 3.24 *Composition of Expenses on Female Clothing in* 1990 (*Source: Based on National Statistical Office, Report of the* 1990 *Household Socio-Economic Survey, Whole Kingdom, OPM, Bangkok,* 1993, *pp.* 1–21.)

Chapter 3 Consumption and Distribution

Clothes must withstand frequent cleaning. The hot and humid climate compels Thais to change outfits often. Garments that are easy to clean and iron have better potential. This also makes blouses and skirts more convenient to wear than dresses.

Clothing is more formal in business circles. In Bangkok, for instance, females usually wear dresses and blouses and skirts because many work in offices. In the provinces, relaxed outfits like slacks are common.

Ethnic costumes are still fashionable in rural areas. In villages, females wear sarongs and *panungs*. These are more common in the Northeast and in the South where they account for up to a quarter of the purchases. In Bangkok in contrast, females don their traditional outfits only at home or for ceremonies and special events.

Children's clothing   There is a large market for children's clothes. Thailand has a young population. Children who go to school wear the compulsory school uniform most of the day. This consists of a skirt and a white blouse for girls and pants and a white shirt for boys. The color of pants and skirts usually differs for private and public schools, but in both cases, it is dark. Households spend about 8 percent of their clothing budget on school uniforms.

Tailoring   Thai tailors are renowned for their speed and quality. They can make suits, dresses, and almost anything else in 24 hours. Tailoring is, however, common only in wealthier areas. In Bangkok, for instance, it captures 12 percent of the expenses on clothing, compared to 6 percent in the provinces. Clients are usually Thai females but Bangkok tailors also work with foreign visitors (see Figure 3.25).

3.4.2 FOOTWEAR

Shoes are a recent addition. Traditionally, people walked with their feet bare. This practice persists, especially in villages, and changes are gradual. Between 1970 and 1991,[16] expenses on shoes doubled in real terms, but this is less than the growth in total consumption. Footwear remains basic. In 1990, the average household spent only US$24 on shoes,[17] confining most purchases to sneakers and slippers.

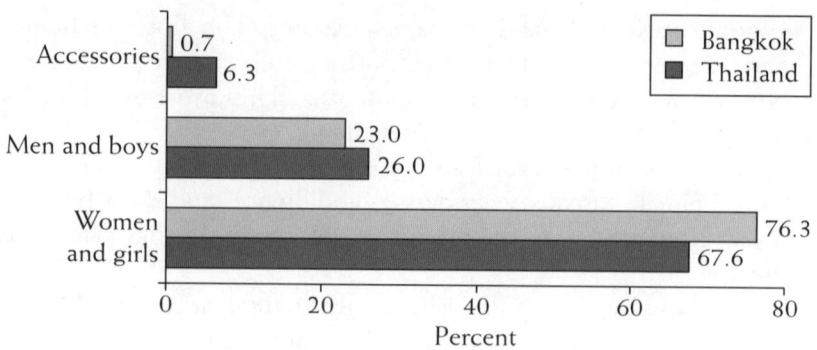

*Figure 3.25   Composition of Expenses on Tailoring in 1990
(Source: Based on National Statistical Office, Report of the 1990 Household Socio-Economic Survey, Whole Kingdom, OPM, Bangkok, 1993, pp. 1–21.)*

Slippers are, probably, the national shoes. Almost everyone wears them and shops keep large supplies of slippers of all shapes and colors. They are cheap and convenient; Thais take their shoes off before entering homes and temples. In addition, rubber slippers resist heavy downpours and floods. Bangkok streets, for instance, are often flooded during the rainy season. Traffic comes to a standstill and people get off the stationary buses and taxis to wade their way through the water.

People, however, wear dress shoes for business, and profession affects expenses. In most provinces, males spend more on shoes because they work outside the home. Thai households allocate about 57 percent of their footwear budget to male shoes and the rest to female shoes. Purchases, however, differ in cities where more females work. In Bangkok, for instance, females spend as much on shoes as males.

Male footwear   Like in the West, male footwear includes sneakers, slippers, and leather shoes. Sneakers and slippers are, however, the most common. Together they account for over two-thirds of the purchases (see Figure 3.26).

Sneakers have, perhaps, become the most successful male shoes, selling well throughout Thailand. They capture 41 percent of the male footwear market. Even tribal people wear sneakers with their traditional costumes. These shoes owe their success partly to their convenience. They are well suited for rugged ground like trails and unpaved roads.

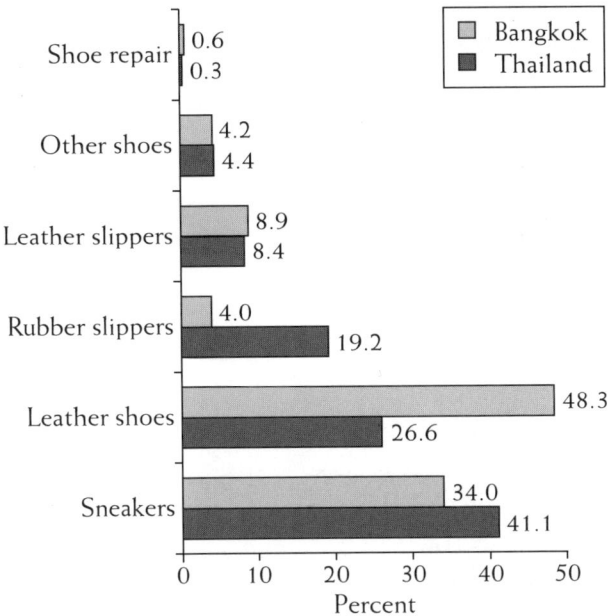

Figure 3.26 Composition of Expenses on Male Shoes in 1990 (Source: Based on National Statistical Office, Report of the 1990 Household Socio-Economic Survey, Whole Kingdom, OPM, Bangkok, 1993, pp. 1–21.)

Slippers are also in high demand. They account for over a quarter of the purchases. Poorer Thais wear rubber slippers and richer ones leather slippers. In the poor Northeast, for instance, males buy rubber slippers almost exclusively, while in Bangkok, leather versions are the most common.

Leather shoes sell better in business centers where office workers wear more formal footwear. Bangkok males, for instance, spend about three times as much on leather shoes as their Northern and Northeastern counterparts.

Female footwear Females have access to a similar range of shoes as males. There are leather shoes, slippers, and sneakers. Slippers and leather shoes, however, top the purchases. Together, they capture 78 percent of the expenses (see Figure 3.27).

Slippers are the most common female shoes. In Thailand, like in the West, females spend more time around the home where they wear slippers. These capture 40 percent of the footwear budget.

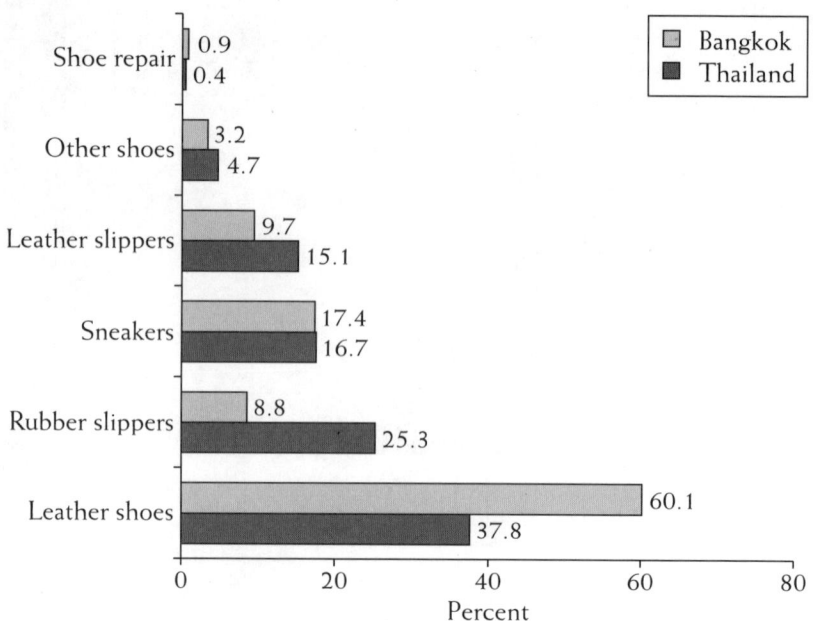

Figure 3.27   Composition of Expenses on Female Shoes in 1990 (Source: Based on National Statistical Office, Report of the 1990 Household Socio-Economic Survey, Whole Kingdom, OPM, Bangkok, 1993, pp. 1–21.)

Leather versions sell better in wealthier areas, especially in Bangkok. In poorer places, rubber slippers prevail.

Leather shoes are the norm for formal occasions. They sell better in Bangkok where many females work in offices, but they also find a sizeable market in the provinces. Leather shoes account for 60 percent of the purchases in Bangkok and for 38 percent in other regions.

Sneakers are less popular. They capture only 17 percent of the market. Sneakers are better suited for females who take long walks. Around the home, however, lace shoes are less convenient than slip-on shoes because of the custom of leaving the shoes outside.

Polish and shoe repair   Polish and shoe repair have a small market. In 1990, the average household spent about 10 cents on these. Expenses are, however, greater in Bangkok where people buy better footwear, especially leather shoes. This suggest that the demand for repair services will increase as income levels rise, raising prospects for repair equipment and supplies.

3.5 MEDICAL AND PERSONAL CARE

Thais are becoming more health-conscious, although their personal and medical expenditures are still small by Western standards. In 1990, the average household spent only US$150 on medical and personal care.[18] Expenses are, however, growing rapidly. Between 1970 and 1991, they increased by almost 700 percent in real terms.[19]

3.5.1 MEDICAL CARE

Health care combines modern and traditional practices. Western medicine has become widespread since its introduction in the nineteenth century, but Thais have cannily maintained their ancestral remedies. The highly respected herbal medicine is the principal alternative to Western treatment. This is an ancient discipline that merchants and travelers brought from India centuries ago. More arcane are the animistic rituals. These superstitions, which belong to the aboriginal cultures of Thailand, are still strongly ingrained in popular beliefs.

The royalty was instrumental in the development of Western medicine. Thai kings were keen to improve health standards. King Mongkut (1824–1851), for instance, invited missionaries to bring medications and vaccines into Thailand. King Chulalongkorn went further, opening the first Thai hospital, Siriraj, in 1886. Many people then opposed these changes. There were few qualified doctors and Thais said they preferred herbal to Western remedies.

Western medicine is better accepted now, but herbal medicine still enjoys a large following. In 1993, the Confederation of Thai Traditional Medicine estimated that 200,000 folk doctors practiced nationwide, although only 30,000 were registered.[20] In Bangkok, several schools train practitioners, while in the provinces, masters transfer their knowledge to apprentices.

Low cost is part of the success of herbal medicine. In most provinces, people spend little on health care. In 1990, the average household paid only US$87 in medical bills. Most of the expenses, some 80 percent, are for services.[21] Medications account for the rest.

Medical services Medical services are poor by Western standards. In 1990, Thailand had only 166 hospital beds per hundred thousand people,[22] compared to 510 in the United States. The same year, there were 23 physicians, 4 dentists, and 72 nurses per hundred thousand people, compared to 216, 59, and 676 respectively in the United States.[23]

Health care is, nonetheless, improving. Medical personnel is expanding. Between 1980 and 1990, physicians and health workers increased by 80 percent, dentists by 120 percent, dental hygienists by 190 percent, pharmacists by 60 percent, and nurses by 110 percent. Medical facilities are also developing. Between 1985 and 1990, clinics and health centers grew by one third and hospital beds by 10 percent.[24]

The quality of health services peaks in Bangkok. The city has, by far, the best medical personnel and equipment in Thailand. In 1990, about half of Thai physicians and dentists practiced in Bangkok and the number of hospital beds per inhabitant was twice as large in Bangkok as in the provinces. Services are often private. Bangkok residents spend most of their health care budget, some 60 percent, on private hospitals and clinics, compared to 41 percent for northeasterners (see Figure 3.28).

Standards are much lower in rural areas. Villagers seldom pay the fees of a physician or a specialist, relying more on health workers and nurses. Dental and eye examination fees combined, for instance, account for only 2 percent of the expenses on medical services in the Northeast, compared to 5 percent in Bangkok. Incidentally, surveys indicate that many villagers suffer from tooth decay and gum diseases.

Thai authorities are trying to improve primary health care in these places. Universities train health workers to treat specific diseases in hospitals. Although they hold junior positions, these people relieve the staff shortage. The administration also emphasizes prevention. Research teams study diseases like malaria and they implement control programs. Health officers also organize information campaigns to raise hygiene standards, while nutritionists introduce new foods to improve diets.

These efforts, however, barely suffice to meet the growing demand for medical services, creating many business opportunities. Thais are investing more in facilities such as health centers, clinics, and medical equipment. Related products, like eye-testing equipment for optical shops, also have potential.

Chapter 3 Consumption and Distribution

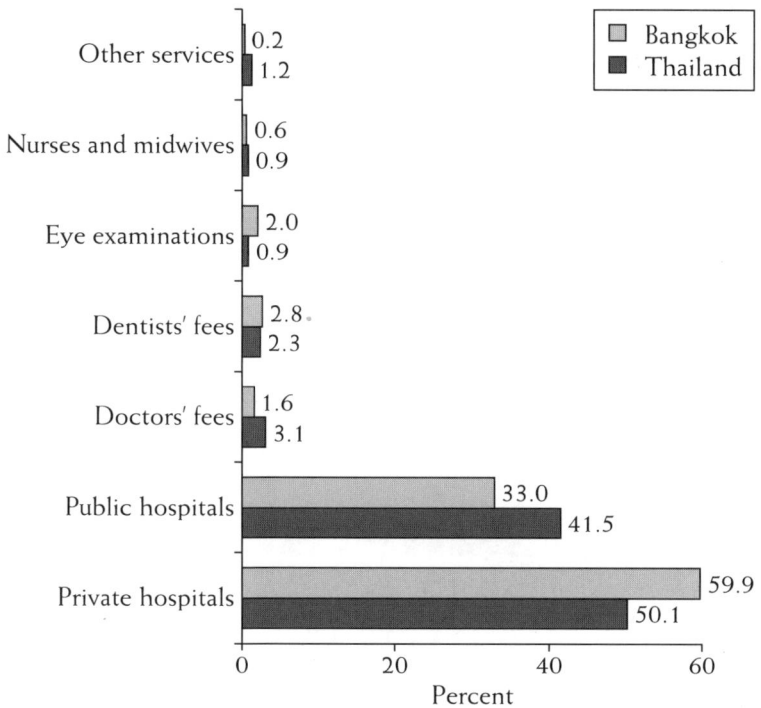

Figure 3.28 *Composition of Expenses on Medical Services in 1990 (Source: Based on National Statistical Office, Report of the 1990 Household Socio-Economic Survey, Whole Kingdom, OPM, Bangkok, 1993, pp. 1–21.)*

Medicines Almost all medicines, from hypnotics and aphrodisiacs to antibiotics, are available in Thailand, most without prescription. Painkillers, cold remedies, and digestive medicines, however, sell best. Together, they account for almost two-thirds of the expenses on medical products (see Figure 3.29).

Consumption differs across regions, reflecting varying health standards. Wealthier Thais, for instance, use more antibiotics, cold remedies, vitamins, and bandages. In poorer places, people spend more on such basic products as digestive medicines and painkillers.

For some time Thais consumed many painkillers, especially in poor areas. Small traders bought them in bulk from pharmacists to resell at a profit in slums. In 1990, there were about two hundred brands of painkillers in Thailand. That year, the most famous brand had an estimated turnover of US$22 million.

127

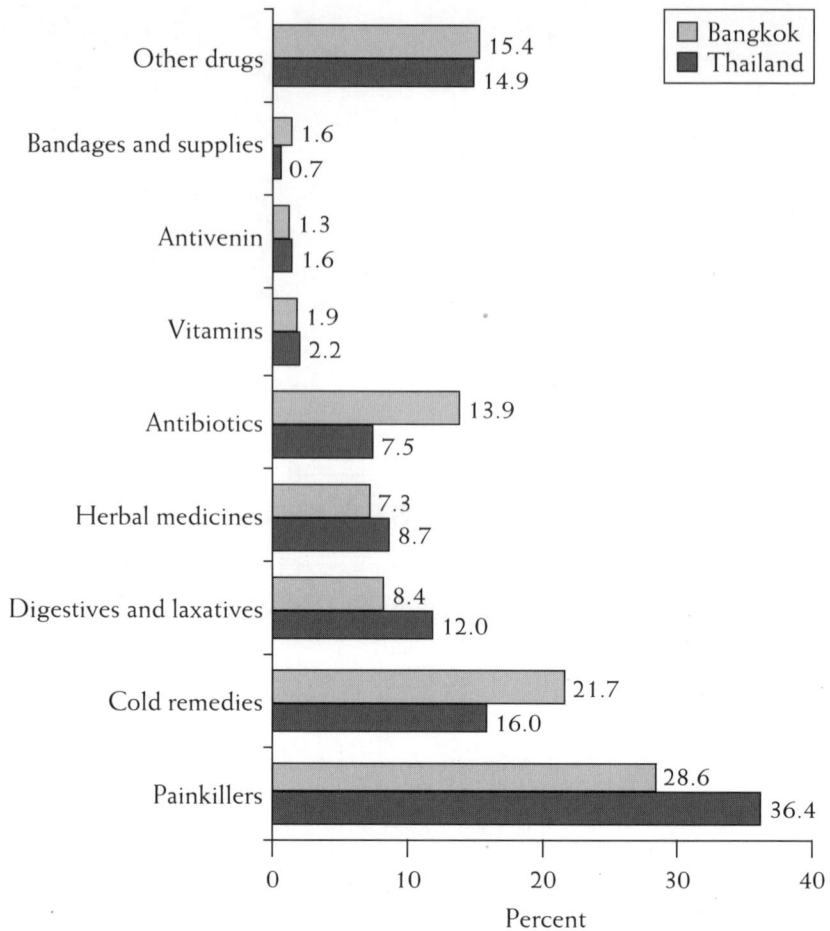

Figure 3.29 Composition of Expenses on Medicines in 1990 (Source: Based on National Statistical Office, Report of the 1990 Household Socio-Economic Survey, Whole Kingdom, OPM, Bangkok, 1993, pp. 1–21.)

Painkillers were popular because they contained caffeine. Many people work long hours at hard manual jobs and they look for stimulants. Male workers consumed packaged painkillers regularly, taking them straight or mixed with tonic drinks.

The extensive use of painkillers was, however, controversial. Lobby groups campaigned for many years to get rid of caffeine in painkillers. They argued that caffeine causes addiction and that misused aspirin causes peptic ulcers, abdominal bleeding, and peritonitis. Eventually, the Thai Food and Drug Administration bowed to pressure. In March 1991, it banned caffeine from painkillers. The move affected 16 formulas of painkillers sold under 200 different brand names.

Amphetamines are also popular stimulants. In 1991, a study by Ramathibody Hospital estimated that 83 percent of Thai truck drivers use them.[25] Even elephants take amphetamines. Thais employ elephants to move logs in forests. Some owners feed them with the drug to make them work longer. In July 1993, the Forest Industry Organization announced its intention to open a veterinary hospital to treat drug-addicted elephants.

Antivenin is an integral part of the medical kit. The many species of venomous snakes living in Thailand claim regular casualties. Snakebites often occur in rice fields because cobra feed on mice. Thai authorities have established several research institutes to study snakes. These centers produce antidotes that are exported worldwide.

Herbal remedies are still widely used. They capture about 9 percent of the expenses on medications and their market share peaks in the South where it reaches 16 percent. In 1993, over 3,400 herbal recipes were registered drugs, but this is only a small part of the vast number of remedies recorded in ancient texts.

Because the cost of Western medicines keeps increasing, the Thai authorities are trying to restore the knowledge of medicinal herbs. In October 1993, the Health Ministry opened a research center, called Institute of Thai Traditional Medicine, to collect scattered recipes and develop uniform standards.

3.5.2 PERSONAL CARE

Personal care is increasing, although not as rapidly as health care. Between 1970 and 1991, it grew by 300 percent.[26] Demand remains basic. In 1990, the average household spent US$63 on personal care the bulk of it, some 80 percent, on products, leaving only 20 percent for personal services.[27]

Personal services Personal services are still luxuries in Thailand. Many are standard. Thais spend about 95 percent of their personal service budget on hairdressing, mostly on haircuts (see Figure 3.30). Personal services are, however, more diverse in wealthier areas. Hair

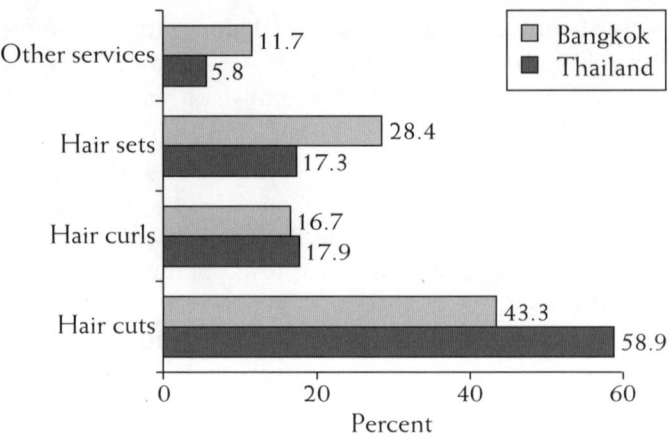

Figure 3.30   Composition of Expenses on Personal Care Services in 1990 (Source: Based on National Statistical Office, Report of the 1990 Household Socio-Economic Survey, Whole Kingdom, OPM, Bangkok, 1993, pp. 1–21.)

sets, facials, and sculptured nails are more common in Bangkok than in other parts of the country. This suggests that high-quality equipment and supplies for salons and beauty parlors have good prospects.

Personal care products   Personal care products are also basic. Hygiene products dominate, accounting for nearly three-quarters of the purchases (see Figure 3.31). People, however, are increasing their expenses on less essential items like cosmetics, perfumes, and hair creams.

Cosmetics have a small but growing market. They account for only one-fifth of the expenses on personal care products and they focus on essential goods. Although lipstick is getting more popular, face powder remains the principal purchase. Shine shows easily in hot and humid weather. Matte face powders help control it. Other cosmetics also have potential, but they must withstand storage in hot temperatures and contain little oil.

Perfumes are new to Asia. They are targeted at wealthier people. They sell primarily in upmarket department stores. Distributors also organize promotional events, setting up booths in shopping arcades to launch new brands and raise consumer awareness.

Chapter 3 Consumption and Distribution

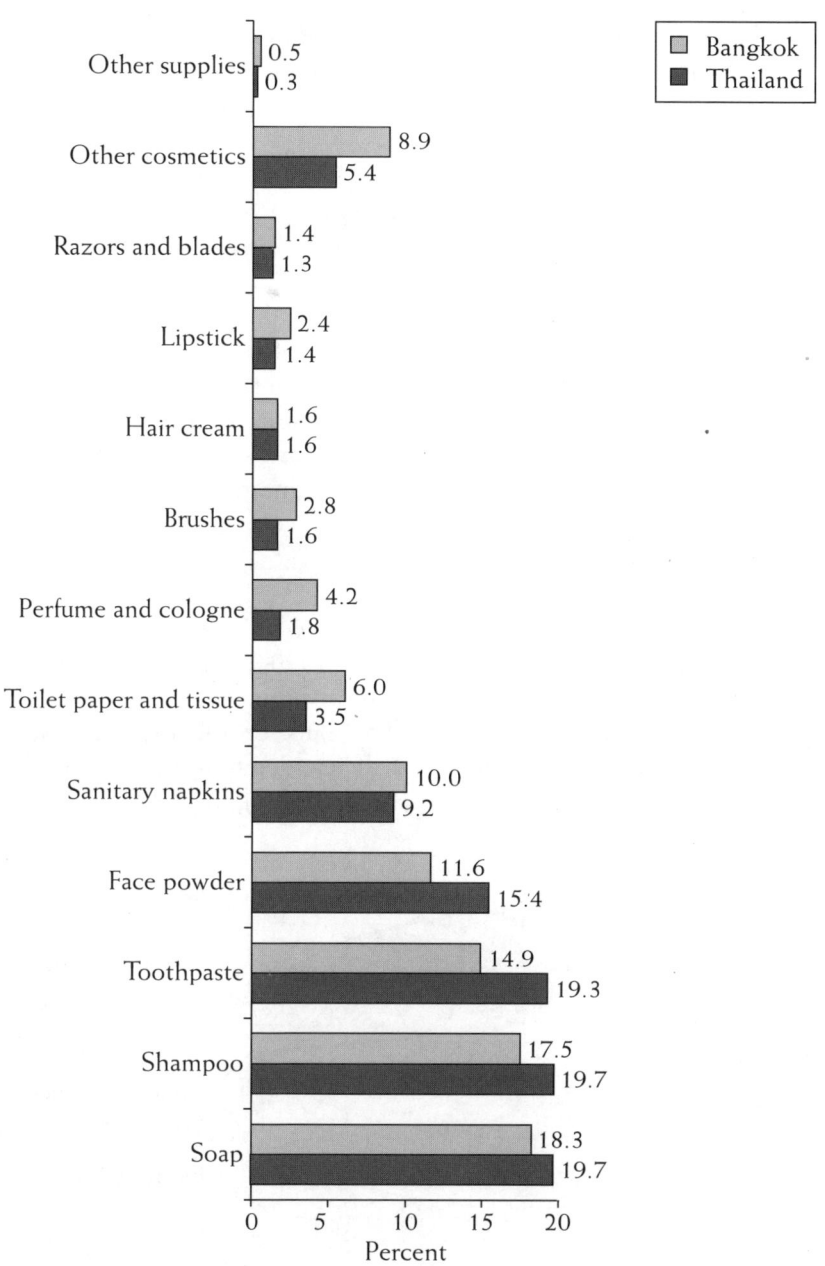

Figure 3.31 Composition of Expenses on Personal Care Products in 1990 (Source: Based on National Statistical Office, Report of the 1990 Household Socio-Economic Survey, Whole Kingdom, OPM, Bangkok, 1993, pp. 1–21.)

Hair-care products have potential. Thai females used to keep their hair cropped short. Contacts with the West, however, made long hair fashionable, increasing the demand for hair creams and other hair treatments.

Consumption is greater and more diverse in wealthier areas. People spend twice as much on personal-care products in Bangkok than in the provinces. Because they often work in offices, Bangkok residents are better groomed. Females wear more makeup and males shave more frequently. These people buy more perfumes, cosmetics, hair creams, shaving creams, razors, and blades.

Wealth also affects the market for other personal products. Richer Thais, for instance, wear better eyeglasses and they use contact lenses more frequently. Contact lenses are especially convenient during downpours in the humid summer months.

3.6 HOUSING

Housing is the second largest expenditure of Thais. It accounts for more than a quarter of consumption. In 1990, the average household spent US$572 on home, utilities, furnishing, equipment, cleaning supplies, and domestic helpers. The bulk of the expenses, some 90 percent, cover home and utilities, leaving little room for equipping and running the household (see Figure 3.32).

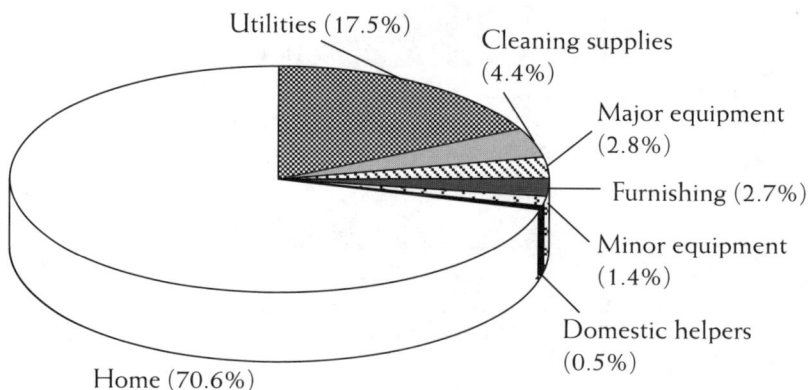

Figure 3.32 Composition of Housing Expenses in 1990
(Source: Based on National Statistical Office, Report of the 1990 Household Socio-Economic Survey, Whole Kingdom, OPM, Bangkok, 1993, pp. 1–21.)

3.6.1 HOME

In Thailand, as in the West, rent is the leading cost of a residence. It accounts for almost three-quarters of the expenses on homes (see Figure 3.33). Rental value of owned dwellings, the cost of living in a owned home, which is supposed to reflect the rental value of the home, is especially prominent because most Thais own their homes.

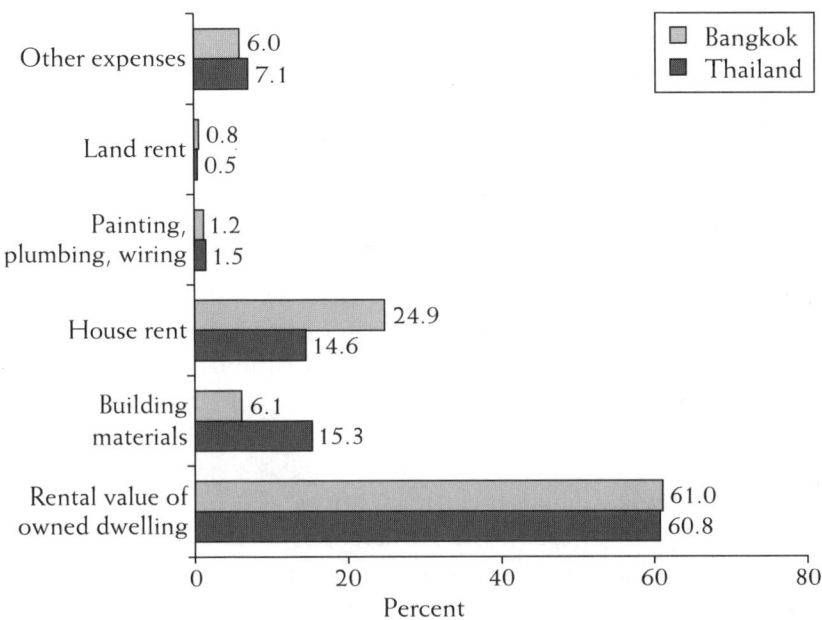

Figure 3.33 Composition of Home Expenses in 1990
(Source: Based on National Statistical Office, Report of the 1990 Household Socio-Economic Survey, Whole Kingdom, OPM, Bangkok, 1993, pp. 1–21.)

This cost is also increasing as people get richer. Until recently, Thais built their own houses. They bought building materials and enrolled their friends and relatives to help them. This practice is disappearing and more people hire builders.

Developers have become active in the residential sector. They build most of the new residential units, especially in wealthier areas. In Bangkok, for instance, condominiums and housing estates are sprouting.

These modern homes are better furnished. They are painted and they have indoor plumbing and electricity. This increases the demand for quality paints, wires, plumbing equipment, and other building materials. Since the tropical climate enhances corrosion, waterproof paints and materials that resist humidity have greater sales potential.

3.6.2 UTILITIES

Utilities are developing gradually. Between 1970 and 1991, the consumption of water and fuels increased by 260 percent in real terms.[28] In Bangkok, most households have electricity and running water, but in rural areas, these are still considered luxuries (see Figure 3.34). Villagers often collect water from wells and rivers, they cook on charcoal and wood, and they light their homes with kerosene lamps.

Water Running water is common only in cities. In Bangkok, for instance, about 90 percent of households have indoor plumbing[29] and people spend almost five times as much on water as other Thais. In the provinces, people rely more on rivers and wells.

Equipment for collecting water is in high demand. Items like buckets, water tanks, and pumps sell well in the provinces. Households who use underground water often install a submersible pump in their well that they activate occasionally to refill their elevated water tank. Many people also store rain and river water in tanks.

Cooking fuels Thais fuel their stoves mainly with charcoal, wood, and gas. For many years, charcoal and wood have been the principal cooking fuels. Wood is now getting scarce but charcoal is still common. Many stalls, for example, cook on charcoal burners. Gas is the new cooking fuel. It sells better in the Central Region and in the South, but it is also becoming popular in other regions. More people are replacing their traditional clay stoves with modern gas cookers.

Electricity New industries, condominiums, and housing estates are increasing the consumption of electricity. Thailand is importing more oil to generate energy. During the Gulf War in early 1991, the government even feared an oil shortage. It banned movie theaters and other businesses from using electrical signboards. Growing consumption is also straining local infrastructure. Production barely meets demand, and Thai authorities are investing in additional power plants.

In the interim, supply is irregular, partly because distribution lines are in poor condition. Blackouts are frequent, sometimes lasting

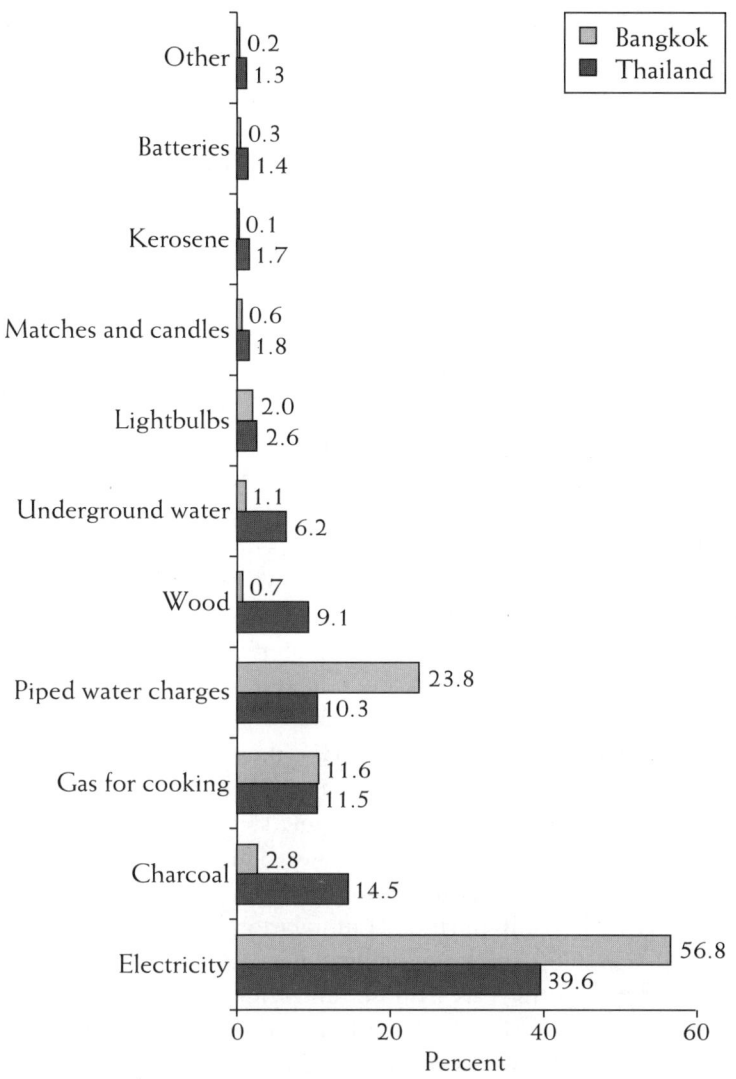

*Figure 3.34 Composition of Expenses on Utilities in 1990
(Source: Based on National Statistical Office, Report of the 1990 Household Socio-Economic Survey, Whole Kingdom, OPM, Bangkok, 1993, pp. 1–21.)*

several hours. People keep candles and matches in anticipation of electricity cuts and factories use automatic switches to protect their machinery. Generators and rechargeable battery items are also becoming valuable.

In the many rural areas which have no electricity, people rely on kerosene lamps and battery-powered goods. Expenses on batteries are about three times as high in the provinces as in Bangkok. Prosperous communities buy generators, but they run them part-time, turning them off for the night in the early evening. After 9 p.m. these places are often in complete darkness.

3.6.3 FURNISHING AND EQUIPMENT

Furnishing and home equipment are the fastest growing expenditures of Thais. Between 1970 and 1991, they increased elevenfold in real terms.[30] These expenses, however, remain small. In 1990, the average household spent only US$40 furnishing and equipping its home.[31]

Furnishing The furnishing of homes is showing signs of changes although it is often basic. Sheets, pillowcases, bedspreads, towels, and washcloths are becoming more common in wealthier areas. In most provinces, however, blankets and mosquito nets remain the leading purchases, together accounting for 60 percent of the expenses on furnishing (see Figure 3.35).

In many places, mosquito nets are a must. The kingdom has no less than 410 species of mosquitoes. Seven of these species are malaria vectors. In infected areas, people sleep under mosquito nets. Some even soak their nets in insecticide. This practice will probably spread because malaria is increasing.

Beds are, perhaps, the principal innovation in household furniture. They are replacing mats gradually. In wealthier regions, mats are disappearing, but they are still common in villages.

Bedroom and bathroom furnishing are the privilege of richer Thais. Sheets, pillowcases, towels, washcloths, bedspreads, and draperies are becoming common in modern homes. In Bangkok, for instance, they account for nearly half of the expenses on furnishing, compared to only 28 percent in the Northeast.

Minor household equipment Minor household equipment is a small expenditure group. In 1990, the average household spent only US$8 on it. Most of this category is, kitchen equipment. Dishes and pottery alone capture 45 percent of the purchases, while pots and

Chapter 3 Consumption and Distribution

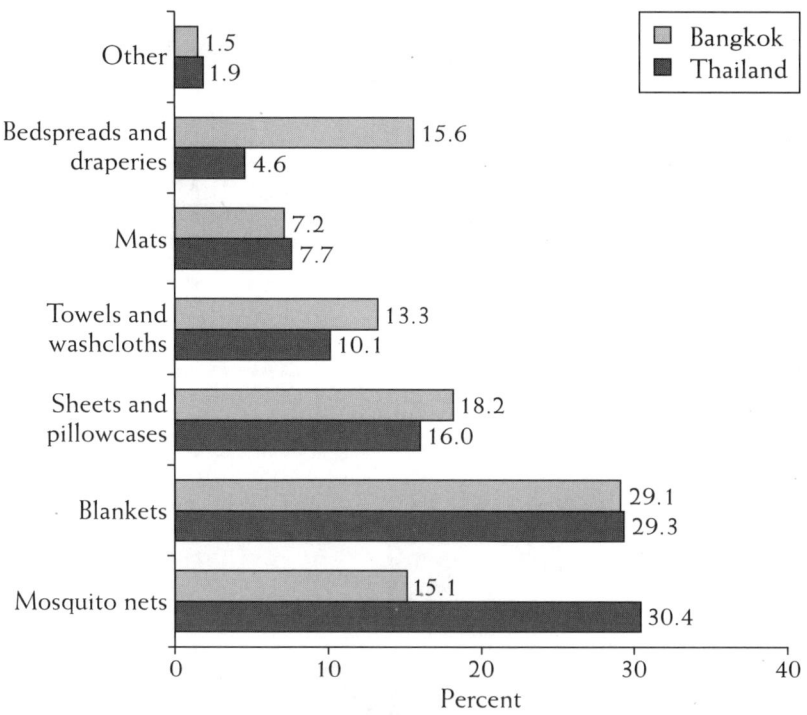

Figure 3.35 Composition of Furnishing Expenses in 1990 (Source: Based on National Statistical Office, Report of the 1990 Household Socio-Economic Survey, Whole Kingdom, OPM, Bangkok, 1993, pp. 1–21.)

pans, glassware, cutlery, vacuum flasks, and small utensils account for most other expenses (see Figure 3.36).

Tools in Thai kitchens are essentially Asian. People use clay pots for making soups, woks for frying, double boilers for steaming, and cleavers and chopping boards for mincing. More peculiarly Thai, perhaps, are the coconut graters, carving sets, and small molds.

This traditional equipment is poorly adapted to modern life. People, for instance, shred vegetables with knives and they pound spices with mortars and pestles. Such slow processes are becoming more expensive as incomes increase. This suggests that time-saving devices, like vegetable graters, slicers, choppers, grinders, beaters, and blenders have potential.

Tableware is minimal but expanding. It often consists of a few serving dishes, plates, and bowls. Traditionally, Thais ate with their

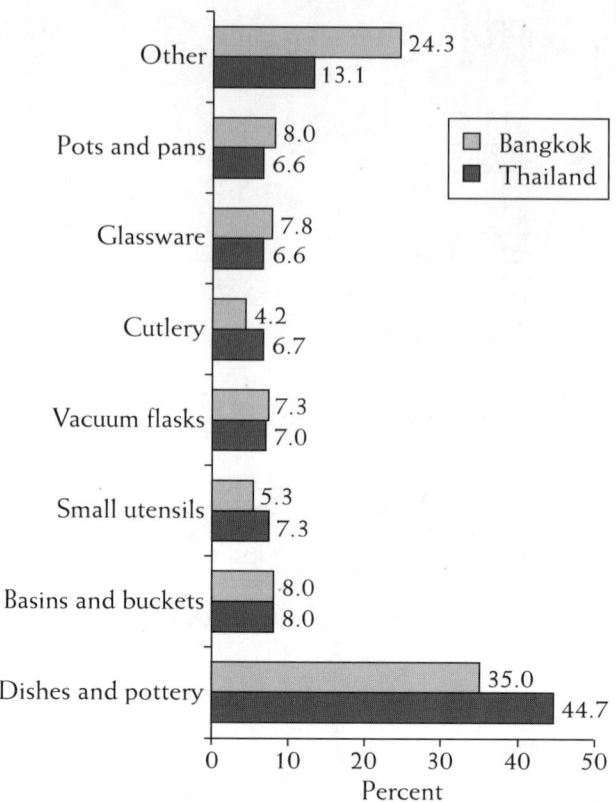

Figure 3.36 Composition of Expenses on Minor Household Equipment in 1990
(Source: Based on National Statistical Office, Report of the 1990 Household Socio-Economic Survey, Whole Kingdom, OPM, Bangkok, 1993, pp. 1–21.)

fingers. While this practice persists, more people are now using Western-style tableware. Forks and spoons, for instance, are becoming common, although knives are rarely in.

Storing food in this tropical country is a hurdle. Many insects like ants and cockroaches eat their way through cardboard boxes and they enter open packages. Thais must keep virtually all foods in jars and sealed containers, increasing the demand for plastic boxes and other airtight containers.

Basins and buckets are integral parts of the household equipment. People who do not have indoor plumbing collect water in buckets and they clean dishes and clothes in basins. These products are in greater demand in remote areas. In the Northeast, for instance, they account for 13 percent of the purchases, compared to less than 8 percent in Bangkok.

Major household equipment Expenses on major equipment are small but growing. In 1990, the average household spent US$16 on it, although expenditures differed greatly, ranging from US$9 in the Northeast to US$43 in Bangkok.[32] Low budgets confine many of the purchases to small electrical items like electric pots (rice cookers), fans, and irons. Wealthier Thais, however, invest in more expensive goods such as refrigerators, air conditioners, furniture, and mattresses (see Figure 3.37).

Small electrical items have been selling for some time and their market is growing steadily. Electric fans, pots, and irons are the most successful. In 1990, about two-thirds of the households had a fan, half an electric pot, and 47 percent an iron. Only wealthier Thais buy less essential items like mixers.

Refrigerators are also in growing demand. Between 1986 and 1990, ownership increased from 21 to 32 percent. Once the privilege of urban Thais, refrigerators are now selling in rural areas. Up-country, they top the purchases of household equipment.

Air conditioners, in contrast, are still luxuries. They have much appeal, but few households buy them. Their electricity cost exceeds most salaries. Air conditioners sell almost exclusively in cities. Bangkok residents are the principal buyers. Cooling systems for offices are also successful. Over the past few years, for instance, many administrations have replaced their fans with air conditioners.

Modern stoves are replacing old cooking devices gradually. Traditionally, Thais cooked on clay stoves fueled by charcoal or wood. They still do so, especially in the provinces. In villages, people even use metallic buckets as makeshift stoves. More households, however, are buying modern cookers.

Gas is the favorite fuel for these new stoves. They produce the high temperatures required for Thai cuisine. Typical gas cookers have a compartment for storing a gas bottle and a single large double-ringed burner fitted with a wok stand. Some of these burners can generate over four kilowatts of power.

Gas cookers are more common in the Central and Southern regions. These areas are closer to the gas fields of the Gulf of

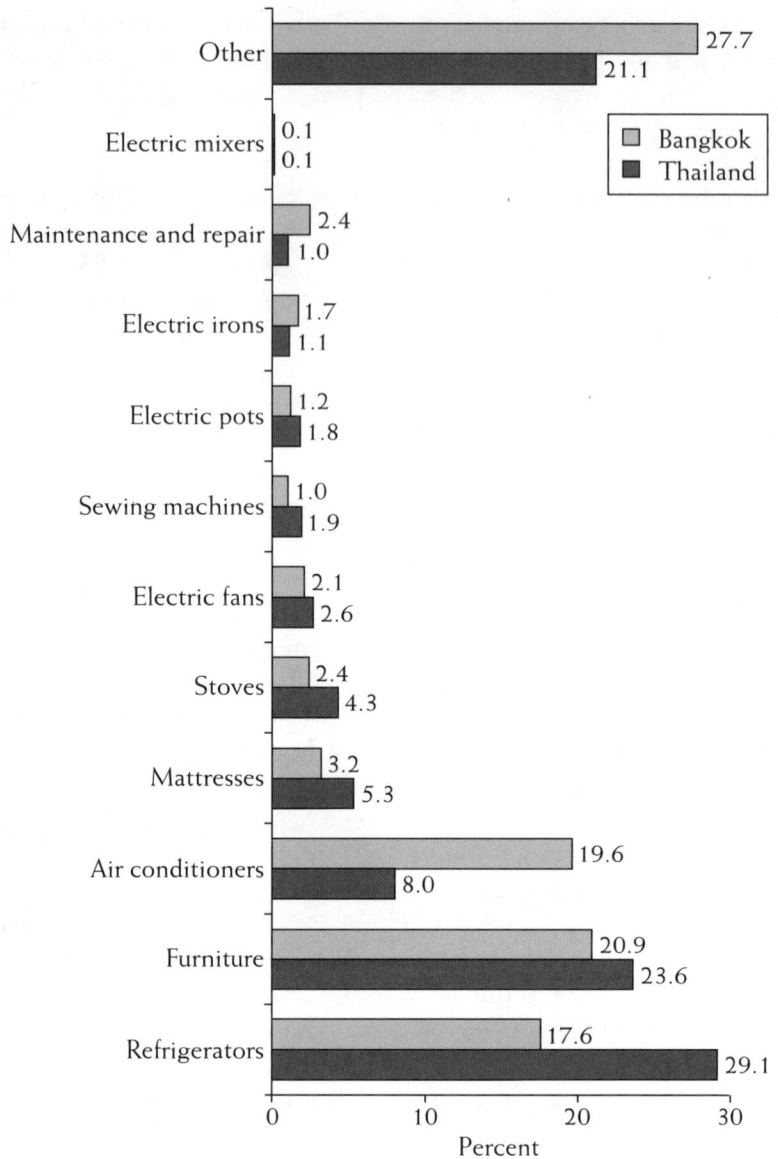

Figure 3.37 *Composition of Expenses on Major Household Equipment in 1990 (Source: Based on National Statistical Office, Report of the 1990 Household Socio-Economic Survey, Whole Kingdom, OPM, Bangkok, 1993, pp. 1–21.)*

Thailand. Between 1986 and 1990, for instance, the proportion of households having a gas stove increased from 33 to 53 percent in the Central Region and from 21 to 45 percent in the South. Electric pots (rice cookers) are the cheap alternative to stoves. They have become fast-selling items in villages.

Mattresses are also becoming popular. People usually lay them on the floor like mats. This is better suited to home interiors than regular beds because Thai furniture is low.

3.6.4 CLEANING

Cleaning is becoming more sophisticated, with wealthier Thais using higher quality products. In 1990, the average household spent US$28 on cleaning, but in Bangkok, expenses reached US$61. Cleaning supplies capture the bulk, some 90 percent, of the expenditures and services account for the rest.[33]

Cleaning supplies Many different cleaning products are now available in Thailand, although people still buy detergents mainly. Powdered and liquid detergents together account for about three-quarters of the purchases (see Figure 3.38). Their market share is especially prominent in villages where they are often the sole cleaning device. Producers tap this vast market through networks of traveling sales people.

Purchases are more diverse in wealthier areas. Since richer people buy better homes and garments, they take greater care of them. They polish their floors, have their clothes dry-cleaned, and sanitize their environment. In Bangkok, for instance, people spend about ten times more on dry cleaning, starch, polish, insecticides, and disinfectants, than in the Northeast.

Domestic helpers Few households employ personnel and they only do so for basic services like housekeeping and child care. Households spend some 59 percent of their domestic helpers budget on maids and over a quarter on nurses and laundresses (see Figure 3.39). The remaining 13 percent pays for drivers and gardeners. Drivers are more common in Bangkok where traffic congestion often forces people to leave their cars and walk or get a motorcycle ride to their destination.

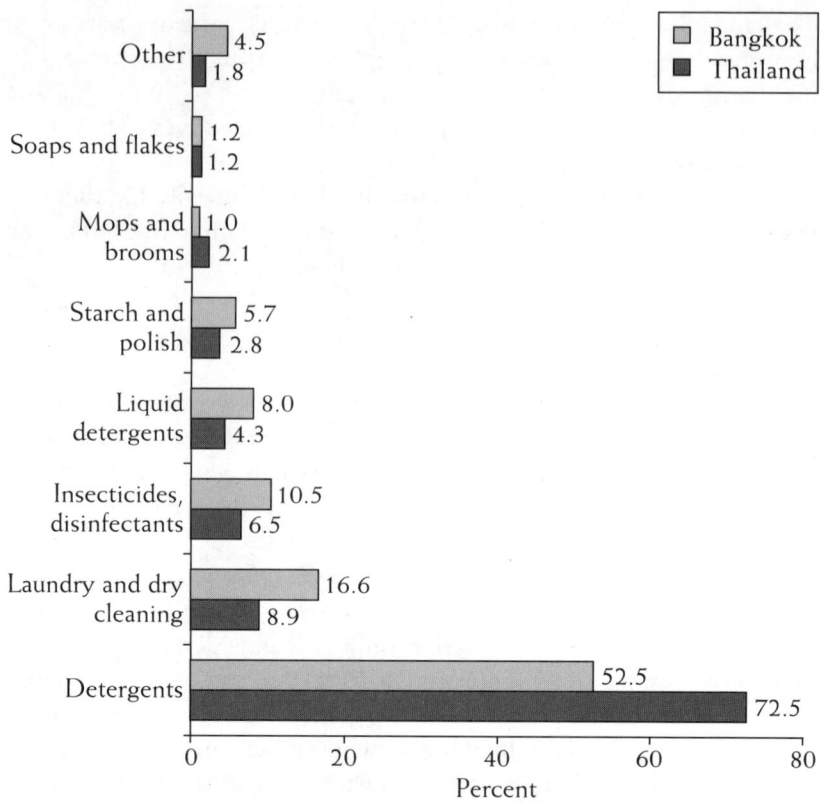

Figure 3.38 Composition of Expenses on Cleaning Supplies in 1990 (Source: Based on National Statistical Office, Report of the 1990 Household Socio-Economic Survey, Whole Kingdom, OPM, Bangkok, 1993, pp. 1–21.)

3.7 TRANSPORTATION AND COMMUNICATIONS

Transportation and communications are the third largest expense of Thais. In 1990 the average household spent US$327 on these; this is about 14 percent of its total consumption. Transportation dominates, capturing 96 percent of this budget (see Figure 3.40).

Services are, however, in short supply. Thailand is notorious for its congested infrastructure. Busy telephone lines and legendary traffic jams are often said to hinder the growth of the country. Thai authorities are speeding up the development of infrastructure, but changes take time.

Chapter 3 Consumption and Distribution

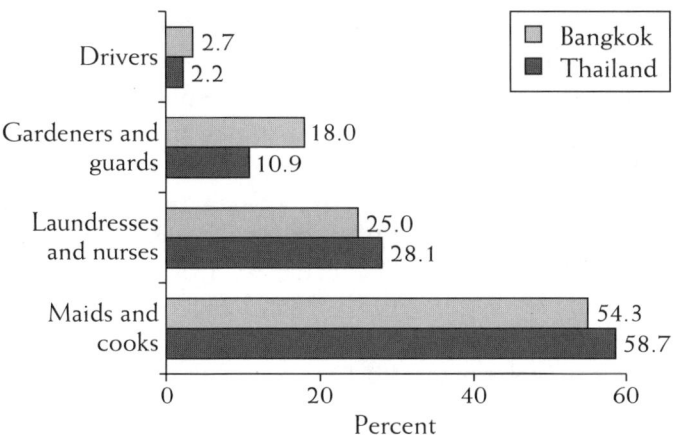

Figure 3.39 Composition of Expenses on Domestic Helpers in 1990 (Source: Based on National Statistical Office, Report of the 1990 Household Socio-Economic Survey, Whole Kingdom, OPM, Bangkok, 1993, pp. 1–21.)

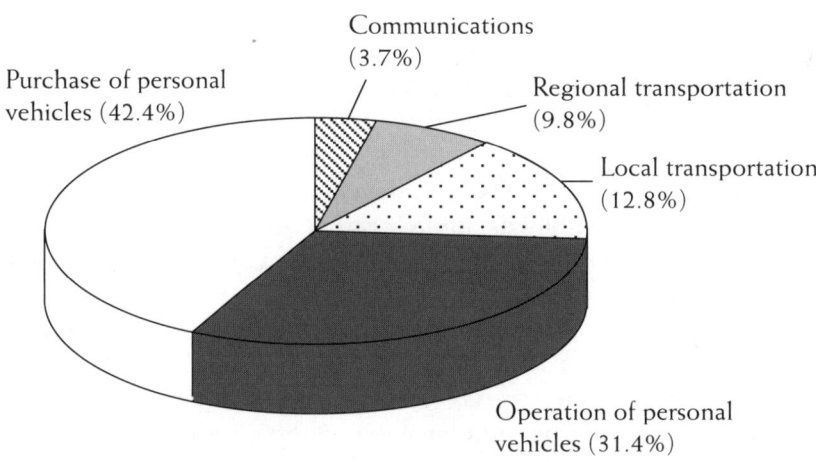

Figure 3.40 Composition of Expenses on Transportation and Communications in 1990
(Source: Based on National Statistical Office, Report of the 1990 Household Socio-Economic Survey, Whole Kingdom, OPM, Bangkok, 1993, pp. 1–21.)

143

In the interim, people stand in line. In Bangkok, traffic often comes to a standstill. Cars move at an average speed of 10–25 kilometers (7–15 miles) per hour. Fumes are thick. At busy intersections, policemen wear oxygen masks and Bangkok hospitals claim that 40 percent of these people suffer from respiratory problems.[34]

Business is another casualty of traffic. Congestion slows down deliveries and often prevents managers from reaching meeting places on time. In October 1991, when Bangkok hosted the annual conference of the World Bank, the Thai government had to declare a two-day national holiday to keep cars off the streets while the delegates moved around the city.

3.7.1 PUBLIC TRANSPORTATION

Public transportation is varied, ranging from pedicabs to airplanes. It is cheap and convenient. People use it for both local and regional trips. In 1990, the average household spent US$74 on public transportation, over half on local fares and the rest on regional travel.[35]

Local transportation Thais have a wide range of local transportation to choose from. There are buses, minibuses, motorcycles, *samlors* (three-wheeled motorcycles and pedicabs), taxis, and boats. People, however, travel mainly by bus. City, school, and office buses combined capture nearly two-thirds of the expenses on local transportation in the whole kingdom and three-quarters in Bangkok (see Figure 3.41).

Buses are the only form of mass transit aside from taxis in Thai cities. Thailand has a large fleet of buses and minibuses of variable quality. The best ones are comfortable and have air conditioning. Buses are usually cheap and convenient although they may be slow at rush hours.

For faster trips, people hire motorcycles and *samlors*. In Bangkok, their drivers weave around cars and they cut through small alleys, apparently unaware of safety standards.

Samlors are an integral part of Thai life. They appeared in 1933 in the form of tricycle rickshaws and soon became widespread. In 1960, however, the Thai government banned these pedicabs in Bangkok because they obstructed traffic. At that time, some 13,000

Chapter 3 Consumption and Distribution

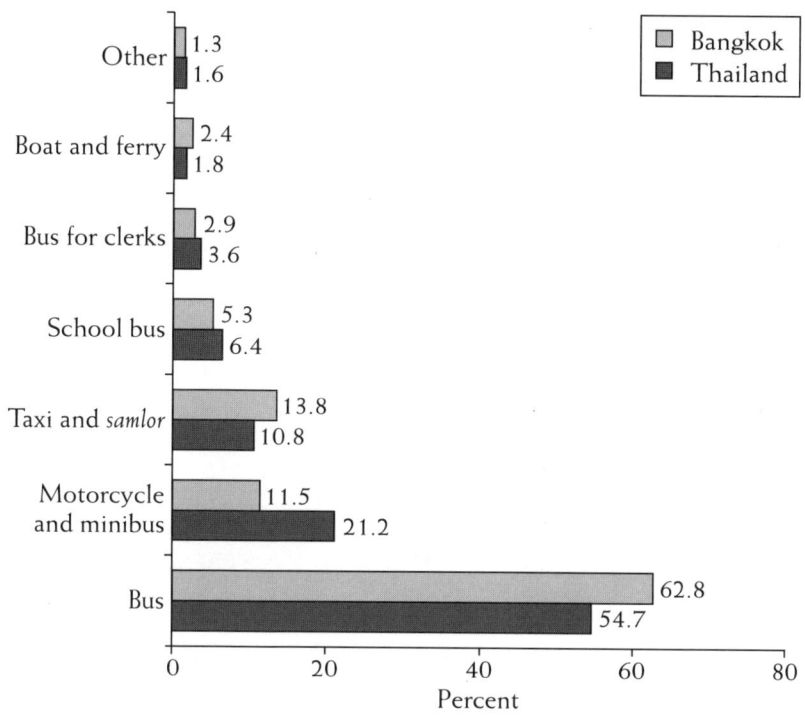

Figure 3.41 Composition of Expenses on Local Transportation in 1990 (Source: Based on National Statistical Office, Report of the 1990 Household Socio-Economic Survey, Whole Kingdom, OPM, Bangkok, 1993, pp. 1–21.)

registered *samlors* circulated in the city. Drivers then replaced their rickshaws with Japanese three-wheeled motorcycles. These are also called *samlors* or *tuk-tuks*. Pedal *samlors*, however, still exist up-country.

Pickup trucks and taxis are safer alternatives. Pickup trucks are fitted with benches. They are collective taxis with no fixed routes. Their drivers arrange trips to suit customers and they take on additional passengers along the way if these people are traveling in the same direction.

Boats are still a common means of transportation in Bangkok. During daytime, barges cross the Chao Phraya river and speedy long-tailed boats ply the canals. These stop at numerous piers and they are a convenient way to avoid the city's chaotic traffic. In the provinces, however, boats play a lesser role.

Regional transportation Buses, trains, planes, and ships share the market for regional transportation. As in Bangkok, buses are the most popular. Thais spend over half of their expenses on regional transportation on bus fares (see Figure 3.42).

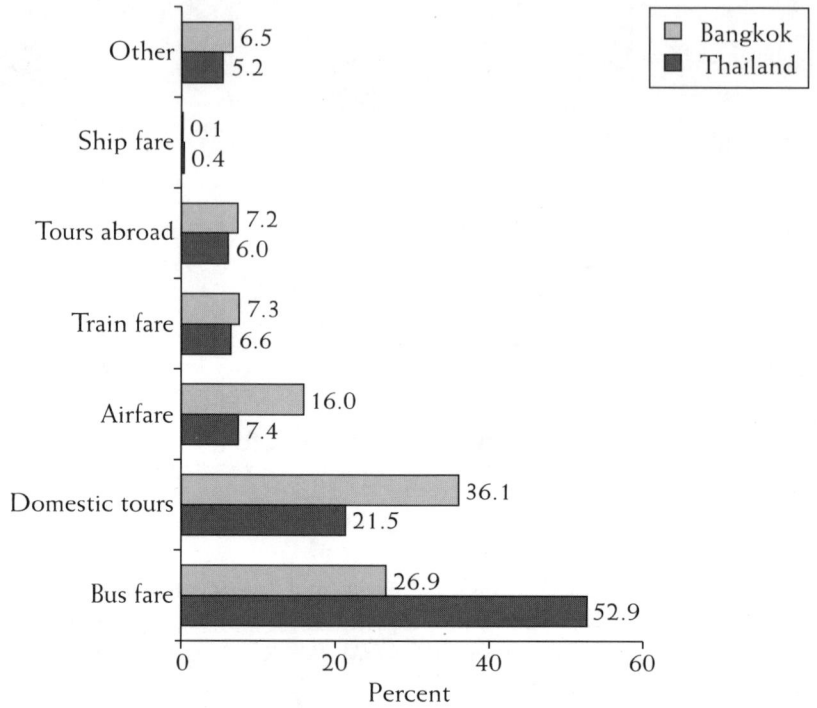

Figure 3.42 Composition of Expenses on Regional Transportation in 1990 (Source: Based on National Statistical Office, Report of the 1990 Household Socio-Economic Survey, Whole Kingdom, OPM, Bangkok, 1993, pp. 1–21.)

A variety of private and public buses cover long-distance routes. The national bus company runs a fleet of coaches between Bangkok and other Thai cities. These coaches are cheap and comfortable. Many have air conditioning, television, and video. Private operators also run intercity buses. Some of these are luxurious coaches. Others have a more local flavor, with fans lining the ceiling and slapstick comedies running on the videos. Conductors solicit passersby and the buses leave only when they have filled their seats.

Train schedules are less flexible and slower. Trains run at the average speed of 50 kilometers (30 miles) per hour. They are, however, cheap. In 1990, the average passenger traveled 135 kilometers (85 miles) and paid only US$1.30.[36] Trains are especially busy during holiday periods and long weekends when workers return home.

Local airlines offer speedier, although more expensive, service. They fly many routes, catering mainly to business people and foreign visitors. Only wealthier Thais travel by plane for private purposes. In Bangkok, for instance, airline tickets account for 16 percent of household expenses on regional transportation, compared to nearly nothing in the provinces.

Tour operators offer many domestic and foreign packages. Domestic tours are the most successful, although more Thais are taking trips abroad. Favorite foreign destinations include Yünnan (the province of Southern China from which Thai people originate) and Malaysia.

3.7.2 PERSONAL TRANSPORTATION

Congestion fails to deter people from using personal transportation. In 1990, the average household spent US$240 buying and operating personal vehicles;[37] this is nearly three-quarters of the total expenses on transportation and communications.

Vehicles Automobiles and motorcycles top the purchases. Together they account for 92 percent of the expenses on personal vehicles (see Figure 3.43). In 1992, 6.3 million motorcycles and 890,000 private passenger cars were registered in Thailand.[38] Cars circulate mainly in Bangkok, but motorcycles are common in all regions.

Motorcycles are very successful. In 1992, they accounted for about two-thirds of all motor vehicles in Thailand. Their appeal is quasi-universal. Teenagers, adults, housewives, workers, and students alike use them. Even pets get an occasional ride. At rush hours, scores of motorcycles pack city streets. In Bangkok, they are a convenient means for weaving through the traffic.

This flourishing trade bodes well for vehicle spare parts and accessories. Helmets, glasses, raincoats, screens, baskets, children's seats, locks, and awnings have potential. Helmets are especially promising because they became mandatory in late 1992.

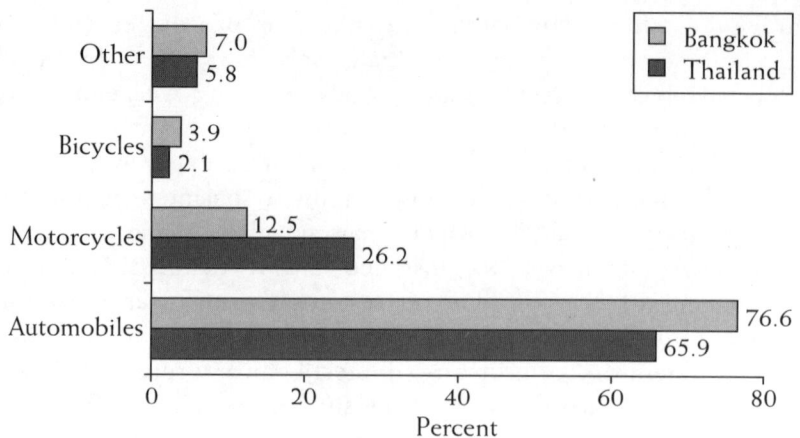

Figure 3.43   Composition of Expenses on Vehicles in 1990
(Source: Based on National Statistical Office, Report of the 1990 Household Socio-Economic Survey, Whole Kingdom, OPM, Bangkok, 1993, pp. 1–21.)

Operation costs   Fuel and repairs are the leading costs of vehicle operation. Together, they capture about 90 percent of the expenses (see Figure 3.44). There are, however, large differences in expenditures across regions, especially on fuel. In the provinces, people use more regular gasoline and diesel fuel. In Bangkok, in contrast, people spend more on premium gasoline.

3.7.3 COMMUNICATIONS

The communications system in Thailand is a headache. In 1992, there were only 31 telephone lines per thousand people,[39] compared to 555 in the United States.[40] The waiting list for would-be telephone subscribers is growing daily and existing lines are overcrowded.

The telephone and telegraph are, however, the principal expenditures. Together they capture over 90 percent of the communications budget (see Figure 3.45). Expenditures are especially high in cities, where more people have regular and cellular telephones and facsimile machines. People, for instance, spend ten times more on telephone and telegraph in Bangkok than in the Northeast.

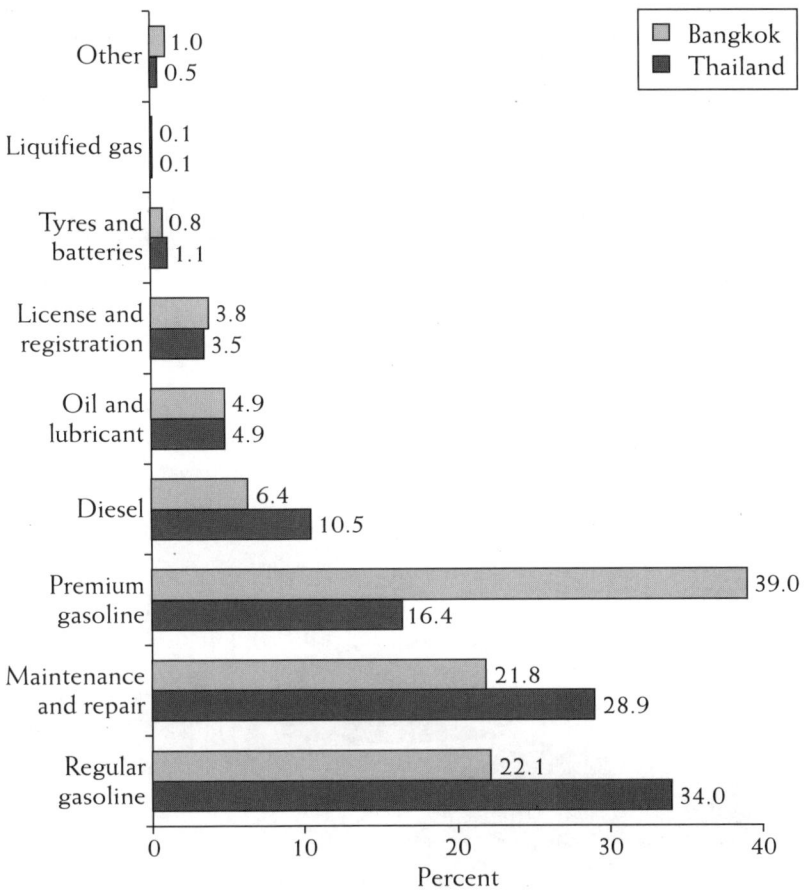

Figure 3.44 Composition of Expenses on Vehicle Operation in 1990 (Source: Based on National Statistical Office, Report of the 1990 Household Socio-Economic Survey, Whole Kingdom, OPM, Bangkok, 1993, pp. 1–21.)

3.8 RECREATION

The leisure industry is expanding rapidly. Between 1970 and 1991, expenses on recreation have increased by about 400 percent.[41] Thailand offers many forms of entertainment, both traditional and modern. Traditional festivities, however, capture most of the expenditures. In 1990, the average household spent US$85 on recreation, of which 57 percent went to religious activities and ceremonies (see Figure 3.46).

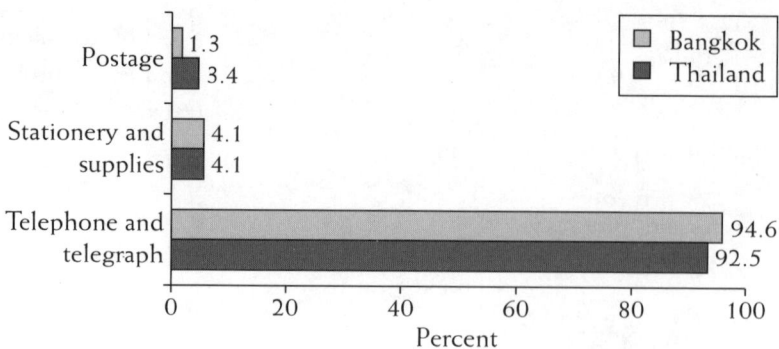

Figure 3.45 *Composition of Communications Expenses in 1990*
(*Source: Based on National Statistical Office, Report of the 1990 Household Socio-Economic Survey, Whole Kingdom, OPM, Bangkok, 1993, pp. 1–21.*)

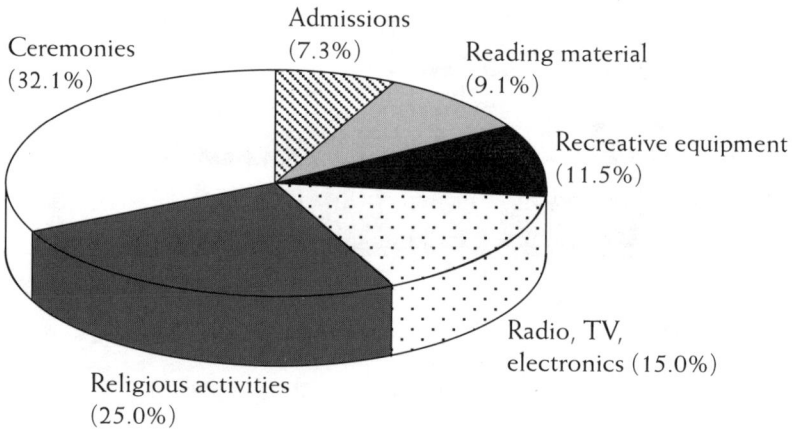

Figure 3.46 *Composition of Expenses on Recreation in 1990*
(*Source: Based on National Statistical Office, Report of the 1990 Household Socio-Economic Survey, Whole Kingdom, OPM, Bangkok, 1993, pp. 1–21.*)

3.8.1 RELIGIOUS ACTIVITIES AND CEREMONIES

Religion is an integral part of Thai life and a source of recreation. The many richly ornate temples and shrines speak of the importance of religion. People spend much time and money supporting temple activities. They are also keen to attend ceremonies. Cremations, wedding parties, and ordinations are popular events.

Religious activities Religious activities are a mixture of Buddhist and superstitious rites. People make donations to Buddhist temples and they buy flowers and joss sticks to appease gods and spirits. Most expenditures, however, sponsor Buddhism. Donations to temples account for three-quarters of religious expenses (see Figure 3.47).

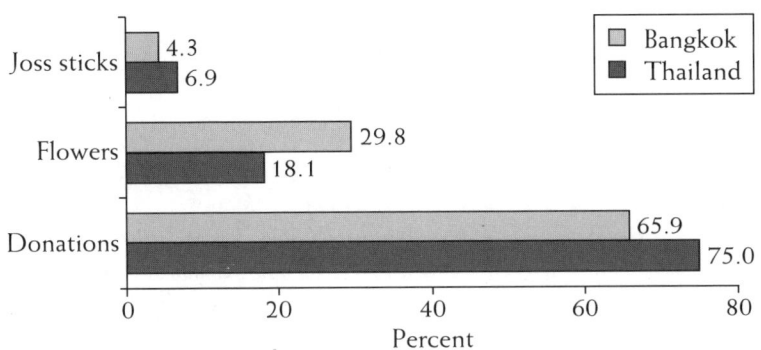

Figure 3.47 Composition of Expenses on Religious Activities in 1990 (Source: Based on National Statistical Office, Report of the 1990 Household Socio-Economic Survey, Whole Kingdom, OPM, Bangkok, 1993, pp. 1–21.)

Superstitions are omnipresent. Almost every home, backyard, and business has a shrine. Vendors sell flower garlands and joss sticks at nearly every street corner and people make regular offerings of foods and decorations. The staff of a Bangkok international hotel, for instance, feeds the gods at the adjacent shrine various delicacies, including Western breakfasts complete with roll, jam, and coffee.

Ceremonies Thais are legendary for their care at preparing ceremonies and social events. Weddings, cremations, and monkhoods (ordaining of monks) remain popular gatherings. They are opportunities for making merit. Weddings are the most costly, capturing over half of the expenses on ceremonies (see Figure 3.48). The South is the only region where ceremonies are rare. Southern Thais are culturally diverse and they seldom attend Buddhist events.

In most regions, however, people are keen to find new causes for celebration. Birthday parties have become fashionable, especially for

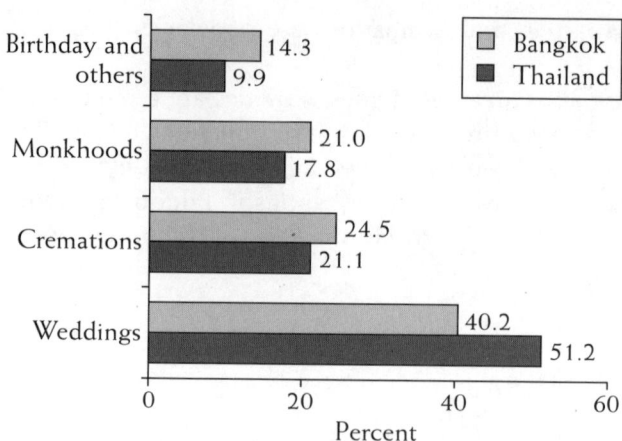

Figure 3.48 *Composition of Expenses on Ceremonies and Social Events in 1990*
(Source: Based on National Statistical Office, *Report of the 1990 Household Socio-Economic Survey, Whole Kingdom*, OPM, Bangkok, 1993, pp. 1–21.)

Bangkok residents whose expenses are double those of other Thais. This suggests that there is a growing market for personal gift items like pens, lighters, and watches.

3.8.2 RECREATIONAL AND ELECTRONIC EQUIPMENT

Modern forms of entertainment are in demand. People allocate about a quarter of their entertainment budget on recreational and electronic equipment.

Recreational equipment Thais have countless ways to entertain themselves, but a few activities capture the bulk of their expenses. Toys, pet and garden supplies, and tapes are the leading recreational material together accounting for about 85 percent of the purchases (see Figure 3.49). Photographic and sports supplies account for the rest.

Pets have been common for some time, but people are now spending more on them. Grooming and veterinary services and pet supplies are in growing demand.

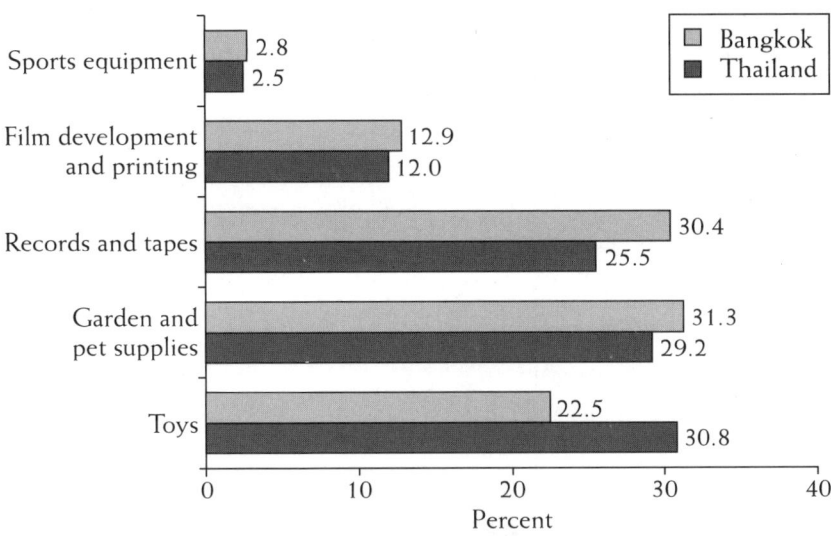

Figure 3.49 Composition of Expenses on Recreational Equipment in 1990 (Source: Based on National Statistical Office, Report of the 1990 Household Socio-Economic Survey, Whole Kingdom, OPM, Bangkok, 1993, pp. 1–21.)

Photography has become a favorite hobby in wealthier areas. Bangkok residents, for instance, spend about eight times more on films than other Thais. This growing market is creating new opportunities for cameras, accessories, films, magazines, and photo-processing equipment. Small labs that develop and print films are sprouting in major cities.

Home entertainment equipment Shops carry a wide range of electronic equipment, but people buy mainly basic products. Television sets are a favorite, accounting for 57 percent of the purchases by value (see Figure 3.50). Other items like stereos, video-cassette recorders, and camcorders sell in wealthier areas.

Sophisticated products are especially popular in cities. In Bangkok, for instance, stereos replace record players, while videos and remote-control devices supplement television sets. Bangkok residents also spend more on maintenance and repair, suggesting that they invest in higher-quality goods. Buyers usually look for the latest models because unscrupulous dealers in Asia repack and sell used equipment as new.

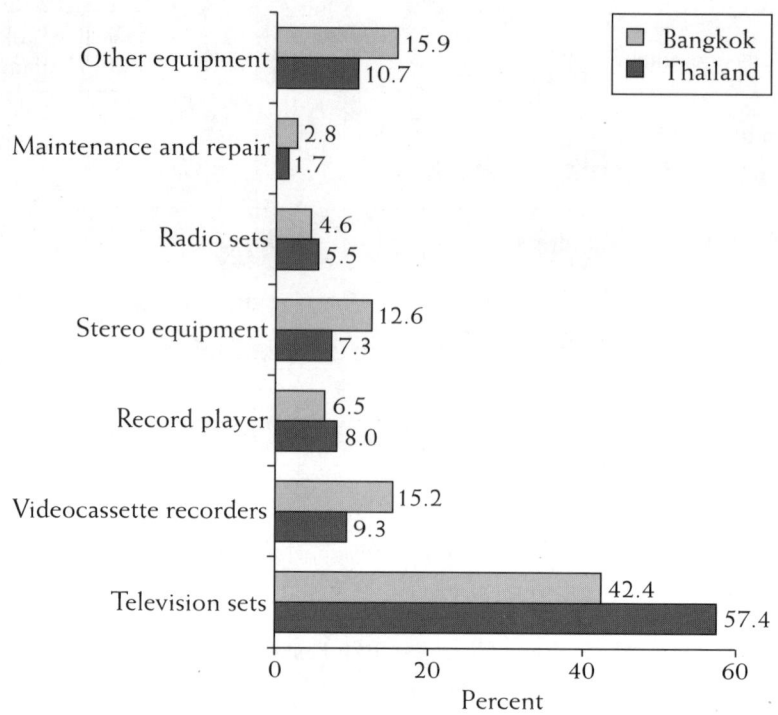

Figure 3.50   Composition of Expenses on Home Entertainment Equipment in 1990 (Source: Based on National Statistical Office, Report of the 1990 Household Socio-Economic Survey, Whole Kingdom, OPM, Bangkok, 1993, pp. 1–21.)

3.8.3 ADMISSIONS AND READING MATERIAL

Thais, like other people, enjoy going out. They go to the movies, visit museums, watch shows, and relax at their clubs. Going to the movies and visiting museums are the most popular activities. Together, they capture over half of the expenses on admissions (see Figure 3.51). Clubs are common only in wealthier areas. In Bangkok, for instance, people spend five times more on membership fees than other Thais.

Shops and libraries have a good supply of reading material, especially in cities. They carry a variety of newspapers, magazines, and books. People, however, read mainly newspapers. These account for 70 percent of the expenses on reading material (see Figure 3.52).

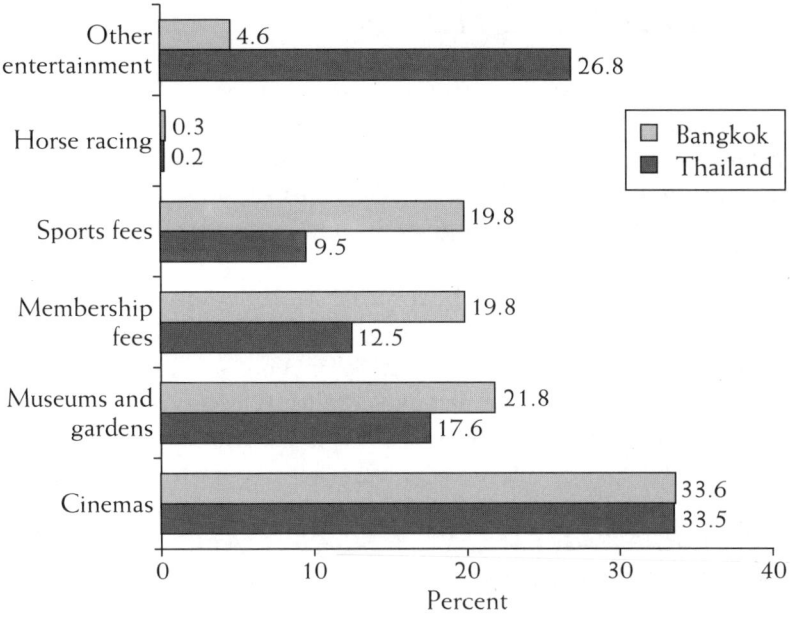

Figure 3.51 Composition of Expenses on Entertainment Admissions in 1990 (Source: Based on National Statistical Office, Report of the 1990 Household Socio-Economic Survey, Whole Kingdom, OPM, Bangkok, 1993, pp. 1–21.)

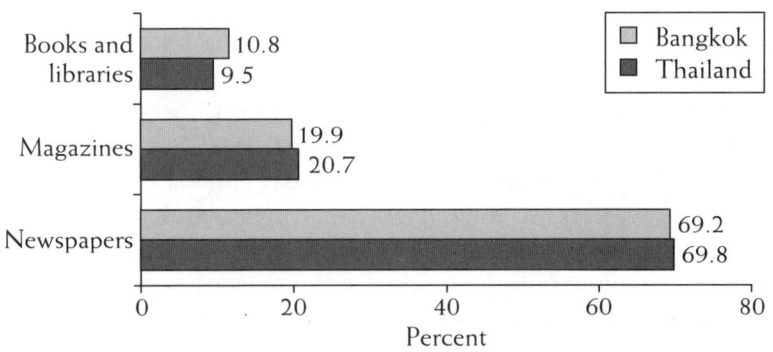

Figure 3.52 Composition of Expenses on Reading Material in 1990 (Source: Based on National Statistical Office, Report of the 1990 Household Socio-Economic Survey, Whole Kingdom, OPM, Bangkok, 1993, pp. 1–21.)

3.9 DISTRIBUTION

Thailand has entered the world of modern distribution. Convenience stores, department stores, and shopping malls are sprouting throughout the country. Shopping has become a new pastime. In 1990, over 5 percent of Thais reported that they went shopping regularly.[42] Although stalls and corner stores still abound, fancy outlets are taking over.

The retail industry is becoming more competitive and its management more sophisticated. Operators offset declining profit margins by reducing costs, especially inventory costs. More chain stores and distributors, for instance, are using computer networks to regulate flows of merchandise between warehouses and minimize expenses.

3.9.1 DEPARTMENT STORES AND SHOPPING MALLS

A wealth of department store chains, both local and foreign, operate throughout the country. They are well established. The first Thai department store opened in Bangkok in the late 1950s when the concept of fixed prices was new to the kingdom. Soon, a Thai-Japanese store joined in. Many others followed. Leading foreign department store chains from Japan, the United States, and Europe are now operating in Thailand. They have outlets in Bangkok and in large provincial towns. Product lines vary. Some discount stores carry medium-quality items. Others cater to the yuppies and they specialize in fashionable upmarket goods.

Department stores provide entertainment and shopping facilities. Many have cafeterias. Some even have private zoos, keeping such animals as tigers, bears, gorillas, macaws, snakes, and crocodiles. They organize temporary attractions like musical performances and sweepstakes. These are opportunities for other industries to advertise their services. Some store exhibitions, for instance, promote tourism in foreign countries.

Shopping malls also offer quality retail space. Many are located in Bangkok. Their clean, quiet, and air-conditioned environment is a pleasant alternative to the dust, heat, and noise of the city. Shopping malls have retail stores, cafeterias, and restaurants. They often rival Western shopping centers in quality.

Malls have grown bigger over the past decade. Since the early 1980s, large multipurpose complexes have sprouted in the outskirts of Bangkok. These usually include department stores, shopping arcades, office buildings, car parks, convention halls, health clubs, theaters, and other amusement facilities. Leading Thai malls are some of the biggest in Asia and they rank among the top retail centers in the world.

These vast shopping centers are trendsetters. Their management is sophisticated. Some malls even employ experienced foreign management teams to supervise their operations. They set new standards in the industry, encouraging other retailers to upgrade their services. Demand for retail management consulting is growing. Specialized companies now provide assistance in store design and decoration, staff training, sales promotion, and marketing.

3.9.2 SUPERMARKETS AND CONVENIENCE STORES

Supermarkets appeared recently and they have had mixed results. The first experiments of Western-style outlets started in Bangkok in the early 1970s. Supermarkets have developed slowly and most have remained independent stores. Chains are difficult to operate. In Bangkok, they face high storage and distribution costs. Because congestion impairs centralized storage and distribution, companies must set up district-based storage facilities.

Convenience stores are more successful. They require a smaller investment and they have fewer storage problems. These outlets appeared in the late 1980s. Subsequently, the convenience store business expanded rapidly. Several chains, both local and foreign, are now well established.

Operators compete for good locations. In Bangkok, stores open in densely populated districts and in high-traffic areas like bus stops and gas stations. In the provinces, convenience stores are often affiliated with department stores.

These new convenience stores contrast sharply with the traditional corner stores. They are modern, well lit, air-conditioned, and they are open 24 hours a day. Some stores even provide additional facilities like fast-food restaurants, photo-developing, and automatic teller machines. Their growing network creates new opportunities to distribute foreign consumer goods nationwide.

The booming convenience store business has sparked the development of other chain stores. Manufacturers set up showrooms for their products nationwide, while distributors develop networks of specialized stores for electrical appliances and electronic equipment. They finance their expansion through direct investment and by selling franchises and sub-area licenses.

3.9.3 DIRECT SELLING

Direct selling has been successful for some time. Mail-order catalogues and door-to-door sales are effective means of reaching people in remote places. Direct-selling companies began operating in the 1970s and by 1993, there were many such distributors ranging from small local operations to multinational groups.

Mail-order catalogues are efficient distribution channels in rural areas. Their product line is extensive, including personal care products, jewelry, cosmetics, cleaning products, household appliances, and foods and beverages. The affiliate of a leading American mail-order concern, for instance, offered some 400 products in its 1993 catalogue.

Traveling sales people also scour the countryside selling consumer goods door-to-door. They are often well received by the naturally hospitable Thais. Their repeated visits have helped some leading international brands become household names.

NOTES

1. Calculations based on National Statistical Office, *Report of the 1990 Household Socio-Economic Survey, Whole Kingdom*, OPM, Bangkok, 1993, pp. 1–21.
2. Panyacheewin, Saowarop, "How crabs help to keep the kids healthy in Isan," *Bangkok Post*, 29 May 1991, Outlook section, p. 28.
3. Supra 1, pp. 1–21.
4. Supra 1, pp. 1–21.
5. Supra 1, pp. 1–21.
6. Calculations based on Center for Agricultural Statistics, *Agricultural Statistics of Thailand, Crop Year 1991/92*, MAC, Bangkok, 1992, pp. 212–3.
7. Supra 1, pp. 1–21.

8. "Anand vows to push for development of children," *Bangkok Post*, 24 January 1992.
9. Supra 1, pp. 1–21.
10. Supra 1, pp. 1–21.
11. Supra 1, pp. 1–21.
12. Source: *Report of the 1990 Household Socio-Economic Survey, Whole Kingdom*, OPM, Bangkok, 1993, p. 109.
13. Calculations based on Office of the National Economic and Social Development Board, *National Income of Thailand*, OPM, Bangkok, various issues.
14. Supra 1, pp. 1–21.
15. Supra 1, pp. 1–21.
16. Supra 13, various issues.
17. Supra 1, pp. 1–21.
18. Supra 1, pp. 1–21.
19. Supra 13, various issues.
20. "Ministry to restore Thai medicine," *Bangkok Post*, 21 October 1993.
21. Supra 1, pp. 1–21.
22. Calculations based on Division of Health Statistics, *Public Health Statistics A.D. 1990*, MPH, Bangkok, 1992, pp. 12, 233–4.
23. Source: US Bureau of the Census, *Statistical Abstract of the United States: 1992*, 112th ed., Washington, D.C., 1992, p. 109.
24. Calculations based on National Statistical Office, *Statistical Yearbook Thailand*, OPM, Bangkok, various issues.
25. "Office launches campaign against use of stimulants," *Bangkok Post*, 25 January 1991.
26. Supra 13, various issues.
27. Supra 1, pp. 1–21.
28. Supra 13, various issues.
29. Supra 12, p. 108.
30. Supra 13, various issues.
31. Supra 1, pp. 1–21.
32. Supra 1, pp. 1–21.
33. Supra 1, pp. 1–21.
34. Moreau, Ron, "Life in the slow lane," *Newsweek*, 30 September 1991, pp. 16–7.
35. Supra 1, pp. 1–21.
36. Calculations based on Finance and Accounting Department, *1991 Information Booklet*, SRT, Bangkok, pp. 42, 55.

37. Supra 1, pp. 1–21.
38. Source: National Statistical Office, *Statistical Yearbook Thailand 1993*, OPM, Bangkok, 1993, p. 240.
39. Calculations based on National Statistical Office, *Statistical Yearbook Thailand 1993*, OPM, Bangkok, 1993, p. 258.
40. Calculations based on US Bureau of the Census, *Statistical Abstract of the United States: 1992*, 112th ed., Washington, D.C., 1992, pp. 8, 553.
41. Supra 13, various issues.
42. Source: National Statistical Office, *Report of the Cultural Activity Participation and Time Use Survey 1990*, OPM, Bangkok, 1992, p. 27.

4 MEDIA AND ADVERTISING

Thailand has a comprehensive network of media. It has cable and satellite television, about 360 radio stations,[1] and scores of newspapers and magazines. Foreign media have also gained a foothold on the market, encouraging local producers to upgrade their services. In addition, the kingdom is opening to advanced technology with the pending introduction of ultrahigh frequency television and interactive cinemas.

Media, once the preserve of urbanites, are now reaching more villages. Radios are widespread, ownership of television is increasing, and more newspapers and magazines are selling in the provinces. Faraway districts, however, have access to fewer media. Newspapers and magazines seldom reach remote communities, while television remains a luxury in these places.

Yet because of its size, the rural population dominates the audience. Radio and television cater primarily to villagers. Newspapers and magazines, which address better-educated and therefore more urban Thais, still have more readers in villages than in cities. Only cable television and a few local radio stations cater to urban audiences exclusively.

Advertising has expanded with the media industry. Between 1980 and 1992, total advertising expenses grew by 575 percent in real terms,[2] about four times the increase in gross domestic product. This has been a windfall for most media, especially newspapers whose advertising revenue grew tenfold in real terms.

Bigger budgets finance more sophisticated campaigns. Advertising agencies introduce new concepts like direct-response advertising and public-service advertisements. They are also offering a broader spectrum of services to clients. Direct marketing and market research, for instance, are getting more common.

These changes reflect the development of the consumer market. Growing competition between brands fuels advertising expenses and increases the quality of market research. The following sections show how producers communicate with consumers. They introduce the media, detail media habits, and analyze advertising expenses and techniques.

4.1 TELEVISION

Television has become a leading form of recreation in Thailand. Television sets probably come first on the purchase list of most households, and the rapid economic growth has helped sales. In 1990, about 62 percent of Thais owned a television, up from 33 percent in 1984.[3] This expansion has also affected related products, with accessories like video, television stands, and remote controls being in growing demand.

Television has become a powerful medium. It is the single most important source of information. In 1989, over 80 percent of the households reported learning about some official news from television.[4]

4.1.1 BROADCASTING

Thailand has entered the world of modern media, opening its television market to sophisticated networks. Cable and satellite television are the latest additions to the existing terrestrial stations. The kingdom is also intent on introducing other services, including ultrahigh frequency (UHF) and interactive television.

Terrestrial television has been established for some time. The first domestic station, Channel 9, started broadcasting in 1955. This may seem like a modest achievement to Americans who already had 450 television stations at that time. By Asian standards, however, this was a significant event; Thailand had become the first Southeast Asian nation to have a television station.

Subsequently, other channels joined in. By the early 1970s, Thailand had five national and five regional stations. National stations broadcast from Bangkok, while regional stations are spread throughout the territory.

Other networks like cable and satellite television were slower to surface. For years, the Thai government refused to grant additional licenses, keeping would-be operators at bay. This, however, ended in 1989 with the introduction of cable services. Communications companies are now preparing the launch of additional cable networks and of Thai satellite television stations. These changes have enhanced competition and they sparked a series of deregulations on broadcasting time and programming.

Terrestrial television Terrestrial television has broad coverage. Except for Channel 11 which reaches less than half of the population, the four other national stations, channels 3, 5, 7, and 9, reach between two-thirds and three-quarters of the households.[5] In addition, regional stations cater to the local audiences.

Broadcasting is in the Thai language. Stations buy material from both local and foreign entertainment companies, but they seldom use subtitles. Channels usually dub foreign programs at their expense and they air the original sound tracks on FM radio.

The use of foreign material, however, fails to improve quality and creativity. Thai national television stations have little to offer. At prime time, they run low-budget soap operas, dubbed Chinese dramas, kung fu movies, old sports tournaments, and other cheap programs.

This combination is, nonetheless, successful for Channel 7. The station tops the rates of popularity, capturing half of the audience.[6] Channel 7 broadcasts a wide range of shows that include series, cartoons, varieties, news, and documentaries. All of these get large audiences, but the station fares especially well with its comprehensive news and documentaries. Viewers also praise the quality of its image, an advantage that Channel 7 derives from its extensive network of relay stations.

Channel 3 ranks second in popularity. It attracts a quarter of the audience.[7] This station specializes in entertainment programs, especially movies and series. It broadcasts daily about ten series of various origins, but mainly Thai, Chinese, Japanese, and English. Programs also include a few cartoons, varieties, talk shows, and brief news coverages.

163

Channel 3 started on a modest budget. For many years, it used the regional television channels as relay stations for its programs and few viewers received clear pictures. In 1988, however, it pooled resources with Channel 9 to set up a joint network of 22 relay stations comparable to that of Channel 7.

Channel 5 is less successful. It captures only 15 percent of the audience.[8] The station telecasts a variety-oriented program, but it also broadcasts some news, documentaries, series, and cartoons. It performs well with its news programs, but moderately with its entertainment programs. It also gets average rating for the quality of its image.

Channel 9 trails behind. Only one-tenth of television viewers watch it.[9] Programs are reminiscent of those of Channels 5, but they are less successful. Channel 9 broadcasts mainly varieties and news, while including a few series, cartoons, and documentaries. Its rating is, nonetheless, improving. For many years, Channel 9 had poor-quality image and its share of audience did not exceed 5 percent. Its popularity increased since the launch of its new network of relay stations (shared with Channel 3).

Channel 11 is the least successful television station. It attracts only 1 percent of the viewers.[10] The Thai government uses this station as an educational service. It spends little on programs, essentially broadcasting news, documentaries, parliament debates, and classes for the country's open universities.

All terrestrial television stations are largely under government control. State agencies and the military own both regional and national stations. The Mass Communications Organization of Thailand, a government agency, owns channels 3 and 9; the Royal Thai Army, channels 5 and 7; and the Public Relations Department of the Thai government, Channel 11.

The only private parties are the channel operators which have leased stations. There are only two such operators. They run Channel 7 and Channel 3. Incidentally, these are the most popular stations, together capturing three-quarters of the audience and nearly as much of the television advertising revenue.

Greater competition is, however, on the way as the Thai government eases regulations. In 1991, the Broadcasting Directing Board, an agency that controls media, lifted restrictions on daytime transmission and permitted television channels to broadcast after midnight. The board also allowed stations to relay foreign news and to show foreign programs after the evening news. Subsequently, broadcasting time on national stations doubled, increasing from 10 to 20 hours per day.

More important, perhaps, is the opening of the industry to the private sector. In 1992, the Thai government allowed private enterprises to set up television stations. Subsequently, it invited companies to bid for a concession to operate Thailand's first ultrahigh frequency television station.

Cable television Cable television is expanding. The service started in 1989 and by 1993, it served some 100,000 subscribers in the Bangkok area.[11] The government had initially limited operating licenses to Bangkok Metropolis. In 1994, however, the administration announced that broadcasters would be allowed to cover the provinces.

Cable services have opened Thailand to a broad spectrum of international productions. Operators broadcast popular foreign programs, including American and British international news services and Western series and movies. So far, programming is mainly in English. As cable services extend to the provinces, however, operators are likely to include more programs in the Thai language and more local news.

Higher-quality programs come at a cost. Cable television is a pay-service, a new concept in the Thai television industry. Stations mainly live off subscription fees. In 1993, they charged connecting fees of about US$100 and monthly fees ranging from US$20 to US$32. These prices restrict viewers to richer people. Cable stations vie for the narrow market of expatriates, foreign visitors, and upper-income Thais. Many subscriptions are also for individual hotel rooms.

Cable television has paved the way for more sophisticated electronic media. Companies say that they will use the newly laid fiber-optic telephone lines to expand the network of cable television and introduce additional services like interactive television and "video-on-demand." Interactive television, so far only available in the United States, allows viewers to communicate directly with television hosts during live shows. Video-on-demand gives subscribers access to a library of programs.

Satellite television The pending introduction of Thai satellite television stations is, probably, the most significant change in the television industry. This project has become feasible since Thailand launched its first communications satellite. So far, Thais could receive only foreign stations.

Satellite television is an emerging medium. It took off in 1991 with the launch of a Hong Kong-based station that operates television for Asian viewers. The station, which relays programs from Europe, Asia, and the United States, broadcasts five channels 24 hours a day featuring sports, news, entertainment, music, and Chinese-language programs. In addition, Thais may receive some Australian-based programs.

Satellite television is, perhaps, the single biggest factor in the deregulation and upgrading of Thai television. As satellite dishes get smaller, they become more difficult to police. The foreign programs that they pick up compete with local productions.

Competition has, however, been limited so far. Satellite television is still the preserve of wealthier Thais. A satellite dish is beyond most budgets. In 1993, the cheapest dish cost about US$600 and only a few homes were connected.

4.1.2 AUDIENCE

Television is popular. Between 1984 and 1990, ownership nearly doubled, and television sets have become common in the provinces. Even tribal villages have television. In these places, however, it is still a luxury and owners sell the right to watch programs. In the Hmong village of Pa Khia Nai near Chiang Mai, for instance, families who have television let neighbors join them for an evening at a one-baht fee (a nickel).[12]

In wealthier areas, television is widespread and it is changing from a family item to a personal good. In Bangkok, where the vast majority of households have at least one television set, producers are now selling small sets for individual use.

Stores also carry higher-quality equipment. Color television sets and videocassette recorders are in growing demand. In 1990, 36 percent of the households had color television and 26 percent black-and-white television, up from 13 and 22 percent respectively in 1984.[13] Videocassette recorders (VCR), which were almost inexistent a few years ago, are also becoming more common. In

1990, 7 percent of the households had a VCR, up from 2 percent in 1984.[14]

Profile Television has quasi-universal appeal, attracting a wide spectrum of people from all age groups and professions. Watching television is especially common among younger generations partly because they are wealthier. Viewing also peaks among professionals and managers, who are the top income earners in Thailand (see Figure 4.1). As they grow richer, however, more Thais buy television sets, and differences become less pronounced.

Figure 4.1 Television Viewing by Occupation in 1984 and 1990 (Sources: Based on National Statistical Office, Report of the Mass Media Survey (Radio and Television) 1984, OPM, Bangkok, p. 33, and National Statistical Office, Report of the Cultural Activity Participation and Time Use Survey 1990, OPM, Bangkok, 1992, Statistical Tables, p. 48.)

People also have many opportunities to watch television outside the home, and audience exceeds ownership. In 1990, about 80 percent of Thais watched television regularly[15] although only 62 percent had a television set at home. Pubs, coffee shops, and intercity buses often show videos. People also watch television at the market place, temple, office, and at neighbors' or relatives' homes. Some administration officers even have a television set in their office.

The typical viewer differs little from the average Thai. Television is no longer the privilege of urbanites, better-educated people, and high-income earners. In 1990, farmers accounted for 45 percent of the audience and over three-quarters of the viewers lived in villages (see Figure 4.2). Since most people, especially villagers, have not studied beyond primary level, the bulk of the viewers are poorly educated.

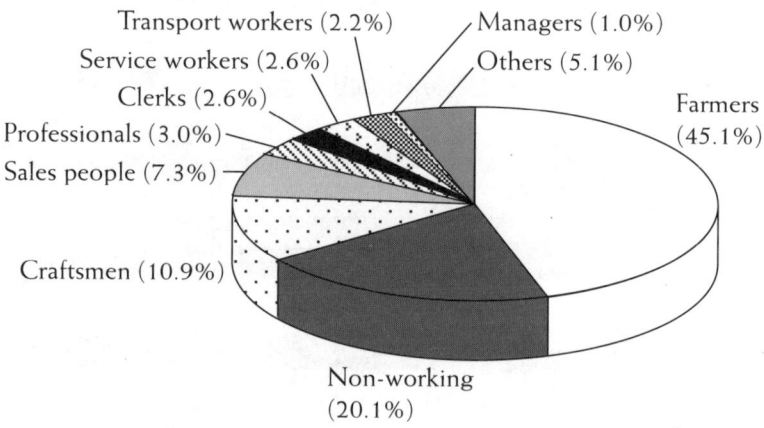

Figure 4.2 Composition of Television Audience by Occupation in 1990 (Source: Based on National Statistical Office, Report of the Cultural Activity Participation and Time Use Survey 1990, OPM, Bangkok, 1992, Statistical Tables, p. 48.)

Viewing habits By Asian standards, Thais spend little time watching television. In 1990, the average viewing time was about two hours per day,[16] one of the lowest in Asia. This is about half the time spent by the average Japanese viewer.

Thais are, nonetheless, enthusiastic viewers. People who have television usually watch it every day. Peak hours are between 8 p.m.

and 10 p.m. on weekdays, while viewing is almost uninterrupted from morning to late evening on weekends.[17]

The biggest fans of television live in poorer areas, where watching television is still a social event. In these places, people organize television parties reminiscent of those held by Europeans forty years ago. They also plan their television sessions, listening to program announcements (see Figure 4.3). The poorer the area, the greater the care at selecting a program. In the Northeast, for instance, almost 60 percent of the people listen to the televised program announcements, compared to only 9 percent in Bangkok.

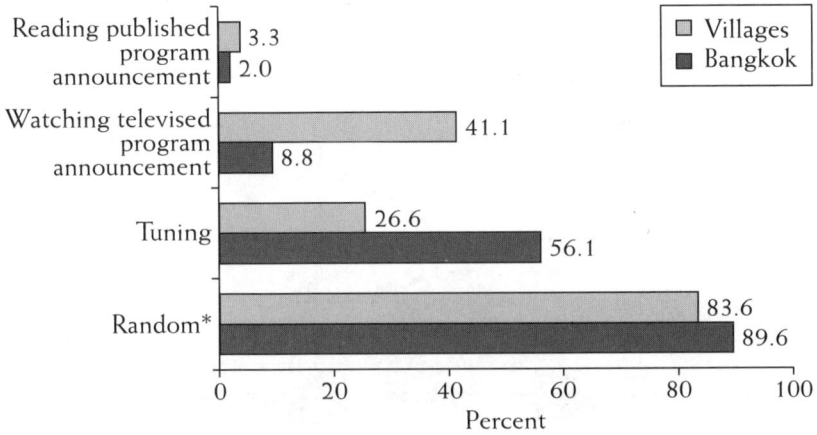

*Called "pursuing the program" in the survey report.

Figure 4.3 Television Program Selection in 1984
(Source: Based on National Statistical Office, Report of the Mass Media Survey (Radio and Television) 1984, OPM, Bangkok, p. 37.)

In wealthier provinces, the novelty has faded, demoting television to an ordinary household item. Richer Thais watch television casually and they rarely listen to televised program announcements. They usually tune in on their favorite station, switching occasionally to check the programs on other channels.

Preferences Many different programs appeal to Thais although viewers have distinct preferences. News and entertainment programs are the most successful. Features and commentaries also do well, but they attract smaller audiences. Educational programs are the only shows which fare poorly. Preferences are similar in urban and rural areas, although villagers are more avid viewers. Most programs do better in villages.

The news draws large audiences. Thais pay much attention to national and international matters, with nearly all viewers, some 98 percent, watching the domestic and foreign news. Sports news also command a large following, with about 90 percent ratings (see Figure 4.4). Local and economic news, in contrast, have less appeal, attracting only a quarter of the audience. These patterns prevail throughout Thailand, although villagers, who often live off agriculture, pay special attention to local news and to the weather forecasts.

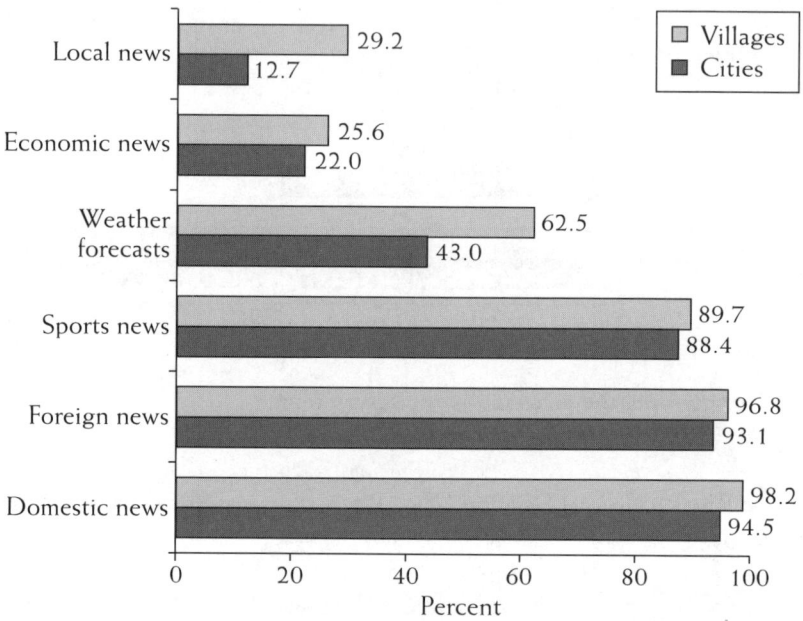

Figure 4.4 Ratings of Televised News Programs in 1984
(Source: Based on National Statistical Office, Report of the Mass Media Survey (Radio and Television) 1984, OPM, Bangkok, p. 39.)

Entertainment programs score highly. Series, movies, cartoons, television games, and popular music are favorites, each attracting over 80 percent of the audience (see Figure 4.5). People watch both local and foreign programs, but Thai productions often fare better, especially pop music. This is more visible in rural areas where people are conservative. This suggests that Thai-made videos are better suited than imported videos for showing in commercial outlets.

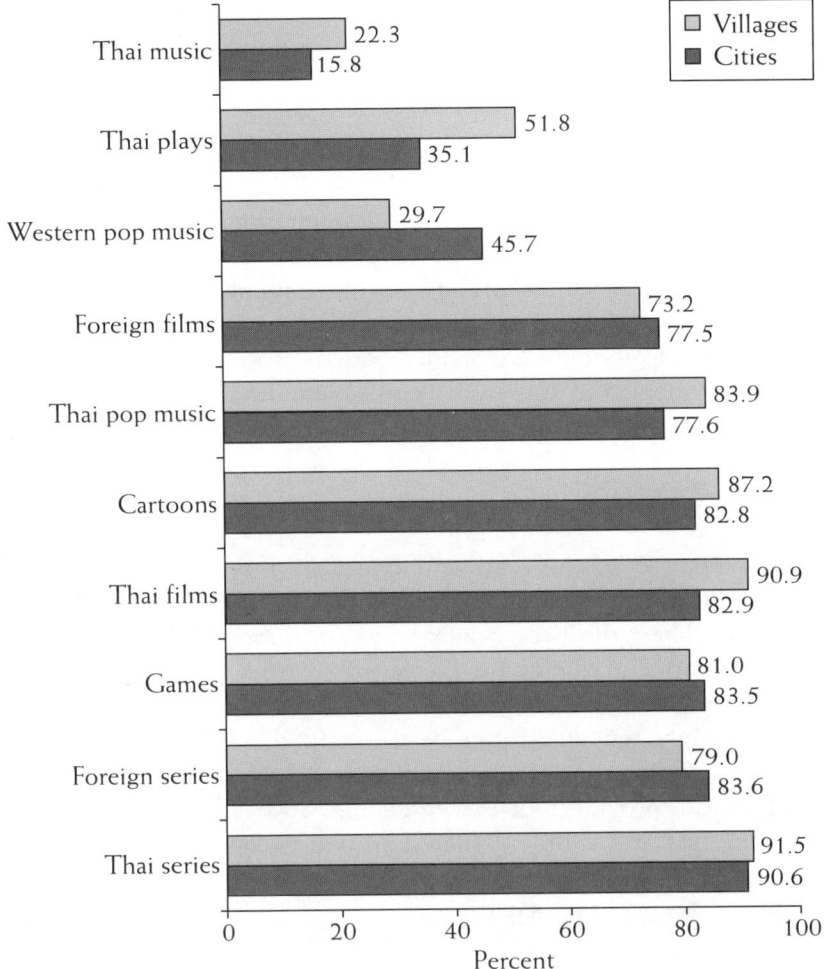

Figure 4.5 Ratings of Televised Entertainment Programs in 1984 (Source: Based on National Statistical Office, Report of the Mass Media Survey (Radio and Television) 1984, OPM, Bangkok, p. 40.)

Feature programs cover a wide spectrum of topics, but they achieve moderate results. Sports, the most popular feature programs, capture about 60 percent of the audience (see Figure 4.6). The next most successful topics, health care, career, and government policy, attract only 40 percent of the viewers. Program selection also differs slightly across areas. Villagers seem more interested in practical topics, like career and health, and urbanites in cultural matters, like arts, language, and technology.

Commentaries draw medium-sized audiences. They focus on foreign, political, economic, and social issues and attract a third to half of the viewers (see Figure 4.7).

Few Thais complain about television programs. Those who do often disagree on the timing, content, and frequency. Complainants find news programs too short and lacking content. They say features and commentaries are short, rare, and empty. Opinions on entertainment programs are divided between too short and too long, or too frequent and too rare. People who find an entertainment program too short usually say that it also comes on too infrequently.

4.2 Radio

Radio sets are widespread and ownership is stable. In 1990, 73 percent of the households had a radio, compared to 75 percent in 1984.[18] The radio is especially valuable in remote areas, where it remains a principal link with the outside world.

This medium is well established in Thailand. Broadcasting started in 1930, only ten years after its debut in the United States. For decades, radio was the leading communications device, reaching the most remote provinces of the kingdom. Most villages had at least one radio set and people gathered around to listen to it.

4.2.1 Broadcasting

The broadcasting industry is competitive. Thailand has a long and growing list of radio stations. In 1992, the kingdom had over 360 commercial stations; this is 20 percent more than in 1989. Government officials say that Bangkok residents alone can tune in to over 70 stations.[19] This expansion, however, coincides with a re-allocation of frequencies from AM to FM. Between 1989 and

1992, the proportion of stations broadcasting on FM frequencies increased from 44 to 60 percent.[20]

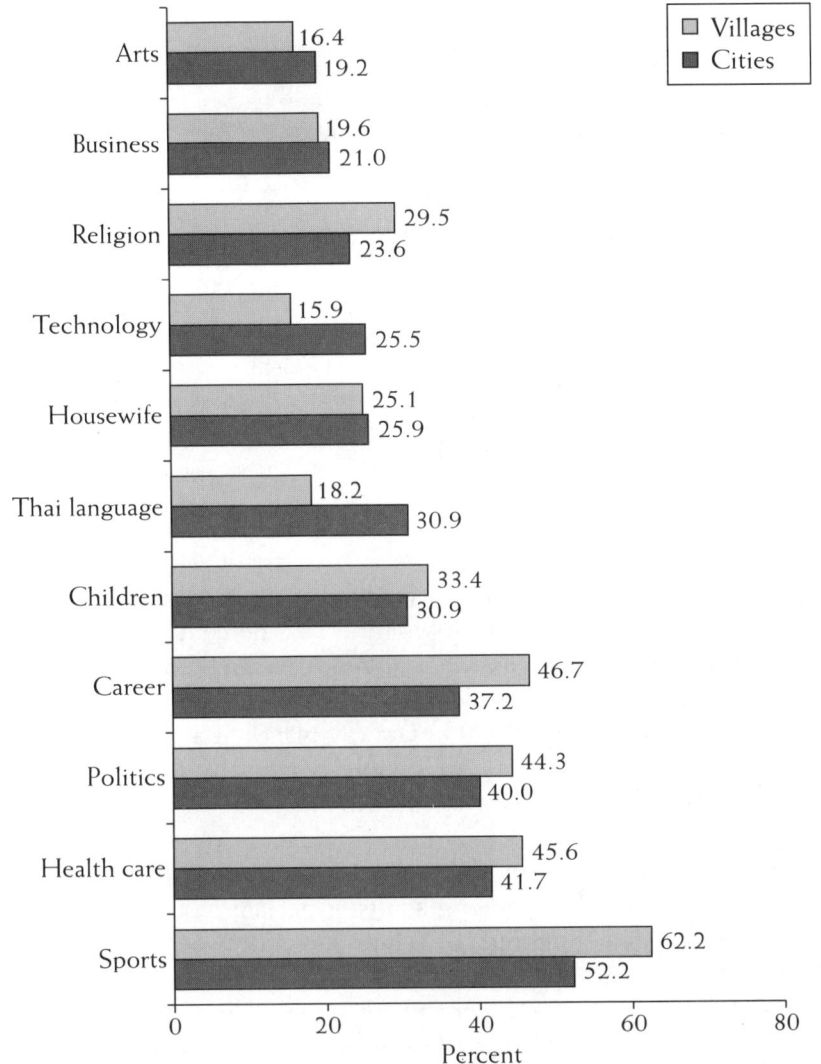

Figure 4.6   Ratings of Televised Feature Programs in 1984
(Source: Based on National Statistical Office, Report of the Mass Media Survey (Radio and Television) 1984, OPM, Bangkok, pp. 39–40.)

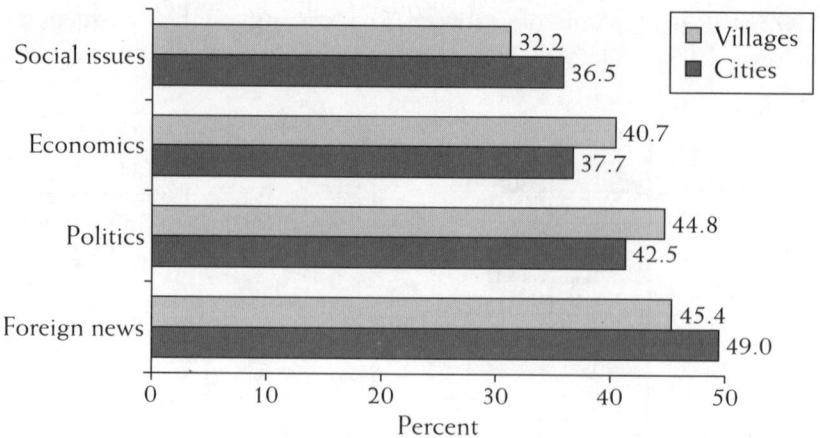

Figure 4.7   Ratings of Televised Commentary Programs in 1984 (Source: Based on National Statistical Office, Report of the Mass Media Survey (Radio and Television) 1984, OPM, Bangkok, p. 40.)

4.2.2 AUDIENCE

Radio is no longer the powerful medium it once was. Audience is falling below ownership. In 1990 only 87 percent of the radio households were regular listeners.[21] Radio remains, nonetheless, an important communications device. It is still a leading source of information and entertainment in faraway places. It also finds steady audiences among a variety of people, especially young adults, commuters, and people who work outdoors.

Profile   Unlike television, radio appeals to selected age groups. It finds a greater following among adults, especially younger ones. In 1990, nearly three-quarters of Thais aged between 15 and 19 listened to the radio (see Figure 4.8). Listening declines steadily with age and it plummets at 42 percent for people above 60 years old.

Profession, in contrast, has less effect on the audience. Radio reaches a broad spectrum of people engaged in all occupations. Only professionals, managers, and clerks tend to listen more to the radio. Incidentally, many live in the Bangkok area and spend much time commuting.

The impact of television is greater. It may be the single biggest influence on radio audience. The growing sales of television sets in

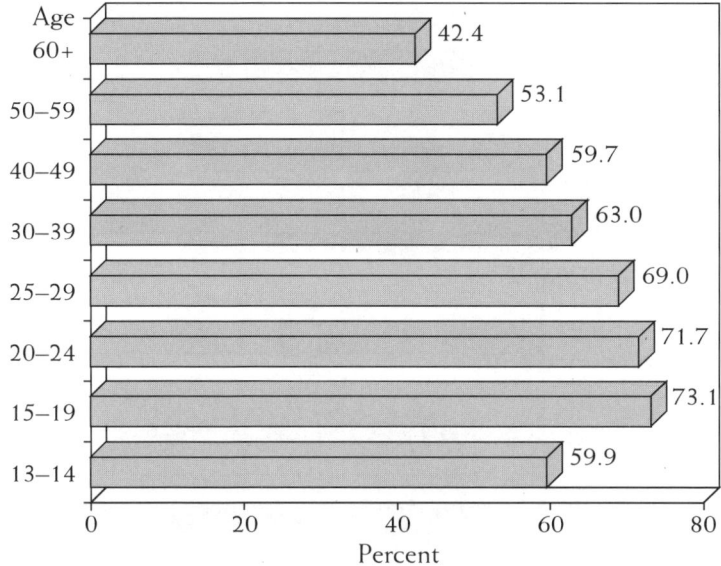

*Figure 4.8   Radio Listening by Age in 1990
(Source: Based on National Statistical Office, Report of the Cultural Activity Participation and Time Use Survey 1990, OPM, Bangkok, 1992, p. 29.)*

villages coincide with a decline in radio listeners. Between 1984 and 1990, for instance, the proportion of farmers listening to the radio dropped from 75 to 63 percent (see Figure 4.9), while the proportion of those viewing television increased from 52 to 74 percent (see Figure 4.1).

Although declining, the audience is still substantial. About two-thirds of Thais listen to the radio. These people are representative of the population; about 80 percent live in villages and nearly half are farmers (see Figure 4.10).

Listening habits   Thais use their radios less intensively than their television sets. Typically, people spend less than two hours per day listening to the radio. There is an uninterrupted stream of listeners throughout the day, although most people turn on their radios in the early morning hours for the news. Total audience peaks between 6 a.m. and 8 a.m.[22]

These hours, however, are not always prime time for individual broadcasters. Most stations air news programs in the morning,

Figure 4.9 Radio Listening by Occupation in 1984 and 1990
(Sources: Based on National Statistical Office, Report of the Mass Media Survey (Radio and Television) 1984, OPM, Bangkok, p. 17, and National Statistical Office, Report of the Cultural Activity Participation and Time Use Survey 1990, OPM, Bangkok, 1992, Statistical Tables, p. 48.)

capturing only a small part of the audience. Prime time varies widely across stations and may be any time of the day or night.

People select radio stations for the quality of the programs and of the reception. They listen to local stations because they can hear them better, but they put up with a poor reception for better programs. In the provinces, for instance, people often listen to the Bangkok stations for the news and they switch to more audible local stations for other programs. Overall, more than half of Thais listen to Bangkok stations for the news but only a quarter for entertainment programs.

Chapter 4 Media and Advertising

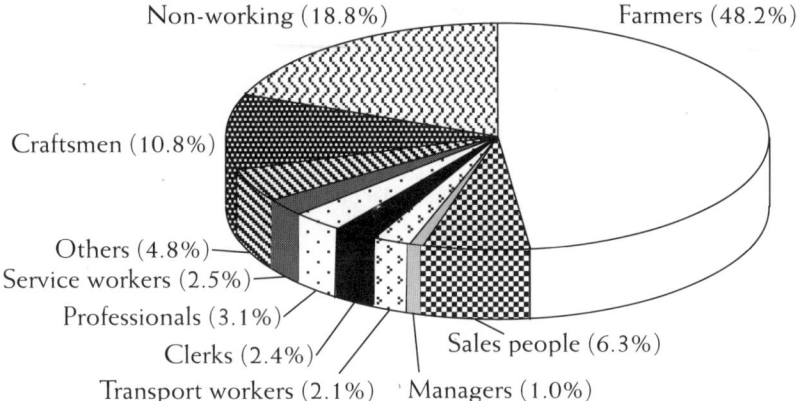

Figure 4.10 Composition of Radio Audience by Occupation in 1990 (Source: Based on National Statistical Office, Report of the Cultural Activity Participation and Time Use Survey 1990, OPM, Bangkok, 1992, Statistical Tables, p. 48.)

Listening is often casual. The mere number of stations precludes careful selection of programs. Most people tune in to their favorite station, switching stations occasionally to check other programs (see Figure 4.11). The audience is, however, more selective in rural areas. Nearly a quarter of the villagers listen to program announcements, compared to only 5 percent in Bangkok.

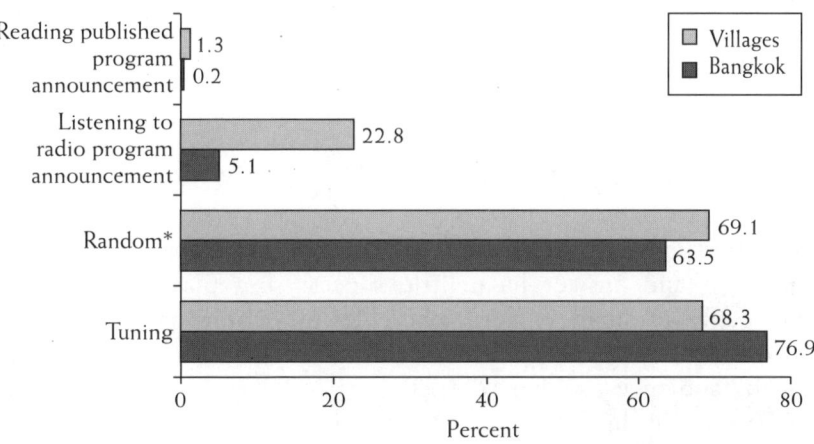

*Called "pursuing the program" in the survey report.

Figure 4.11 Radio Program Selection in 1984 (Source: Based on National Statistical Office, Report of the Mass Media Survey (Radio and Television) 1984, OPM, Bangkok, p. 20.)

177

Preferences Preferences are well defined. People listen mainly to the news and to entertainment programs. Features and commentaries draw small audiences, while educational programs get hardly any notice. These patterns prevail throughout the country, although there are slight differences between cities and villages.

The news programs are the most successful. They attract up to 90 percent of the audience (see Figure 4.12). Foreign and domestic news, sports reports, and weather forecasts rank high in the ratings. People, however, seldom listen to official announcements.

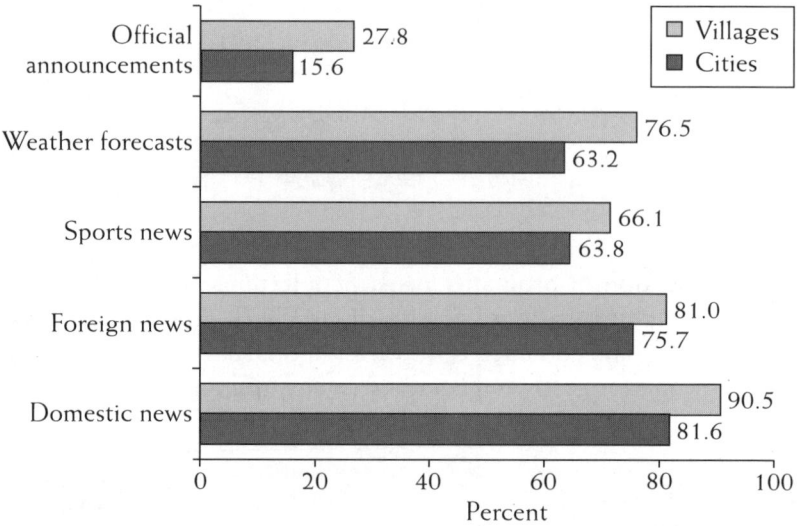

Figure 4.12 Ratings of Radio News Programs in 1984
(Source: Based on National Statistical Office, Report of the Mass Media Survey (Radio and Television) 1984, OPM, Bangkok, p. 22.)

Entertainment programs get variable response. Games like question and answer have little success, but plays are popular, especially in small villages where fewer people have television. Music shows, however, are a favorite. They attract up to 90 percent of the audience (see Figure 4.13).

Music is an important industry in Thailand. Artists train to meet international standards and they become celebrities in the kingdom and in neighboring countries. Thai pop music, a quick dance-beat music, is the most popular, while Western pop music fares well only in cities. Since provincial audiences are more conservative, local

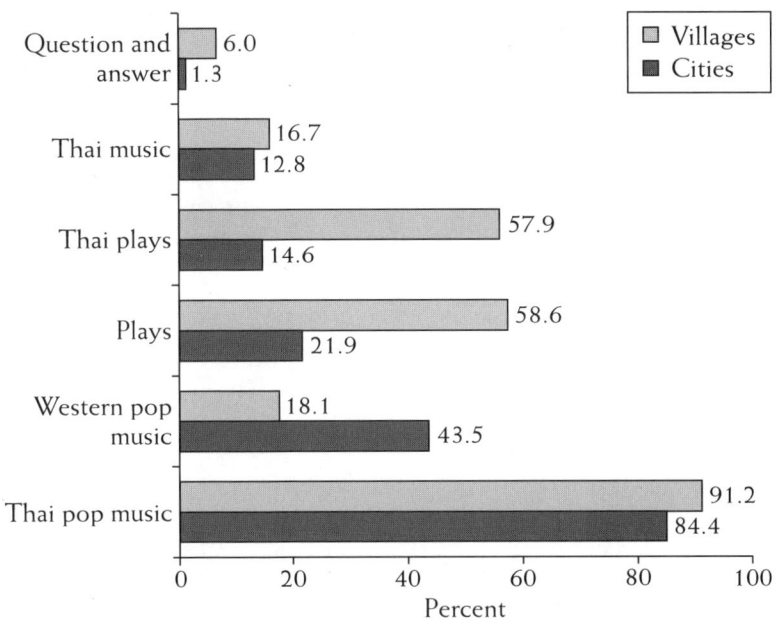

Figure 4.13 Ratings of Radio Entertainment Programs in 1984 (Source: Based on National Statistical Office, Report of the Mass Media Survey (Radio and Television) 1984, OPM, Bangkok, p. 23.)

recording companies produce two main kinds of pop music, one more country-style for the provinces and the other with Western-like sounds for the cities.

Feature programs are diverse, but their success is moderate. Audiences rarely exceed 30 percent, especially in cities (see Figure 4.14). Some feature programs, however, do well in rural areas, especially those on agriculture, sports, health, career, politics, and religion.

Commentaries also attract small audiences. These news-related programs analyze political, foreign, social, economic, and cultural issues. Except for critics, which draw 60 percent of the public, most commentaries capture less than a quarter of the audience (see Figure 4.15).

Few people complain about radio. Those who do often find the programs too short and lacking content.

Business Prospects in Thailand

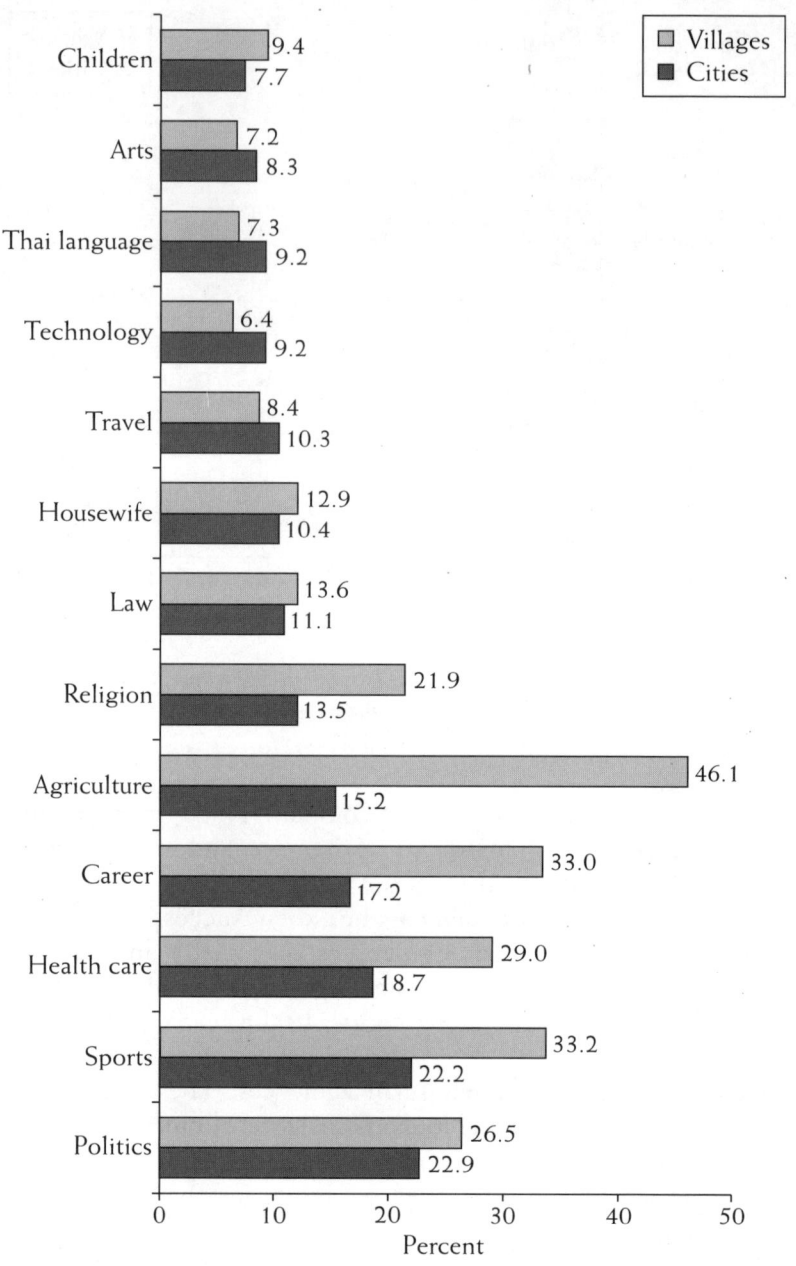

Figure 4.14 Ratings of Radio Feature Programs in 1984
(Source: Based on National Statistical Office, Report of the Mass Media Survey (Radio and Television) 1984, OPM, Bangkok, p. 22.)

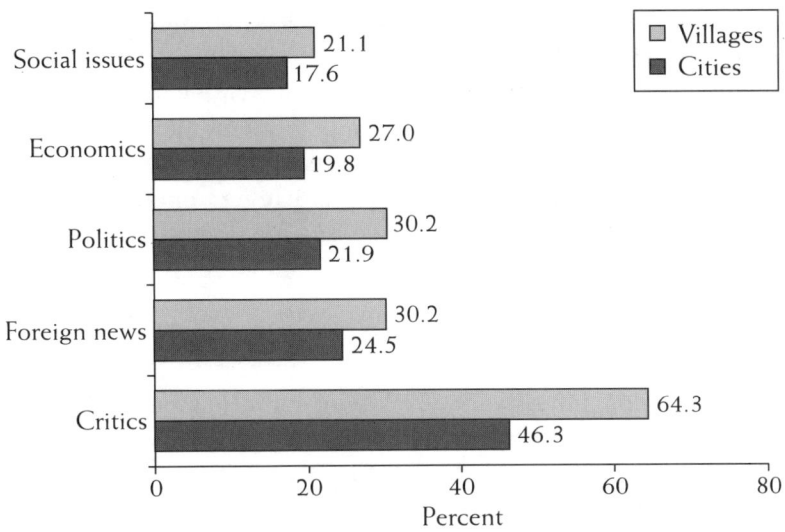

Figure 4.15 Ratings of Radio Commentary Programs in 1984 (Source: Based on National Statistical Office, Report of the Mass Media Survey (Radio and Television) 1984, OPM, Bangkok, pp. 22–3.)

4.3 PUBLISHING

Thailand has a thriving press industry and the ambition to become an international publishing center. Newsstands sell many different newspapers, magazines, and other periodicals, both local and regional. Bookstores carry extensive collections of local and imported books, while businesses produce newsletters and reports for their clients.

Most publications are in the Thai language, but not all. A few local newspapers and magazines are in Chinese and English. Bookstores also sell regional and imported publications in English, Chinese, and Japanese.

The market is expanding, especially for books and magazines. New generations of well-educated professionals and managers seek industry news in business, financial, and other trade reviews, while the emerging middle class is buying a greater array of consumer magazines on such topics as car, travel, entertainment, and fashion. Even youngsters, who study longer, seek their own books and magazines. Publications have also become a marketing tool, with businesses producing newsletters to promote their products and boost the image of their company.

These changes are increasing the demand for newsprint and other printing paper. Thailand used to import all its newsprint, buying mainly from producers in Canada, Sweden, New Zealand, and the United States. Growing demand, however, encouraged local companies to set up newsprint factories for domestic consumption and export.

4.3.1 PUBLICATIONS

The publishing industry is developing rapidly. Companies launch new titles and they buy additional machinery. They also extend their distribution network to the rural areas, opening offices in the provinces. Because these investments are expensive, top publishers resort to public offerings. Between 1990 and 1992, the number of publishers listed on the stock exchange more than doubled, increasing from three to eight.

These companies have extensive interests. They produce their own titles, they run business information services on subscription basis, and they use their typesetting and printing equipment for other publications. Leading publishers, for instance, act as local agents for foreign titles, providing editorial, production, and distribution services. They also print leaflets, brochures, and company reviews for enterprises like banks, sports clubs, and hotels.

Major publishing companies have regional operations. Their overseas offices sell advertising space in Thai publications and they control foreign titles. The most ambitious publishers are even investing in the United States, buying majority stakes in small American publishing houses.

Thai publications often meet international standards and some are sold abroad. The English-language dailies, Bangkok Post and The Nation, for instance, sell in Thailand and in other large Asian cities, while some Thai-owned magazines are distributed throughout the Asia-Pacific region.

Newspapers A host of high-quality newspapers, dailies, weeklies, and semiweeklies, circulate in Thailand. Most are in the Thai language, but there are also some English and Chinese titles. Thai newspapers cater to the local audiences, English titles target expatriates and upper-income Thais, while Chinese newspapers sell to the Chinese community.

Thai-language newspapers have the widest and most diverse audience. In 1992, the most popular Thai newspaper had an estimated readership[23] of about 12 million, while the next most successful title followed at 6 million.[24] Many newspapers cater to the general public, reporting local, political, economic, and business news, although some titles specialize in specific issues like sports.

Some of the biggest publishers of Thai-language newspapers are listed on the stock exchange. In 1992, there were three such companies. These are also the producers of some of the best Thai-language newspapers that target upper-income young professionals, top managers, and government officials.

English-language newspapers have a narrower market. They cater to expatriates and better-educated Thais and they sell in Bangkok and in large provincial cities. Readers have access to both regional and local newspapers. The two leading dailies, however, are local titles: the Bangkok Post and The Nation. Their combined readership reached 246,000 in 1992.[25]

Thailand has a long tradition of producing newspapers in English. The first such title came upon in 1844. It was a Thai-English semi-monthly newspaper produced by American missionary Dan Beach. English was also the language of the first Thai daily, the Siam Daily Advertiser, which started publication in 1868.

Decades of publishing in English have nurtured quality. The kingdom is renowned for its fine English-language newspapers. The Bangkok Post, for instance, is often regarded as one of the best English-language newspapers in Asia, while The Nation also commands a large readership. Publishers of these newspapers are well established and they are listed on the stock exchange. They also act as advertising representatives, printers, and distributors for foreign titles.

Chinese-language newspapers cater to smaller audiences. In 1992, the three leading Chinese-language titles had a combined readership of 62,000.[26] The Chinese press has, nonetheless, a representative on the stock exchange. Compared to other listed publishers, it is small and it targets a less-educated audience.

The mere number of newspapers speaks of their success, but actual circulation figures are difficult to find. In Thailand, as in other Asian countries, production is seldom audited. Some publishers claim grossly inflated figures of actual circulation.

Readership is often more informative. It is estimated independently by monitoring agencies and it accounts for multiple reading: people often pass newspapers around. Readership of audited titles may be several times the circulation. For non-audited titles with an inclination for swelling figures, however, readership may be lower than alleged circulation. Some Chinese-language newspapers, for instance, claim circulation of up to four times the estimated readership.

Magazines Magazines have a large and growing market. A number of professional reviews cater to specific occupational groups like engineers, pharmacists, physicians, builders, bankers, programmers, etc. Most titles, however, target the general public, with topics ranging from health and child care, to travel, art, culture, fashion, entertainment, stereo, furniture, home, cars, and sports. In addition, publishers produce general-interest magazines and comics for the expanding children's and teenage market.

Comics are very popular. Their wide audience has encouraged American animation companies to enter the market. Translated American comics are now available. Since 1993, some bilingual versions of major cartoons have been distributed in Thailand. These come with Thai-language bubbles and English subtitles. Prospects are good for consumer products bearing these cartoon characters.

4.3.2 READERS

With over 90 percent literacy rate, one of the highest in Southeast Asia, Thailand offers good prospects for the publishing industry.[27] In 1990, about a quarter of Thai adults read newspapers regularly and 17 percent magazines.[28] This is small for such a literate population, but the market is expanding rapidly. Between 1985 and 1990, the proportion of Thais reading books and magazines increased by one-third.[29] Newspapers are also in growing demand, with more people buying them instead of borrowing them.

Profile Education is, perhaps, the single most important factor in readership. Newspapers and magazines cater to the better-educated Thais. The vast majority of university-educated people, some 90 percent, read newspapers, compared to two-thirds of high school graduates and only one-fifth of primary school graduates. Overall, 43 percent of newspaper readers have at least secondary education (see Figure 4.16).

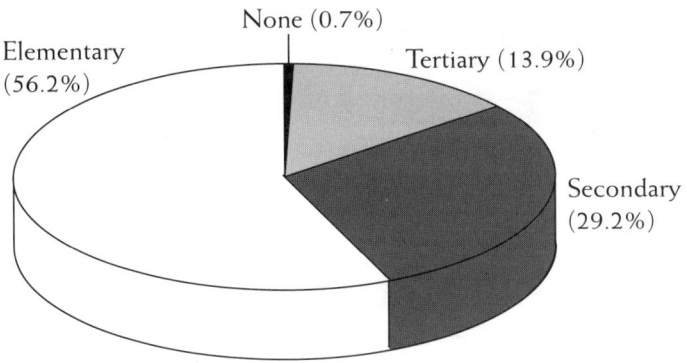

Figure 4.16   Composition of Newspaper Readers by Educational Level
in 1989
(Source: Based on National Statistical Office, Report of the Newspaper Reading Survey 1989, OPM, Bangkok, p. 20.)

These well-educated readers often work at higher-paid jobs. Professionals, for instance, are the most active, with about 90 percent reading newspapers and two-thirds books and magazines (see Figure 4.17). Farmers, in contrast, are the least involved; only 9 percent read newspapers and 7 percent books and magazines.

Such differing reading patterns produce an odd audience. Readers are not representative of the Thai population. They comprise relatively few farmers, only 19 percent in 1990, and many managers, professionals, and clerks (see Figure 4.18). Because many educated people live in cities, readers comprise a large proportion of urbanites. While only 19 percent of Thais live in cities, 44 percent of newspaper readers and 37 percent of magazine readers are urbanites.

The composition of the audience also reflects distinct preferences. Newspapers attract more males and mature people. In 1990, 60 percent of the readers were male and readership peaked among people aged between 25 and 39 (see Figure 4.19). This bias is more pronounced in poorer areas. In the Northeast, for instance, males account for about two-thirds of the readers, compared to half in Bangkok. Magazines, in contrast, address a younger and more

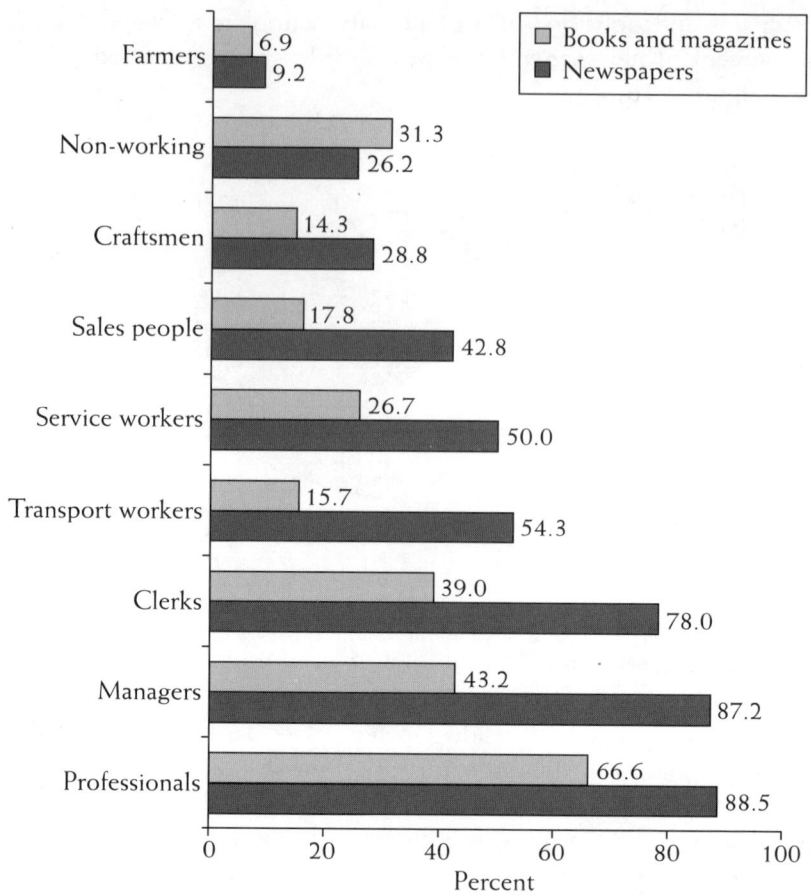

Figure 4.17 Newspaper, Book, and Magazine Reading by Occupation in 1990 (Source: Based on National Statistical Office, Report of the Cultural Activity Participation and Time Use Survey 1990, OPM, Bangkok, 1992, Statistical Tables, p. 48.)

balanced audience. Teenagers are the leading buyers and about half of their readers are male.

Reading habits Reading is not yet a national pastime. About half of Thais say that they do not read newspapers because they are not interested.[30] Readership remains low, especially in rural areas. In 1990, only one-sixth of villagers read newspapers and one-eighth books and magazines, compared to over half and one-third respectively of urbanites (see Figure 4.20). Lack of interest is the

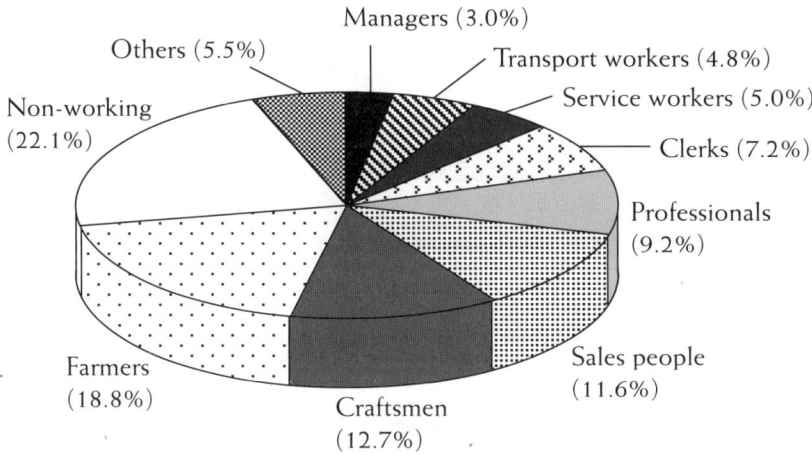

Figure 4.18 Composition of Newspaper Readers by Occupation in 1990 (Source: Based on National Statistical Office, Report of the Cultural Activity Participation and Time Use Survey 1990, OPM, Bangkok, 1992, Statistical Tables, p. 48.)

main obstacle to readership, but it is not the only one.

The next biggest hurdle is distribution. Few publications reach remote villages and about a quarter of Thais claim that they do not read newspapers because they are geographically isolated. Even the villagers who read newspapers give up doing so regularly. In rural Thailand, only 40 percent of the readers peruse the newspaper at least 4 days a week, compared to 77 percent in cities.[31] Books and magazines are not so affected, partly because the timing of distribution is less critical.

Poor distribution has bred comradeship. People often share reading material. In 1989, over half of Thais did not buy the newspapers they read,[32] suggesting that every newspaper sold changed hands at least twice. Passing newspapers is especially common in the countryside where they are difficult to get. In villages, only one-third of readers buy their newspapers, compared to three-quarters in cities.

People are flexible, reading newspapers whenever they find them. Many go to the village's reading place, but it is also customary to stop by a friend's or relative's home to read the newspaper.

Whether they buy or borrow publications, people spend about the same time reading them. The average reader spares about

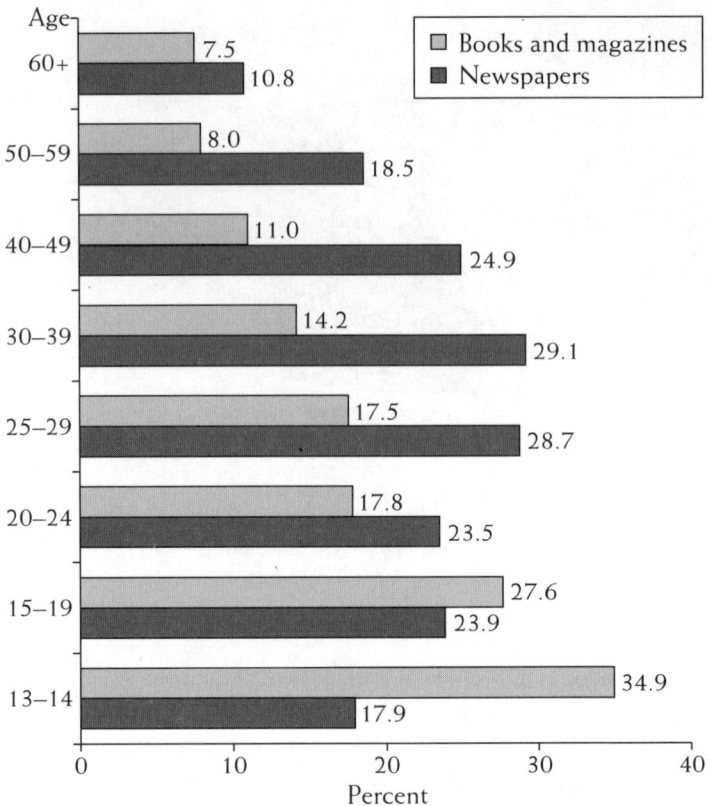

Figure 4.19 Newspaper, Book, and Magazine Reading by Age in 1990 (Source: Based on National Statistical Office, Report of the Cultural Activity Participation and Time Use Survey 1990, OPM, Bangkok, 1992, p. 29.)

50 minutes daily reading newspapers and one hour reading books and magazines.[33] Readers are also likely to peruse several different publications. Over half of the households reading newspapers also read books and magazines. This is especially common in cities, where nearly two-thirds of the households read several publications.

Selection of articles Thai newspapers are concise. Many contain only 16 to 20 pages of news, features, and commentaries. People look at the news mainly and they read the features and commentaries if they find them interesting.

News sections cover a variety of topics, many of which are popular. Nearly all readers follow the general news and about

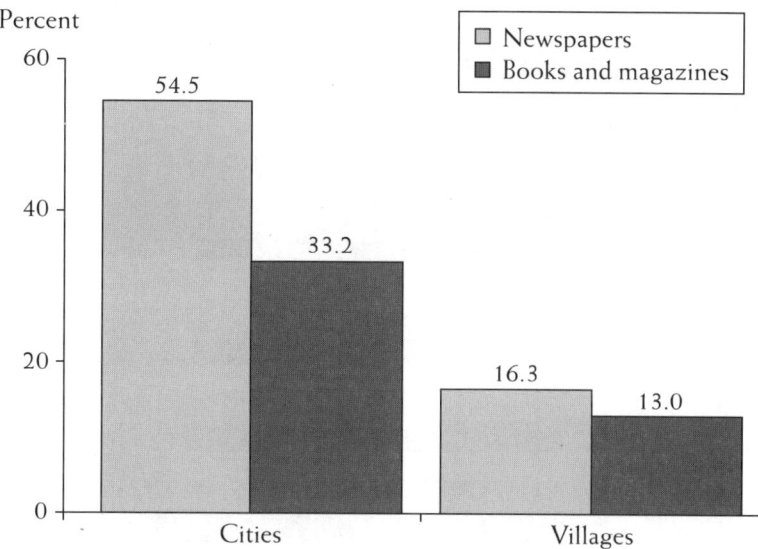

Figure 4.20 Newspaper, Book, and Magazine Reading by Area in 1990 (Source: Based on National Statistical Office, Report of the Cultural Activity Participation and Time Use Survey 1990, OPM, Bangkok, 1992, p. 27.)

80 percent the political news, while economic, foreign, and sports matters attract over two-thirds of the readers (see Figure 4.21).

Features and commentaries address many different issues with variable success. Readership ranges from about a quarter to two-thirds. Politics, economics, and government score the highest, while health care also has a large following. Other topics are less successful (see Figures 4.22 and 4.23).

Males and females have similar reading patterns, although their interests differ slightly. Females are practical, reading more articles on health care, children, women, and entertainment. They are more mystic too, often looking at the horoscope. Males, in contrast, pay greater attention to politics, economics, foreign affairs, and sports.

Although these patterns persist throughout Thailand, some topics are more popular in cities. Articles which appeal to females, for instance, fare better in cities, where more females read newspapers. Urbanites also read more articles on art because they have exposure to cultural activities. In addition, they pay greater attention to politics and foreign affairs.

Thai readers are usually satisfied with their newspapers, although they have suggestions for improvement. Most fundamental

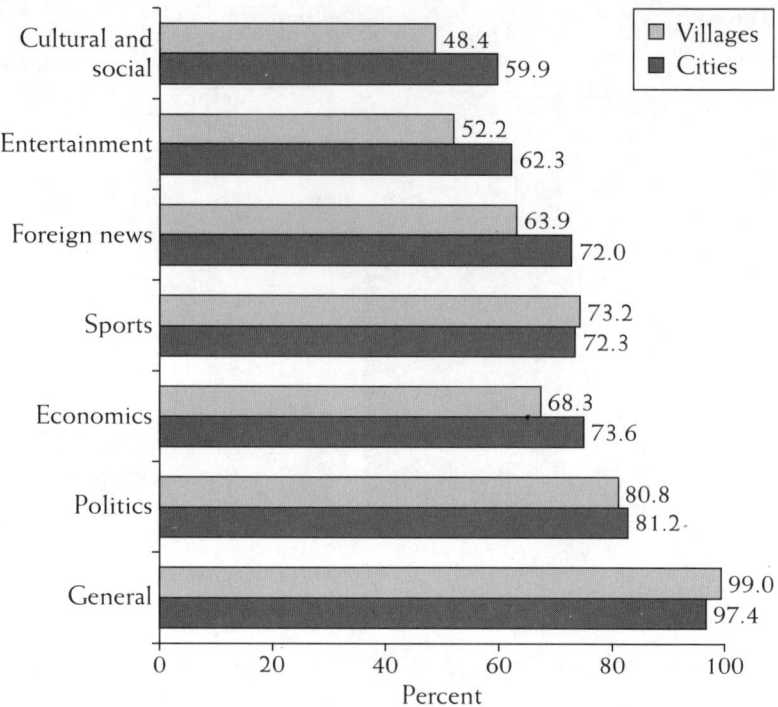

Figure 4.21   Reading of News by Type in 1989
(*Source: Based on National Statistical Office, Report of the Newspaper Reading Survey 1989, OPM, Bangkok, p. 28.*)

comments pertain to the contents. People would like to have more detailed and factual articles and less advertising. In addition, readers agree that publishers should use correct and simple language.

The format of newspapers is also an issue. Thai newspapers have a printed area of 37.8 × 53.3 cm ($14\frac{7}{8}$ × 21 inches) and most people would prefer smaller newspapers. A vast majority of readers, however, some 93 percent, would also like bigger print. Thais enjoy illustrations, and many wish their newspapers would use colorful designs as well as more and clearer pictures.

More controversial, perhaps, is the marketing strategy. In rural areas, people complain that newspapers are difficult to get and that they arrive late. As expected, nobody says that newspapers are cheap. An overwhelming majority of people find them too expensive and hardly anyone is willing to pay more to get a better-quality newspaper.

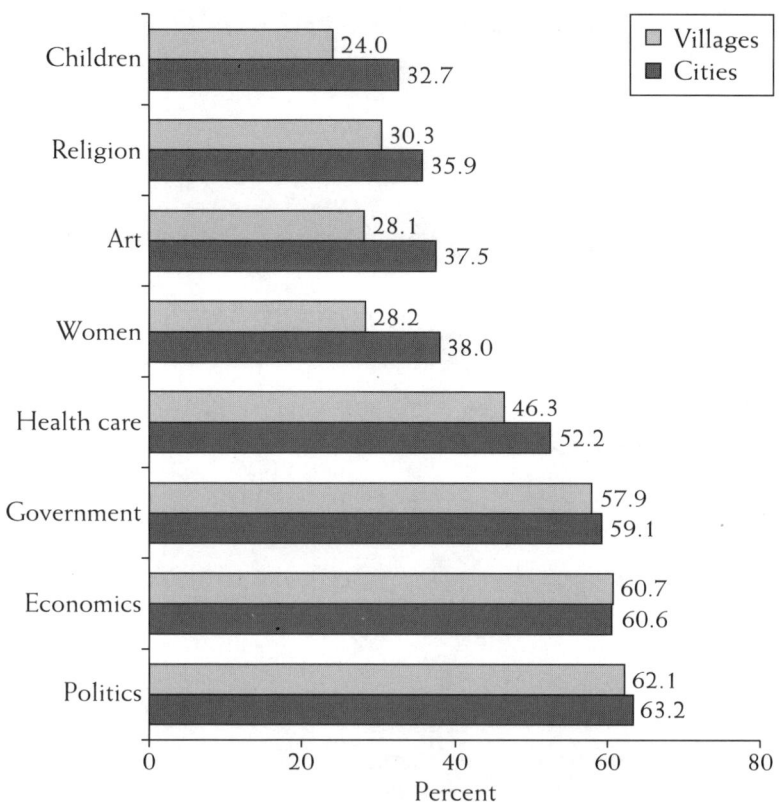

Figure 4.22   Reading of Features by Type in 1989
(Source: Based on National Statistical Office, Report of the Newspaper Reading Survey 1989, OPM, Bangkok, p. 28.)

4.3.3 PRINTING

Unlike publishing companies, printing businesses are developing slowly. Enterprises remain small and traditional. They are often family-run and they lack marketing strategy. Many, however, are technically up to international standards. Their qualified workers are especially skilled at artwork and hand-finishing jobs.

Main problems stem from poor management and trade restrictions. Slack quality controls often fail to detect inconsistencies in the output. The industry's low standards of English also impair communication, especially on technical specifications. In addition, high tariffs on imported raw materials and slow customs clearance

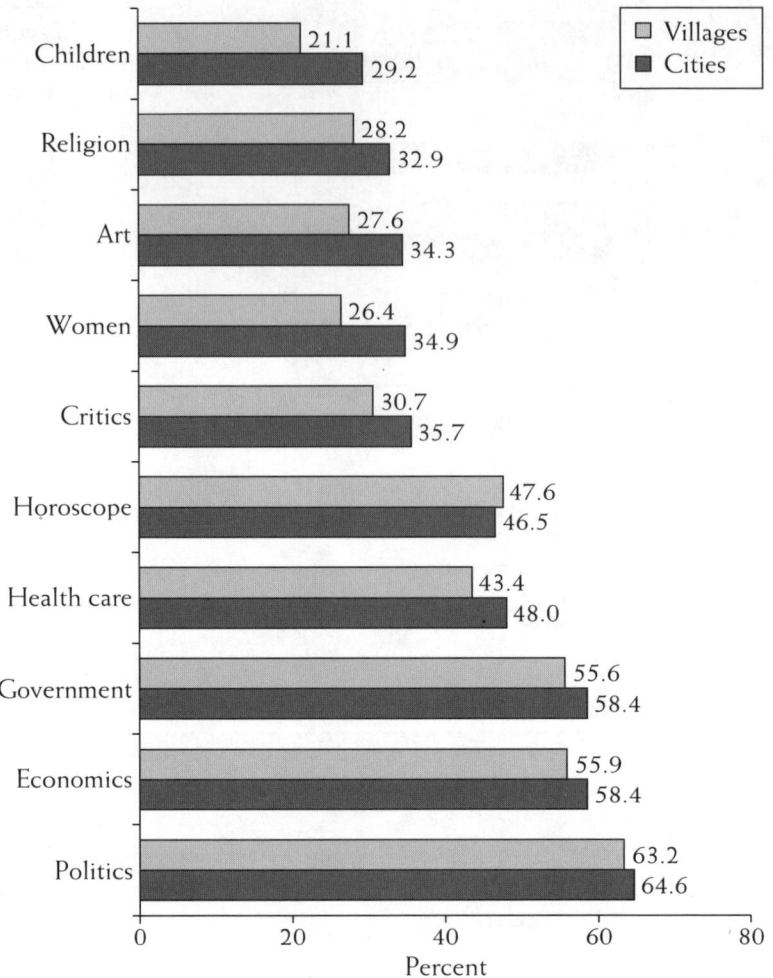

Figure 4.23 Reading of Commentaries by Type in 1989 (Source: Based on National Statistical Office, Report of the Newspaper Reading Survey 1989, OPM, Bangkok, p. 28.)

mar efficiency and lower the quality of the products. Bindings, for instance, are often substandard because of the lack of materials.

4.4 CINEMA

Cinema was once a top attraction, but its appeal is fading. In 1990, only 6 percent of Thais reported going to the movies, down from

21 percent in 1985.[34] Admissions are declining and theaters are getting scarce. By 1992 there were only 613 cinema screens,[35] one for every 93,000 people. This is low by Asian standards. Singapore, for instance, has one screen per 29,000 people and South Korea one per 55,000 people.

4.4.1 PRODUCERS

The local motion picture industry is still alive, but it specializes in low-budget movies. The average Thai movie costs between US$120,000 and US$160,000 to produce, a hundred times cheaper than its American counterpart.[36]

There is little room for quality. Most releases are B-grade movies. Script and shooting take little time to complete and screenwriters often clone successful movies. Blockbusters are either comedies, action, ghost, or sex movies. These follow simple guidelines. Comedies, for instance, include standard jokes, while action films feature much violence.

Thai movie theaters are relying increasingly on foreign films. In 1992, over three-quarters of the movies shown were imported, up from half in 1987.[37] The bulk of these foreign movies come from Hong Kong because Chinese films are cheap and profitable. Most others are American, British, Japanese, Italian, and French.

The Thai film industry has, nonetheless, potential. Top directors produce quality movies that combine artistic and commercial value. Some of these people even team up with foreign screenwriters to make English-language series and movies for worldwide distribution.

The movie industry is also expected to benefit from cuts in import duties on film and equipment. In 1993, the Thai government agreed to reduce duties on lighting, acoustic equipment, unexposed film, foreign movies, and Thai movies filmed abroad.

4.4.2 AUDIENCE

Cinemas cater mainly to the youth. In 1990, over half of the audience was aged between 15 and 24. These people are the most avid viewers, with about 11 percent going to the movies. Attendance is lower in older age groups and it drops to only 1 percent for people above 60 years old (see Figure 4.24).

Education and profession, in contrast, have little influence on

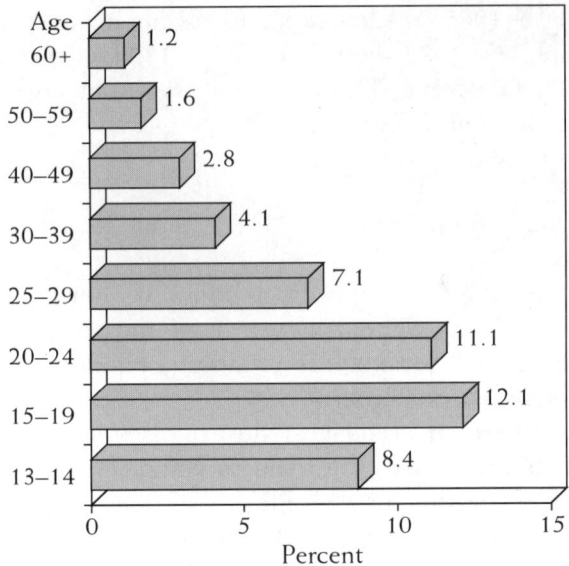

*Figure 4.24 Going to the Movies by Age in 1990
(Source: Based on National Statistical Office, Report of the
Cultural Activity Participation and Time Use Survey 1990,
OPM, Bangkok, 1992, p. 29.)*

attendance. About 6 percent of Thais in most occupational and educational groups go to the movies.[38] That clerks go to the movies more frequently and managers less often reflects only age differences—clerks tend to be younger and managers older. The cinema audience is, therefore, a collection of young Thai adults of mixed background.

Because most Thais live in rural areas, the bulk of the viewers, some 80 percent, are villagers.[39] These people are often less sophisticated. They want to watch simple stories that they can understand. Chinese and low-quality Thai movies are successful in these places.

In cities, especially Bangkok, people are more discerning. They watch the better-quality movies that seldom reach the villages. They also have access to better theaters. In Bangkok, for instance, a fifty-seat simulation cinema with a domed screen and computer-programmed seat platforms moving with on-screen action opened in 1994.

4.5 ADVERTISING AND PUBLIC RELATIONS

By Asian standards, Thailand has a substantial advertising market. In 1992, total advertising expenses reached US$802 million, well above the US$435 million recorded in Malaysia and US$454 million in Singapore.[40] These figures, however, do not reflect the relative weight of advertising in each country.

The Thai advertising industry owes its size more to the number of advertisers rather than the size of individual accounts. In 1992, the top Thai advertiser spent a hundred and twenty times less than his Japanese counterpart and nine times less than his Malaysian peer in publicity. Even in small countries like Hong Kong, Singapore, and New Zealand, advertisers have bigger budgets than in Thailand.

Thais invest little per person in advertising. In 1992, per capita advertising expenses reached US$14, a modest achievement if compared to US$266 in Japan.[41] This pattern is, however, changing rapidly. Between 1980 and 1992, per capita advertising expenses increased by 370 percent in real terms (see Figure 4.25).

Economic growth and competition fuel the demand for advertising. There are more advertisers both in the public and private sectors. The Thai government now calls on advertising agencies to promote various social and political goals. In February 1992, for instance, the administration in power launched a television, newspaper, and billboard campaign nationwide to discourage vote buying during elections.

Even scientists use advertising. Researchers at Mahidol University, for instance, organized an advertising campaign to increase the intake of vitamin A in the Northeast. They used posters, T-shirts, and radio commercials to promote ivy gourd, a creeper of edible leaves rich in vitamin A.[42]

Incidentally, children proved to be effective vehicles in conveying messages to adults. During their campaign, researchers asked school teachers to assign pupils to grow ivy gourd at home. Parents helped their children, hoping that this would improve their grades. In the process, parents perceived the benefits of the change in the diet.

4.5.1 MEDIA

Advertisers have access to the whole range of media including

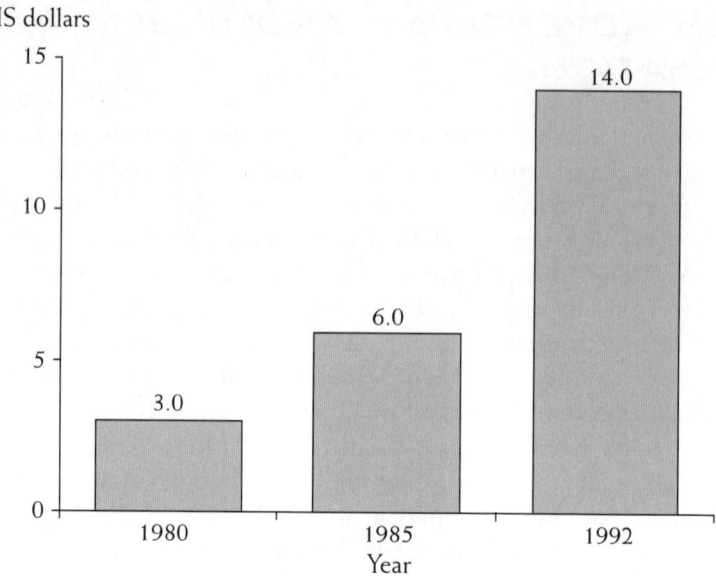

Figure 4.25   Evolution of Per Capita Advertising Expenses at 1992 Constant Prices
(Sources: Based on Zenith Media Worldwide, Asia Pacific Market & MediaFact, London, various issues, and National Statistical Office, Statistical Yearbook Thailand 1993, OPM, Bangkok, 1993, p. 27.)

television, radio, press, cinema, and outdoor. Television, however, dominates, capturing about half of the advertising expenses (see Figure 4.26). Newspapers and magazines combined account for over one-third of this market. Other media are less prominent. Radio gets one-eighth of the expenses, outdoor 5 percent, and cinema is marginal.

Countless products are advertised through all these channels, especially fast-selling consumer goods. In 1992, for instance, the most advertised product categories included pharmaceutical products, dairy products, cosmetics, shampoos, alcoholic beverages, and gasoline, along with services, like retailing and real estate.

Advertisers call on local celebrities to promote their products. They say that Thais relate more to local heroes than to foreign idols. Leading American manufacturers of soft drinks, for instance, often sponsor Thai musicians and they attribute part of their success to this marketing strategy.

The development of advertising is a boon for the media industry,

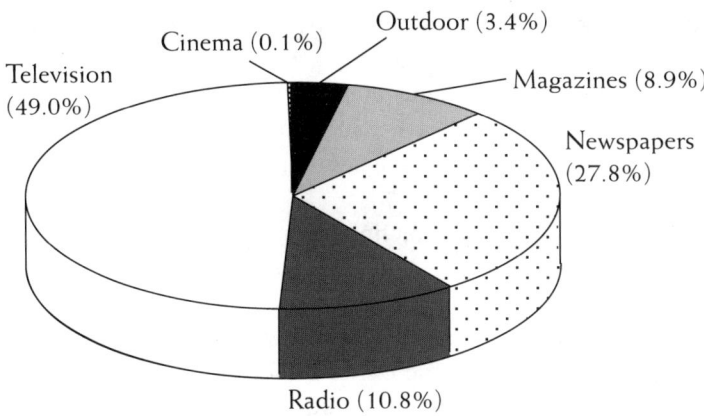

Figure 4.26   Composition of Advertising Expenses by Medium in 1992 (Sources: Based on Zenith Media Worldwide, Asia Pacific Market & MediaFact 1993, London, 1993, p. 2.)

although benefits vary. Press and outdoor advertising are in growing demand, while radio and cinema are becoming less popular. Television is the only medium which is maintaining its market share.

Several companies monitor these trends. They conduct regular surveys on the size, composition, and behavior of the mass media audiences and on advertising expenses.

Television   Television is the most attractive medium because animation and color appeal to Thais. In the past decade, it has consistently captured about half of the advertising expenses. In 1992, television stations collected a total of US$393 million in advertising revenue.[43]

Although effective, television campaigns are expensive. The costs of air time and of producing spots are high. In 1993, terrestrial stations charged between US$1,600 and US$3,000 for running a thirty-second spot at prime time[44] (from 7 p.m. to 11 p.m.) That year, most spots also cost between US$80,000 and US$120,000 to produce and prices exceeded US$400,000 for the most expensive ones.[45]

Because of its high cost and wide audience, television is better suited for fast-selling consumer goods. Top spenders promote personal care products, detergents, beverages, and gasoline. Advertisers use messages that help build brand names nationwide and boost sales.

Commercials are often conventional. Most spots are mass-market advertisements. Thais seldom use direct-response messages, which present a product and invite viewers to call a telephone number. Although some agencies have conducted successful direct-response campaigns, few advertisers have enough telephone lines to cope with a flood of calls.

Campaigns require some planning, especially for booking air time. Advertisers usually reserve their slot six months in advance, although they may do so up to 15 days before the airing date if space is available. Procedures are, however, simple as advertisers may buy commercial air time either directly from the station (or the company leasing it) or from a broker.

The advertising load on television stations has grown dramatically over the past few years mainly because broadcasting time increased. In 1992, the four leading national channels combined broadcasted 79 hours of advertising per week,[46] nearly twice as much as in 1989. This is high by Asian standards. Thai stations broadcast twenty hours a day, bringing their average hourly advertising load to about 8 minutes per hour, almost as much as in Japan. At peak hours, Thai television stations run advertisements every 15 minutes.

Viewers, however, seem to have little interest in watching commercials. Recent findings by monitoring companies show that people tend to switch channels during commercials, especially if they have remote control. They miss all spots but the first and last ones. Although few Thais, less than 1 percent, have remote control, this behavior stresses the importance of using creative advertisements that keep viewers interested.

Newspapers Newspaper advertising is in high demand. It is the second largest and the fastest-growing form of advertising in Thailand. In 1992, newspapers captured 28 percent of total advertising expenses, up from 16 percent in 1980.[47]

This medium owes its popularity to its low advertising cost. In 1992, the top-selling Thai-language dailies charged US$7,000–9,000 for a full page black-and-white advertisement, compared to US$150,000–200,000 for Japanese newspapers with similar readership. English-language newspapers were cheaper at US$5,000, while the Chinese-language dailies charged as low as US$1,500.[48] The premium for color advertisements is variable across titles, ranging from 14 to 75 percent.

Because the press caters to upper-income and business people, it is valuable for advertising upmarket and business products. Leading press advertisers include developers, department stores, airlines, hotels, car manufacturers, and distributors of computers, electronic equipment, and alcoholic beverages.

Placing an advertisement in newspapers is simple and fairly speedy. Advertisers buy space directly from the publishers. Lead time varies. Some newspapers require as little as three days in advance, while top-selling dailies require up to a month in advance.

Most advertising is in Thai, but newspapers also carry advertisements in other languages, especially in Chinese and English. English-language newspapers advertise products, services, and events to Westerners and upper-income Thais. They are leading vehicles for English-language advertising—they claim that they get most of the English-language advertising.

Magazines Magazines are in growing demand, but their advertising revenue is increasing slowly. In 1992, they captured 9 percent of total advertising expenses, up from 7 percent in 1980.[49] Growth is also irregular, with the share of magazine advertising fluctuating substantially from year to year.

Magazine advertising rates, although variable, are usually lower than those of newspapers. In 1992, top-selling business magazines charged US$1,200 for a full page black-and-white advertisement,[50] a third of the rate charged by a newspaper with similar distribution. Advertisements in color command a high premium over those in black and white. Many magazines charge at least 80 percent more for advertisements in color and some as much as 170 percent more.

Booking advertising space in magazines is easy, but it may require planning. Advertisers buy advertisement space from publishers. Many magazines set a monthly booking deadline. Others specify a time period before publishing. In these cases, lead time is often 30 to 45 days, but it may be up to one year.

Radio Radio, once a prized vehicle for advertising, is losing out to other media. Between 1980 and 1992, its share of advertising declined from 25 to 11 percent.[51] For many years, radio was the principal communications medium in Thailand and, in some places, the primary link with the outside world. It was the only medium whose commercials could reach people in the most remote parts of the country.

Radio remains, nonetheless, a valuable vehicle. Its share of advertising expenses is among the highest in Asia. Radio is also expected to pick up because recent changes in programming have boosted listening, attracting more spenders. In addition, radio advertisements are relatively cheap to produce and to air. In 1992, the cost of running a thirty-second spot at prime time could be as low as US$25.[52]

Because it targets narrow segments of the population through its numerous stations, radio is useful in promoting products and services locally. Leading advertisers include department stores, shopping arcades, hotels, and restaurants along with producers of fast-selling items like personal care products, beverages, gasoline, and household appliances.

Booking commercial air time is easy. Most advertisers buy slots through brokers, although some deal directly with the stations. Lead time is usually short. Advertisers must book about 20 days in advance for running a commercial and 60 days in advance for sponsoring a program.

Outdoor Outdoor advertising has grown slowly, but it is becoming more popular. Until the mid-1980s, this medium was insignificant and research companies did not monitor it. By 1992, it was still marginal, capturing only 3.4 percent of the advertising expenses,[53] but it had become an integral part of advertising. A year later, it featured for the first time as an award category in the Top Advertising Contest of Thailand.

There is a wide selection of outdoor billboards. The most common are paper poster panels, but there are also electronic panels, painted bulletins, and balloon billboards. Outdoor posters are located in many venues including shopping centers, roadside, train and bus stations, airports, expressway light boxes, bus shelters, boats, buses, and pickup trucks.

Bus posters are usually on the sides, backs, and interiors of the vehicles, but some advertisers use whole buses. They paint the entire vehicles with their company logo and colors. Such advertising is more commonly used on modern vehicles. In 1992, for instance, the Bangkok Mass Transit Authority granted an advertising agency a concession to use its new fleet of buses for extensive advertising.

Sophisticated neon and electronic signs have much appeal, but they are subject to restrictions and frequent electricity cuts. During the Gulf War in early 1991, for instance, Thai authorities, fearing an oil shortage, banned movie theaters and other businesses from using electrical signboards.

Outdoor advertising targets commuters and shoppers. It is suited for advertising fast-selling consumption items, especially personal care products, beverages, and household appliances. Few companies use billboards for other purposes like building corporate identity.

Booking procedures depend on the type of poster. Advertisers contract with the management of shopping arcades for posters in these places. They arrange booking for painted panels though the suppliers of such panels and they hire brokers to rent space in public transportation.

Cinema   Advertising in cinemas is negligible. Movie theaters have lost much of their appeal, driving down advertising revenue. Between 1980 and 1992, the share of cinema advertising dropped from 6 to 0.1 percent.[54]

Cost is declining. Rates did not keep pace with inflation. Between 1982 and 1992, theaters have kept their advertising rates almost unchanged, increasing them only once by 5 percent. Slots may be purchased through brokers.

Because cinemas cater to young people, they are valuable in promoting goods to the youth. Cinema advertising focuses on such products as cosmetics, cars, soft drinks, snacks, sportswear, and casual wear.

4.5.2 ADVERTISING AGENCIES

Thailand has a host of advertising agencies, both local and foreign. Many leading international agencies, especially Japanese, have set up affiliates or representative offices. This large international presence has created a highly competitive environment. Market shares seldom exceed 5 percent. In 1991, only four agencies achieved this feat. Because advertising is in growing demand, competition is increasing. New agencies are setting up, while existing ones are opening offices in the provinces.

Quality   This rapid expansion is stretching the industry's resources. Agencies are short of qualified personnel, especially creative directors. Staff turnover is high as employees find better-paid jobs in competing firms or set up their own business. Agencies change names frequently, recording departures and new alliances of associates. More people are training for creative jobs, but they need experience. In the interim, advertising departments resort to technological expedients; eye-catching computer graphics often make up for the lack of creativity.

The industry is, however, trying to maintain quality. It organizes two major awards competitions, the Top Advertising Contest of Thailand Award and the Bangkok Art Directors' Award. Both events reward creativity and organizers withhold prizes when entries do not meet their standards.

Image Quality problems add to the difficulty of gaining public acceptance. The industry uses its representative, the Advertising Association of Thailand (AAT), to improve its public image. The AAT promotes the understanding of communications services and their effectiveness. It also fosters social contributions, encouraging corporate advertisers to sponsor campaigns on such public issues as pollution and road safety.

These public-service advertisements are new to Thailand, although they have existed for some time in the West. Until recently, the only such campaigns were low-budget government productions. In the past few years, however, more private firms have sponsored quality public-service advertisements. Advertisers tag their product brand names to the spots to build their company image and boost sales.

Services Agencies provide a wide range of services, but advertising is their core business. Some agencies claim that it accounts for some 95 percent of their services, compared to 80 percent in the United States. Related services, like direct marketing and public relations are, however, in growing demand.

Direct marketing is becoming more common, although human resources in this sector are scarce. Agencies began setting up direct-marketing divisions in the mid-1980s and the trend is rising. Their services are diverse, covering in-house activities like direct-mail campaigns, as well as field work like store promotional events. Agencies, for instance, use their trained sales staff to conduct product demonstrations and give away samples. They also monitor and analyze sales and stocks movements.

For some industries, direct marketing is a cheaper alternative to advertising. It is especially useful in promoting products like perfumes and wines to a selected public.

4.5.3 REGULATIONS

Most advertising regulations aim at protecting consumers. Thailand's Consumer Protection Act advocates truth in advertising. It is administered by the Committee on Advertising (COA), a section of the Consumer Protection Committee.

The COA controls both the content and the method of advertising. It prohibits false or exaggerated statements (unless obviously so), as well as misleading, immoral, degrading, and potentially subversive messages. The committee also ensures that the advertising method is not harmful to the physical or mental health of consumers.

Corrections await advertisements which do not meet these criteria. The COA may request changes in the message or in the method of advertising. In more serious cases, it may prohibit the advertising or forbid the use of certain media. Advertisers may ensure that they fulfill the COA requirements by requesting (for a fee) its written opinion.

The powers of the COA extend beyond advertising per se. The committee may intervene if it considers that some goods are harmful to consumers. It may request to include a warning in the advertisement, limit advertising to certain media, or prohibit advertising.

While these regulations cover most goods, specific rules apply to a few products. These rules fall under the jurisdiction of the Food and Drug Administration (FDA), a department of the Ministry of Public Health. The advertising of FDA-controlled products may be prohibited, subject to approval, or subject to surveillance.

Drugs The FDA controls the advertising of medications of all kinds, including Western and herbal medicines. It classifies medicines into various categories and advertising rules depend on them. The FDA prohibits the advertising of drugs classified as dangerous or controlled and it subjects the advertising of other drugs to approval. In the latter case advertisers must submit the text, sound, and pictures of their advertising message for licensing.

Regulations discourage misleading advertisements, but criteria are vague. Decisions rest on subjective evaluations. The licenser decides what a message suggests or how people interpret it. The FDA, for instance, prohibits advertisements which "suggest" that a drug is capable of miraculous relief, cure, or prevention of illness. It also rejects advertisements which "create the understanding" that the drug is an abortifacient, a strong emmenagogue, an aphrodisiac, or a birth-control device.

More clear-cut, perhaps, are the rules on the style of advertising. The FDA forbids the advertising of drugs by songs or by showing the suffering of a patient.

Narcotic drugs The advertising of narcotic drugs is restricted. The FDA prohibits the advertising of narcotic drugs unless it is made directly to a medical practitioner, a first-class practitioner of dentistry, a first-class veterinarian, or unless the advertising is on the label of the package. The law defines narcotic drugs as chemicals and substances which affect the body and mind in such prominent ways that they produce unpleasant aftereffects from abstinence and that their dosage must be increased regularly.

Psychotropic substances Similar regulations apply to psychotropic substances. The FDA specifies that these may be advertised directly only to a medical practitioner, a first-class practitioner of dentistry, a pharmacist, or a first-class veterinarian. Advertising is also permitted on the label or accompanying leaflet of the package. The law covers both natural and synthetic psychotropic substances, that is, opiates, tranquilizers, and other chemicals that modify mental activity.

Medical devices The advertising of medical devices is more open. It is permitted provided that the FDA approves the text, sound, and picture of the advertisement. The FDA ensures that the advertisement neither exaggerates nor falsifies the capabilities, quality, quantity, and origin of the product. Medical devices cover instruments, products, and articles used for medical, nursing, midwifery, and veterinary practices.

Food The advertising of any kind of food is subject to approval. Advertisers must submit text, sound, and pictures or motion pictures to the FDA to ascertain that the message does not contain false or deceptive statements on the qualities or benefits of food.

The FDA's licenser has large powers. He may refuse to grant advertising licenses and may even ban the production, importation, or distribution of the food concerned if it does not have the qualities advertised. Ignoring his decisions carries harsh penalties including fine and imprisonment.

The rules and their interpretations are controversial. Advertising agencies complain that rules are not specific, making approval arbitrary. Several years ago, for instance, an agency proposed to advertise a brand of marshmallows by showing several children carrying a giant marshmallow. The FDA turned down the idea, arguing that the message falsely suggested that this product gave supernatural powers.

Poisonous substances The advertising of poisonous substance is subject only to surveillance. The FDA inspects advertisements in all media regularly to ensure that they are neither false nor misleading. Offenders are liable for fine and/or imprisonment. Poisonous substances cover products likely to be harmful to persons, animals, and plants.

Various administrations control these substances. The Ministry of Agriculture handles agricultural poisonous substances; the Ministry of Industry, industrial poisonous substances; and the Ministry of Public Health, other poisonous substances.

Tobacco Restrictions on the advertising of tobacco are, probably, the most stringent. The tobacco control bill of 1992 prohibits all forms of cigarette advertising and marketing promotions, including at points of sale. This is one of the kingdom's most-enforced laws. Penalties are harsh. Mandatory jail term and fines await offenders. This is a main departure from the previous legislation which had banned radio and television advertisements on tobacco but had kept penalties minimal.

NOTES

1. Source: Zenith Media Worldwide, *Asia Pacific Market and MediaFact 1993*, London, 1993, p. 206.
2. Calculations based on Zenith Media Worldwide, *Asia Pacific*

Market and MediaFact, London, various issues, and Office of the National Economic and Social Development Board, *National Income of Thailand, Rebase Series 1980–1991*, OPM, Bangkok, 1993, pp. 10, 15.
3. Sources: National Statistical Office, *Report of the 1990 Household Socio-Economic Survey, Whole Kingdom*, OPM, Bangkok, 1993, p. 121, and National Statistical Office, *Report of the Mass Media Survey, (Radio and Television) 1984*, OPM, Bangkok, p. 26.
4. Calculations based on National Statistical Office, *Report of the Newspaper Reading Survey 1989*, OPM, Bangkok, p. 69.
5. Supra 1, p. 198.
6. Supra 1, p. 198.
7. Supra 1, p. 198.
8. Supra 1, p. 198.
9. Supra 1, p. 198.
10. Supra 1, p. 198.
11. Miller, Lee, "Thai TV: On the brink of change," *Asian Advertising and Marketing*, 19 November 1993, p. 11.
12. Mekloy, Pongpet, "Hooked on heroin," *Bangkok Post*, 23 December 1991, Outlook Section, pp. 31–2.
13. Supra 3, various issues.
14. Sources: National Statistical Office, *Report of the 1990 Household Socio-Economic Survey, Whole Kingdom*, OPM, Bangkok, 1993, p. 121, and National Statistical Office, *Report of the Mass Media Survey, (Radio and Television) 1984*, OPM, Bangkok, p. 29.
15. Source: National Statistical Office, *Report of the Cultural Activity Participation and Time Use Survey 1990*, OPM, Bangkok, 1992, p. 27.
16. Calculations based on National Statistical Office, *Report of the Cultural Activity Participation and Time Use Survey 1990*, OPM, Bangkok, 1992, Statistical Tables, p. 50.
17. See National Statistical Office, *Report of the Mass Media Survey, (Radio and Television) 1984*, OPM, Bangkok, p. 35.
18. Sources: National Statistical Office, *Report of the 1990 Household Socio-Economic Survey, Whole Kingdom*, OPM, Bangkok, 1993, p. 121, and National Statistical Office, *Report of the Mass Media Survey, (Radio and Television) 1984*, OPM, Bangkok, p. 12.
19. "Board lifts restrictions on radio commercials," *Bangkok Post*, 24 May 1991.
20. Calculations based on Zenith Media Worldwide, *Asia Pacific Market and MediaFact*, London, various issues.

Chapter 4 Media and Advertising

21. Calculations based on National Statistical Office, *Report of the Cultural Activity Participation and Time Use Survey 1990*, OPM, Bangkok, 1992, p. 27, and National Statistical Office, *Report of the 1990 Household Socio-Economic Survey, Whole Kingdom*, OPM, Bangkok, 1993, p. 121.
22. Supra 17, p. 18.
23. Readership has a broad coverage as it refers to people who have read or just looked at the latest issue of a publication.
24. Supra 1, p. 200.
25. Supra 1, p. 200.
26. Supra 1, p. 200.
27. Supra 17, p. 18.
28. Calculations based on National Statistical Office, *Statistical Handbook of Thailand 1989*, OPM, Bangkok, p. 32–3.
29. Calculations based on National Statistical Office, *Report of the Cultural Activity Participation and Time Use Survey*, OPM, Bangkok, various issues.
30. Supra 4, p. 41.
31. Supra 4, p. 52.
32. Calculations based on National Statistical Office, *Report of the Newspaper Reading Survey 1989*, OPM, Bangkok, p. 24.
33. Supra 4, p. 55.
34. Supra 29, various issues.
35. Source: National Statistical Office, *Statistical Yearbook Thailand 1993*, OPM, Bangkok, 1993, p. 425.
36. Pornpitagpan, Nilibol, "Playing safe for box office hits," *Bangkok Post*, 7 February 1991, Outlook section, p. 23.
37. "Film body fears impact of tariff cut," *Bangkok Post*, 3 August 1993, Business Post section, p. 24.
38. Supra 16, p. 46.
39. Supra 16, pp. 46–7.
40. Supra 1, p. 2.
41. Calculations based on Zenith Media Worldwide, *Asia Pacific Market and MediaFact 1993*, London, 1993, p. 2, and International Monetary Fund, *IFS*, various issues.
42. Panyacheewin, Saowarop "Tamlueng: Nature's recipe for health," *Bangkok Post*, 13 June 1991, Outlook section, p. 23.
43. Supra 1, p. 197.
44. Calculations based on Zenith Media Worldwide, *Asia Pacific Market and MediaFact 1993*, London, 1993, p. 198.

45. Miller, Lee "Ad industry outgrows its strength," *Asian Advertising and Marketing*, 19 November 1993, p. 12.
46. Supra 44, p. 198.
47. Supra 20, various issues.
48. Supra 44, p. 200.
49. Supra 20, various issues.
50. Supra 44, p. 201.
51. Supra 20, various issues.
52. Supra 44, p. 206.
53. Supra 1, p. 2.
54. Supra 20, various issues.

5 PRODUCTION AND TRADE

Thailand is, perhaps, better known for its agriculture and fisheries than for its other industries. The kingdom is a world's leading producer of rubber, pineapples, and prawns and a top exporter of rice and fishing products. It is one of the few net exporters of food in the world. Thailand's agricultural industry also employs the majority of the Thai labor force. This vast sector, however, accounts for only a small part of the Thai GDP.

Mining is also an important activity. Thailand is reputed for its gemstones, especially sapphires and rubies, but it produces about 40 different minerals and prospecting uncovers new resources regularly. The recent findings of oil and gas are, perhaps, the most important changes in this industry. They have contributed to the rapid growth in mining revenue and during the 1980s, the returns from mining expanded by 16 percent per year in real terms.[1]

The manufacturing sector remains, however, Thailand's main success story. Within a few decades it has become the biggest and one of the fastest-growing sectors of the economy (see Figure 5.1). In 1991, the manufacturing industry accounted for 28 percent of the GDP, up from 16 percent in 1970.[2]

Rapid growth has created business opportunities in many sectors. Foreign investment is increasing and it targets a growing range of activities. The following sections introduce the industries of Thailand, review their development, and evaluate their prospects.

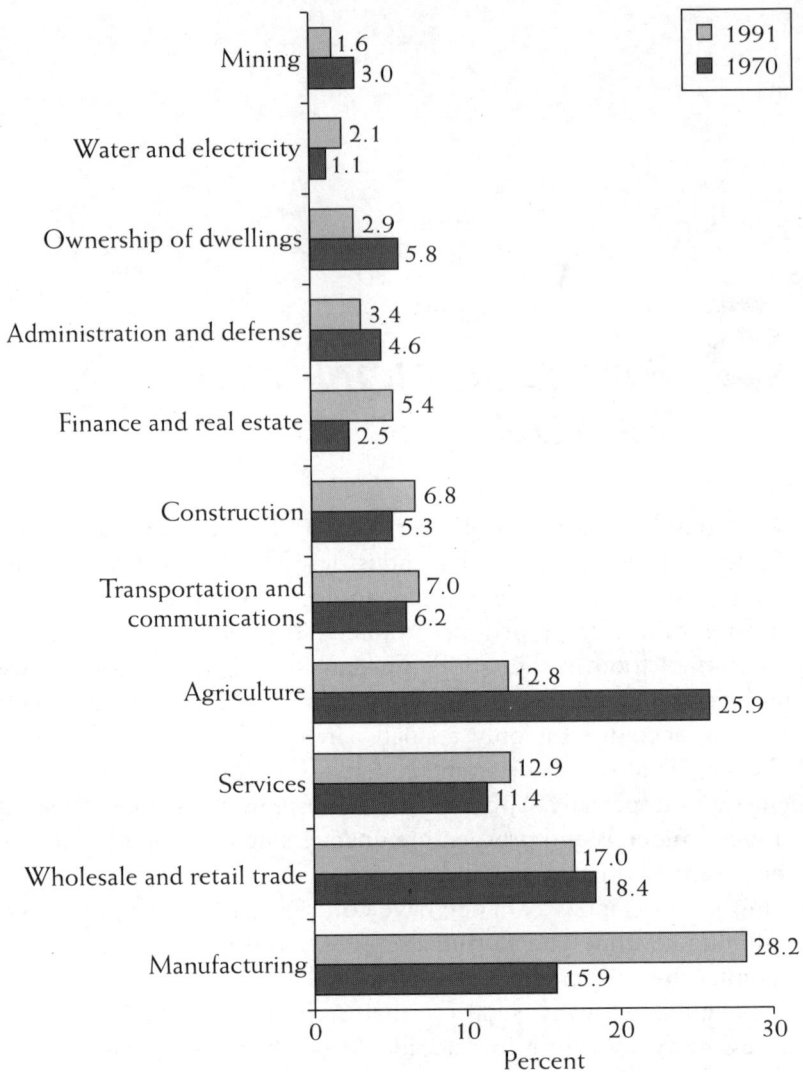

Figure 5.1   GDP by Industrial Origin in 1970 and 1991
(Source: Based on Office of the National Economic and Social Development Board, National Income of Thailand, OPM, Bangkok, various issues.)

Chapter 5 Production and Trade

5.1 AGRICULTURE, FISHERY, FORESTRY

Thai agriculture is diversified, although crops are the mainstay. The kingdom derives about 60 percent of its agricultural revenue from crops (see Figure 5.2). The rest comes from livestock, fisheries, forestry, simple processing, and other agricultural services.

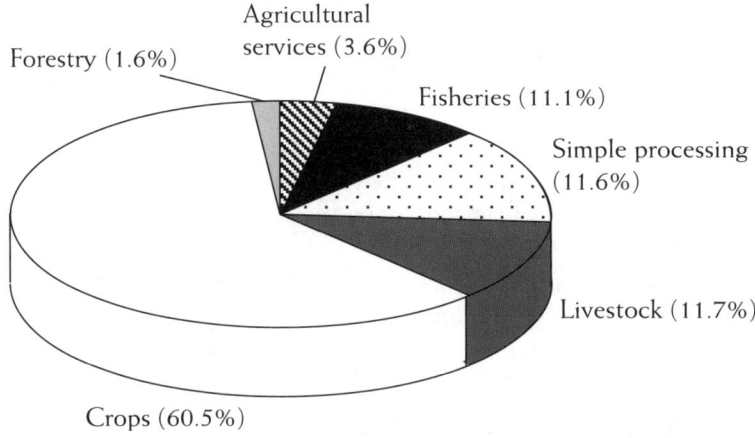

Figure 5.2   Composition of Agricultural Product in 1991 (Source: Based on Office of the National Economic and Social Development Board, National Income of Thailand, Rebase Series 1980–1991, OPM, Bangkok, 1993, p. 11.)

Agriculture is the most traditional industry of Thailand. For over a thousand years, this sector has been the livelihood of the country. At the turn of the century, it still employed nine-tenths of the population and until 1980, it remained the kingdom's single largest source of revenue. Agriculture has now lost its lead, generating only one-eighth of Thailand's GDP in 1991.[3]

This sector is, however, unrivaled in its social role. It employs the largest and poorest segment of the population. In 1991, some 60 percent of Thais were farmers,[4] but they earned only 12 percent of the total income. These people often cultivate the land with meager resources. They lack equipment, fertilizers, pesticides, and quality seeds. Their production is vulnerable to floods, droughts, and pests.

211

Poverty is partly an outcome of the demographic expansion. As families pass farmland to their children, properties have been partitioned. In some places, the land has been so divided that plots are no longer viable.

Because these villagers have no training, their job alternatives are bleak. Those who move to the cities must work at arduous low-paid jobs that make farming look appealing by comparison. Those who work on farms are often indebted and they must take up odd jobs during slack agricultural periods.

Farm incomes are irregular. A poor harvest or a decline in prices may wipe out a family. Some farmers protect themselves by entering into contract farming agreements with processing companies. Farmers then buy raw material from the companies and they sell their crops at a predetermined price. Such agreements are, however, difficult to enforce. People are tempted to default when market prices differ from contract prices.

These arrangements are, nonetheless, the sole regulatory mechanism. There is no futures market in Thailand. Past attempts to organize one have failed because taxes on transactions made the scheme too cumbersome. The idea of a futures market has, however, resurfaced recently. Its proponents argue that it will help farmers stabilize their incomes and encourage them to select their crops carefully. The Securities and Exchange Commission of Thailand announced that it expects to open a futures and option market by 1996.

In the interim, farmers rely on government intervention, and there is no lack of it. Successive administrations have used subsidies and price controls to influence production and support incomes. They have erected trade barriers and for some items, the market is virtually sealed off. A host of agencies and committees organize these interventions, but the Public Warehouse Organization (PWO), established in 1955, is especially powerful.

The PWO is, probably, the principal instrument for intervention. It buys agricultural products to support prices, organizes exports of commodities under government contract, provides low-cost and temporary storage facilities, and grants loans at preferential rates. Its activities have had mixed results. They are expensive, protracted, and not always effective. In addition, they often encourage non-profitable ventures.

Thai agriculture has also received much external support.

International agencies and foreign governments have offered technical cooperation and subsidies. Between 1987 and 1991, technical cooperation, alone, brought US$124 million. Japan was by far the biggest donor, contributing about US$80 million, while Europe followed with US$29 million.[5]

Foreign subsidies to Thailand take different forms. Japanese aid is comprehensive, covering crops, livestock, fisheries, and processing. European aid, in contrast, focuses on crops. In addition, Europe subsidizes Thai farmers indirectly through purchases of certain products above market prices.

5.1.1 CROPS

Thailand's fertile soil and tropical climate are propitious to agriculture. Farmers grow many different products, including cereals, sugar, vegetables, fruits, nuts, peppers, flowers, tobacco, and cotton (see Figure 5.3). Paddy is, however, the biggest output. It makes up a third to a half of the crop revenue depending on production and market value. Other important crops include rubber, cassava, sugarcane, and maize.

Plant species abound. Thailand is one of the most biologically diverse countries in the world. Its vast genetic material supplies both the domestic and foreign agricultural industry. These plants are used in engineering high-yield stronger strains. Domestic research has, however, been limited and many better-quality varieties are developed abroad.

Rice Rice is Thailand's most important crop. In 1991, it accounted for one-third of the revenue from crops. Rice grows in paddy fields throughout the country and especially in Northern, Northeastern, and Central Thailand. Together, these regions yield about 95 percent of the rice crops (see Figure 5.4). The Northeast has the largest planted area but the lowest productivity. Fields in the North and Central, in contrast, have the highest yield per acre. Some of the most fertile areas, especially in the Central Region, produce two crops. This second crop, however, often fetches a lower price because it contains more moisture.

Rice is also a leading source of export revenue. In 1992, the kingdom exported 4.9 million tons of rice worth US$1.43 billion.[6] Although this is below the record high six million tons exported in

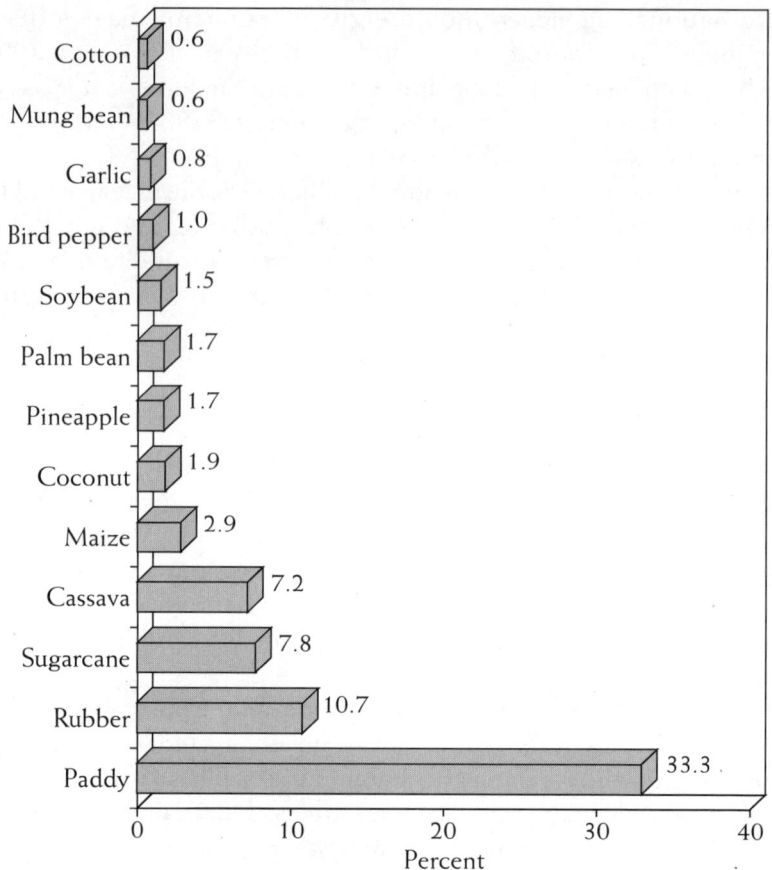

Figure 5.3 Principal Elements of Crop Revenue in 1991
(Source: Based on Office of the National Economic and Social Development Board, National Income of Thailand, Rebase Series 1980–1991, OPM, Bangkok, 1993, p. 20.)

1989, it still makes Thailand the world's largest exporter of rice. The chief product is long-grain white non-glutinous rice, accounting for over 95 percent of the exports. Thai rice supplies foreign markets worldwide, and major buyers include the Middle East, Africa, Asia, and the United States.

Growing rice is the most traditional occupation in Thailand. For centuries, the rice paddy has governed all aspects of life and it was the main source of wealth. The kings rewarded nobles with rice land and before banks existed, people invested their money in rice fields.

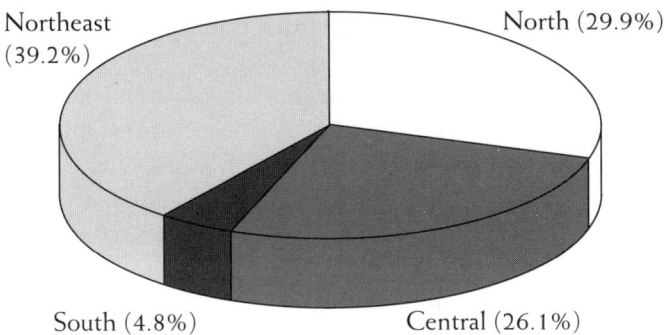

Figure 5.4 Composition of Rice Crop by Region in 1992 (Source: Based on Center for Agricultural Statistics, Agricultural Statistics of Thailand, Crop Year 1991/1992, MAC, Bangkok, 1992, pp. 14–9.)

Rice was then the sole food for almost everyone. Low-grade rice made animal feed, while fermented grains produced alcohol and husks fed furnaces. In those days, a girl's skill at planting rice enhanced her marriage prospects; so did a boy's ability to tie rice bundles.

Thailand has countless indigenous species of rice, but few farmers use them. In 1991, local gene banks stored no less than 19,000 strains of wild rice.[7] Most farmers, however, use high-yield crossbred seeds. About five major strains are said to produce the bulk of the brown, white, glutinous, and non-glutinous rice harvested nationwide.

Crops are often of high quality. The top grade, 100 percent white non-glutinous rice, for instance, accounts for about a third of the exports by volume. The kingdom is also renowned for its fine fragrant rice, a variety which grows mainly in the Northeast. High-quality rice sells primarily in Asia and the Middle East. The lower grades end up in poorer countries.

Lower-quality rice faces much competition from low-cost producers like Vietnam and Pakistan. Its prospects are poor. The Thai government encourages farmers to produce high-grade varieties and it promotes the image of Thai rice abroad. In 1991, for instance, the Commerce Ministry launched a new advertising logo bearing the mention "Original Quality Rice from Thailand" and it organized a rice festival.

Rice trade is controlled. Trading must conform to the Rice Trade Act of 1946 and to the Export Standard Act of 1979. The Rice Trade Act compels exporters to provide details of their purchases and stocks while the Export Standard Act on food staples requires exporters to obtain an export license. Traders must also obtain special permission for importing rice. Until recently, this provision amounted to a virtual ban, but Thailand is now set to let rice in and to restrict imports only through duties.

These laws are remnants of the postwar era, when Asian food supply was limited. At that time, two countries had large export surpluses, Burma and Thailand. Under the peace treaty with Britain, Thailand was obligated to export to Malaysia and to a few other countries a certain quantity of rice, part of it for free and the rest at a given price. High market prices, however, encouraged Thai producers to smuggle rice out of the country. This prevented the government both from fulfilling its obligations and from collecting export tax. Subsequently, the government set up controls on rice milling and trading.

Decades of regulations have restricted competition. Only a few companies trade rice. The top ten traders handle about 60 percent of the rice exports. Distributors in the domestic market are also few. The two leading brands, for instance, control the bulk of the sales of small rice packages.

Rubber   Rubber is Thailand's second most important agricultural product. In 1991, the total output of 1.15 million tons of Para rubber contributed 11 percent of the total revenue from crops. Rubber plantations occupy 1.8 million hectares (4.4 million acres); this is 8 percent of the cultivated land.[8] The vast majority of plantations are located in the South, but there are also a few experimental stations in the Northeast.

Rubber is a fairly recent crop, but it has evolved dramatically. The first rubber trees were introduced at the turn of the century. Initially, growers planted both rubber trees and fruit trees on their land. For many years, production remained below 50,000 tons. It began expanding after the Second World War, following a surge in demand. In the mid-1960s, the Thai government encouraged planters to replace their old rubber trees with new high-yield species and to end mixed planting. Modern plantations with neat rows of rubber trees gradually replaced the old-style forestlike plots.

These changes helped improve yields. Over the past decade, production doubled, although planted area increased by only 20 percent.[9] By 1991, Thailand had overtaken Malaysia as the world's largest producer of rubber.

Expanding crops have encouraged the development of the processing industry. Some two hundred rubber factories operate in the country. They range from small operations set up by local groups of planters to international concerns. Producers of leading brands of tires, for instance, have subsidiaries in Thailand.

These factories produce mainly for the foreign markets. In 1991, Thailand exported US$1.3 billion of rubber products. These comprised 30 million tires, 31 million inner tubes, 1.1 billion pairs of gloves, and 1.3 million tons of other articles of rubber. Leading products are, however, smoked rubber sheets and rubber blocks. Together, they account for 70 percent of the exports by value.[10] Main buyers are Japan, China, Singapore, and the United States.

Aside from producing Para rubber, plantations feed the wood industry. After 25 to 30 years, rubber trees cease to produce latex. Thai planters, then, harvest the wood for furniture and carpentry and they replant their lots with new trees.

Sugar Thais have a good supply of sugar-producing plants, especially sugarcane, coconut palm, and palmyra palm. They yield various kinds of sugars that differ both in taste and texture. Coconut and palm sugars are thick and brown, raw cane sugar makes molasses, and refined cane sugar, the dominant produce, is white and crystalline.

Sugarcane is the principal raw material and a growing source of income. Between 1970 and 1991, its share of crop revenue increased from 1 to 8 percent.[11] In 1992, planted areas occupied 850,000 hectares (2.3 million acres). They are located in upper Thailand and especially in its fertile Central Region, which produces over half of the total crop.[12]

This trend is fairly recent; sugarcane has had various fortunes. In the nineteenth century, production was substantial and Thailand seemed well geared to become a major supplier. By the late 1800s, however, beet sugar from the West replaced cane sugar. Thai exports ceased, domestic production declined, and imports increased. Farmers grew sugarcane only for molasses. Production, however, resumed in the late 1930s with the introduction of foreign, more productive, varieties of sugarcane.

Thailand is now a major supplier of sugarcane. In 1992, growers harvested 47.5 million tons of sugarcane, 4 percent of the world's output, and they exported about US$800 million of sugar and molasses. These products reach foreign markets worldwide, but leading buyers are Asian countries. In 1992, Japan, Malaysia, Indonesia, and South Korea combined purchased about two-thirds of the exported sugar.[13]

The Thai government keeps a tight control over production and distribution. The Cane and Sugar Board, an agency of the Industry Ministry, is the regulator. It controls millers and traders and it sets prices. In 1993, the board instructed Thailand's 46 sugar mills to set aside 1.28 million tons of sugar for domestic consumption. It also set the price of sugarcane gauged at ten CCS (Commercial Cane Sugar, a measure of sweetness) at US$16.5 per ton.

Cassava and tapioca products Thailand is a leading supplier of cassava. In 1992, the kingdom produced 20.4 million tons of fresh cassava root; this is about 13 percent of the world's output. Cassava grows in upper Thailand. About 60 percent of the crop comes from the Northeast and 30 percent from the Central Region. The North accounts for the rest.[14]

Cassava roots feed the tapioca factories. These process the annual 20 million tons of fresh root into about 1.3 million tons of flour and 5.6 million tons of pellets. The bulk of their output supplies foreign markets, especially the European Community (EC), which absorbs about two-thirds of Thai exports of tapioca products.

Until recently, the EC was instrumental in supporting the production of cassava in Thailand. For some time, the community let in about five million tons of Thai tapioca pellets per year at a low import duty. Because the price of tapioca in European markets fetched about three times the world price, Thais kept on producing it.

Throughout this period, the EC encouraged Thai farmers to switch crops, but in vain. Production remained stable. The decline in European intervention prices that started in 1993 is, however, likely to be more effective.

Oil crops Thais grow a variety of oil seeds for the vegetable oil industry, but output is still short of demand. In 1992, the kingdom imported some US$55 million oils and fats.[15] Local production of oil seeds is diverse. Farmers grow soybeans, palm fruits, groundnuts, coconuts, castor beans, sesame seeds, and sunflower seeds. Only palm fruits and soybeans, however, are of any significance. Both benefit from price support and crops are increasing. Between 1982 and 1992, planted areas for each product nearly tripled.[16]

Oil palms grow mainly in the South. Almost all plantations are located in this region. In 1991, they occupied over 146,000 hectares (360,000 acres) and they produced 1.3 million tons of fresh palm fruits.[17] These yielded over 220,000 tons of crude palm oil, most of which supplied the vegetable oil industry. Yet, productivity is lower than in Malaysia, the world's biggest producer, and since Thai prices are higher too, smuggling is rife.

Soybeans grow throughout Thailand, but they are more common in the North. Some 80 percent of the crops come from this region. Planted areas are substantial, covering 348,000 hectares (860,000 acres) in 1992. That year, production reached 436,000 tons.[18] Most of the output supplies the factories of cooking oil and the rest is for animal feed.

Pineapples Pineapples are Thailand's biggest fruit crop. In 1992, the kingdom produced 1.9 million tons of pineapples; this is 19 percent of the world's harvest.[19] Most plantations are located in the Central Region. The bulk of their crops supply processing factories for making juices and other canned products.

Coffee Coffee production is small but growing. In 1992, Thailand produced about 80,000 tons of coffee, up from 19,000 in 1983. Almost all the coffee produced, some 98 percent, comes from the South and the rest from the Central and Northern regions.[20] Producers grow the robusta variety in the South and arabica beans in the North.

Coffee has become a popular drink in Thailand, but growers export the bulk of their crops. They usually sell the beans non-roasted. Leading buyers are the United States, Singapore, Japan, and Europe.

Tobacco Tobacco has been cultivated for some time, especially in the North and in the Northeast. In the 1930s, international brands were already producing cigarettes in Thailand. In 1991, tobacco contributed about 1 percent of the total revenue from crops.[21] Farmers grow four main varieties; Virginia, burley, Turkish, and native. Virginia and burley are more common, together accounting for 87 percent of the crop.

Fibers Thais grow various fibers but in small quantities. The returns from cotton, jute, kenaf, kapok, and silk combined barely exceed 1 percent of the value of all crops.[22] Fibers are, nonetheless traditional products.

Cotton has, perhaps the longest history. It was introduced from India some 26 centuries ago and for many years, it was cultivated for domestic needs. When Thailand opened to international trade in the middle of the nineteenth century, foreign cotton goods became easily available and local production declined. Modern Thais import most of their cotton.

Silk is also an ancient production. Findings in Ban Chiang in the Northeast suggest that Thais produced silk some 2,000 years ago. Following generations kept up with the craft but only for domestic consumption. At the turn of the century, King Chulalongkorn tried to modernize production and improve its commercial potential. The king set up a Department of Sericulture, hired Japanese experts, and opened experimental nurseries to train farmers.

This was not successful. Weaving remained a cottage industry. In the Northeast, where mulberry trees grow well, silk weaving is still a common way of earning money between harvests. Production in this region is often substandard.

5.1.2 LIVESTOCK PRODUCTS

Raising livestock has traditionally been a side occupation in villages. Almost all farmers raise pigs and poultry. They usually sell the pigs and keep the poultry for family consumption. Some also keep dairy cows, goats, sheep, and geese. In addition Thais use cattle and buffaloes as draft animals and they employ elephants to haul logs in the forests and horses to carry bundles in the mountains.

Chickens, swine, cattle, and buffaloes are, however, the principal sources of income. Together they account for over 80 percent of the revenue from livestock (see Figure 5.5). Most breeding areas are in upper Thailand, although each province has its specialties.

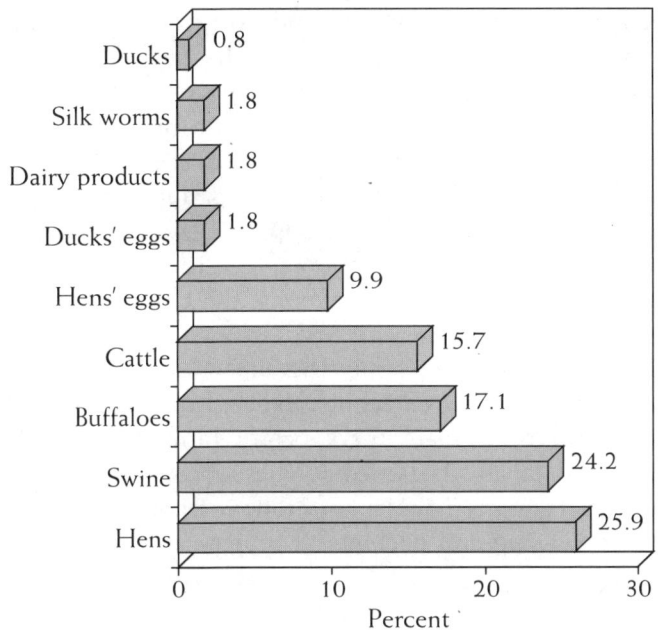

Figure 5.5   Principal Elements of Livestock Revenue in 1991 (Source: Based on Office of the National Economic and Social Development Board, National Income of Thailand, Rebase Series 1980–1991, OPM, Bangkok, 1993, p. 22.)

The Central Region is the main livestock breeding area. Farmers in this region raise over half of Thailand's sheep, swine, and ducks, nearly two-thirds of its chickens and three-quarters of its geese and dairy cows.[23]

The Northeast comes next. It has the biggest herd of buffaloes and cattle in Thailand. This region harbors about 80 percent of the kingdom's buffaloes and a third of its cattle. The Northeast is also renowned for its many swine, ducks, chickens, geese, and horses.[24]

The North stands out for its large number of horses and elephants. About two-thirds of the country's elephants and 43 percent of its horses live in this region, especially in the hilly areas. In addition, northern Thais raise many sheep, goats, cattle, and swine.[25]

The South, in contrast, has little livestock. Only goats and sheep thrive here. The region produces about two-thirds of Thailand's goats and one-fifth of its sheep.[26]

Chickens and swine Chickens and swine, the traditional farm animals, are in growing demand. Over the past decade, numbers increased by two-thirds for swine and by three-quarters for chickens. By 1991, Thailand had 8.2 million pigs and 131 million chickens.[27] This is a large market for animal feed.

Although breeding is often a side occupation for small farmers, companies have set up large-scale operations. This began in the 1970s when an American foundation agreed to provide expertise for raising poultry industrially. Subsequently, the United States supplied parent stock to Thai breeders.

Chickens and pigs now supply the expanding industry of frozen meat. Leading processing companies export frozen chicken and pork worldwide and their main markets are Hong Kong, Malaysia, Singapore, and Japan. These companies operate in a competitive environment. They keep abreast of modern techniques, investing in advanced processing and packing machinery and equipment.

Dairy cows Dairy farming is a cottage industry. In 1991, about 15,000 farmers raised Thailand's 191,000 dairy cows.[28] This is an average of 13 cows per farmer. Breeders often lack experience because dairy farming developed only recently. In the past, only the Indian community produced milk. Modern Thai farmers usually join cooperatives which provide training, equipment, veterinary assistance, and sales support.

The industry relies on government incentives. It expanded after 1971, when the Thai government set up the Dairy Farming Promotion Organization to produce and promote dairy products. The administration also required that factories buy part of their raw milk from local producers and that they increase production regularly.

Prospects are good. Although the consumption of milk products is still low, it is increasing gradually. The Bangkok Bank estimates that between 1985 and 1991 per capita consumption increased from 2 to 12 liters of milk (0.5 to 3 gallons).[29]

This has encouraged Thai farmers to upgrade their cattle breeding stock. Many import heifers from overseas. Leading suppliers are Australia, New Zealand, and the United States. American breeding stock usually comes from Texas. It is more expensive than its Australian counterpart, but it is highly regarded by Thai farmers. Thailand has even become a leading export market for Texan heifers.

Elephants Elephants, once revered as the emblem of the royalty and as symbols of power, are becoming scarce. Between 1981 and 1991, their number has declined from 3,700 to 2,900.[30] The logging ban of 1989 has enhanced the trend. It put scores of elephants out of work and made them more valuable dead than alive. Poachers are now preying on them for hides and ivory.

5.1.3 FISHERY

Thailand has a large fishing industry that ranks among the biggest in the world. The annual catch reaches about three million tons, some 92 percent of which is marine fish and the rest freshwater fish. Marine fishing takes place in coastal, offshore, and deep-sea areas and inland fishing in rivers, reservoirs, and inundated areas.

Activities concentrate in the Central and Southern regions. In 1990, 43 percent of the 21,500 fishing vessels registered in Thailand were based in the Central Region and the rest in the South.[31] The catch is diverse, but it comprises many fishes. In 1990, fishes made up some three-quarters of the catch by volume; shellfish and mollusks accounted for the rest (see Figure 5.6).

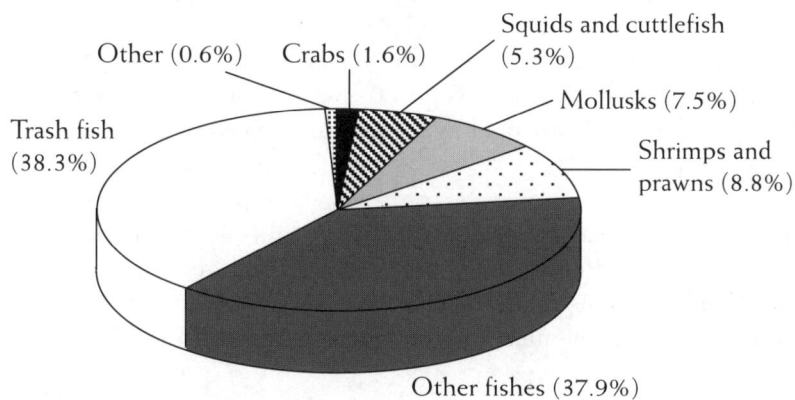

Figure 5.6 *Marine Fish Caught by Type in 1990*
(*Source:* Based on Center for Agricultural Statistics, *Agricultural Statistics of Thailand, Crop Year 1991/1992*, MAC, Bangkok, 1992, pp. 123–4.)

Factories process much of the output. Better quality products are canned or frozen, while the trash fish that is cheap or not suitable for consumption supplies the fishmeal industry. Processing plants are often located inland, although some floating factories collect trash fish from fishermen and process it on board.

The industry is well established because fishing is a traditional activity. At the turn of the century, fish was the main source of protein. It was served at almost every meal, especially in sea coastal areas. People consumed then fresh, dried, preserved, and salted fish. Traders even exported Thai preserved fish to Hong Kong and Singapore. Thailand has maintained its prominence and it is especially renowned for prawn and tuna.

Prawn farming Fishing activities have taken a new stimuli with the development of aquaculture, especially prawn farming. Between 1981 and 1990, the number of aquaculture farms quadrupled. By 1990 16,300 farms operated in Thailand and they occupied 66,000 hectares (163,000 acres). These farms have become the kingdom's principal suppliers of prawns and shrimps. In 1990, they accounted for over half of total production, compared to 10 percent in 1980.[32]

Aquaculture has existed for some time, but it became important with the introduction of black tiger prawns. Production started in the early 1980s in the Bangkok area. Later, prawn farms spread east toward Cambodia and south toward Malaysia. This helped Thailand become a top producer and exporter of prawns.

Thai prawns are sold mainly on foreign markets. In 1992, Thailand exported some 143,000 tons of prawns worth about US$1.3 billion.[33] Principal buyers are Japan, Europe, and the United States.

Prawn farming is, however, controversial. Operators often settle in mangrove forest areas because these have fairly level ground and are close to the sea. Prawn ponds then replace the forest and pollute the environment. The main problem is the waste water containing excrements and chemicals that farmers release into the sea.

Tuna Tuna is the second most important fishery product in Thailand. In 1991, the kingdom exported over 300,000 tons of processed tuna worth US$720 million.[34] Principal products are frozen and canned tuna.

5.1.4 FORESTRY

Forestry is declining. Its contribution to the nation's GDP has become negligible and the bulk of its output is charcoal and firewood (see Figure 5.7). The size of the forest has also declined dramatically. Between 1950 and 1991, the proportion of land covered with forest dropped from 62 to 27 percent.[35] Logging companies are still active, but they operate outside Thailand. They work concessions in Burma, Laos, and Cambodia and they supply Thai sawmills.

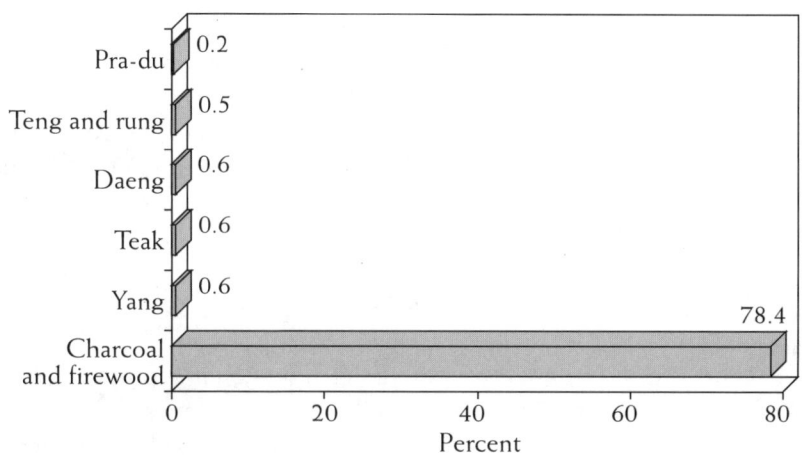

Figure 5.7 Principal Elements of Forestry Revenue in 1991
(Source: Based on Office of the National Economic and Social Development Board, National Income of Thailand, Rebase Series 1980–1991, OPM, Bangkok, 1993, p. 24.)

Forestry is an old industry, but it officially started at the end of the nineteenth century. In 1896, the Thai government set up a Forest Department to control logging. The department prohibited work in unleased areas and it appointed forest officers to enforce the leases.

Thai forests were then prized for their teak wood. This valuable tree from Northern Thailand supplied foreign markets, especially India and Europe. At the turn of the century, Thailand exported 45,000 tons of teak per year. Loggers killed the trees by girdling them at the base and they left them to season for a couple of years before felling them. Elephants dragged the logs to the rivers and floated them to Bangkok.

Most of Thailand's valuable trees have now disappeared. Thai forests have suffered from extensive logging and from the activities of the military and of the farmers. In the 1970s, Thai armed forces burnt large tracts of forest to dislodge communist guerillas. This has ceased, but a new threat has come from landless farmers. These people encroach the forest to cultivate crops. Thai officials estimate that encroachers occupy about six million hectares (15 million acres); this is nearly half the size of the remaining Thai forest.[36]

Attempts to stop deforestation have been ineffective. The 1989 logging ban failed to stop illegal logging, while reforestation programs on encroached land met strong resistance. Villagers fight eviction and they oppose plans to develop commercial eucalyptus plantations, contending that these fast-growing hardwood trees reduce the water table.

Few commercial reforestation projects gain acceptance. Those which do often provide benefits to the local communities. Some pulp and paper plants, for instance, treat their waste water and release it to nearby agricultural areas.

5.2 EXTRACTIVE RESOURCES

Thailand is rich in extractive resources. The country produces over 40 different minerals, including lignite, zinc, tin, limestone (for the cement industry), gypsum, and gemstones. Prospecting regularly uncovers new resources. Recently found gas and oil, for instance, are now top earners of mining income.

Returns from mining are variable. They are sensitive to fluctuations in commodity prices. A one-time top income earner may become non-profitable when its price drops. Tin, for instance, has been a casualty of price changes. The sharp decline in tin prices have reduced the contribution of tin to the mining revenue from 69 percent in 1980 to 0.8 percent in 1991 (see Figure 5.8).

A host of mining companies operate in Thailand. They range from small operators to major international concerns. Some of the biggest local and multinational companies are prospecting and exploiting resources both inland and offshore.

5.2.1 OIL AND GAS

Thailand has sizeable deposits of petroleum. Sites are located inland

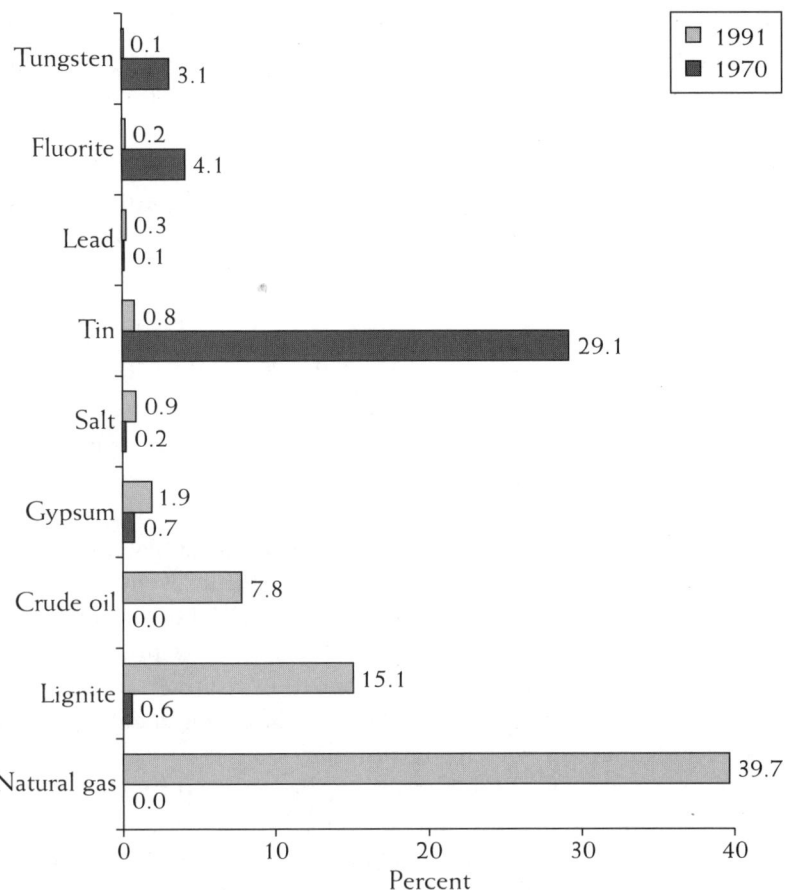

*Figure 5.8 Principal Elements of Mining Revenue in 1991
(Source: Based on Office of the National Economic and Social Development Board, National Income of Thailand, Rebase Series 1980–1991, OPM, Bangkok, 1993, p. 260.)*

in various regions and offshore in the Gulf of Thailand and in the Andaman Sea. They yield natural gas, crude oil, and condensate. Natural gas is, however, the principal output. In 1992, Thai wells produced 301,700 million cubic feet of natural gas, 9.6 million barrels of condensate, and 9.1 million barrels of crude oil.[37]

Thais have known about their petroleum resources for some time, but large-scale exploration did not start until recently. At the turn of the century, people found oil in remote parts of Northern Thailand near the Burmese border. They dug shallow pits and they skimmed the oil from the water that collected in the pits. The amount produced was insignificant, but no systematic prospecting and exploration could be envisaged until communications and technology improved.

The oil industry has since become large and competitive. Some of the world's biggest oil companies are now operating in Thailand and smaller enterprises have also joined in. They are involved in all aspects of production, including exploration, extraction, refining, transformation, and distribution of oil products.

Domestic production, however, falls short of consumption. In 1992, only 30 percent of the petroleum consumed was produced locally.[38] The rest comes from various places, but especially the Middle East and Southeast Asia.

Gas   Gas has become Thailand's principal extractive resource. In 1991, it accounted for 40 percent of the mining revenue.[39] Most of the natural gas comes from the Gulf of Thailand, but recent findings suggest that the Korat plateau in the Northeast has potential. Some of the natural gas deposits that prospecting teams have discovered there are commercially viable. These findings are encouraging and more companies are seeking exploration licenses.

The potential of the kingdom is, however, difficult to assess because systematic prospecting is recent. It started in 1962, when an American company drilled Thailand's first exploration well. The company had then obtained the first petroleum exploration license ever issued in Thailand. It discovered gas fields in the late 1970s and extraction started in 1981. By 1983, natural gas had become Thailand's biggest mining resource.

Crude oil   The production of crude oil is small. In 1991, it accounted for only 8 percent of the mining revenue.[40] Wells supply domestic refineries, which produce gasoline, diesel fuel, kerosene, and liquefied petroleum gas.

Oil fields are spread out and companies operate both inland and offshore. Onshore fields are often small reservoirs formed by sedimentary rocks, but some are viable. Offshore fields are scarce. By 1991, only three oil fields had been uncovered in the Gulf of Thailand. The Andaman Sea may have resources, but exploration is limited because sites are located in deep areas.

5.2.2 LIGNITE

Lignite, an inferior form of coal, has become a prized mineral. In 1991, its output made up 15 percent of the mining revenue.[41] Production has increased to meet the growing demand for energy. Between 1988 and 1992, it doubled, increasing from 7.2 to 15.6 million tons.[42] Thais use the bulk of their lignite, some three-quarters, to produce electricity. The rest supplies other industries, notably the cement factories, where coal often fuels furnaces.

Thailand has many small seams of coal in the North and in the South, but the bulk of the production comes from the northern mines of Lampang and Lamphun. The state-owned Electricity Generating Authority of Thailand is the kingdom's biggest producer. It mines coal for its own power plants.

5.2.3 TIN

Thailand is a major producer of tin and a member of the Association of Tin Producing Countries.[43] For many years tin has been a leading income earner. In 1980, for instance, it accounted for 69 percent of the mining revenue. Growing production of other resources, like oil and gas, and reduced tin mining activities have, however, lowered this figure to only 0.8 percent in 1991.

Deposits are located in the Central, Northern, and Southern regions, but the biggest mining areas are in the South, both inland and offshore. Mining in this region is a traditional occupation which has attracted a regular influx of Chinese migrants over the past centuries.

Smelting, in contrast, started recently. Thai tin ore used to supply Malaysian and Singaporean smelters. This ended in 1965 when a private company set up Thailand's first tin smelter. Others followed.

Smelters were established when prices were high and production was substantial. They obtained ample supplies of ore from the many mining companies. These ranged from large-scale concerns to individual operations. Among the biggest was the state-owned Offshore Mining Organization, which was set up in 1975 to operate concessions in the Gulf of Thailand.

Companies then used the gamut of mining techniques. Offshore, they employed both large-scale dredgers and small suction boats. Inland, they resorted to gravel pumping, ground sluicing, and open-pit mining.

Falling prices in the mid-1980s halted many of these mining and smelting activities. Production declined rapidly as the number of active mines dropped from 735 in 1983 to 140 in 1992.[44] Smelters ran short of raw material and scaled down their operations, while the Offshore Mining Organization accumulated losses. The company is now earmarked for dissolution. Many other operators converted their mining land into development projects, especially golf courses.

Tinplate is perhaps the only prosperous activity. Output is increasing with the growing demand in the canning industry and in some export-oriented products like electrical appliances and computers.

5.2.4 ZINC

Known deposits of zinc are small. Thailand's only mine is a forty-hectare (hundred-acre) site in the Tak province, 400 kilometer (250 miles) north of Bangkok. In 1992, it produced 422,000 tons of ore.[45] Because reserves are nearing depletion, quality is declining. In 1992, the average zinc content of the ore was 18 percent, down from 28 percent in 1984 when exploitation began. In addition, the ore holds much sulfur and it needs sophisticated purifying techniques.

It took a combination of tariff protection, government subsidies, and high zinc prices for zinc production to remain profitable. These factors contributed to the success of the mine operator and refiner, which has emerged as a top mineral-based conglomerate. In 1992, it produced 61,000 tons of zinc ingot and 9,000 tons of zinc alloy[46] and it held interests in the prospecting and mining of various minerals, including gold, potash, and copper.

Despite the depletion of local resources, zinc smelting still has potential. Thai companies intensify prospecting in neighboring countries, especially in Burma and Vietnam, where they have obtained rights to mine minerals.

5.2.5 OTHER MINERALS

Gemstones Gems are, perhaps, the most celebrated mining products in Thailand. The kingdom is renowned for its abundance of colored gemstones, especially sapphires and rubies. Years of mining have depleted local resources and high-quality stones are now scarce. Mines are nonetheless still active, producing sapphires, rubies, zircons, quartz, and garnets. The Central Region is the main gem-producing area. Principal mines are in Chantaburi and Trat near Cambodia and in Kanchanaburi near Burma. In 1990, these three areas combined produced 3.6 million carats of gemstones.

Chantaburi is especially important for the gem trade. It is located at the heart of a large gem-bearing tract of land that runs from Trat in Thailand to Pailin in Cambodia. Pailin is reputed for its high-quality sapphires and rubies. The vast majority of people in this area live off gem-related businesses. These people are leading suppliers of gems to Bangkok dealers.

Gypsum   The production of gypsum is expanding rapidly. Between 1986 and 1992, it increased from 1.7 million tons to 7.1 million tons.[47] The main producing areas are in the North and in the South. This mineral is especially valuable for producing gypsum boards and cement. The bulk of the output is exported, especially to Japan. In 1992, the kingdom exported 5.7 million tons of gypsum ore, 60 percent of which went to Japan. Other important buyers include Taiwan, South Korea, Malaysia, and Indonesia.

Rock salt   Thailand has large reserves of rock salt that are said to be some of the world's largest. Deposits are located in the Northeast, where about 30 percent of the land has high salt content. Known reserves approach 5 billion tons, enough to supply the domestic market for decades. Rock salt is not valuable, but it has many applications. It is used in the production of chlorine, plastic, batteries, corrugated iron, dyes, Freon, soap, detergent, seasoning powder, toothpaste, and fish sauce.

The mining of rock salt started a long time ago, but intensified recently. In the early 1900s the Northeast produced salt for domestic consumption and for export. In those days, people dug wells to collect the brine that they crystallized by boiling. In the mid-1970s, when prospecting uncovered large deposits, production increased.

Producers are diverse. They range from small family businesses to large producers. Only a few companies, however, have large-scale operations. They mine their own salt and buy raw material from smaller operators.

Ceramic clay Reserves of ceramic clay, which include both ball clay and kaolin, are substantial. The biggest deposits are located in the North and there are a few other mines in the Central and Southern regions. The bulk of the output supplies mainly local producers.

5.3 MANUFACTURED PRODUCTS

Manufacturing is the prime beneficiary of Thailand's economic growth. In 1981, it superseded agriculture as the biggest sector of the economy and by 1991, it accounted for over 28 percent of the GDP. Manufacturing is also developing rapidly. Between 1970 and 1991, it has grown annually by 10 percent in real terms, compared to 7.4 percent for the whole economy.[48]

The manufacturing sector owes its expansion partly to international investment. Over the past two decades, many foreign companies, especially Japanese businesses, have relocated their labor-intensive production lines to low-cost areas. Because of its cheap and large labor force, Thailand has been a prime destination for these companies. Investors have diverse interests, but they are especially involved in the production of electrical goods, machinery, textiles, transportation equipment, footwear, and clothing. Incidentally, these industries have become some of the biggest contributors to the manufacturing product (see Figure 5.9).

Manufacturers further benefited from a sheltered environment. The Thai government granted investors tax holidays, trade protection, and on occasions, exclusive rights to produce for a specific period. New businesses may still expect tax incentives, but they operate in a more competitive environment because of the gradual decline of trade restrictions.

Production is also getting more capital-intensive. Increasing wages are eroding Thailand's labor-cost advantage. The kingdom no longer competes with low-cost areas like China and Vietnam. Manufacturers are upgrading their output and production processes. Sophisticated labor-saving machinery is in high demand. Companies are also keen on improving their human resources; training programs for technical staff and middle management are successful.

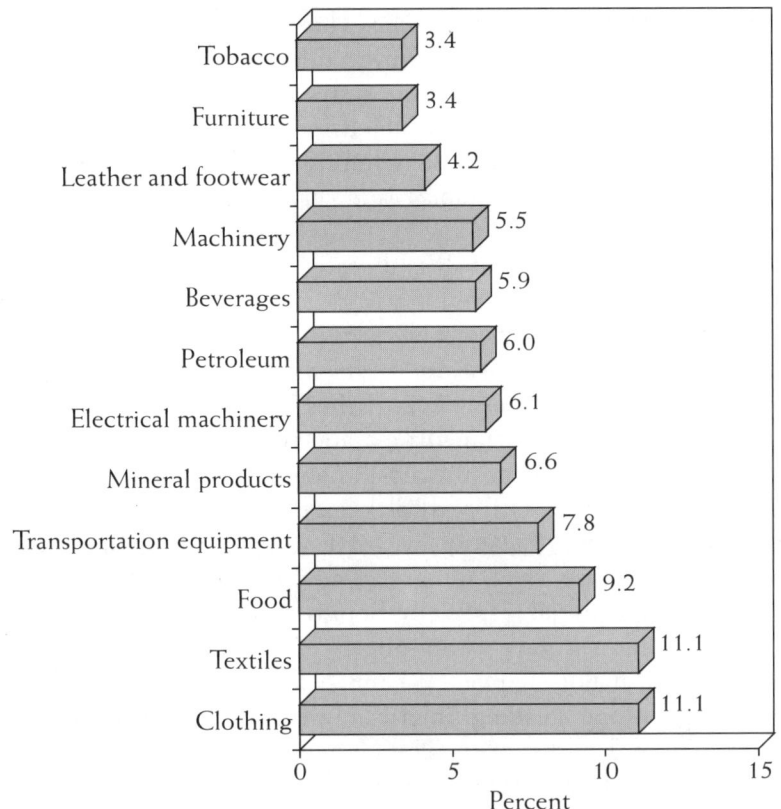

Figure 5.9 Principal Elements of Manufacturing Revenue in 1991 (Source: Based on Office of the National Economic and Social Development Board, National Income of Thailand, Rebase Series 1980–1991, OPM, Bangkok, 1993, p. 28.)

5.3.1 FOOD PROCESSING

The food processing industry is an outcome of Thailand's extensive agriculture. It was once the country's biggest manufacturing industry. Food processing has expanded steadily although not as rapidly as other industries and it has lost its preeminence. In 1991, it accounted for about 9 percent of the manufacturing output, down from 20 percent in 1970. Although no longer a leader, the food processing industry remains an important export earner. Its products are sold worldwide.

Processing techniques are diverse. Thais can, freeze, preserve, and dehydrate food. Canning is, however, the most common method. It applies to fruits, vegetables, fish, and seafood products. Freezing, introduced more recently, is confined to few items, mainly seafood and poultry. Preserving and dehydrating are less popular and used only for a few fruits, vegetables, and seafood products.

Fish and seafood The fish and seafood processing industry is a main income earner. Thailand is a world's leading supplier of fishery products. In 1992, exports reached US$3 billion.[49] Factories produce mainly canned and frozen seafood. They can shrimps, squids, clams, crab, and tuna, and they freeze fishes and prawns. Their main products, however, are canned tuna and frozen prawns.

Canned tuna is, perhaps, the most renowned Thai fishery product. Since the mid-1980s, Thailand has been the world's biggest supplier of canned tuna. In 1992, exports totaled US$530 million.[50] A few products dominate the industry. They process both local and imported raw material, especially bonito and skipjack.

Thai products figure prominently on foreign markets. The kingdom is a major supplier of canned tuna to Japan, the United States, and Europe. Leading American brands, for instance, buy their products from Thai factories. The United States accounts for about half of Thailand's exports of canned tuna.

Frozen prawns is a more recent produce, but it has become a top income earner. In 1992, frozen prawns accounted for about one-third of the kingdom's exports of fishery products by value. Black tiger prawns are the main produce. They fetch high prices, and they are especially prized in Japan.

Chicken The processing of chicken has expanded with the development of industrial breeding. In the early 1970s, large-scale breeders set up processing plants to slaughter, cut, bone, pack, and freeze chickens. Frozen Thai chicken has now gained acceptance worldwide. Main markets are Japan, Europe, and Singapore. Thai producers are, however, facing growing competition from companies in China and Brazil, which have lower costs of production.

Animal feed The growing breeding activities have increased the demand for animal feed. Local producers are well established and several are listed on the stock exchange. These companies are some of the biggest suppliers of animal feed in Asia and they have operations worldwide. Product lines are extensive covering feed for poultry, cattle, pigs, horses, dogs, cats, shrimps, and fishes.

Fruits and vegetables Thai factories process large quantities of fruits and vegetables. Their products are sold worldwide and in 1991, exports reached US$700 million.[51] Processed fruits are especially important, accounting for some three-quarters of the exports by value.

The industry relies on local raw material. Thais grow vast quantities of high-quality fruits and vegetables year-round, and factories process many of these. Nuts, peaches, grapes, citrus, apples, cherries, pears, longans, rambutans, mangoes, guava, pineapples, bamboo shoots, young corn, peas, beans, asparagus, sweet corn, tomatoes, and turnips are some of the products that factories process. A few goods, however, dominate. Pineapples are, by far, the principal raw material. They account for about 80 percent of fruits processed. Among vegetables, bamboo shoots and young corn are especially prominent.

Canning is the single most important processing method. Over 90 percent of the fruits and most of the vegetables processed are canned. Preserving, drying, and freezing are marginal by comparison. Processing plants operate near the growing areas. Many pineapple canneries, for instance, are located in the Central Region in Rayong and Prachuap Khiri Khan.

Factories often process different products to keep active year-round. In the North, plants can both longans, lychees, and baby corn, all of which are harvested locally but at different periods. Similarly, tomato processing plants in the Northeast also produce canned pineapples.

Thai canned products are reputed for quality. They have secured steady sales in North America and Europe, and they are also distributed in Asian markets. The main competition comes from producers in China and the Philippines, whose products are cheaper, although of a lower quality.

This successful industry has attracted both local and foreign investors. Leading international producers have set up operations in Thailand and some of the biggest manufacturers grow their own fruits and vegetables.

5.3.2 BEVERAGES AND TOBACCO

The industries of beverages and tobacco are developing less rapidly. Between 1980 and 1991, production increased by 6 percent per year in real terms for beverages and by 2 percent for tobacco.[52]

Non-alcoholic beverages Thai companies produce and distribute a wide range of non-alcoholic beverages. Many have entered into agreements or joint ventures with international brands to manufacture and sell their products. Stores carry a variety of soft drinks, health drinks, energy drinks, iced teas and coffees, mineral water, and fruit juices. They cater to a small, but growing, market.

Soft drinks are getting especially popular. In 1992, local factories produced 1,300 million liters (330 million gallons) of soft drinks, up from 800 million liters (210 million gallons) in 1988.[53] As almost all the output is for domestic consumption, this suggests that the average Thai consumes 67 cans of soft drinks annually.

Both regular and diet versions are now available. Diet drinks gained official acceptance in 1991, when the Food and Drug Administration (FDA) agreed to classify aspartame, a sweetener used in diet drinks, as a food instead of medicine. This cleared the way for distribution in grocery stores. These beverages, however, still have a narrow market, selling mainly to upper-income health-conscious Thais and to tourists. They are available at major supermarkets, hotels, and tourist shops.

Other beverages have much broader coverage. They sell throughout the country in supermarkets, corner stores, and stalls. Distributors have set up networks of warehouses covering most provinces and they run fleets of delivery trucks and *tuk-tuks* (three-wheel motorcycles).

Alcoholic beverages Alcoholic beverages are less diverse. Consumption focuses on beer and whiskey. Distributors also import small quantities of foreign liquors and wines for expatriates, upper-income Thais, and foreign visitors.

Beer is in growing demand. Between 1988 and 1992, total consumption almost tripled, increasing from 130 to 325 million liters[54] (34 to 85 million gallons). However, consumption remains small by Western standards. In 1992, it was only 6 liters (1.5 gallon) per person per year,[55] compared to 30–50 liters (8–13 gallons) in the West.

There are few producers. The two leading local brands share the bulk of the market. Until recently, imports have been marginal, capturing less than 1 percent of sales. Years of protectionism had sheltered local breweries. New policies, however, advocate a freer market and they open the industry to new entrants.

Competition is increasing. Breweries expand their capacities and they introduce new products, while foreign companies set up new plants. The industry has much potential, although high taxes have restricted demand.

The production of liquor is more stable. Between 1988 and 1992, output has been virtually unchanged at about 600 million liters[56] (158 million gallons). The Thai government holds a large stake in the industry through its company, Liquor Distillery Organization, and it restricts entry.

Whiskey is the principal produce. It is the national drink, and in poorer places it is often the sole alcoholic beverage. Thai whiskey is cheap, but it is often low quality. Distilleries are, however, keen to upgrade their products to international standards, and they set up liquor-aging facilities.

Distributors of foreign beverages cater to a smaller market. Their imported Western-style wines, beers, and liquors are sold only in pubs, wine bars, international hotels, resorts, and golf courses.

Packaging of beverages The packaging of beverages is traditional but changing. Until recently, most factories bottled their products. Increasing wages are now discouraging such time-consuming techniques. Producers are turning to alternative methods, especially canning.

Few companies produce packaging material for beverages. The principal one was set up in 1968 as a joint venture between a Japanese manufacturer of packaging products and Thai producers of beer, water, and soft drinks. The company has the marketing advantage of selling almost all its products to its shareholders. Until recently, it specialized in producing bottle caps. Since 1990, however, it has also been producing two-piece aluminum-can bodies.

Tobacco products The Thai administration controls the production of tobacco. The state-owned Thailand Tobacco Monopoly, established in 1939, is the sole manufacturer of cigars and cigarettes. Between 1974 and 1990, it was also the sole legal supplier of tobacco products because the Thai government banned imports of foreign cigarettes. Smuggling, however, was rife and most street vendors sold foreign cigarettes. This allowed top international brands to gain a foothold on the market.

The ban no longer exists, but regulations on distribution have become tighter. In 1992, the government enacted the Non-Smokers' Health Protection Act and the Tobacco Product Control Act. They require owners and operators of public places and vehicles to arrange for non-smoking sections. The laws also prohibit the sale of cigarettes to people under 18 years old and sales through vending machines. In addition, cigarette warnings must cover at least 25 percent of the surface of the packet and they must be printed in black and white.

More controversial perhaps are the restrictions on advertising. Regulations ban all types of advertising and marketing promotions, including at points of sale. Distributors must rely on indirect publicity and low pricing to increase sales. Indirect publicity comes from products with similar brand names. Some local goods like shoes, clothes, and audio equipment are sold under popular foreign labels. Those bearing the names of famous brands of cigarettes have become valuable sources of "free" advertising.

Nonetheless the Thailand Tobacco Monopoly remains profitable. Sales keep growing. In 1992, the company produced 40,700 tons of cigarettes, up from 34,000 tons in 1988.[57] It is a substantial source of income to the Thai government, contributing to excise and retail taxes and profits.

5.3.3 TEXTILE, CLOTHING, AND FOOTWEAR

Textile, clothing, and footwear are leading industries in Thailand. They have expanded rapidly over the past few decades as foreign entrepreneurs relocated their labor-intensive production lines in low-cost areas. In 1991, they accounted for over a quarter of Thailand's manufacturing product.[58] A host of producers are now operating. They range from small family businesses to large multinational groups. In 1992, 29 were listed on the stock exchange.

Large-scale manufacturing is, however, fairly new to Thailand. Until World War II, textile and clothing were cottage industries. Most homes had a loom to cater to the needs of the household.

People made silk and cotton cloth, often using imported yarn. The production of footwear was also minimal because most people walked with their feet bare.

Textile and clothing Textile and clothing are large and diverse industries. They are Thailand's biggest sources of manufacturing revenue. Companies produce a wide array of goods both in natural and synthetic fibers. They operate at all stages of production, including spinning, knitting, weaving, dyeing, printing, and finishing.

Heavy duties on imports of semifinished and finished products have encouraged this vertical integration. Producers rely mainly on domestic goods for inputs and they import only goods that are not available locally.

Cotton is the principal such product. It is the only material imported in large quantities. In 1992, Thais bought US$543 million of cotton in raw form from a variety of suppliers, including Pakistan, the United States, Australia, Sudan, Ivory coast, and China.[59]

Factories also use various other natural fibers, but silk is, probably, the most renowned. For centuries, Thais have been weaving silk for domestic consumption. Larger-scale commercial production started only after World War II, when American engineer Jim Thompson convinced weavers to produce cloth in longer length than the traditional sarong-size and to use colorfast chemical dyes.

Subsequently, the industry expanded, but it was soon regulated. Thai authorities required that weavers buy their thread from local spinners at a predetermined price. The local thread remained substandard and the reputation of Thai silk abroad deteriorated. Requirements are now less stringent, but they change frequently and they affect production. The quality of silk goods is still variable.

Man-made fibers are less famous, but they are in growing demand. In 1992, factories produced 360,000 tons of synthetic fibers, up from 156,000 tons in 1988.[60] The industry is competitive. Some of the leading international manufacturers have set up large production plants in Thailand.

These have based their expansion almost entirely on low labor costs. For many years, manufacturers have relied on labor-intensive production techniques, investing little in machinery. They produced medium- and low-quality goods. Processes which require skills, like dyeing and printing, seldom met international standards.

Increasing wages are now changing these strategies. Leading producers are investing in modern labor-saving equipment. They are also keen to employ higher-quality personnel. Trade associations provide members with information on the latest technology and they help them upgrade the quality of labor. They also organize special courses to train staff.

Footwear The footwear industry is more specialized, but it is successful. Between 1970 and 1991, it has grown annually by 12 percent in real terms.[61] Expansion was especially rapid during the 1980s when Taiwanese and Hong Kong companies relocated their factories in Thailand. Products are, however, restricted. Most are sports shoes and rubber slippers.

Producers supply mainly foreign markets. In 1992, exports of footwear totaled about US$1 billion.[62] Leading American brands of sports gear buy their products from Thai manufacturers. Quality is improving steadily and some local suppliers are now capable of producing entire lines of shoes, including the top-end goods.

5.3.4 OIL AND CHEMICALS

Findings of oil and gas in the Gulf of Thailand have boosted the development of the petroleum industry. A host of new plants for heavy petrochemical and related products are under construction. Many are located in Map Ta Phud, 190 kilometers (120 miles) southeast of Bangkok. The industrial estates and deepwater industrial port in this area are especially designed to service the petrochemical industry.

The Thai government has invested heavily in the oil industry. It has set up companies and has formed joint ventures with the private sector. Its enterprise, Petroleum Authority of Thailand, for instance, is a key player. It holds a monopoly over the distribution of gas and it is the sole supplier of fuel oil and diesel oil to the state-owned Electricity Generating Authority of Thailand. The Petroleum Authority of Thailand also has majority stakes in local oil companies and refineries.

Foreign firms have, nonetheless, gained a strong foothold on the market. Long-established American, Dutch, and British companies have become major players, while various other companies from Europe and the Middle East also operate in the kingdom.

Oil refineries Competition is increasing. Oil refineries were among the first petroleum industries to be deregulated. In 1990, the Thai government eased restrictions on the establishment of new refineries, attracting foreign investors. Until then, only three companies, a leading American concern and two partly state-owned enterprises, had operated refineries.

Growing competition encourages companies to upgrade their products. They install sulfur-recovery and hydro-treating units to produce high-quality low-sulfur diesel fuel. They also invest in octane-upgrading units and catalytic reformers to produce high-octane unleaded gasoline.

Gasoline Gasoline is in growing demand and gas stations are sprouting in all regions. In March 1993, there were over 3,800 gas stations nationwide.[63] Because most vehicles circulate in the Central Region, many stations, nearly half, are located in this area. The rest are spread throughout the country (see Figure 5.10).

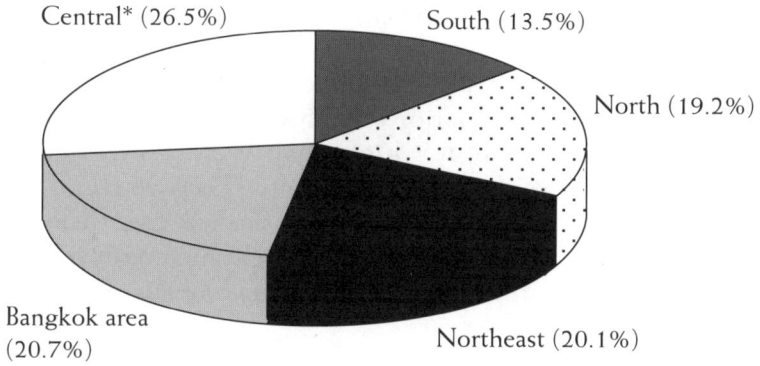

*Excluding the Bangkok area.

Figure 5.10   Distribution of Gas Stations by Region in 1993 (Source: BANGKOK POST/Thailand Department of Commercial Registration— July 9, 1993, Motoring section, p. 3.)

Operators are a mixture of small local enterprises and large international companies. Until recently, the four leading distributors controlled about 85 percent of the market. Their preeminence is, however, eroding as new companies join in. The most active ones open several new outlets each month.

241

Marketing strategies differ. International operators emphasize distribution in Bangkok and in Central Thailand. Local concerns focus on the provinces, especially those in the North, Northeast, and South. Some target the rural areas, setting up small one-pump stations for high-speed diesel. In addition, independent distributors, usually small local marketing firms selling gasoline under unfamiliar brand names, are prominent in the North and the Northeast.

The industry has become more competitive. The relaxation of controls on oil prices in June 1991 sparked a marketing war. Distributors cut prices and they upgraded their product line. They introduced unleaded gasoline, increased the Research Octane Number from 83 to 87 in regular gasoline and from 95 to 98 in premium products, and reduced sulfur in diesel oil from 1 to 0.5 percent.

Service is also improving rapidly. Operators display prices on large panels, adjusting them for fluctuations in prices of raw material. They introduce new facilities like credit-card payment, computerized dispensers, and supermarkets. They also try to improve their image. Some hire consultants to redesign their outlets.

Lubricating oil The market for lubricating oil is also getting more competitive. New regulations on low-smoke emissions have increased the demand for high-quality oils. Producers are introducing more sophisticated lubricants. They cater to various needs, including racing and high-performance cars, heavy-duty trucks, and taxis. They also target owners of motorcycles with high-performance oil for four-stroke engines and low-smoke oil for two-stroke engines.

Asphalt This industry has developed under the protection of the government. Few companies manufacture asphalt, but they include both local and foreign investors. They produce mainly for the domestic market. The industry is, however, set to become more competitive. The government is reducing regulations, cutting import duties and lifting price controls and import restrictions.

These changes bode well for the industry. They coincide with a growing demand for asphalt; the Thai government has stepped up its road-building program.

Chemicals The production of chemicals is new, but growing. It started in the late 1980s, following the development of the production of natural gas and in 1991, it accounted for only 2.3 percent of the manufacturing output. The Thai government encourages the development of this industry. In the 1980s it established Mab Ta Phud as a center for petrochemical industries. This area is especially convenient because it is located near reserves of natural gas. Industries in Mab Ta Phud extract and separate natural gas and they produce olefins (unsaturated hydrocarbons), especially ethylene and propylene. Aromatic plants are also under development.

Output is getting diverse as more plants start operating. Principal products include vinyls, polyvinyls, and chloride for the plastic industry; bleaching agents for the textile industry; ingredients for making synthetic fibers; and resins for making paints.

Many of these plants are partly state-owned, but the Thai government also encourages private ventures through incentives, especially tax holidays (that is, tax breaks). This policy has attracted many foreign investors. The principal ones are from Japan, the United States, and Taiwan, but a host of other companies from Europe, the Middle East, Asia, and Central America also hold stakes in this industry.

Large enterprises dominate. In 1992, nine companies producing chemicals and plastics were listed on the stock exchange. These included both chemical conglomerates and affiliates of large diversified groups.

Pharmaceutical products The pharmaceutical industry is less open. Poor legal protection has impaired development. For many years, local manufacturers could copy foreign formulas freely. Pharmaceutical products, however, became patentable in 1992.

This is an improvement, although the new law is still contentious. It empowers the Pharmaceutical Patent Board to define acceptable prices for drugs and to revoke licenses of patent holders whose prices are "too high." It also requires licensees to disclose manufacturing processes. Foreign companies complain that the Pharmaceutical Patent Board comprises too many members from the local pharmaceutical industry and that this may affect decisions.

Many foreign manufacturers still refrain from operating in Thailand, but not all. Some leading American and European companies have been producing and distributing their brands for some time. The industry also comprises a few large private and state-owned local concerns.

5.3.5 ELECTRICAL AND ELECTRONIC EQUIPMENT

Electrical and electronic equipment is Thailand's fastest-growing manufacturing industry. Between 1970 and 1991, it has expanded annually by over 16 percent in real terms. During this period its contribution to the manufacturing output has tripled, reaching 6 percent in 1991.[64]

The industry owes its development to Thailand's cheap labor force. Over the past few decades, foreign investors, especially Japanese, have moved their labor-intensive production lines to low-cost areas. This has helped them remain competitive in international markets while avoiding high import duties on the products they sell locally.

Production has since developed steadily. The first Japanese companies which came to Thailand set up assembly lines for simple electrical equipment such as black-and-white television sets and electric fans. Subsequently, they trained local staff to handle more complex products.

Most major Japanese manufacturers of electrical and electronic equipment have now set up factories in Thailand. They produce a wide range of goods, including electrical appliances, electronic components, consumer electronic products, communications equipment, and computer and industrial electronic equipment. Their brands have gained a strong foothold in the Thai market, catering to almost every household and business need.

Investors from other countries have followed the Japanese example. Taiwanese, South Korean, European, and American companies are producing and distributing their brands in Thailand. Competition is intense, especially for household electrical and electronic products and for communications and office-automation equipment. Only a few products like transformers and generators escape this fate.

5.3.6 TRANSPORTATION EQUIPMENT

Transportation equipment is a large and expanding industry.

Between 1970 and 1991, production grew annually by 12 percent in real terms and the industry's contribution to the manufacturing output increased from 5 to 8 percent.[65]

Prospects are good because demand is increasing. In 1992, some 9.6 million vehicles circulated in Thailand, up from 6.4 million in 1988.[66] Motorcycles are, however, the principal transportation, composing two-thirds of the vehicles (see Figure 5.11). Passenger cars, trucks, and buses account for the rest.

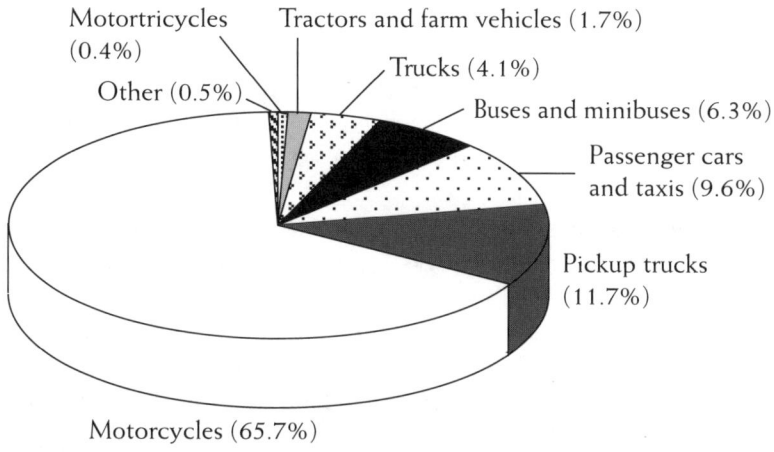

Figure 5.11 *Composition of Vehicles Registered by Type in 1992 (Source: Based on National Statistical Office, Statistical Yearbook Thailand 1993, OPM, Bangkok, 1993, p. 240.)*

Demand varies widely across regions. It peaks in Bangkok. About a quarter of all vehicles and nearly three-quarters of the passenger cars circulate in the capital. Sales are lower in the provinces, especially in poorer areas. In these places, pickup trucks and motorcycles are the most popular vehicles (see Figure 5.12).

The industry has been protected for some time. High import duties, import bans, and local content requirements have closed the market to outsiders. Protection has also affected productivity. Production cost is high, quality lags behind international standards, and product lines are small. Manufacturers are, however, a powerful lobby, and they resist deregulation.

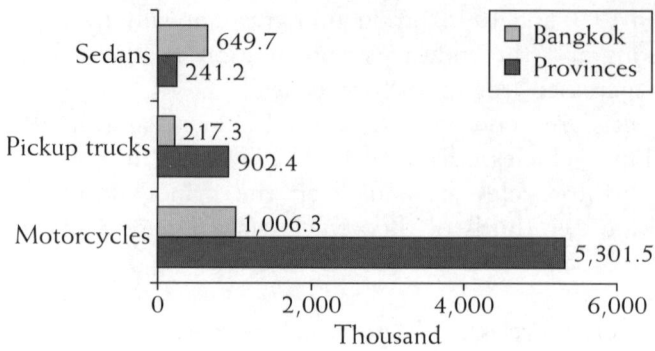

*Figure 5.12   Private Vehicles by Type in 1992
(Source: Based on National Statistical Office, Statistical Yearbook Thailand 1993, OPM, Bangkok, 1993, pp. 242–5.)*

Cars and commercial vehicles   Thai manufacturers produce passenger cars, buses, and trucks, catering mainly to local buyers. In 1992, they assembled about 324,000 vehicles, about a third of which were passenger cars and the rest commercial vehicles.[67] Light pickup trucks, which come in standard and four-wheel drive, are the biggest segment of the industry, accounting for the bulk of the trucks produced.

Production relies entirely on foreign technology, especially Japanese and European. The vast majority of the vehicles assembled locally are Japanese. Most others are European.

The car industry has developed with the help and protection of the Thai government. At its creation in the early 1960s, it was one of the first industries to receive investment incentives. Protection came in the form of import bans, prohibitive import duties on competing products, and restrictions on the number of assembly lines. Manufacturers also had to meet local content requirements for parts.

These regulations have inhibited efficiency. Until recently, prices of cars were some of the highest in the world, while quality remained substandard. Manufacturers also failed to meet demand during periods of high economic growth. In the late 1980s, for instance, buyers had to leave large reserve deposits and wait a long time for delivery.

Competition is, however, picking up with the gradual deregulation of the industry. In 1990, the Thai government lifted the limit on car series and models to be assembled locally. A year later, it repealed the import ban on cars with engines of less than 2300 cc, and it reduced import duties. These measures brought in lower prices and a greater variety of models. Within a year, sales of passenger cars nearly doubled, increasing from 67,000 in 1991 to 121,000 in 1992.[68]

Inspection procedures are also being improved. The Land Transport Department, which registers vehicles, proposed to transfer its inspection process to the private sector. In 1993, it invited private companies to open 137 inspection centers in the Bangkok area, including 30 for cars and 107 for motorcycles.

Car parts The car parts industry has expanded mainly because of the local content requirement. A variety of companies, including car manufacturers, opened factories to produce parts. This trend accelerated in the 1980s as the administration increased the requirement. This compelled assemblers to source sophisticated parts locally. Subsequently, foreign producers set up new plants in Thailand to manufacture these parts, while local suppliers upgraded their product lines.

Thai assemblers now rely on many different suppliers. A typical car manufacturer buys parts from 40 to 50 different companies. These are either affiliates, associates, or general vendors. Affiliates are joint ventures or fully owned subsidiaries of car manufacturers, associates are regular sub-contractors, and general vendors are occasional suppliers. Local parts are, nonetheless, substandard, and suppliers resist deregulation.

Motorcycles Thailand produces most of its motorcycles locally. The industry comprises two main segments: manufacturing of parts and assembly lines. There are four major companies producing engines and other essential parts and five assembly lines. These produce mainly Japanese models.

The industry is protected. It has developed for import substitution. In 1978, the government banned imports of motorcycles and it increased the local content requirement. Assemblers must now use 70 percent locally made parts. Product lines are limited. Factories assemble mopeds and sports motorcycles with engines below 150 cc, while Thai law bans the production and importation of bigger models.

Most locally produced vehicles are equipped with a two-stroke engine, either air- or water-cooled. In 1993, Thailand was one the world's top manufacturers of two-stroke motorcycles, partly because many countries have stopped producing these models. Two-stroke engines are popular because they are compact, light, and cheap to produce. They also have a high power-weight ratio. These engines are, however, noisy and they emit smoke and other pollutants.

Their shortcomings encourage manufacturers to change products. Four-stroke engines are set to replace existing models. Thai authorities have indicated plans to promote their production. These engines are already dominant in industrial countries where pollution regulations are stringent.

The industry has good prospects. In 1992 some 6.3 million motorcycles circulated nationwide; this is one for every other household. Production is increasing steadily. In 1993, manufacturers assembled almost a million motorcycles, twice as much as in 1988. Most vehicles, however, are sold locally. Exports are limited and they usually target neighboring countries, especially Vietnam and Laos.

5.3.7 GEMS AND JEWELRY

Thailand is at the heart of Asia's booming gem and jewelry trade. The kingdom's 400 gem and jewelry factories employ 1.3 million people. They produce mainly for foreign markets and in 1992, exports reached US$1.5 billion.[69] This makes Thailand a world's leading exporter of gems and jewelry. Principal buyers are the United States, Japan, Belgium, Hong Kong, and Germany.

The industry is keen to strengthen its international reputation. It keeps upgrading facilities for foreign trade. In 1993, it opened a center for the production and trade of diamonds, gems, and jewelry. This center, called Gemopolis Industrial Estate, occupies 28 hectares (68 acres) of land and it is located in the eastern suburb of Bangkok. It houses factories, industrial condominiums for small production plants, trading and exhibition centers, and a hotel.

Gem cutting Thailand has gained international recognition as a gem cutting center. Factories cut and polish colored gemstones and diamonds. They supply foreign markets worldwide. Gem-producing countries like Australia, Sri Lanka, and Burma have their stones cut in Thailand, where labor is skilled and cheap.

Gem cutting, although a natural outcome of the mining activities, started recently. After World War II, Thailand had only a few cutters and they were poorly skilled. The kingdom's ample supply of gemstones and cheap labor force, however, attracted European entrepreneurs. They set up factories, trained workers, and expanded gradually.

Later, these producers entered the more difficult field of diamond cutting. Thailand's first diamond cutting factory began operation in the late 1970s. More followed. The kingdom now has many gem and diamond factories and a large supply of well-trained cutters.

Production has, so far, focused on small stones. Thai factories usually produce one- to five-point diamonds in a fancy cut, called Bangkok cut, which ensures least carat-loss. Many are trying to obtain bigger rough to produce larger stones, but this requires more skill. Top producers hire foreign experts to upgrade their manufacturing processes and they send their staff to Belgium and Israel, two leading cutting centers, for training.

All diamonds are imported. Factories purchase their rough directly from De Beers's trading arm, the Central Selling Organization (CSO), which is often said to control 80 percent of the world's trade of diamonds. They also secure stones from dealers in Belgium, Israel, India, and Hong Kong.

Thailand has become a substantial force in the trade. De Beers has officially recognized the kingdom as a diamond-polishing center and its agents have opened consulting practices in Bangkok. The company also has accredited some of the leading Thai factories as sight-holders and sight-dealers. A sight-holder may buy rough directly from the CSO, while a sight-dealer may sell rough on behalf of the CSO.

Jewelry Thailand is renowned for its jewelry. In Bangkok, countless retail shops offer locally made pieces to foreign visitors, while factories export their products worldwide. Principal markets include the United States, Japan, and Europe. The industry is competitive, with producers ranging from small family businesses to large public companies. In 1993, five manufacturers were listed on the stock exchange.

The industry is, however, fairly recent. In the early 1980s, it was still in its infancy. Its designs did not appeal to foreign customers

249

and they lacked originality. Jewelry making had, nonetheless, potential. Local craftsmen could produce good traditional designs and imitate foreign creations. Their skill attracted foreign manufacturers.

These companies trained staff to produce for exports. Initially, they specialized in medium-quality goods for the United States. Later, they upgraded their products for the European markets. Thai productions are now well received and top local designers win international awards regularly.

5.4 CONSTRUCTION AND BUILDING MATERIALS

The construction industry is expanding, although its progression varies widely with economic activity. Between 1986 and 1991, for instance, annual growth rate reached 24 percent in real terms, compared to only 5 percent in the 1970s.[70]

5.4.1 CONSTRUCTION

Rapid economic growth has spurred the development of the construction industry. Factories, office buildings, commercial space, condominiums, and golf courses are in growing demand. A host of contractors, both foreign and local, cater to this expanding market.

Foreign enterprises have established a strong foothold in the industry. They are usually large multinational companies with stronger capital bases than local contractors. They also have better access to cheap overseas funds, an advantage for financing construction projects. These enterprises are often the principal bidders for major infrastructure projects like ports, airports, and roads.

Japanese contractors are especially prominent. They handle many different kinds of works that range from large and complex projects to simpler constructions, like office towers, housing, and factories. Part of their success stems from the extensive Japanese interests in Thailand. Japanese contractors handle virtually all projects linked to Japanese grant aid. They also build most factories and offices for Japanese manufacturers.

Local companies play a lesser, but growing, role. Many set up joint ventures with foreign contractors and they enter into agreements for technology transfer. Some also use internal resources to expand. A few local companies have become leading concerns. Their interests are diverse, spanning engineering, construction services, and rental of construction equipment.

Many buildings, however, fail to meet safety standards. Unqualified contractors do not follow original designs and they use poor-grade materials. Owners also make extensions to their buildings without approval and they do not implement safety measures. Problems have worsened during the recent construction boom, as enforcement became more difficult. A series of incidents plagued the industry. In 1993, for instance, a hotel in Nakhon Ratchasima collapsed while undergoing illegal extension work.

5.4.2 BUILDING MATERIALS

Booming business in the construction industry has fueled the demand for construction materials, but imports are regulated. Thai authorities have encouraged the local production of building materials for import substitution. High import duties, import bans, and exclusive production rights are effective barriers to trade. Entering into joint ventures with local companies to manufacture goods is often easier than trading them.

Such regulations were conducive to the development of large enterprises. The most remarkable example is, perhaps, the Siam Cement Group, a diversified conglomerate whose activities cover nearly all aspects of the building-material business. In 1993, the company had about 100 subsidiaries and affiliates. It holds major interests in cement and refractories, construction materials, machinery, vehicle parts, pulp and paper, petrochemicals, and trading. Product list is extensive. For residential construction alone, the group manufactures over 8,000 different items. In addition, it trades raw materials, construction materials, communications and electrical equipment, computers, and heavy equipment.

The Siam Cement Group also owes its preeminence to its unique position. It is a royal company. The group was founded in 1913 by royal decree. Its largest shareholder is the Crown Property Bureau, an independent investment agency for the Crown, which holds over a third of the shares.

The company plays a pivotal role in the economy. It has invested in most of Thailand's fast-growing industries, becoming a choice partner for foreign investors. It has formed joint ventures with world-leading producers. Although growing competition in the Thai market has eroded its profits, Siam Cement remains the top player in most construction-related businesses. People often say that it is a barometer of the Thai economy.

Cement Thais produce cement mainly for the domestic market. The kingdom is almost self-sufficient and suppliers keep expanding their facilities to meet the growing demand. Plants have developed more quickly in the past few years because of the rapid economic growth. Between 1988 and 1992, per capita consumption doubled, reaching about 400 kilograms (880 pounds) of cement per person per year;[71] this is two-thirds of the Japanese consumption.

This industry has developed under government protection. Until recently, Thai authorities limited the number of producers and they controlled prices. Deregulations have now opened the market, but large companies still dominate the industry. The five top manufacturers together account for about 95 percent of total production. They control sales through their network of distributors, and they also sell part of their production to independent distributors.

Steel Thailand has a substantial steel industry. In 1992, the kingdom's ten producers of ingot and billets had a combined capacity of 1.23 million tons per year.[72] Local factories also produce a variety of transformed goods, including reinforced steel bars, wire rods, shapes, pipes, tin plates, castings, cold-formed sections, and sheets. Local production, however, does not meet demand. In 1992, Thailand brought in some seven million tons of steel products, including bars, rods, sheets, and plates.

The production of steel is fairly new. It is not indigenous, because there is little domestic supply of iron. Although Thais used to mine and smelt iron to make weapons, they ceased to do so when the country opened to international trade in the mid-nineteenth century. The kingdom now imports iron and its steel mills rely on imported scrap.

The industry developed because of the policy of promotion for import substitution. Until recently, the government banned imports of certain steel products and it restricted the establishment of new steel mills. These regulations have, however, been relaxed, encouraging manufacturers to upgrade machinery and improve productivity.

Glass Manufacturers supply a wide range of glass products to the domestic and foreign markets. They produce sheet, float, safety, and insulating glass and mirrors. These come in various grades like polished, figured, wired, heat-absorbing, heat-reflecting, laminated, and tempered. Local buyers are diverse, but the construction, automobile, and furniture industries dominate. Thai factories also export glass worldwide, and major markets are in the Asia-Pacific region.

The industry has been protected for many years. It started in the 1960s and until 1990, one company held a quasi monopoly over the production. This has changed. The government is granting production licenses to new entrants, and the market is getting more competitive.

Prospects are good. Principal raw materials, glass sand, dolomite, lime stone, and feldspar, are available locally. Demand is also increasing, especially with the construction of many high-rise buildings and the growing production of vehicles.

Ceramics Ceramic products are diverse. They include refractory materials, tiles, receptacles, sanitary ware, tableware, and ornaments. They supply the domestic and foreign markets. Manufacturers export about US$40 million of ceramic products annually, over half of which are tableware and ornaments. Leading markets are the United States, Japan, and Europe.

Thailand is a choice base for making ceramics. The kingdom has large reserves of kaolin and ball clay and a long tradition of making pottery. At the end of the eleventh century, potters already manufactured imitations of Chinese Sung Dynasty cracked ware. Production continued for centuries, but only on a small scale. Large-scale manufacturing started recently for import substitution.

Quality is, however, average. Production is labor-intensive and local raw materials, although abundant, are of low quality. Prime ceramics produced in Thailand are often made of imported materials.

The industry is a mixture of producers of various sizes. Some of the biggest manufacturers are listed on the stock exchange. In 1992, there were six such companies, including affiliates of foreign enterprises. There are also a host of small local companies, especially in the Central and Northern regions. Their operations are similar to a cottage industry, with factories employing people at home for painting and engraving.

5.5 ELECTRICITY AND WATER

Demand for electricity and water is increasing with economic growth. The expanding commercial and manufacturing sectors are the biggest influences on consumption, but the better quality of housing also counts. More homes have electricity and running water. Growing demand has strained resources, and Thai authorities are speeding up the development of new facilities.

5.5.1 ELECTRICITY

Consumption of electricity, although small by Western standards, is increasing rapidly. In 1991, sales reached 43.2 billion kilowatt-hours, up from 15 billion in 1982;[73] this is an annual growth of 12 percent per year. Commercial and industrial concerns are the leading users, together buying 78 percent of the electricity sold by volume. Households account for an additional 21 percent (see Figure 5.13).

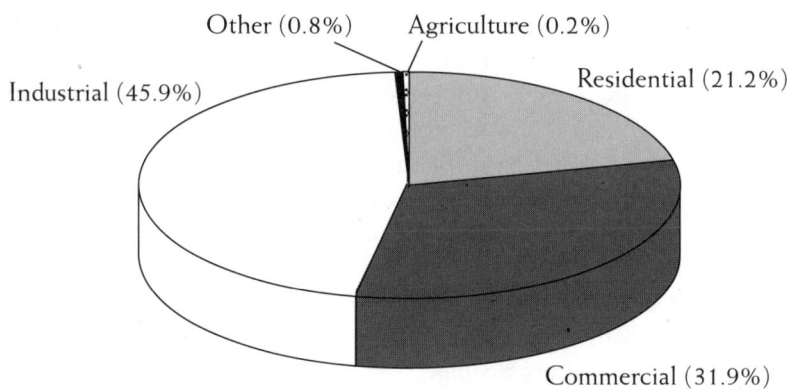

Figure 5.13 Volume of Electricity Consumed by Sector in 1991
(*Source: Based on National Statistical Office, Statistical Yearbook Thailand 1993, OPM, Bangkok, 1993, p. 414.*)

The production of electricity relies heavily on foreign sources of energy. In 1992, 59 percent of Thailand's primary energy was imported, mainly as crude oil (see Figure 5.14). Principal local resources are petroleum and lignite, together accounting for 38 percent of consumption. Hydroelectricity plays a lesser role as it supplies only 3 percent of total energy.

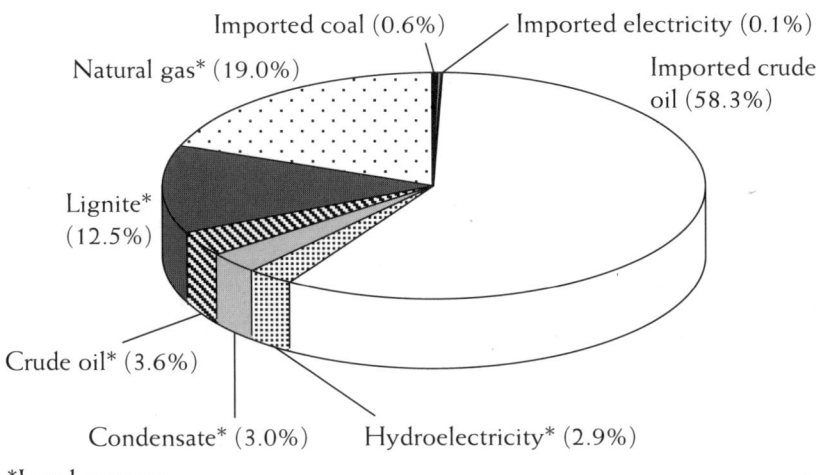

*Local sources

Figure 5.14   Sources of Energy in Crude Oil Equivalent in 1992
(Source: Based on Bank of Thailand, Annual Economic Report 1992, Bangkok, p. 23.)

Thai authorities are seeking new sources of energy. They are negotiating purchases of natural gas from Indonesia and Burma, which have extensive reserves. There are also suggestions to exploit the potential of the Mekong River which flows through China, Burma, Thailand, Laos, Cambodia, and Vietnam.

Years of conflicts in Indochina have left the river virtually untouched, but development plans are now surfacing. Thais are keen to build dams along the tributaries of the Mekong, both in Thailand and abroad. Thai companies are already building several dams on the Nam Theun, a feeder of the Mekong in Laos, to supply electricity to Thailand.

Less conventional sources of energy are also under study. In 1993, for instance, the Bangkok Metropolitan Administration hired consultants to evaluate possibilities for setting up gas-fired electricity-generating stations using methane gas from garbage dumps. Municipalities are also testing the potential of solar energy. Some have installed solar power generators to supply electricity for lighting and audio-visual equipment in schools.

Solar energy is especially attractive for remote places that are costly to reach through electricity lines. Many villagers are now relying on rechargeable batteries to power lightbulbs and other appliances like television sets, but recharging takes time. Solar energy may be more convenient. Several companies already specialize in solar systems, selling solar panels, batteries, and solar-powered household appliances, like water pumps and refrigerators.

5.5.2 WATER

Water is getting scarce. Over the past few years, almost every dry season had its water crisis. In 1994, Thailand had 26 large- and medium-sized dams and water reservoirs with combined storage capacity of 43 billion cubic meters[74] (1,520 billion cubic feet). Thai authorities are keen to build additional facilities, but planned new reservoirs meet strong opposition from nearby villagers and environmental lobby groups. The former seek greater compensation for their land and the latter object to the ecological damages.

Reservoirs supply water mainly for general and irrigation uses, but they also serve specific purposes. Thais, for instance, release fresh water in the Chao Phraya River to counter the sea water which flows up during dry seasons.

However, these needs are small compared to those of farmers. In the central plains, where farmers cultivate the land year-round, irrigation is a major function. It accounts for about 40 percent of the annual requirements of the large Bhumipol and Sirikit dams, the two principal sources of water in the area.

In these places, irrigation dictates agricultural production. Periods of low rainfall deplete reservoirs and compel farmers to replace second rice crops with other crops that need less water like soybean, mung bean, and corn.

Water is also an issue for the manufacturing sector. The rapid development of large-scale industries is straining resources. In industrial areas, the government builds new reservoirs, while industrial estates have their own reservoirs and they advertise good water supply. Heavy users, like oil refineries, also rely on their own resources, setting up desalination plants for sea water.

Part of the problem stems from pricing. Most users pay a small flat fee for open access to public water and they have no incentives to reduce consumption. Experts estimate that a third of Bangkok's water supply is wasted through leaky pipes.

5.6 TOURISM

Thailand is reputed worldwide to be a tourist destination. It is one of the most-visited places in Asia. In 1993, the kingdom recorded 5.8 million visitor arrivals; this is more than arrivals in Japan, South Korea, and Indonesia, for example.

Tourism is a major industry and a leading earner of foreign exchange. In 1992, it generated US$4.8 billion in revenue; this is greater than the export earnings from textile products. Prospects are encouraging as visitor arrivals keep increasing. Between 1960 and 1993, they grew annually by 14 percent (see Figure 5.15).

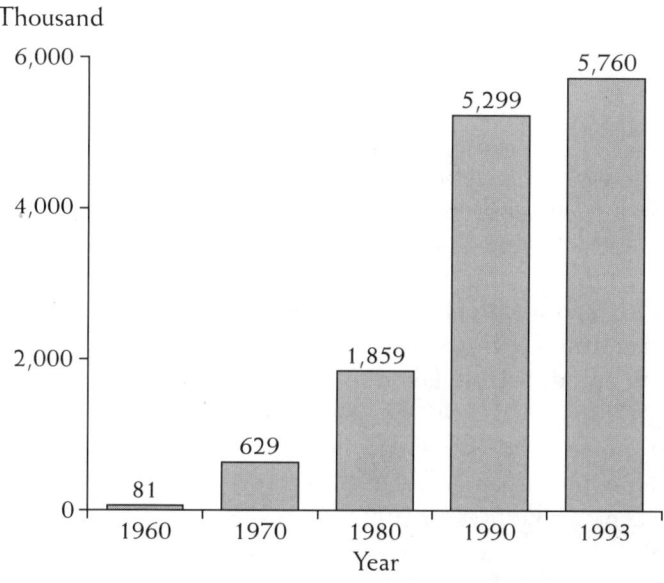

Figure 5.15 Visitor Arrivals
(Source: Based on Statistics and Research Division, Tourism Authority of Thailand, Bangkok.)

People of all nationalities visit Thailand, but most reside in nearby countries. Overall, about two-thirds of the visitors come from the Asia-Pacific region, while a quarter are European, and only 7 percent are American (see Figure 5.16). Neighboring Malaysians, are the single largest group of visitors, accounting for 14 percent of the arrivals, while Japanese follow at 11 percent. Males also predominate, accounting for some two-thirds of the visitors.

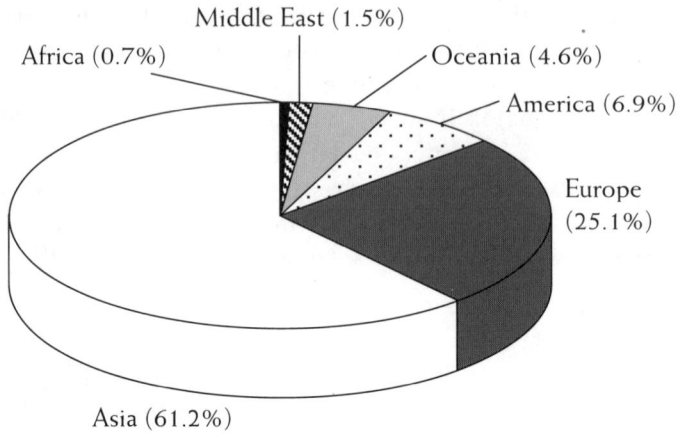

Figure 5.16   Visitor Arrivals by Country of Residence in 1992 (Source: Based on Statistics and Research Division, Tourism Authority of Thailand, Bangkok.)

The kingdom offers many attractions at reasonable prices. Domestic tours, shows, sites, museums, beaches, dining, and shopping are affordable favorites. In 1992, the average visitor spent only US$135 per day, 40 percent of which was on shopping and 14 percent on food (see Figure 5.17).

Most people organize their own trips, although practices differ greatly across countries. In 1992, 57 percent of the visitors came by themselves. Tours are, however, popular with certain groups of people, especially Asians. Some three-quarters of the Korean and Taiwanese visitors, for instance, come on tours, compared to only 20 percent of the Americans.[75]

Accommodations are widely available throughout the country. In 1992, 4,250 establishments in major cities offered some 205,000 rooms. Bangkok has the best facilities with over 48,000 rooms, but

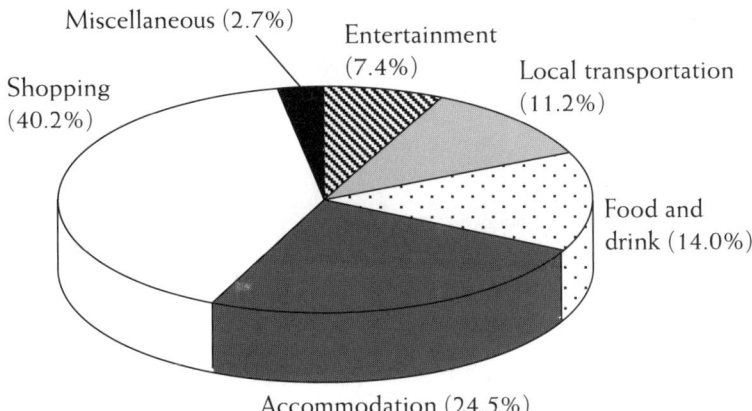

Figure 5.17 *Composition of Visitor Expenses in 1992* (Source: Based on Statistics and Research Division, Tourism Authority of Thailand, Bangkok.)

other important destinations like Pattaya, Phuket, and Chiang Mai are also well stocked. Accommodations range from small bungalows and family-run guest houses to first-class international hotels and exclusive resorts. The average tourist, however, stays in a medium-quality establishment, spending US$33 daily on accommodation in 1992.

These good facilities encourage extended stays. In 1992, the average visitor stayed a week, up from three days in 1960 (see Figure 5.18). The length of stay, however, depends on the country of residence. People from distant places such as Europe, America, Australia, and the Middle East stay longer while Asians make shorter, but more frequent, visits.

Thailand is also a destination for people doing business. Some 10 percent of the visitors are business people. They too have a wide choice of facilities. First-class hotels provide many services, including meeting rooms and business centers. The kingdom is also equipped for major events, with specialized centers handling major international conventions. The principal and newest such compound, the Queen Sirikit National Convention Center in Bangkok, hosted the annual conference of the World Bank in 1991. That year, international organizations held about 450 conventions in Thailand.[76] Bangkok is the main venue, but Phuket, Chiang Mai, and Pattaya are also important destinations.

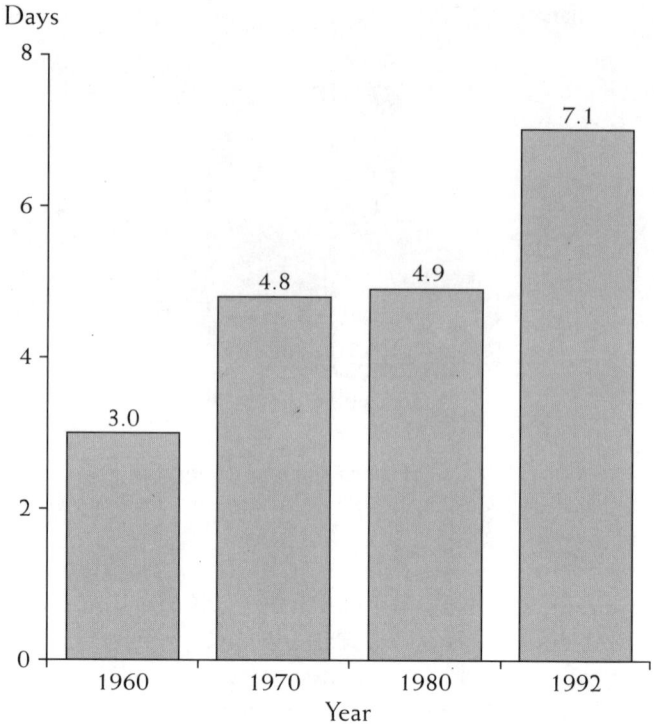

Figure 5.18   Length of Stay of Visitors
(Source: Based on Statistics and Research Division, Tourism Authority of Thailand, Bangkok.)

5.7 INTERNATIONAL TRADE

International trade is developing rapidly, although it is still small by Asian standards. Between 1987 and 1992, total foreign trade increased annually by 24 percent in real terms (see Figure 5.19). By 1992, imports and exports, combined, reached US$73 billion. This is, however, still lower than the trade of Malaysia, Taiwan, and South Korea, for example.

Trading partners are mostly from Asia, North America, and Europe. Japan and the United States are especially important, together accounting for 40 percent of both imports and exports. The share of the European Community is also substantial at 20 percent of exports and 14 percent of imports (see Figures 5.20 and 5.21).

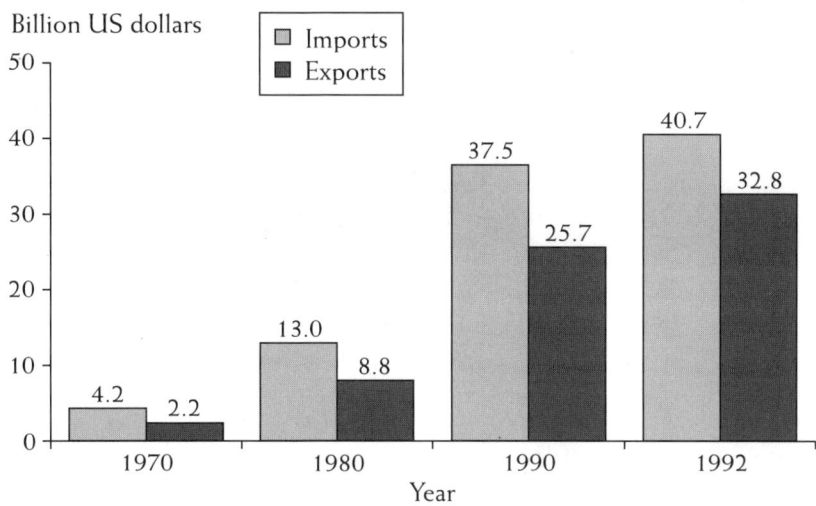

Figure 5.19 Evolution of Imports and Exports at 1992 Constant Prices (Source: Based on National Statistical Office, Statistical Yearbook Thailand, OPM, Bangkok, various issues.)

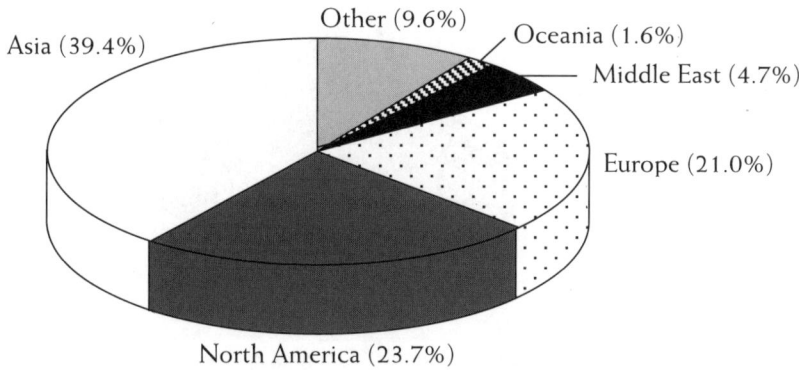

Figure 5.20 Exports by Destination in 1992 (Source: Based on Bank of Thailand, Annual Economic Report 1992, Bangkok, p. 86.)

Exports focus on consumer goods. Food alone accounts for a quarter of the exports by value. Main products are rice, sugar, and canned goods (see Figure 5.22). Manufactured products and machinery also comprise many consumer products. Leading items for instance, include textile, footwear, jewelry, fans, air conditioners, refrigerators, calculators, and household appliances.

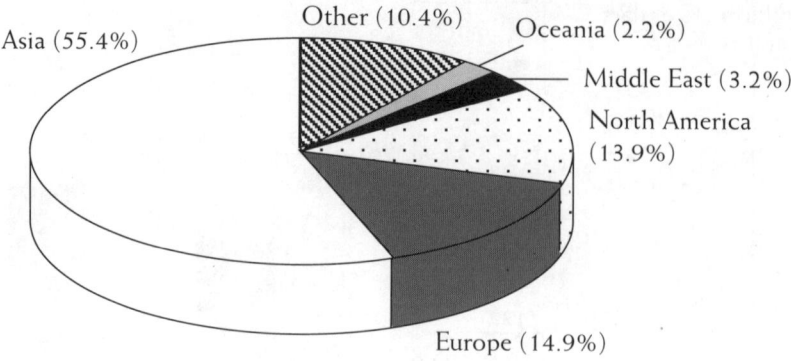

Figure 5.21 Imports by Origin in 1992
(Source: Based on Bank of Thailand, Annual Economic Report 1992, Bangkok, p. 86.)

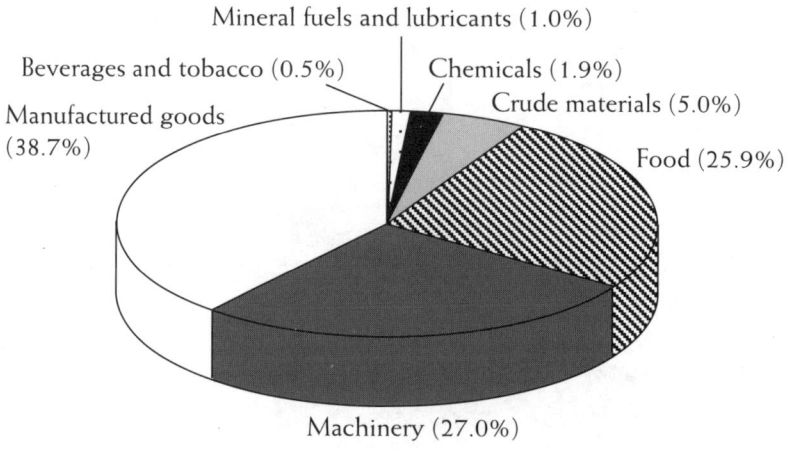

Figure 5.22 Exports by Category in 1992
(Source: Based on Bank of Thailand, Quarterly Bulletin, March 1993, p. 40.)

Imports are more industry-oriented. Principal categories are petroleum, chemicals, and machinery (see Figure 5.23). The last comprises mainly industrial equipment and parts. Imported manufactured goods also include many semifinished products for industrial use.

Past governments have often supported policies of import substitution that inhibited international trade. High duties protected local producers. Many ranged between 25 and 60 percent and some even exceeded 500 percent. The administration also imposed trade restrictions like bans, licenses, permits, and special fees on items deemed too competitive. Less obvious, but also effective, were the customs valuation procedures that foreign traders often described as arbitrary.

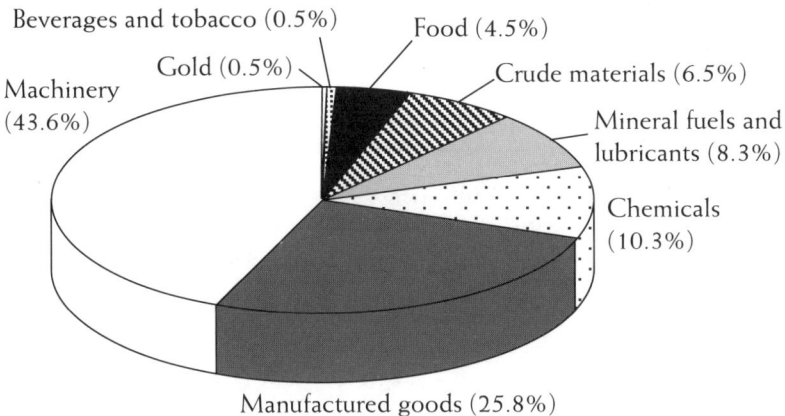

Figure 5.23   Imports by Category in 1992
(Source: Based on Bank of Thailand, Quarterly Bulletin, March 1993, p. 40.)

Recent policies, however, emphasize freer trade. Customs duties are declining. Between 1990 and 1992, Thai authorities have cut tariffs on over 1,500 items, including machinery, capital equipment, automobiles and parts, ore, iron, steel, and chemical products. Trade restrictions are also being removed and there are fewer controlled products.

Thailand is also intent on developing special links with trading partners in the region. The kingdom was instrumental in reviving the old idea of setting up an ASEAN[77] Free Trade Area. It convinced members to abolish all tariffs on intra-ASEAN trade over a 15-year period starting 1993.

NOTES

1. Calculations based on Office of the National Economic and Social Development Board, *National Income of Thailand, Rebase Series 1980–1991*, OPM, Bangkok, 1993, p. 15.

2. Calculations based on Office of the National Economic and Social Development Board, *National Income of Thailand*, OPM, Bangkok, various issues.
3. Supra 1, p. 10.
4. Calculations based on National Statistical Office, *Statistical Yearbook Thailand 1993*, OPM, Bangkok, 1993, pp. 56–7.
5. Source: Department of Technical and Economic Cooperation, *Government of Thailand Technical Cooperation under the Seventh National Economic and Social Development Plan (1992–1996)*, OPM, Bangkok, 1992, p. 102.
6. Supra 4, p. 286.
7. Ekachai, Sanitsuda, "Winners and losers," *Bangkok Post*, 13 March 1991, Outlook section, pp. 27, 31.
8. Calculations based on Center for Agricultural Statistics, *Agricultural Statistics of Thailand, Crop Year 1991/92*, MAC, Bangkok, 1992, p. 97.
9. Supra 8, p. 97.
10. Supra 8, p. 155.
11. Supra 2, various issues.
12. Supra 8, pp. 36–7.
13. Supra 4, p. 294.
14. Supra 8, pp. 28–31.
15. Supra 4, p. 266.
16. Supra 8, pp. 54, 64.
17. Source: Center for Agricultural Statistics, *Agricultural Statistics of Thailand, Crop Year 1991/92*, MAC, Bangkok, 1992, p. 64.
18. Supra 17, pp. 54–5.
19. Supra 17, pp. 86–7.
20. Supra 17, pp. 84–5.
21. Supra 1, p. 20.
22. Supra 1, p. 20.
23. Calculations based on Department of Livestock Development, *Yearly Statistic Reports 1991*, MAC, Bangkok, pp. 49–51.
24. Supra 23, pp. 49–51.
25. Supra 23, pp. 49–51.
26. Supra 23, pp. 49–51.
27. Source: Department of Livestock Development, *Yearly Statistic Reports 1991*, MAC, Bangkok, p. 181.
28. Supra 27, p. 52.

29. "Growing demand brightens prospects for dairy market," *Bangkok Post*, 25 August 1992, Business Post section, p. 19.
30. Supra 27, p. 181.
31. Supra 8, p. 127.
32. Supra 8, p. 127.
33. Supra 4, p. 292.
34. Supra 8, p. 163.
35. Calculations based on National Statistical Office, *Statistical Yearbook Thailand*, OPM, Bangkok, various issues.
36. "Logging ban retained in new policy on forest," *Bangkok Post*, 13 March 1993.
37. Source: Bank of Thailand, *Quarterly Bulletin*, March 1993, p. 82.
38. Calculations based on Bank of Thailand, *Annual Economic Report 1992*, Bangkok, p. 23.
39. Supra 1, p. 26.
40. Supra 1, p. 26.
41. Supra 1, p. 26.
42. Supra 37, p. 82.
43. The Association of Tin Producing Countries comprises Australia, Bolivia, Indonesia, Malaysia, Nigeria, Thailand, and Zaire. The combined output of these countries accounts for some 60 percent of the world's production.
44. Source: National Statistical Office, *Statistical Yearbook Thailand 1993*, OPM, Bangkok, 1993, p. 221.
45. Supra 37, p. 82.
46. Source: Department of Mineral Resources, *Thailand's Metal Statistics 2528-2535* [1985–1992], Bangkok, 1993, Appendix II.
47. Sources: Department of Mineral Resources, *Mineral Statistics of Thailand*, Bangkok, p. 29, and National Statistical Office, *Statistical Yearbook Thailand 1993*, OPM, Bangkok, 1993, p. 217.
48. Supra 2, various issues.
49. Supra 4, pp. 304–5.
50. Supra 4, p. 305.
51. Supra 8, pp. 149–51.
52. Supra 1, p. 28.
53. Supra 37, p. 84.
54. Supra 37, p. 86.
55. Calculations based on Bank of Thailand, *Quarterly Bulletin*, March 1993, p. 86, and National Statistical Office, *Statistical Yearbook Thailand 1993*, OPM, Bangkok, 1993, p. 27.

56. Supra 37, p. 84.
57. Supra 37, p. 84.
58. Supra 1, p. 28.
59. Supra 44, p. 281.
60. Supra 37, p. 84.
61. Supra 2, various issues.
62. Supra 4, p. 307.
63. Source: BANGKOK POST/Thailand Department of Commercial Registration–July 9, 1993, Motoring section, p. 3.
64. Supra 2, various issues.
65. Supra 2, various issues.
66. Source: National Statistical Office, *Statistical Yearbook Thailand*, OPM, Bangkok, various issues.
67. Calculations based on Bank of Thailand, *Quarterly Bulletin*, March 1993, p. 84.
68. Supra 37, p. 86.
69. Supra 4, p. 269.
70. Supra 2, various issues.
71. Supra 55, p. 27.
72. Supra 46, p. 2.
73. Supra 44, p. 414.
74. Source: Bank of Thailand, *Annual Economic Report 1992*, Bangkok, p. 16.
75. Source: Statistics and Research Division, Tourism Authority of Thailand, Bangkok.
76. Source: Tourism Authority of Thailand, *Thailand Tourism Statistical Report 1991*, Bangkok, p. 52.
77. ASEAN, the Association of Southeast Asian Nations, includes Thailand, Malaysia, Indonesia, Brunei, the Philippines, Singapore and recently, Vietnam.

6 Finance and Real Estate

Finance and real estate are, perhaps, the sectors of the economy that are changing the most. Thailand has embarked on a major program of deregulation, removing controls and restrictions in most aspects of financial activity. Increasing incomes have also fueled an unprecedented surge in property development. Condominiums, office buildings, factories, industrial estates, shopping centers, resorts, and golf courses are sprouting throughout the country.

Competition has intensified, increasing efficiency. Financial institutions are upgrading the collection of savings and allocation of funds, while real-estate companies advertise better designs and settings. Product lines are expanding, offering a greater array of financing tools and investment opportunities.

Raising capital is getting easier. The recent introduction of offshore banking has attracted more foreign funds and reduced the cost of investment. It has also induced banks to upgrade their private, merchant, and investment banking divisions, providing better information and advisory services to clients.

The following sections explain which facilities the finance and real-estate sectors offer and they highlight the leading trends in these industries.

6.1 Bank of Thailand

The Bank of Thailand is the central bank and the kingdom's sole monetary authority. It plays a major role in the economy, advising the government on both monetary and fiscal issues. The bank implements monetary policies and it uses them to maintain stable growth and to balance the government's fiscal policies.

Duties extend to monitoring the financial system. The central bank supervises financial institutions, prescribing bank operating ratios such as the reserve ratio and the ratio of capital funds to risk assets. It also provides managerial assistance during periods of difficulties. Its Fund for Rehabilitation and Development of Financial Institutes, for instance, rescues troubled financial institutions and auctions them off when their performance improves.

The Bank of Thailand also provides banking services to a few institutions. It is a banker to commercial banks, state enterprises, and the government. All commercial banks must maintain legal reserves with the Bank of Thailand, which is also the lender of the last resort.

Like most other such institutions, the central bank issues bank notes. These come in ten different denominations ranging from 50 satang (there are 100 satang in a baht) to 1,000 baht. The most common denominations, however, are 1, 10, 20, 100, and 500 baht notes. Together, they account for over 90 percent of the bank notes in circulation by volume.[1]

Central banking is a recent function. Its establishment coincides with the development of domestic banks. The first central banking institution, the Thai National Banking Bureau, was set up in 1939 when Thailand had only four local commercial banks. It operated until the creation of The Bank of Thailand in 1942. Subsequently, local commercial banks multiplied.

6.1.1 MONETARY ACTIVITIES

The Bank of Thailand controls money supply through direct interventions mainly. It extends discretionary loans to commercial banks against government or government-guaranteed bonds and it trades government bonds on the repurchase market. This market, set up in 1979, has become a prime tool for intervention. It allows the central bank to buy and sell bonds with the agreement to resell or repurchase them later. In addition, since 1987, the Bank of Thailand has been issuing its own bonds.

The Bank of Thailand has earned a reputation for maintaining strict controls over the money supply. This policy has kept inflation low and helped stabilize the exchange rate. Except for a brief period of depreciation in the early 1980s (which coincides with an increase in the value of the US dollar) the exchange rate has been remarkably stable (see Figure 6.1). Since 1986, it has hovered around 25.5 baht per US dollar.

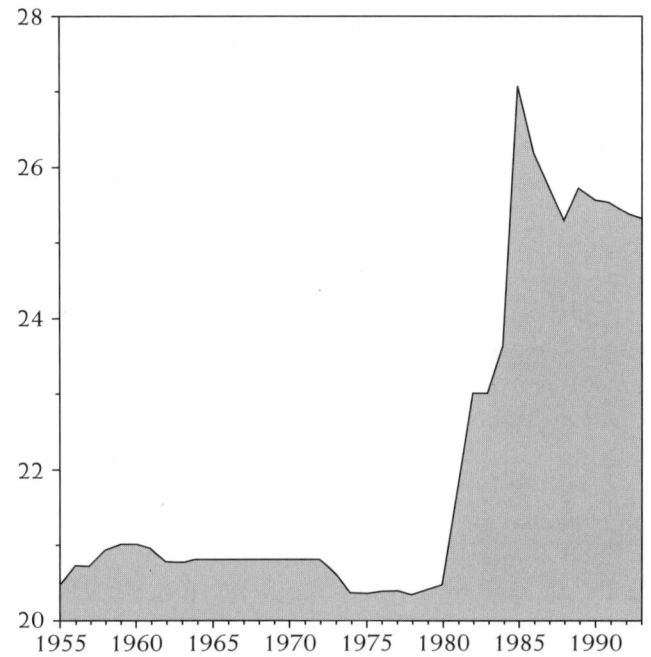

Figure 6.1 Exchange Rate of the Baht 1955–1993
(Source: Based on International Monetary Fund, IFS, various issues.)

Fluctuations in exchange rate, although small, are frequent. The Exchange Equalization Fund, an agency of the Bank of Thailand, determines the value of the baht daily. Since November 1984, the baht has been pegged to a basket of currencies of main trading partners. The Bank of Thailand does not disclose the exact composition of the basket, but approximate weights are 80 percent for the US dollar, 15 percent for the yen, and 5 percent for the German mark and other currencies. Incidentally, the large weight of the US dollar reflects its importance in transactions. Traders label most of their import and export prices in US dollars.

6.1.2 FINANCIAL REFORMS

The Bank of Thailand has initiated a series of reforms that are making profound changes in the financial sector. Officials say that the program, which started in 1989, aims to establish Thailand as a regional financial center similar to Singapore and Hong Kong. They argue that this will increase the role of Thailand in the development of Indochina.

Reforms focus on deregulating and monitoring the financial system. The central bank has lifted many restrictions on interest rates, foreign exchange, portfolio management, and financial services. It has also strengthened its supervision of financial institutions to increase their credibility. Additional measures to facilitate payments and develop the money market are under way.

Deregulations have eased transactions and broadened financial activities. Most financial institutions may now underwrite and trade debt instruments, manage mutual funds, extend leases, and provide information and advisory services. New products like negotiable certificates of deposits are also developing rapidly.

Foreign exchange Many of the old controls on foreign exchange have been removed and remaining restrictions are being lifted gradually. Commercial banks may now process all transactions of foreign exchange and they may make greater transfers of money without asking permission from the Bank of Thailand.

Both the deposit and borrowing of foreign exchange are getting easier. Newly introduced foreign currency accounts allow holders to pay for business transactions abroad, transfer money to other foreign currency accounts in Thailand, and convert their balance into baht. Non-resident baht accounts have also become more flexible, letting holders credit and remit funds freely in and out of the country.

Exchange procedures for travelers are convenient. People may bring in any amount of foreign and Thai currencies and take out all the foreign exchange that was brought in. Travelers may change money in many places, including authorized banks, moneychangers, tour agents, and hotels and guest houses. In tourist areas, banks even run fleets of moneychanger vehicles that they post near major attractions.

Administrative operations, once lengthy and tedious, have improved dramatically. Reforms have reduced paperwork and delays in remitting funds overseas, enhancing the financial appeal of the country.

International trade Financial transactions for international trade are open. There are no exchange restrictions on exports and imports. Exporters may deposit their proceeds on a foreign-currency account or convert them into baht. Importers may buy foreign exchange, draw from their foreign currency account, and open letters of credit to pay for their purchases. Any currency is acceptable in settling accounts, although the US dollar is the most common medium. Some 70 percent of exports are said to be transacted in US dollars.

New agencies facilitate international trade. In 1993, the Bank of Thailand established the Exim Bank to assist traders. This new institution extends loans, and provides guarantees, insurance, and information services. It helps exporters grant better credit terms to foreign buyers, especially for new markets like Indochina and Russia. Its services replace the cumbersome and controversial packing credits. Trading partners had often retaliated against these preferential financial plans that they viewed as government subsidies.

International investment International investment is getting more attractive. Foreign investors may freely repatriate investment capital, dividends, profits, and loan and interest repayments. They may also transfer foreign exchange between subsidiaries without changing those funds into baht and they may send abroad securities, promissory notes, and bills of exchange without restriction.

Residents may also invest abroad more easily. The central bank allows direct investment and lending to affiliated companies abroad of up to US$5 million without prior authorization. Only the transfer of capital for the purchase of immovable properties and investment in foreign stocks is still restricted.

Gold The trade of gold is no longer restricted. Thai authorities have removed import quotas, licenses, and specific taxes. The only tax applied on imports of gold is the 7 percent value-added tax, which is refunded upon re-export.

Interest rate Interest rates are now fully flexible. The Bank of Thailand has gradually removed ceilings on deposits and lending rates for commercial banks, finance companies, and *credit-foncier* companies (real-estate-financing companies). It also lets commercial banks adjust their lending and borrowing rates.

6.2 BANKS

A variety of banks operate in Thailand. There are commercial and specialized banks as well as branches and representative offices of foreign banks. Banking is well established. It started in November 1865 when the Hong Kong & Shanghai Banking Corporation, then an eight-month-old company, appointed agents in Bangkok. In 1888, the bank upgraded this agency to a branch, becoming the first bank to open a branch in Thailand. Others followed, although it took nearly two decades for a local company to join in.

In those days, banks kept direct contact with their clients. Bill-collecting offices, for instance, employed teams of fit young men to remind late customers of their overdue loans. They also kept chains, nails, and padlocks to seal the warehouses of recalcitrant debtors.[2] These days are gone. Thailand now has a modern banking sector.

6.2.1 COMMERCIAL BANKS

Commercial banking is changing rapidly. Banks are providing a greater array of services. They accept time, savings, and demand deposits and they lend money through overdrafts, loans, bill discounts, and leasing. Activities also include fee-based services such as feasibility studies, loan syndication, consulting for mergers and acquisitions, and custodian services. In addition, banks may underwrite, issue, and trade debt instruments and issue negotiable certificates of deposit (time deposits with variable maturity).

Commercial banks have traditionally played the most important role in collecting savings and financing investments. They are the biggest financial institutions in Thailand, although they are not numerous. Until recently, the Thai government restricted entry in the industry. In 1993, the kingdom had only 15 local commercial banks and 14 foreign banks with branch offices.

Thai banks Thai banks are small compared to their European, American, and Japanese counterparts, although some are prominent by regional standards. Thailand's leading bank, for instance, is also one of the top commercial banks in Southeast Asia.

A few of these prominent banks dominate the local market. In June 1993, the top three local banks controlled over half of the domestic market. Together, they accounted for about 54 percent of the deposits, lendings, and assets of domestic banks. They also operated large networks of branches in excess of 400 each.

Most Thai banks, regardless of size, are profitable. In 1992, the average Thai commercial bank earned US$50 million in net profits. The bulk of the revenues came from the spread between lending and borrowing rates. Because of protection, these spreads remained high, at times nearing five percentage points.

This is, however, changing. Recent reforms have increased competition between Thai commercial banks and other local and foreign financial institutions. Local banks must now rely less on interest income and more on fee-based services. These are expanding. Since 1992, commercial banks may underwrite, issue, and trade debt instruments, and provide information and advisory services. Banks responded by expanding their investment-, merchant-, and private-banking divisions.

The most visible changes are, perhaps, those of retail-banking services. Operations are getting more efficient as banks upgrade computer technology. They also offer new products like telephone banking, and they expand their network of branches and automatic teller machines (ATM). Some of these machines are even linked to a pool so that people may use the ATM of any affiliated bank. So far, over half of the local banks have joined the pool.

Operations are also getting closer to international practice. Since 1993, banks have adopted international capital guidelines set by the Bank of International Settlements for accounting. The Bank of Thailand also requested commercial banks to declare their criteria for deposits and loan rates, putting an end to negotiable rates.

Thai banks have had little exposure to international markets. Until recently only leading local banks provided international support. This usually consisted in financing Thai trade and extending commercial loans in foreign currencies through foreign branches.

These activities are now expanding. Banks are opening new branches in such places as Singapore, Hong Kong, and the Cayman Islands. They are also keen to expand their network in neighboring countries. Many operate in Cambodia, Laos, and Burma and in 1992, some Thai banks became the first foreign banks to obtain licenses for opening branches in Vietnam.

Local banks, however, are still too small to finance the growth of the Thai economy. The rapid development of capital-intensive industries is straining resources. Large-scale projects require international financing through syndicated loans.

Offshore banking Foreign banks are playing a more prominent role in Thailand. In 1993, the Bank of Thailand granted 47 licenses for the newly created International Banking Facility (IBF), an offshore banking service. Although over half of the licenses went to local banks and to branches of foreign banks in Thailand, recipients also included 20 foreign banks with no branch operation in the kingdom.

This is a major change in the financial system. The IBF opened Thailand to international finance and its licenses were the first granted to foreign banks since 1978. Until recently, Thai laws had restricted the presence and operations of foreign banks, granting few licenses and letting recipients open only one branch office. These foreign branches were profitable, but they accounted for a minute proportion of total financial assets.

The new IBF licenses cover a wide range of services. They allow banks to make foreign exchange operations, finance trade and investment, manage syndicated loans, underwrite debt, and provide information and advisory services. While these activities may not help foreign banks make strong inroads in the hinterland, where companies are small and traditional, they allow them to take a greater part in financing investment and servicing foreign companies and joint ventures.

The principal consequence is the greater access to cheaper international capital. The IBF licenses allow banks to source funds overseas for extending loans in foreign currency in Thailand. Capital comes from deposits by non-residents and juristic persons and from borrowings abroad. Since interest rates are lower outside Thailand, the IBF helps companies finance investment at lower cost. Businesses may also expect better merchant- and investment-banking services.

6.2.2 SPECIAL-PURPOSE BANKS

Special-purpose banks finance specific economic sectors. They are state-owned companies whose activities are controlled by the Thai administration. They extend loans at preferential interest rates, but they may deal only with specific clients and projects. There are three such banks; the Government Savings Bank, the Bank for Agriculture and Agricultural Cooperatives, and the Government Housing Bank.

Government Savings Bank The Government Savings Bank specializes in collecting small savings. It obtains most of its funds through demand, savings, time, and fixed deposits and through premium savings bonds. The bank has an extensive network of offices throughout the country. By the end of 1992, it operated 512 branches, 11 mobile units (both on land and water), and one district representative.[3] Most of these offices, some 87 percent, are located outside Bangkok.

The bank makes great efforts to collect savings from small depositors. In Bangkok, for instance, it has been running a door-to-door floating service for some 30 years. Its vessel plies the city's canals 6 days a week. Customers put a small flag outside their homes to indicate that they want to make a transaction and get the floating bank to stop at their door.

Collecting small savings is a long-standing goal for the Thai government. The Government Savings Bank finds its origin back to 1913 when King Rama VI set up the Savings Office. The office was later transferred to the Post & Telegraph Department and in 1947 its assets and liabilities were finally taken over by the newly created Government Savings Bank. Because of the large and poor rural population, small savings are still an important source of funds.

These funds have traditionally financed government projects, but this is changing. Until recently, the Government Savings Bank invested most of its funds in government securities, bonds, and promissory notes. Dealings with the private sector are, however, increasing as the bank extends more loans to enterprises and individuals. In 1992, claims on households and businesses accounted for 10 percent of total assets, up from only 1 percent in 1986.[4]

The Government Savings Bank has now embarked on a major program of diversification. It has formed joint ventures with many private and public enterprises to expand its activities. Its large network of offices is especially valuable for distributing financial products like mutual funds, insurance, and leasing services nationwide. The bank is also keen to improve efficiency, setting up training programs for staff and investing in computers.

Bank for Agriculture and Agricultural Cooperatives The Bank for Agriculture and Agricultural Cooperatives is the bank of the farming community. It deals exclusively with the agricultural sector, extending credits to farmers and cooperatives at low interest rates. The bank also fosters the development of agricultural marketing cooperatives and it takes part in product-development projects, providing credit, technology, and personnel to participating farmers. It operates an extensive network of offices which, in 1992, comprised 74 branches, 192 subbranches, and a large number of field offices.[5]

Institutional investors and the general public are the principal sources of funds. Their deposits accounted for 59 percent of the bank's liabilities in 1992. The bank is, however, relying increasingly on the general public for capital. Between 1986 and 1992, the share of deposits by households and businesses in the funds collected increased from 19 to 44 percent, while those of commercial banks dropped from 37 to 15 percent.[6]

Social goals often prevail over commercial operations. Since its creation in 1966, the bank has extended loans below market prices to poorer farmers. These are usually small short-term advances; average size was only US$600 in 1992.[7] The bank is also a tool for government intervention. In 1993, for instance, Thai authorities requested that the bank buy paddy rice pledged as collateral for loans. Since the price of rice used in loan agreements exceeds market price, this amounts to a farm subsidy.

The Bank for Agriculture and Agricultural Cooperatives is broadening its activities, although only within the field of agriculture. Until recently, it financed exclusively non-processed agricultural products. In 1992, it added agricultural-related businesses. Changes, however, are gradual because the social importance of the farming population slows down expansion plans.

Government Housing Bank The Government Housing Bank finances private housing. It deals mainly with small borrowers and it is not allowed to lend funds to developers. Since most housing developments are in the Bangkok area, the bank has many branches there. In 1992, it operated 12 of its 18 branches in Bangkok; it also ran 15 subbranches and a few mobile units.[8]

Government control over the bank's activities is declining. Since it obtained the "efficient government enterprise" status in 1993, the Government Housing Bank has gained more freedom. It is now expanding its activities, especially the information business; its extensive database on customers, loans, and repayments is valuable, especially to the real-estate sector.

6.3 FINANCE AND CREDIT INSTITUTIONS

Finance and credit institutions provide financial and investment services to individuals and businesses. The principal institutions are the finance and securities companies whose activities are wide-ranging. Other credit institutions, while varied, offer fewer services.

6.3.1 FINANCE AND SECURITIES COMPANIES

Finance and securities companies are the second most important financial institutions in Thailand. They are the principal alternative to banks for lending and borrowing. The ability of these companies to grab market niches is a major challenge to commercial banks. In 1992, assets of finance and securities companies were about one-quarter those of commercial banks,[9] a remarkable achievement for an industry which started only in 1969.

Until recently, finance and securities companies were closely related. Most finance companies held both finance and securities licenses. By the end of 1992, Thailand had 71 finance and securities companies, 21 finance companies, and 12 securities companies.[10] In 1993, however, Thailand's Security and Exchange Commission resolved to separate the finance and securities businesses.

Finance companies   Finance companies fund a variety of projects. They extend loans for investment, organize syndicated loans, grant commercial credit, provide call loans to securities companies, and take stakes in business ventures (many invest heavily in the real-estate sector). Finance companies also deal with individuals, providing credit for housing and personal consumption, especially through hire-purchase agreements.

Liberalization has expanded the range of services that finance companies may provide. Principal changes concern advisory and portfolio services. Financial companies are now allowed to provide information services and to sponsor companies seeking listing on the stock exchange. They may also underwrite debt instruments, manage provident funds, and take custodian service for securities, certificates of deposits, and debt instruments. In addition, they may act as representatives for holders of debentures and as supervisors for mutual funds.

The principal sources of funds are households and businesses. Together, they supply about two-thirds of the capital collected. Other lenders include commercial banks, foreign investors, and the Bank of Thailand. Until recently, finance companies collected most of their funds by issuing promissory notes. Since 1992, however, they are allowed to accept deposits and to issue negotiable certificates of deposits.

Securities companies Securities companies provide services related to portfolio investment. They handle trading, brokerage, and custodian services of stocks, and they act as registrars of securities and paying agents for securities. They also advise clients, providing information services and sponsoring companies for listing on the stock exchange. Securities companies finance these activities by issuing stocks and by borrowing from financial institutions.

The statuses and activities of these companies vary. Those who are members of Thailand's stock exchange are brokers and they may place orders directly on the stock market. Others are subbrokers and they must place orders through brokers. In 1994, 40 securities companies were members. The stock exchange determines the brokerage fees and in 1993, they were 0.5 percent of the value traded for stocks and preferred shares, 0.1 percent for debentures and bonds, and 0.3 percent for unit trusts.

Trading is now automated. Brokers key in their orders and, in most cases, the computer of the stock exchange matches these orders automatically. For certain transactions like big lots and foreigners' dealings, however, the system advertises orders and it links interested parties so that they can conduct negotiations directly.

Stock trading is still new to Thailand. Companies lack expertise and skilled local staff is scarce. Many brokers employ expatriates in senior positions. The industry is especially short of analysts. The Securities Analyst Association has set up programs to train financial analysts and investment and securities analysts. Standards are high, with courses modeled on American training programs and taught by foreign instructors.

Brokerage services are, however, getting more sophisticated. Leading securities companies have trading floors with electronic display boards for their clients and they operate provincial stock-trading offices. The first such offices were set up in 1990 in major provincial towns like Chiang Mai in the North, and Hat Yai, Phuket, and Songkhla in the South. Subsequently, brokers expanded their network and by 1994, they operated 142 trading offices in 26 provinces.

While brokerage is the principal source of income, fee-based earnings may be substantial. The biggest securities companies usually provide corporate and property finance services. Corporate finance is becoming especially valuable because many Thai companies are trying to find new ways of raising capital.

6.3.2 REAL-ESTATE-FINANCING COMPANIES

Real-estate-financing companies, called *credit-foncier* companies, finance the purchase of immovable properties. They may perform a variety of operations related to real estate including lending money on mortgage, buying immovable properties with the right of redemption, and selling properties by hire-purchase. Since 1992, these companies may also invest up to 20 percent of their funds in specific debt instruments. Most of the business, however, is mortgage loan.

In many ways, *credit-foncier* companies operate like finance companies. They raise capital from the public by issuing debentures and by borrowing and they are subject to similar registered and paid-up capital requirements. *Credit-foncier* institutions, however, operate fewer business licenses than finance institutions, although they may now apply for licenses to underwrite debt instruments.

While the scope of these services is limited, it is likely to expand with the deregulation of the financial industry. Thai authorities are encouraging *credit-foncier* companies to merge and to increase their registered capital in preparation for more diverse operations.

6.3.3 INDUSTRIAL FINANCE INSTITUTIONS

Industrial finance institutions are development finance companies set up to promote Thai industries. There are three such institutions: the Industrial Finance Corporation of Thailand, the Small Industry Finance Corporation, and the Small Industry Credit Guarantee Corporation. All are partly state-owned, but they raise most of their capital from the public and operate as private companies.

Industrial Finance Corporation of Thailand The Industrial Finance Corporation of Thailand finances fixed assets of companies through medium- and long-term loans. It was set up in 1959 to support the policies of import substitution and to promote export-oriented industries. This semigovernmental enterprise is owned at 85 percent by private companies and at 15 percent by the Ministry of Finance. Clients are mainly private enterprises because the corporation may not extend loans to companies with over one-third state ownership.

The corporation also takes an active part in the development of the capital market. It has helped create the first Thai credit rating agency, called Thai Rating and Information Services Company, and it is instrumental in setting up corporate bond markets for non-listed debentures.

Capital comes from various sources, but domestic funds are getting more important. In 1993, they accounted for over three-quarters of the liabilities, up from half in 1986. The Industrial Finance Corporation of Thailand issues bonds, promissory notes, and debentures to raise funds locally. It sources foreign capital from international aid agencies, especially the Japanese Overseas Economic Cooperation Fund. This Japanese fund grants loans with special advantages like grace periods for repayment and low interest rates.

Small Industry Finance Corporation The Small Industry Finance Corporation provides financial and technical assistance to small industrial enterprises. Its loans finance the establishment, expansion, and upgrading of small-scale industries. The corporation may also engage in other businesses like underwriting securities.

Although assistance to small companies had existed for some time, the corporation began operation recently. It was established in 1992 to replace the Small Industries Finance Office. Unlike its predecessor, the new corporation is a juristic entity allowed to raise funds from the public.

Small Industry Credit Guarantee Corporation The Small Industry Credit Guarantee Corporation guarantees small, but sound, projects. It helps individuals without enough collateral obtain credits from financial institutions. It also underwrites securities and invests in stocks. Because it is a juristic entity, this financial institution raises funds from the public.

6.3.4 MUTUAL FUND MANAGEMENT COMPANIES

Mutual fund management companies operate mutual funds and they sell unit trusts. There are two main types of funds, domestic and foreign. Domestic funds are registered and sold in Thailand. Foreign funds are listed abroad and registered either in Thailand or abroad. Those which are registered in Thailand and managed by Thai companies are called onshore funds; others are offshore funds.

Fund management is a growing activity. In 1992 the government ended the 17-year monopoly of the partly state-owned Mutual Fund Company, granting licenses for the management of funds to seven new operators. Subsequently, investment funds multiplied. By the end of 1992, there were 20 domestic funds, up from 6 the year before. Their number keeps increasing as new funds, both closed-end and open-end, are being launched regularly.

The fund market is set to expand further with the pending introduction of asset-backed unit trusts. This service is similar to American securitization. It allows financial institutions to transfer their asset-backed loans to specialized fund companies which turn them into securities.

6.3.5 FACTORING

Factoring is now available in Thailand. This service, which allows companies to convert accounts receivable into cash by selling them to a factor, is a recent addition to the finance industry. It started in 1986 when a world's leading factoring company set up an affiliate in Thailand. Since factoring allows traders to import or export goods without issuing a letter of credit, it is likely to grow with international trade.

6.3.6 COOPERATIVES

Thailand has many cooperatives of various types, although the principal ones are agricultural and savings cooperatives. In 1992 the kingdom had over 3,400 cooperatives, 49 percent of which were for agriculture and 28 percent for thrift and credit.[11] The rest were consumer, services, fishery, and land-settlement cooperatives. Cooperatives are traditional institutions that date back to 1916 and they remain popular.

Agricultural cooperatives Agricultural cooperatives are organized by farmers to improve their financial status. Members pool resources to buy equipment, distribute their production, and obtain credits at low interest rates. The main source of funds are borrowings from the Bank for Agriculture and Agricultural Cooperatives while deposits are a negligible source.

Savings cooperatives Savings cooperatives, also called credit unions, are formed by members of certain professions. There are, for instance, savings cooperatives for school teachers, university employees, provincial police units, and public sector employees. Members must contribute a minimum monthly subscription. Cooperatives extend loans to members for various purposes ranging from unforeseen expenses to purchase of durable goods, repairs in homes, and acquisition of houses.

6.3.7 PAWNSHOPS

Pawnshops cater to low-income groups. They grant loans for consumption against a variety of personal items like gold jewelry, watches, sewing machines, and electrical appliances. Loans are small and in 1992, their average value was US$130.[12]

Pawning is a well-established practice. It began in 1866 and it has developed steadily. At the end of 1992, there were 367 pawnshops in Thailand. Although widespread, pawnshops remain small. Staff seldom exceeds ten people and there are no branches.

Most of these businesses are private, but government and municipalities (city councils) also run pawnshops. Private pawnshops rely on their own resources and occasionally on commercial banks for funds. Government and municipal pawnshops receive an initial capital from government and municipal budgets but they may also borrow from other sources.

6.4 STOCK EXCHANGE

The Stock Exchange of Thailand (SET) is the secondary market for trading quoted securities. These include common and preferred stocks, unit trusts, warrants, debentures, and government bonds. Shares are, however, the principal and most actively traded securities. In 1992, they accounted for 89 percent of the issues by volume and for 97 percent of the total trade by value. Bonds, in contrast, are less successful, and trading remains small.

Compared to Western stock exchanges, the Thai stock exchange is still new. The first Thai equity market, called the Bangkok Stock Exchange Co Ltd, was set up in 1962 by a private group. Trading was then small and the exchange ceased operation in the early 1970s. In 1975, a new organization, the Securities Exchange of Thailand, later renamed Stock Exchange of Thailand, revived trading. Activity remained moderate for some time, but it picked up later.

The new stock exchange started as a small local operation with only 16 securities. Trading did not increase significantly until the mid-1980s (see Figure 6.2). The stock exchange has since expanded dramatically and by 1992, quoted companies numbered 320. This stock market owes its rapid expansion partly to its open policy. It has granted listing to companies of various sizes.

Selection criteria are now getting more stringent. The stock exchange no longer distinguishes between registered and authorized listings. The latter used to apply to smaller companies with less registered capital. All new listings must be registered, while authorized companies must change their status to registered.

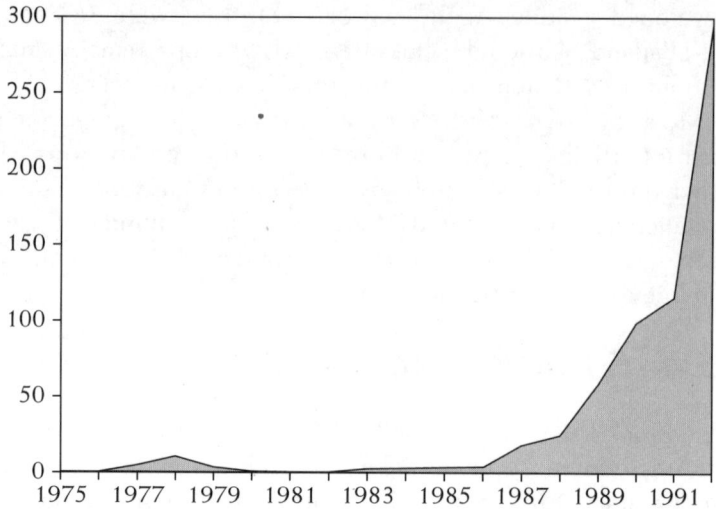

*Figure 6.2   Average Daily Turnover of Corporate Securities 1975–1992
(Sources: Based on Research and Development Department, The Stock Exchange of Thailand, Bangkok, and International Monetary Fund, IFS, various issues.)*

6.4.1 TRADING

The Thai stock exchange has now acquired regional stature. In 1992, the average daily turnover reached US$296 million, up from US$165,000 in 1975.[13] This expanding trade reflects the rapid economic growth, but it also stems from large inflows of foreign capital. Each year since 1987, these have accounted for 8 to 15 percent of total turnover. Much of this capital comes from the United States and in 1993, the American Securities and Exchange Commission endorsed securities companies listed on American exchanges to place their stock scrips with the Thai depository center.

Efficiency is improving. In 1991, the stock exchange replaced the old trading floor and its open auction with an automated trading system which matches orders and broadcasts securities quotations and news. This computerized system helps diffuse information and it speeds transactions.

The growing activity has resulted in longer trading hours. In 1992, the stock exchange added a second session, increasing trading time by one hour. Trading is now open Monday to Friday from

10:00 a.m. to 12:30 p.m. and from 2:30 p.m. to 4:00 p.m. This schedule is set to increase further. In 1994, the stock exchange and its members agreed to extend trading by an additional half hour.

The exchange organizes transactions through three separate boards called the main, the special, and the foreign boards. The main board is for regular trading, that is, lots of 100 shares called board lots. The special board cater to odd and special lots that are not multiples of 100 shares and to big lots of over US$400,000 or 10 percent of the paid-up capital of a company. The foreign board is for transactions by foreign investors.

Trading on the foreign board must comply with legal limits on share holding. Thai law prescribes ceilings on foreign ownership of local companies. These range from 15 to 100 percent, but the most common ceiling is 49 percent. Limits may also be self-imposed by any Thai company in its articles of association. Trading on the foreign board stops when foreign ownership has reached the ceiling.

These limitations are, however, declining. Thai authorities are increasing the ceilings on foreign ownership. In addition, the creation of new mutual fund management companies has expanded investment opportunities. The SET is also considering the introduction of non-voting shares for foreign investors.

Investment procedures are also getting easier. Since the relaxation of foreign-exchange controls, foreign capital needs no longer be registered and investors may repatriate investment funds, dividends, and profits freely. In 1992, the Thai government also reduced taxes on dividends, interest payments, and capital gains.

Potential gains are high, although prices of stocks are volatile. High economic growth and brisk business produce a rapidly changing environment where prices adjust frequently. Because of the importance of trade and foreign investment in the economy, prices are especially sensitive to international events. Trade agreements between the United States and China, for instance, affect Thai stocks substantially. The large flows of international capital aggravate these fluctuations.

Several indices measure the changes in prices of securities. There are thirteen such indicators, a general index, called the SET index, and twelve sectorial indices. The SET index compares current market value of securities with that of the 1975 base year. Because domestic commercial banks account for a substantial proportion of the market capitalization, about half in 1994, they weigh heavily in the general index.

6.4.2 SUPERVISION

Supervision is a major problem in Asian stock exchanges and the Thai stock exchange is no exception. Asian countries often lack the regulatory and administrative background to support stock markets. Insider trading and other financial malpractices are rife.

Thai authorities are, however, keen to improve the image of their stock exchange. In 1992, the Bank of Thailand set up the Securities and Exchange Commission to supervise securities companies, monitor trading, and promote new financial instruments.

The commission leads regular campaigns against stock manipulation and other forms of malpractice. In 1992, soon after its creation, it charged twelve people for buying and selling shares with the intent to mislead the public. Such actions usually depress the market, although only for short periods.

Takeover bids also follow strict rules. Investors must notify the Securities and Exchange Commission when buying more than 5 percent of a company. They are required to inform the company concerned for purchases of over 10 percent. Bids in excess of 25 percent must be accompanied by a tender offer for all other shares at the highest price paid for the stake.

Curbing speculation is often a challenge on the volatile Asian stock markets. The Thai stock exchange uses limits on margin loans to control investment. These change occasionally. In 1993, for instance, the exchange specified that at least 50 percent of portfolio value should be in owner's equity. Investors must inject funds or sell part of their portfolio if their margin falls below the required levels.

Brokers who do not abide by the rules face disciplinary action. The exchange may fine and censor brokerages for misdeeds, such as extending credit to clients beyond the margin limit and cutting brokerage fees to attract business. In addition, brokers who make mistakes or whose clients default must usually pay for the losses incurred.

Fraud prevention also relies on the detection of irregular patterns in prices and volumes. In case of unusual transactions, the stock exchange may request an explanation from the company concerned. Failure to respond results in suspension of trading. These actions are public as the stock exchange informs investors of its dealings with companies by posting signs.

Several signs may be posted, but the most controversial is,

probably, the Designated Security one. This sign warns investors of substantial changes in price or volume and it changes trading rules. Investors may trade designated securities only in cash, while brokers may not trade these stocks from their own portfolio.

These rules create much discontent. Brokers maintain that quality of information is the principal problem. The stock exchange insists on full disclosure of information but lags between filing and disclosure encourage insider trading. In addition, since companies may not file unaudited informations, rumors spread until the audited report comes out.

6.4.3 GETTING LISTED

The institutions listed on the stock exchange are juristic companies, government enterprises, and mutual funds. Foreign companies qualify only if they are registered under Thai commercial laws. Companies must also meet administrative requirements especially regarding management and accounting. Boards of directors must comprise at least two outsiders, while financial statements must be verified by accredited auditors.

The principal step in getting listed is to appoint a sponsor, that is, an authorized finance or securities company. Sponsors provide financial advice, prepare application documents, guarantee that applicants are suited for listing, and coordinate with the stock exchange.

Listing takes time. Until recently, procedures could take up to six months. The recent introduction of the sponsoring method for applications, however, has improved processing. Officials say that waiting time has now declined to about three months.

6.5 RAISING CAPITAL

Thailand is short of funds. Domestic savings are usually short-term and they lag behind investment. Businesses still rely heavily on direct credit, especially loans from financial institutions and overdrafts from commercial banks. Public companies also raise funds by issuing stocks.

Raising capital is, however, becoming easier. The licensing of offshore banks has facilitated the borrowing of foreign funds. Reforms of the financial system have also broadened the activities of financial institutions and corporate finance services are developing rapidly.

6.5.1 DEBT INSTRUMENTS

Debt instruments are expanding with the relaxation of financial regulations. Since 1992, limited companies may issue commercial paper and launch euro-convertible debentures to collect funds. Commercial banks have also been allowed to issue negotiable certificates of deposit, that is, time deposits ranging from three months to three years.

The issuance and trade of commercial paper has become a means of raising short-term capital. Enterprises appoint commercial banks and finance companies to auction off bills of exchange. The winning bid is the one with the lowest interest rate. These auctions are popular with large investors because rates are higher than on the bond repurchase market. The Government Savings Bank, for example, is a regular investor in this market.

The most important innovation is, perhaps, the introduction of international bonds. Euro-convertible debentures have become popular debt instruments in Thailand. These are usually US dollar-based bonds with the option to be converted into shares within a specific period. The option to convert the bonds is attractive to foreign investors, especially in Europe and America where Thailand is less known. Since such instruments became available in 1992, many companies have issued international bonds to tap cheaper foreign capital.

Euro-convertible debentures, however, are valuable mainly in financing large investments. Issues are usually over US$50 million. Principal users are real-estate companies whose projects require much capital. In addition, only large companies with good track records find subscribers easily. Brokers claim that only 20 to 40 of the companies listed on the stock exchange meet these standards.

Smaller companies must often turn to the local market were liquidity is lower and interest rates are higher. Issues are diverse, including ordinary, unsecured, convertible, and subordinated long-term debentures, but their success is variable. Small companies must often attach guarantees to attract investors.

Debentures may, however, become more successful with the development of related financial facilities. In 1993, the Securities and Exchange Commission permitted banks and finance companies to underwrite debt instruments, while the Bank of Thailand set up a credit rating agency.

This agency, called Thai Rating and Information Services Company, is the agent of a leading American credit rating agency. It handles only the local rating business. The Thai rating agency uses its parent company's AAA to D format, but it bases ratings on a local scale that takes local characteristics into account. It released its first rating in October 1993.

The Thai Rating and Information Services Company is the first credit-rating agency in Thailand, but it does not hold a monopoly over this business. The law provides for the creation of other agencies, although only limited or public companies that receive technical assistance from a credit-rating company of international repute qualify.

Companies that are not listed on the stock exchange will further benefit from the creation of over-the-counter markets. New laws authorize any 15 securities companies to form a trading center for non-listed securities. Brokers are now trying to organize over-the-counter markets for common stocks and debt instruments, but this takes time.

6.5.2 EQUITIES

Equities play a major role in raising capital. For many years, stocks, especially common shares, have been a major instrument in funding new projects. Companies sell new issues through public offerings and by granting subscription rights to shareholders.

A variety of securities are traded on the stock exchange. Listed juristic companies may issue ordinary and preferred shares and convertible debentures, while mutual fund companies issue unit trusts. Equities have also benefited from the introduction of warrants in 1990. These are rights to purchase stocks and they may be issued only in conjunction with them.

6.5.3 FINANCING JOINT VENTURES

Joint ventures are often opportunities for Thai companies to have access to foreign technology and to inject capital in their operations. Foreign partners usually source funds outside Thailand although procedures depend on the size of the project. For small projects, local financial institutions may provide financing, but for major investments, companies usually seek international funds. Syndicated loans and foreign stock exchanges are common sources of international capital. The Asian Development Bank also grants loans, especially for infrastructure. While these loans are often denominated in US dollars, the currency risk is minimal because of the link between the Thai baht and the US dollar.

6.6 INSURANCE

The insurance industry is still regulated, but it is earmarked for liberalization. Pending reforms are expected to open the market to international investors and enhance competition. So far, there are few foreign insurance businesses. In 1994, only five foreign companies had branches in Thailand although several others operated through joint ventures with local enterprises.

Insurance companies cater to two principal markets, life and non-life. These have similar sizes, each accounting for about half of all direct premiums. Life insurance companies, however, are bigger businesses, partly because they are less numerous. In 1991, the industry comprised 75 insurance companies: 7 selling life insurance, 5 offering both life and non-life policies, 62 providing non-life insurance, and 1 specializing in reinsurance services.[14]

The markets for both life and non-life insurance are expanding rapidly. Between 1982 and 1991, premiums increased annually by 15 percent in real terms for life insurance and by 13 percent for non-life insurance.[15] Yet taking insurance is seldom a priority for both individuals and companies. Even some public transportation companies are not insured.

Aside from a few large concerns, most insurance companies are small businesses. The top ten companies generate about two-thirds of total direct premiums. In 1991, these large enterprises collected an average of US$110 million in premiums each, compared to only US$10 million for other operators.[16]

The industry also suffers from a bad image. Many companies are small family-run businesses. They invest little in marketing and public relations and they lack qualified staff, especially agents. Clients often say that insurers are slow to pay claims. Although the Department of Insurance, a government agency, monitors the activities of the industry by checking solvency and organizing training classes, complaints keep piling up at its offices.

6.6.1 LIFE INSURANCE

The market for life insurance is still small by international standards, but it has potential. In 1991, only 6.8 percent of Thais had a life insurance policy, compared to a quarter of Japanese and half of Americans. In wealthier areas like Bangkok, however, the proportion of policyholders reaches 16 percent and sums insured are bigger. Bangkok residents alone account for a quarter of the policies in force nationwide and 39 percent of the premiums paid.[17]

Companies offer three main types of policies: ordinary, industrial, and group. Ordinary life insurance is designed for individual needs. Industrial policies are low-value insurance contracts. Group policies apply to groups of five people and over, usually co-workers.

Individuals are the principal clients. In 1991, ordinary life insurance accounted for over half of the policies in force and 83 percent of the premiums paid (see Figure 6.3). Industrial insurance is also widespread but less lucrative, accounting for 48 percent of the policies but only 15 percent of the premiums. Group insurance, in contrast, is rare, generating only 2 percent of the premiums.[18]

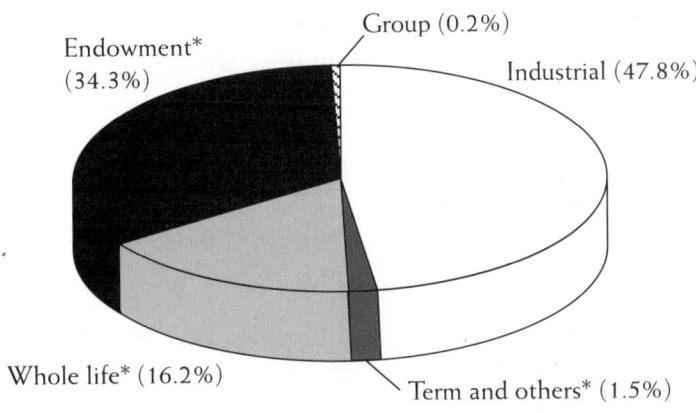

*Ordinary Policies (52.0%)

Figure 6.3 Life Insurance Policies in Force by Type in 1991 (Source: Based on Department of Insurance, Annual Insurance Report of Thailand 1991, Bangkok, p. 6.)

Life insurance in Thailand is often a means of savings. The most popular policies are endowment plans, accounting for nearly half of the sum insured in 1991. These policies run for 10 to 20 years and they redeem the capital invested upon maturity. Because Thai authorities encourage long-term savings, they grant fiscal privileges to policy owners. Life insurance premiums are partly deductible from taxable income.

A few key players dominate the industry. In 1991, the three biggest life insurance companies combined captured 84 percent of the market. The most important one, a branch of a large American company, collected 46 percent of total life insurance premiums. Its market share is especially large for ordinary and group policies, exceeding 50 percent.[19]

6.6.2 NON-LIFE INSURANCE

Non-life insurance companies offer a wide array of services. These fall into five broad categories: fire, marine and transportation, automobile, miscellaneous, and health. Most companies provide coverage in the first four categories. Health insurance is the only separate business. In 1991, six companies offered such policies and they specialized in it.

The industry is developing rapidly. Between 1982 and 1991, direct premiums tripled in real terms. Automobile and health insurance are the fastest-growing sectors, with premiums increasing annually by about 20 percent in real terms, compared to only 6 percent for fire insurance (see Figure 6.4).

Fire and automobile insurance remain the most popular policies. Together, they captured about three-quarters of the non-life insurance market in 1991 (see Figure 6.5). Most other premiums are for freight and miscellaneous policies, while health insurance is marginal.

Fire Fire insurance is the most common non-life coverage and a lucrative business. In 1991, insurance companies issued 1.2 million fire insurance policies, accounting for 46 percent of the non-life policies and a quarter of the direct premiums. Although cheap, these policies are profitable. Claims usually account for only 20 percent of the premium earned, compared to about 60 percent for other coverages.[20]

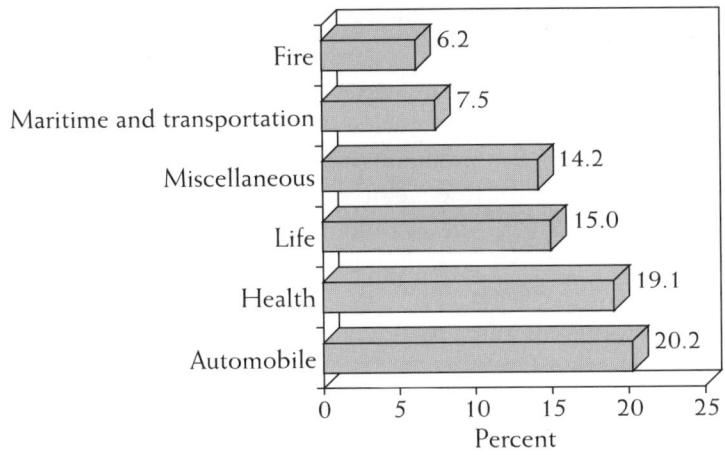

Figure 6.4   Average Annual Growth Rate of Insurance Premiums 1982–1991
(Source: Based on Department of Insurance, *Annual Insurance Report of Thailand 1991*, Bangkok, pp. 41, 173.)

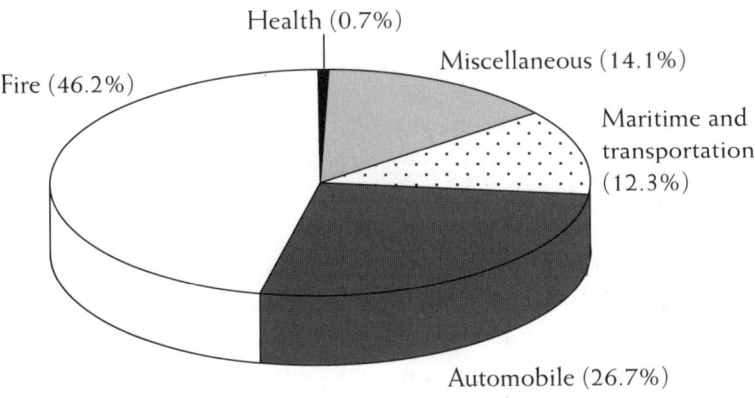

Figure 6.5   Non-Life Insurance Policies Issued by Type in 1991
(Source: Based on Department of Insurance, *Annual Insurance Report of Thailand 1991*, Bangkok, p. 141.)

Many people buy these policies because fires are frequent and destructive. They cause US$25 to US$60 million of damages annually. Because many houses are built of wood and are clustered, blazes spread quickly, especially during the dry season. Fires are also difficult to put out because of the lack of fire-fighting equipment.

Automobile Automobile insurance is the fastest-growing non-life insurance and the principal source of premiums. By 1991, it accounted for a quarter of the non-life policies and for over half of the direct premiums.[21] Yet profits are low because claims account for about two-thirds of the premiums earned.

These policies are set to develop further. The rapid growth of the car fleet combined with the introduction of compulsory third party insurance in 1993 are a boon for the industry. Insurers are prompt to introduce new services. Some have arranged to distribute application forms for third party coverage in public places like post offices.

Maritime and transportation Maritime and transportation insurance is developing slowly despite the rapid expansion of international trade. Between 1982 and 1991, it has grown annually by 7.5 percent in real terms.[22] Since Thai importers usually place orders CIF (cost, insurance, and freight) and exporters conclude deals FOB (free on board), foreign parties often make arrangements for transportation and insurance.

Policies fall into two broad categories: cargo and hull. Cargo is by far the most important business, accounting for about 90 percent of the premiums in this category.[23] Most non-life insurance companies offer this coverage. Hull policies are less common and only one-third of the insurance companies sell them.

Miscellaneous This category comprises a wide range of products. Companies offer coverages against various hazards, especially accidents. Standard golf insurance policies, for instance, provide third party liability and they cover loss or damage of equipment and injuries sustained during a game. More specific are the policies covering the cost of the grand prize that a sponsor of golf games must offer when a contender scores a hole-in-one.

Health Health insurance is a small industry. In 1991, the six health insurance companies combined collected only US$8.6 million direct premiums; this is less than 1 percent of the non-life insurance market.[24] The most popular policies cover personal health and personal accident.

6.7 REAL ESTATE

The real-estate sector has changed dramatically over the past few years. Development projects started throughout the country and more investors established real-estate companies that introduced new products. Holiday time-sharing properties and serviced apartments, for example, are recent additions.

Business is brisk in the Bangkok area. In 1992, construction projects in Bangkok Metropolis accounted for three-quarters of the construction space approved nationwide.[25] In the city center, prestigious office buildings, condominiums, and commercial centers are multiplying. In the suburbs, developers build satellite towns.

In the provinces, projects are related to tourism and manufacturing. Developers build industrial estates, factories, and infrastructure in industrial areas and condominiums, resorts, hotels, and golf courses in tourist places.

Prices, nonetheless, remain low by Asian standards. Property prices in Bangkok are lower than in most Asian cities including Tokyo, Hong Kong, Singapore, and Taipei. In 1993, monthly rental of prime office space in Bangkok approached US$2 per square foot, about one-fifth of the price in Tokyo.

6.7.1 INVESTORS

High profits have attracted a wide range of investors. Manufacturers, bankers, stockbrokers, and almost anybody with capital dabbles in property development. Even academics have entered the market. In 1993, for instance, Thammasat University auctioned the right to develop some of its land. Related businesses like appraisal, brokerage, property consulting, and real-estate information services are also expanding.

A number of companies have become major players in the market. They handle some of the biggest and most ambitious development projects in Thailand. The most spectacular ones are probably the satellite towns that developers build in the Bangkok area. They combine housing, industrial estates, shopping centers, schools, and recreational facilities.

Financing may be a hurdle. Because real-estate projects require large capital investment, developers often presell their residential and office buildings to finance construction. Developers usually request buyers to make a 10 percent deposit before construction starts and to pay an additional 30 percent during construction. The rest is due upon completion.

The biggest real-estate companies have sought listing on the stock exchange. Until recently, issuing stocks was a principal means of raising capital. Funding, however, became easier in May 1992, when new regulations allowed limited and public companies to issue debt instruments. Property developers were the first Thai companies to use this financial tool.

Many local developers have also funded their expansion by entering into joint ventures with foreign partners. This gave international companies opportunities to invest in real estate, an activity otherwise restricted to Thai nationals. Aliens, that is, businesses and partnerships with over 49 percent foreign interest and foreign nationals, may not own land. The Thai Land Code specifies that they may only rent land and own buildings.

There are, however, a few exceptions to the law. Oil concessionaires and companies that are promoted by the Board of Investment may own some land for their activities. Since 1991, the Thai government has also allowed aliens to buy up to 40 percent of the units in condominiums. These are buildings where individual ownership extends only to the units of the building. Land and other facilities such as swimming pools and parking lots are undivided property. Because condominiums include a variety of structures like housing, office buildings, and shopping complexes, investment possibilities are varied.

6.7.2 MARKET

Housing is, perhaps, the aspect of Thai life that is changing the most. The traditional household with several generations living together is gradually disappearing. As they grow richer, people leave the extended family for a private home. The average household is getting smaller. Well-educated single young professionals seek separate accommodation. Wealthier Thais also buy second homes. Houses and flats are in growing demand, and with fewer people building their own homes, real-estate and construction companies supply most of the new units.

High-rise residential buildings are getting more common in cities, but individual homes remain the favorite habitations. In 1990, the vast majority of Thais, some 94 percent, lived in houses.[26] These are also the principal accommodation in Bangkok although a quarter of the city's population lives in rooms and flats. Modern apartment buildings are developing mainly in the city center where land is more expensive.

This trend has accelerated with the growing congestion in the city. Bangkok residents seek accommodations close to their workplaces to reduce commuting time. Favorite residential sites are located near the business districts, but they are more expensive. Condominiums and serviced apartments in these areas cater to expatriates and upper-income Thais. Cheaper sites for middle-income Thais are being developed near planned rail terminals and along highways.

Low-cost high-rise buildings are rare. The National Housing Authority, a government agency, remains the principal provider of cheap housing. There are long waiting lists for its subsidized flats. The agency has recently accelerated its construction programs, planning joint ventures with the private sector. In 1993, it obtained approval to build a new city near Bangkok for 60,000 families. A few real-estate companies also began developing condominiums for the low-income groups. A local company, for instance, used cheap prefabricated construction parts made by a Japanese partner to build low-cost housing.

Because land is getting scarce, investors redevelop slums. Poorer people traditionally rented vacant land to build informal housing. Over time, large shanty communities have developed in various parts of the city, some of which are now valuable. The biggest slum area, for instance, is located in Klong Toey, a prime site adjacent to Bangkok Port. Although slum dwellers resist eviction, shanty areas are being cleared gradually.

The scarcity of land also affects the development of office buildings. The traditional central business districts of Bangkok can no longer accommodate the growing demand. Several new business centers in peripheral areas are cropping up. Biggest developments are located in the northern edge of the city toward Don Muang Airport and on the eastern side near Bangkok Port.

Competition for all types of development projects is fierce. Location is no longer the sole sales criteria. New constructions also emphasize quality. Office towers are automated and they have helicopter landing pads. Condominiums offer additional facilities like swimming pools and clubs and they advertise clean and quiet neighborhood and green spaces. Some upmarket residential properties are even surrounded by orchards.

NOTES

1. Calculations based on Bank of Thailand, *Quarterly Bulletin*, March 1993, p. 6.
2. Pendragon, Victor, "Recalling early days of banking in Siam," *South China Morning Post*, 11 November 1990.
3. Source: Bank of Thailand, *Annual Economic Report 1992*, Bangkok, p. 55.
4. Supra 1, pp. 22–3.
5. Supra 3, p. 57.
6. Supra 1, pp. 22–3.
7. The bank reported that in March 1992, its US$2 billion outstanding loans had been extended to 3.4 million households. See "BAAC to raise capital to 6,000 million baht," *Bangkok Post*, 22 September 1992, Business Post section, p. 26.
8. Supra 3, p. 60.
9. Supra 1, pp. 11, 31.
10. Supra 3, p. 52.
11. Calculations based on Center for Agricultural Statistics, *Agricultural Statistics of Thailand, Crop Year 1991/92*, MAC, Bangkok, 1992, pp. 254–5.
12. Calculations based on Bank of Thailand, *Annual Economic Report 1992*, Bangkok, p. 60.
13. Calculations based on Research and Development Department, The Stock Exchange of Thailand, Bangkok, and International Monetary Fund, *IFS*, various issues.
14. Source: Department of Insurance, *Annual Insurance Report of Thailand 1991*, Bangkok, pp. 3, 139, 413.
15. Calculations based on Department of Insurance, *Annual Insurance Report of Thailand 1991*, Bangkok, pp. 41, 173.
16. Supra 15, pp. 36, 171–2.
17. Supra 15, pp. 112–6.
18. Supra 14, p. 6.
19. Supra 15, p. 36.
20. Supra 15, pp. 141, 143, 147.
21. Supra 15, p. 141.

22. Supra 15, p. 173.
23. Supra 15, p. 141.
24. Supra 15, p. 172.
25. Supra 12, p. 34.
26. Source: National Statistical Office, *Report of the 1990 Household Socio-Economic Survey, Whole Kingdom*, OPM, Bangkok, 1993, pp. 107–8.

7 TRANSPORTATION AND COMMUNICATIONS

Transportation and communications are, probably, Thailand's biggest problem. The kingdom is renowned for its interminable traffic jams, shipping delays, and poor telephone lines. Congestion peaks in Bangkok, Thailand's most densely populated area. The city seems to be in a permanent state of chaos, with traffic often coming to a standstill.

Improving infrastructure has become a pressing issue. It makes the headlines in newspapers and it fuels political debates. Even the king donated money to improve the situation. The task, however, is formidable and expensive. High costs have delayed long-planned projects for years and they have impaired the maintenance of existing infrastructure.

The government is now turning to the private sector for funds. It has recently granted some of the biggest concessions ever issued for transportation and communications. In 1992, the kingdom's top eight concessionary projects included three mass transit systems, two expressways, and three communications systems.[1]

International aid agencies, especially Japanese, have also come to the rescue, offering low-interest loans for infrastructure. These finance a variety of projects, like roads, railways, and ports.

Relief is in sight, although it will take time. The following sections review the current facilities and their shortcomings and they outline the changes that are taking place.

Chapter 7 Transportation and Communications

7.1 MARITIME TRANSPORTATION

Maritime transportation is a leading vehicle for commerce. The bulk of the merchandise entering and leaving Thailand is sea-bound. The kingdom has five major commercial ports: Klong Toey in Bangkok, Laem Chabang and Mab Ta Phud southeast of Bangkok, and Songkhla and Phuket in the South.

Klong Toey is the kingdom's busiest and oldest port. Because of its location on the Chao Phraya river, Bangkok was, for centuries, the major port of call for both merchants and travelers. In the past, the river played a strategic role linking the northern provinces and the central plains with the outside world. Foreign sailing vessels even called there during the Ayutthayan period. Shipping was also crucial to the country. Until the development of inland transportation, Thai kings relied on maritime transportation for trade, communications, and political control.

Facilities at the port have improved steadily with the changes in navigation. Klong Toey was initially built to accommodate steamers and their conventional cargo. It was later remodeled to handle various types of vessels, especially container ships. Its operator, the state-owned Port Authority of Thailand (PAT), also added new berths and midstream anchorages to keep up with the growing traffic.

The PAT was once the principal manager of commercial ports in the kingdom, but it is facing growing competition. Newer ports have greater autonomy. Private enterprises run their terminals. More shipping lines are calling at these ports, although changes take time. Bangkok remains the hub for shipping.

7.1.1 PORT OF BANGKOK–KLONG TOEY

Klong Toey, located 20 miles upstream the Chao Phraya River, is Thailand's major and best equipped commercial port. It handles the bulk of the trade of merchandise and it has the largest handling equipment and the biggest number of tug boats and other service crafts.

Berthing facilities combine quays and anchorage. The port can accommodate a total of 38 ships. Klong Toey wharves, called East Quay and West Quay, have ten berths for conventional ships, six for container ships, and two for lighters. Midstream dolphins and mooring buoys provide space for an additional 20 vessels. Ships mooring in these spaces rely on a fleet of 550 privately operated lighters for service.

Turnover peaks at the wharves. In 1992, some three-quarters of the 3,400 ships calling at Bangkok Port berthed at the quays.[2] The Port Authority of Thailand (PAT), which runs Klong Toey, reserves wharves for discharging. Ships move later to midstream anchorage for loading. The PAT allocates space daily although major shipping lines have secured exclusive rights to use some of the port's container berths.

The port handles various types of freight, but containers dominate. In 1992, these accounted for about 80 percent of the cargo throughput by volume. This is a recent trend that started in the early 1980s. Until then, most cargo was conventional (see Figure 7.1). Containers come in various sizes, but the vast majority are twenty- and forty-feet boxes.

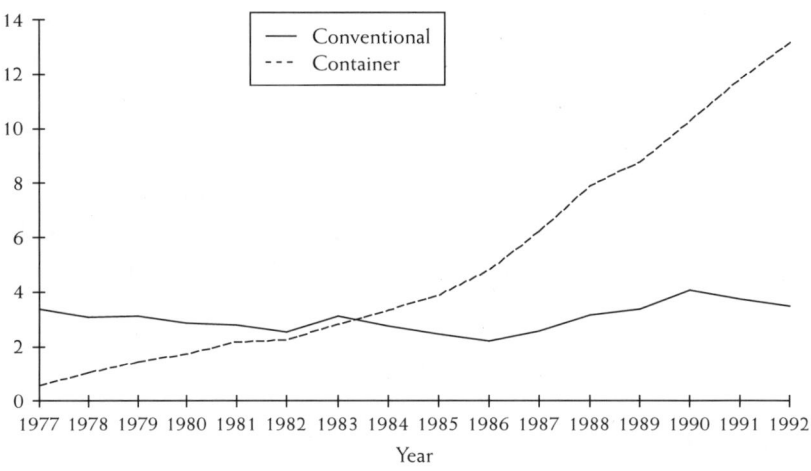

Figure 7.1   Cargo Throughput at Klong Toey Wharf 1977–1992
(*Source: Based on Data Processing Department, Port Authority of Thailand, Bangkok.*)

Traffic is intense. In 1992, container throughput at Klong Toey wharves reached 1.3 million twenty-feet equivalent units[3] (TEU). Although this is only a fraction of the volume at the world's leading container ports of Hong Kong and Singapore, it remains sizeable by international standards. Klong Toey ranks among the top twenty container ports in the world. Its activity is similar to that of the

American ports of Oakland, Seattle, and Tacoma.

The PAT is the principal port operator in Bangkok, but it is not the only one. Over 70 private wharves cater to bulk-cargo ships. They are often run by private traders like rice and tapioca exporters for their business purposes. In 1992, import cargo at private wharves reached 8.35 million tons, compared to 8 million tons at Klong Toey.[4]

Klong Toey, however, can accommodate only small ships. The dredged channel at the entrance of the Chao Phraya River allows in vessels that are up to 172 meters (565 feet) in length, 8.2 meters (27 feet) in draft, and 12,000 dead weight tons (dwt) in capacity. Bigger long liners must tranship merchandise on smaller vessels in Singapore or Hong Kong.

These small feeders, although convenient for regional navigation, can no longer handle Thailand's growing international trade. Shippers are seeking direct service to distant destinations in America and Europe.

Klong Toey is also approaching full capacity. Congestion has worsened, although this is a long-standing problem. The port is notorious for work stoppages, delays, and inefficiencies, a condition that observers have dubbed the "Klong Toey disease." The development of new privately operated ports, however, has introduced competition.

7.1.2 SATTAHIP

Sattahip Commercial Port is no longer active, but it relieved congestion at Bangkok Port for a brief period. The port of Sattahip was set up at the Chuk Samet Naval Base, 185 kilometers (115 miles) southeast of Bangkok. The base was built by the United States between 1966 and 1969 and transferred to the Thai Government in 1972. In 1979, it passed under the control of the PAT. Commercial activities lasted until 1991 when the port reverted to the navy.

During its commercial years, Sattahip was never much active. The port could berth 5 vessels at a time and it could handle 2 million tons of cargo per year, but throughput did not exceed 250,000 tons. Freight consisted mainly of tapioca products, parts and equipment for the automobile industry, and exploration and mining equipment for the gas industry in the Gulf of Thailand.

7.1.3 LAEM CHABANG AND MAB TA PHUD

The new ports of Laem Chabang and Mab Ta Phud are Thailand's answers to the shortcomings of Bangkok Port. They can accommodate bigger ships and they have greater links with the private sector. The ports, which started operation in 1991, are expected to relieve congestion at Klong Toey and to assist the development of industries in the Eastern Region.

Both ports are part of the development plan in the Eastern Seaboard. This is a vast program that involves the construction of roads, railroads, utilities, office buildings, industrial estates, and export processing zones. The Eastern Seaboard, located southeast of Bangkok, is divided into two major areas, the Laem Chabang area for light industries and the Map Ta Phud area for heavy petrochemical complexes.

The port of Mab Ta Phud is an industrial port that services nearby plants. It is located 210 kilometers (130 miles) southeast of Bangkok and it is equipped to handle petroleum, bulk raw material, and factory products. The port may accommodate vessels of up to 60,000 dwt and it has a capacity of 3.4 million tons of cargo per year.

Operations are still confused. The developer of the port, the Industrial Estates Authority of Thailand, leaves the management of the port to private companies. Users, however, have complained of poor service and of insufficient infrastructure.

The port of Laem Chabang has a broader purpose. Officials say that it is expected to become a leading commercial port. Its seven terminals cater to conventional, container, and bulk cargo. Their combined capacity is moderate at about seven million tons of cargo throughput per year, but there is room for expansion.

The port also plays an important role in domestic trade. It links upper Thailand and the South through roll-on roll-off service (*ro-ro*). Trucks coming from upper Thailand may board *ro-ro* vessels at Laem Chabang toward major destinations in the South.

The capacity of berths, however, remains the principal advantage. The port can accommodate vessels of up to 300 meters (984 feet) in length, 14 meters (46 feet) in draft, and 50,000 dwt in capacity. Long liners from major ports in Europe, the United States, and Japan may call there and transshipment is no longer necessary.

The private sector has a large stake in the management of the port. Although the PAT supervises the overall administration, private companies operate the container and bulk terminals. Only the multipurpose terminal remains under the PAT's direct control.

Laem Chabang had a slow start, but traffic has picked up lately. Much of the planned infrastructure was not completed when the port opened, deterring potential users. Rail links and container depots, for instance, were still under construction. Activity improved later although it is still low compared to the traffic at Bangkok Port.

The Port of Laem Chabang has potential, but it needs time to attract customers. Factories in the Eastern Seaboard, although prime targets, are a small proportion of Thai industries. In addition, few importers have warehouses near Laem Chabang. This is inconvenient and it prevents the inspection of incoming merchandise.

7.1.4 PHUKET, SONGKHLA, AND SI CHANG

The ports of Phuket, Songkhla, and Si Chang are specialized. Phuket services the tin industry, Songkhla the rubber factories, and Si Chang the oil companies. They are located near production centers. Phuket and Songkhla are in the South and Si Chang is on an island off Sri Racha in the Eastern Seaboard.

These ports are managed by private companies. The Harbor Department has granted a private operator a concession to run the ports of Phuket and Songkhla, while the port of Si Chang is a private venture. Traffic is fairly low at the Southern ports. Phuket is almost idle, catering only to tourist cruises, while Songkhla is moderately active.

The port of Si Chang, currently under development, has potential. It can accommodate large oil tankers of up to 100,000 dwt and unload their cargo through pipelines, an improvement over the current arrangements. So far, these large ships must berth at sea and transfer oil into smaller vessels.

7.1.5 SHIPPING LINES

Despite its dependence on maritime transportation, Thailand has a small merchant marine. Its fleet is among the smallest in the region and it consists of the smallest vessels too. Thai shipping lines have a low market share, handling less than 10 percent of the exports and imports of merchandise. They are often small family businesses. In 1994, only three companies were listed on the stock exchange.

Shippers have done little to upgrade their services. During most of the 1980s, the number of vessels sailing under the Thai flag remained constant. Ships are old and poorly equipped. Few are fit for carrying containers. The vast majority are oil and gas tankers and general-cargo vessels. Because they are old, these ships are also more costly to operate; they need more maintenance and they spend more time in the docks.

Thai authorities tried to help the industry by protecting it. The Law requires all Thai shipowners to register their vessels under the Thai flag. It also provides for reserving cargo for Thai vessels, especially exports under the control of government agencies. Besides, cabotage laws restrict domestic shipping to locally registered vessels. These efforts, however, were unsuccessful.

Financing investment has perhaps been the principal difficulty of shipowners. Until recently, there were no specific laws on ship mortgage and maritime lien. Companies could not obtain capital by mortgaging a vessel and they had to finance the investment with their own funds. This is, however, changing. A bill passed in 1993 recognizes ships as fixed assets, allowing financial institutions to accept ship mortgage.

7.2 AIR TRANSPORTATION

Air transportation is well organized in Thailand. The kingdom has good facilities for both passengers and cargo. The industry has developed steadily with tourism and the vast majority of its customers are foreign travelers.

For many years, the industry has been closely associated with the military. Commercial aviation started in 1922 under the supervision of the Thai air force. After the Second World War, the Civil Aviation Board took over this responsibility, but the air force maintained close links with the industry. Until 1992, it controlled the management of the national carrier. Recent changes have, however, weakened this role.

7.2.1 AIRPORTS

Air transportation covers many destination. Thailand has 26 major airports, five of them international. The principal one is Don Muang located 22 kilometers (14 miles) north of Bangkok. Other international airports are Chiang Mai in the North, U-Tapao (near Pattaya) in the East, and Phuket and Hat Yai in the South.

Airports have been instrumental in the development of tourism. Many are located in tourist areas. There are, for instance, nine airports in the North and eight in the South; both regions are important tourist destinations. By comparison, only three airports are located in Central Thailand and six in the Northeast. Travelers on international flights also account for the bulk, some two-thirds, of the passengers handled nationwide. In addition, domestic flights cater to many foreign visitors.

Don Muang Airport in Bangkok is a hub for transportation. It is the port of entry of most visitors to Thailand and it is a convenient transit point for European and Australian airlines, especially because it has no curfew. Don Muang also caters to many domestic flights. In 1992, over three-quarters of the 22 million passengers at Thai airports passed through Bangkok.[5] Activity keeps increasing with the development of new regional services and the growth in charter and cargo flights.

Growing traffic is causing congestion. In 1992, Don Muang handled 13 million international and 3.5 million domestic passengers.[6] It is expected to reach full capacity by the end of the 1990s. The airport keeps upgrading its facilities, but expansion is limited by the terminals, parking space, and runways. At peak hours, for instance, there is barely enough parking to accommodate all planes.

Bangkok, like many other leading Asian cities, is planning a second airport. The new site, Nong Ngu Hao, is located about 30 kilometers (20 miles) east of the capital. This is a vast project that provides for two terminals and room for up to 80 million passengers. The first terminal, due for completion in the year 2000, will initially accommodate 30 million passengers.

Private airports are also developing. They cater to smaller aircraft and they handle both scheduled and chartered flights. Some are part of development projects for owners of private planes. They provide various services like a flying club, a maintenance center and accommodations.

7.2.2 AIRLINES

Thailand is well connected to many cities in the world. In 1993, over 60 airlines called at Thai airports. The number is growing steadily as more carriers in the region schedule flights to the kingdom.

Thai Airways International Company is the national carrier and the principal operator in Thailand. In 1993, its fleet of 66 aircraft carried over eight million passengers. The airline covers both domestic and international routes. It flies to major destinations in Thailand, Asia, Europe, Australia, and North America and its network is expanding steadily. Thai Airways International also carries most of Thailand's air cargo. The rest travels on other passenger airlines with cargo facility and on a few all-cargo airlines.

The company is renowned for quality service although its reputation has slipped recently. Until the first part of the 1980s, it was considered one of the best carriers in Asia. Part of this success stems from an early association with a European airline. This partnership covered technical expertise, marketing support, and staff training.

Thai Airways International, like other Asian airlines, has expanded dramatically over the past few decades. It benefited from a rapidly growing market and low competition from European and American airlines. This favorable environment ensured good profits despite loose financial control. A recent slowdown in the industry, however, has encouraged closer supervision.

Management is also changing. In 1992, the government amended the charter of the company so that the commander-in-chief of the air force could no longer be *ex-officio* chairman of Thai Airways International. Subsequently, most air force officers left the board and control was passed to the Transport and Communications Ministry. The company is also being privatized although only 7 percent of its stock has been made public so far.

The new management team faces a competitive environment. As more international airlines fly to Asia, Thai Airways International focuses on developing intraregional routes. These are often profitable and some destinations like China, Vietnam, and Indonesia have potential for becoming high-growth markets.

Competition also arises from local operators. Since the Thai government opened the airways to private interests in 1986, small private companies began offering scheduled flights. They fly small airplanes to tourist destinations in Thailand and in neighboring countries. More recently, companies started amphibian air links between major Thai cities.

Other flying services, especially transportation by helicopter, are expanding. Until 1993, only large companies could operate these, but growing demand from smaller enterprises has encouraged the government to relax its regulations. Operators cater mainly to business people. Large hotels in Bangkok are also turning to helicopters to ferry their clients to the airport and to other destinations in the city.

Deregulation also extends to private flying. In 1991, the Civil Aviation Department allowed private individuals to own aircraft and it eased registration procedures and regulations on flight plans. These changes have rekindled interest in private flying, with many individuals and companies applying for registration licenses.

7.3 RAILROADS, ROADS, AND WATERWAYS

Thais rely on railroads, roads, and waterways for domestic transportation. Roads are especially important, although they are the most recent addition to Thailand's infrastructure. They are still poor by Western standards, but they are a major improvement over traditional means of transportation.

Before roads and railroads existed in Thailand, transportation was basic. People traveled from Bangkok to the South by sea and they used inland routes for other regions. Trips were slow, especially to the Northern provinces, then only accessible by rivers. Early visitors report that the 600-kilometer (375-mile) journey from Bangkok to Lampang took three weeks.

7.3.1 RAILROADS

Railroads radiate from Bangkok, linking the capital with the provinces. The network passes major cities in each region and it reaches border towns near Laos, Cambodia, and Malaysia. It connects with the Malaysian railroad at Padang Besar and Sungai Kolok, allowing people to travel from Singapore to Bangkok. Trains also used to link Thailand and Cambodia, but this service stopped in 1974. Traffic may, however, resume soon because Thais are repairing tracks near the border.

Thai trains cover major routes, leaving out less-frequented destinations. They connect only 42 of the 73 Thai provinces and they are more suited for long-distance transportation than for commuting. In 1992, the average passenger traveled 160 kilometers[7] (100 miles).

Passenger traffic is the principal activity by value. It accounts for about two-thirds of the total revenue. In 1992, trains carried 88 million passengers.[8] Traffic is especially intense during public holidays when workers return to their home towns. Seats are then fully booked and many people ride on the roofs of the trains.

Railroads are attractive because they are cheap. In 1990, a 100-kilometer (60-mile) trip cost only US$3.30 in the first-class compartment and US$0.90 in third-class. The vast majority of Thais, however, some 95 percent, travel third-class. These people usually make shorter trips averaging 140 kilometers (85 miles), compared to 720 kilometers (445 miles) for first-class passengers.[9]

Transporting merchandise is, however, the principal activity. The vast majority, some 90 percent, of the rail cars are freight cars (see Figure 7.2) and in 1992, they transported 7.6 million tons of freight. Most is raw material, especially petroleum and cement. Together these account for three-quarters of the goods transported and for two-thirds of the freight revenue. Containers are also becoming important. Between 1988 and 1992, their volume grew from 82 to 600 tons.[10]

The State Railway of Thailand, a government enterprise, operates the network. The company has been in charge of the rail system since its inception in 1890. Its powers are, however, restricted. Pricing policy, for instance, is subject to government approval and political issues often prevail over business decisions. Management has also been plagued by red tape and the company is now heavily indebted.

Nonetheless, railroads have a more glorious past. They were built to tighten political control over the provinces and borders, but they soon became profitable carrying freight. As they predated roads, railroads enjoyed a quasimonopoly over all-weather inland transportation. They dominated the freight industry until the completion of a network of paved highways in the 1970s.

The competition from roads reduced the profitability of railroads

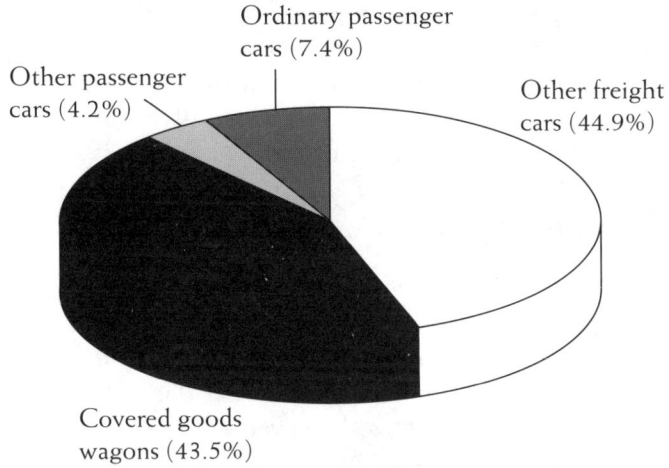

Figure 7.2   *Train Cars by Type in 1992*
(Source: Based on Finance and Accounting Department, State Railway of Thailand, Bangkok.)

and halted their development. Over the past two decades, the length of track has remained virtually unchanged. In 1992, Thailand had 3,960 kilometers (2,460 miles) of running tracks and 660 kilometers (410 miles) of siding tracks, about as much as in 1970. The network has also become obsolete. In 1992, the average diesel locomotive and passenger car were about 22 years old, while the average freight car was 31 years old.[11] This fleet of ageing cars and locomotives run on narrow gauge and mainly one-track lines, while stations still use manual traffic control systems.

Growing congestion, however, has revived interest in trains. Plans focus on extending and upgrading the network. The State Railway of Thailand is considering building lines for high-speed trains on popular routes. It is also improving its services. In 1991, for instance, the company introduced new express trains traveling at up to 120 kilometers per hour (75 miles per hour), the fastest in Thailand.

Planners also envisage developing railroads for regional transportation. New lines to border towns are under review. These are the first steps toward linking Thai railroads with other networks. In 1994, the Asian Development Bank, which sponsors projects in Asia, announced plans to coordinate the financing of a regional system of railroads that will eventually allow travel from Singapore to London.

These ambitious plans are expensive and the State Railway of Thailand is getting more active raising capital. It has been putting some of its vast tracts of land to commercial use, auctioning off rights for development. The company also started granting concessions to private operators of railroad and mass transit lines.

7.3.2 ROADS

Thai roads vary greatly in size and quality. Main roads in urban areas and highways are paved, usually with asphalt. Rural roads, in contrast, are of lower quality. Many are poorly maintained dirt roads, which are often impracticable during the wet season.

The network of highways is, however, well developed. In 1991, provincial and state highways combined stretched over 46,000 kilometers[12] (28,600 miles). State highways are the kingdom's main roads. They radiate from Bangkok, connecting the capital with major cities in each region. Provincial highways are regional feeders. Their network is extensive, accounting for about 60 percent of the highways.

Paved roads are new to Thailand. At the turn of the century, they were inexistent and until 1940, their length remained negligible. Initially, roads were built as feeders to the railroads, not as a separate network. Railroads were then the principal mode of transportation and the Thai government, eager to keep them solvent, held back the construction of highways until the 1950s.

The completion of a paved system of highways provided an efficient alternative to railroads. Trucks and buses made transportation cheaper, faster, and more flexible. They soon became popular, and by 1992, some 79,000 buses and 398,000 trucks circulated in Thailand.[13]

Buses play an important role in public transportation. Their extensive network covers a wide range of local and regional routes nationwide. In Bangkok, for instance, long-distance buses leave for almost every city in Thailand. The state-owned Transport Company runs many routes throughout the country, but it also grants concessions to private operators. In addition, a host of private concerns operate tour, school, and business buses.

However, roads are getting congested. The growth of the traffic outweighs the development of the network. During the 1980s, the number of vehicles has been increasing about twice as fast as the length of highways. Along popular routes, traffic is intense.

The Thai government is stepping up its road-building program, but administrative procedures delay construction. Expropriation is the principal difficulty. The administration bases compensation on the value of land at the time of approval of a project, which may be years before the time of expropriation. In the Northeast, for instance, a road still in construction in 1993 based its compensation on 1981 prices, the start-up date for the project. With the soaring cost of land, people often resist eviction and they lobby for greater compensation.

The Thai administration is also keen to develop international links. Major projects include highways to Southern China, Laos, and Vietnam. While the idea to build Asian highways has been floating for some time (it was initiated in the 1960s), it was stalled by economic and political problems. These projects are resurfacing now because of the high economic growth in the region.

7.3.3 WATERWAYS

Thailand has an extensive network of waterways that is often said to be unparalleled in Asia. For centuries, people have cut canals, called *khlongs*, to connect places. Bangkok is, perhaps, the most visible example of this tradition. The city is legendary for its crisscross of canals and it was once nicknamed the "Venice of the East."

Waterways are an integral part of Thai life. Cities have developed along rivers and canals and until recently, everyone traveled by boat. People even lived on houseboats. They anchored in the countryside where they tilled their fields, gardens, and orchards until the time of the harvest. Then they moved to Bangkok to sell their products.

In Bangkok, rivers and canals were once the only roads. The large ones lined with houseboats functioned as highways and the small ones as alleys. Life by the water was well organized. There were houses, shops, floating omnibuses, restaurants, and markets.

These communities survive, but the importance of waterways is declining. In Bangkok, many canals have been filled to build roads. Barges still ply the Chao Phraya river, but traffic concentrates in the Central Region because navigation up north is seasonal. Thai authorities also invest little in maintaining the system, leaving a minority of rivers and canals navigable year-round.

Waterways may nonetheless regain importance for international

313

transportation. Propositions to alter the Mekong River to accommodate heavy barges have surfaced at international conferences. The river, which flows through China, Burma, Thailand, Laos, Cambodia, and Vietnam has potential to become a major link between these countries.

7.4 TRANSPORTATION IN BANGKOK

Transportation in Bangkok is a nightmare. Congestion in the city is unrivaled in Asia. Vehicles move at the average speed of 10–25 kilometers per hour (7–15 miles per hour) and at peak hours, the traffic often comes to a standstill. Motorists are said to waste a month and a half per year in traffic jams. Exhaust fumes are overpowering, compelling traffic policemen to wear oxygen masks.

Traffic jams have become part of life in Bangkok. Drivers fall fast asleep at the wheel. Families leave their homes at dawn to drive their children to school and they dress and feed them on the way. Business people install cellular telephones, portable facsimile machines, and television sets in their limousine. Accessories for trapped motorists keep increasing and gas stations are now selling portable urinals.

Bangkok owes its chaotic situation partly to its rapid and uncontrolled development. Office and apartment buildings are sprouting throughout the city, with no regard for infrastructure planning. The construction of roads lags behind the expansion of the fleet of vehicles. The police claims that the population of Bangkok drives two million cars everyday on only 2,900 kilometers (1,800 miles) of roads.[14]

7.4.1 ROADS

Roads in Bangkok are ill-adapted to modern life, being scarce and often too narrow. They cover only 3 percent of the land area in the whole metropolis and 11 percent in the city center, compared to about 20 percent in major Western cities. Bangkok also has a host of small lanes, called *sois*, that are narrow and crowded. In these alleys, stalls and street vendors overflow the sidewalk, while some structures intrude permanently.

The layout is also at fault. Railroad crossings on main avenues slow down the traffic, while roads fail to act as a system of feeders and collectors. There are no secondary roads, only *sois* and large arteries. Because *sois* are poorly connected with each other, vehicles must use large arteries even for short trips. This increases the traffic and forces slow movers and frequent stoppers on main roads.

These defects largely result from poor planning. Projects are rarely part of a general design. Many are the conception of a government agency or a politician. Construction techniques are also questionable. The city, for instance, has been filling canals to build roads, an initiative now blamed for causing floods. In addition, the many roads built before the completion of the work on telephone, electricity, and water must be reopened later. Continuous digging to replace utilities slows down the construction of roads and it leaves them in substandard condition.

Bureaucratic red tape may be the biggest hindrance to change. No less than twelve agencies handle the development of roads in Bangkok, creating coordination problems. The Bangkok Metropolitan Administration (BMA), for example, builds roads, puts up signs, and repairs streets and walkways, but it cannot move bus stops, which are controlled by the Land Transport Department. The BMA cannot repair bridges either, although its responsibility extends to the maintenance of bridge ramps.

The Thai government is, however, intent improving the situation. It has launched a vast project to develop expressways. By 1994, 50 kilometers (30 miles) of highway linked the city center with the outer areas of the east, north, and west. Planned extensions will link Bangkok with neighboring provinces. Besides, various roads, including a tollway connecting Don Muang airport with central Bangkok, are under construction.

New highways are usually elevated over existing roads. This reduces the cost of expropriation but constrains routes. Observers contend that original roads are poorly aligned because of the random development of buildings. They say that expressways built over these roads perpetuate this fault.

Expressways are only part of the solution to congestion. They too get blocked if their users cannot exit because the streets of the city are jammed. Other measures include the creation of satellite towns that will divert the traffic away from Bangkok and the development of mass transit systems. These changes, however, take time.

In the interim, the city is trying to control its traffic. The aviation police runs helicopters and broadcasts reports to help motorists avoid congested areas and to assist traffic policemen. The BMA has installed closed-circuit televisions at intersections and it has invested in an Area Traffic Control (ATC), a computerized system that regulates traffic lights. Although an ATC has been operating in some parts of Bangkok since 1978, the government postponed its expansion for financial reasons.

7.4.2 MASS TRANSIT

Buses are, so far, the only form of mass transit in Bangkok. City buses are the principal vehicles, but there are also many school and office buses. The Bangkok Mass Transit Authority is the main operator of city buses. In 1993, it ran some 6,000 vehicles, both regular and air-conditioned. However, the company, which was set up in the 1970s, is debt-ridden and some of its buses are poorly maintained and overcrowded.

The Bangkok Mass Transit Authority blames its financial problems on poor operating conditions. It argues that congestion prevents buses from making more runs and reduces their profitability. It also complains of low fares. Since the government opposes fare increases, the company is trying to raise money from other sources. In 1992, for instance, it granted a concession to run extensive advertising on some of its vehicles.

Service is also improving. The Bangkok Mass Transit Authority is replacing older vehicles with new air-conditioned buses and in 1993, it awarded a private enterprise a concession to run upmarket minibuses on ten routes. These small vehicles offer high-quality service. They have daily newspapers, mobile phones, and an attendant on board.

These are only part of the efforts to promote public transportation. Thai authorities have also granted new taxi licenses and they set up a radio network so that people may call for taxis to pick them up. In addition, they are considering possible locations for car parks on the outskirts of Bangkok. These will allow commuters to leave their vehicles and ride a shuttle to the city center.

The most important change is, probably, the introduction of new mass transit systems. Over the past two decades, government agencies have proposed various mass transit plans including rail systems and subways. By 1994, three projects had been accepted, all of which are elevated railways, but it is unclear whether any one will be built because of red tape and infighting.

These projects are controversial. City planners question their effect on traffic. They point out that rail lines are suited to high-density areas, not to the sprawling low-density suburbs of Bangkok. They argue that the systems will attract only a small proportion of the commuters and that rail transit will help transportation only in the inner city.

Although poor, mass transit has a long history in Bangkok. It started in 1887 with the laying of a tram line. The system, which was operated under concession, used horse-drawn trams for the first five years before switching to electricity. Subsequently, the network expanded and by the late 1950s, Bangkok had ten tram lines with a combined length of track of 50 kilometers (30 miles). Trams disappeared later, leaving public buses as the only mass transportation.

7.5 COMMUNICATIONS

Investment in communications has been low in developing Asian countries, and Thailand is no exception. The production of telephone, radio, and other communications services has lagged behind economic growth. Telephone lines are congested and people must wait several years to be connected.

The industry is, however, undergoing profound and rapid changes. Since the late 1980s, Thai authorities have invited the private sector to tender on many different projects. By 1993, 15 concessions had been granted in various sectors of communications. Private enterprises are now investing in satellites, telephone lines, and cellular telephone and paging systems.

New companies specializing in communications have appeared. Some are key players in the market. They have developed into diversified conglomerates, with interests in computers, telephone, radio paging, cable television, data transmission, and satellite communications.

7.5.1 TELEPHONE, RADIO, PAGING

Telephone, radio, and paging services are under government control. They are the responsibility of two agencies, the Telephone

Organization of Thailand (TOT) and the Communications Authority of Thailand (CAT). The TOT manages local telephone lines, while the CAT handles international operations. Their duties, however, overlap because both agencies grant concessions to operate mobile telephones and pagers.

Telephone Telephone lines are still scarce. In 1992, Thailand had only 1.79 million telephone lines; this is 31 lines per thousand people,[15] compared to 440 in Hong Kong and 415 in South Korea. By 1994, the average waiting time for a telephone line was about four years, while some applicants had been waiting up to eight years.

Financing is the principal difficulty. The administration cannot keep up with demand because of its low budget. The TOT and the CAT can install only a few circuits and telephone lines each year.

The problem is, however, easing. Since 1990, the government has been granting private companies concessions to install and operate telephone lines. The biggest projects are the installation of two million lines in the Bangkok area and of one million in the provinces. These are due for completion in 1997 and they will double the telephone network. More modest but important for the links with the provinces is the concession to lay trunk lines along the railroad tracks nationwide.

Providing basic services is already a huge task, but Thailand has set its sights higher. Its new equipment is sophisticated, consisting of advanced computer-controlled exchanges and optical-fiber telephone lines. These will provide a wide range of services including videotext, high-speed data transfer, call waiting, conference calling, video conference, hot lines, and cable television. Thailand even aims to become the second country in the world after the United States to offer voice-dialing service.

Progress is already noticeable. In 1993, for instance, Thailand conducted its first international video conference with Malaysia. Public telephones that use credit cards have also appeared in Bangkok and in other major cities.

Improved telephone lines are especially valuable to businesses. They allow offices to use more telephones, facsimile machines, key-line systems, and private branch exchanges. A sign of growing demand, producers of office equipment are opening retail outlets to distribute these items.

The expansion of the telephone network has created business opportunities for foreign enterprises. Companies in Europe, Japan, and the United States supply equipment and they provide technical assistance. Prospects extend beyond Thailand because concessionaires of telephone services are expanding abroad. They have secured contracts to build and operate telephone lines in China, Vietnam, and Laos.

Radio In rural areas, Thai authorities resort to radio services. Base stations relaying ultrahigh frequency signals are easier to install and cheaper to operate than conventional telephone lines. The first such system was built between 1984 and 1992 to connect over 1,800 sparsely populated areas. An additional network covering 4,500 remote communities is scheduled for completion in 1996.

Cellular telephone Alternative systems of communications, especially cellular telephones, are thriving. Sales have boomed over the past few years and both the TOT and the CAT have granted private companies concessions to provide this service. By 1993, Thailand had about 300,000 users of cellular telephones.

Competition between these operators has increased the quality of service. In 1994, they introduced digital networks. These have greater capacity than the analog systems that had been used so far. Companies are also extending their coverage to include more highways and provincial cities.

Paging The pager industry is developing rapidly. The service started in 1986 and by 1993, there were some 300,000 users. Operators upgrade their products regularly. Paging services now have nationwide coverage; they use Thai-English alphanumeric display; and they supply additional information like foreign exchange rates, stock exchange listings, and gold prices.

In Bangkok, subscribers may combine their pagers with CT-2 cordless telephones. These allow people to place calls, but not to receive them. Users must call within 200 meters (650 feet) of a cell site. In 1994, there were 2,500 such sites in the city and more were in the planning. Because they do not require high-power radio transmitters, the CT-2 units are cheap to operate. Clientele has, however, developed slowly, with only 12,000 subscribers in 1994.

7.5.2 SATELLITE

Thailand has joined the race for communications via satellite. In 1991, the Thai government granted a local company a concession to launch and operate Thailand's first two commercial satellites. These serve the Thai communications industry primarily, although their coverage extends from Singapore to Korea and from Burma to Vietnam.

Satellite communications are not entirely new to the kingdom. Asian and Pacific-based television stations have beamed their programs into Thailand for some time. State agencies and private companies have also been leasing transponders from overseas satellites. Uses were, however, restricted to the transmission of data and to telephone services.

Thai-owned satellites open new opportunities. Planned services include telephone, paging, video conference, transmission of data, and Thai television stations. While diverse, benefits are especially valuable to businesses. Satellite communications will ease congestion and upgrade services.

Thailand is also expected to benefit from the launch of foreign satellites. American companies, for instance, are planning to provide telephone services worldwide independently of the local phone systems through satellite networks.

7.5.3 COMPUTERS

The market for computers is booming. Since the Thai government lowered import duties on computers and parts in 1991, prices have decreased dramatically and demand has increased. Competition for office automation systems has become fierce, with major international brands of computers opening shops in Thailand.

The financial sector has been, perhaps, the leading investor. Commercial banks have installed automatic teller machines and other electronic equipment, while in 1991, the Thai stock exchange introduced computerized trading.

The use of computers has spread to various administrations. The Port Authority of Thailand and the Thai Customs Department, for example, have invested in computer systems recently. The most spectacular change, however, was probably the launch by the highway police of computerized patrol cars in the Bangkok area.

These cars are linked to the police department's computer center and they retrieve information through the cellular telephone.

The manufacturing industry is also a growing market for computers. The growing cost of labor encourages manufacturers to invest in sophisticated computer-controlled equipment. Factories had been using computers for some time, but mainly for office tasks such as accounting, inventory, and payroll. They are now turning to computer technology for sales, manufacturing, and product design.

Years of high taxes, however, has impeded computer literacy. The industry suffers from lack of qualified personnel, especially programmers. Few students have had computer training because, until recently, hardly any school could afford computers.

Copyright protection for software is also a problem. Companies are reluctant to develop software packages because they cannot get good copyright protection. Sought-after goods like Thai software are difficult to obtain.

7.5.4 MAIL

Mail can be slow and sometimes unreliable. Expatriates, for instance, complain that foreign magazines sent by mail do not reach their destination. Courier services, are, however, well established. A local company started Thailand's first courier service in 1968 and others have since followed.

NOTES

1. Source: Bank of Thailand, *Annual Economic Report 1992*, Bangkok, p. 19.
2. Calculations based on the Port Authority of Thailand, *Annual Report 1992*, Bangkok, p. 35.
3. Source: Data Processing Department, the Port Authority of Thailand, Bangkok.
4. Supra 2, p. 36.
5. Calculations based on National Statistical Office, *Statistical Yearbook Thailand 1993*, OPM, Bangkok, 1993, pp. 232–3.
6. Source: National Statistical Office, *Statistical Yearbook Thailand 1993*, OPM, Bangkok, 1993, p. 232.
7. Calculations based on Finance and Accounting Department, State Railway of Thailand, Bangkok.

8. Source: Finance and Accounting Department, State Railway of Thailand, Bangkok.
9. Supra 7.
10. Supra 8.
11. Supra 8.
12. Supra 6, p. 231.
13. Supra 5, p. 240.
14. Agence France Presse, "Thai traffic 'more serious than AIDS,'" *South China Morning Post*, 18 September 1993.
15. Supra 6, pp. 27, 258.

8 DOING BUSINESS

"The king does not levy a rate on his people ... Whoever wants to trade in elephants, trades. Whoever wants to trade in horses, trades. Whoever wants to trade in gold and silver, trades."

So wrote King Ramakamhaeng (Rama the Brave) in 1292. His words capture the spirit of freedom of the first Thai settlers. It is the same spirit that animates modern Thais. In many ways, Thailand remains the "Land of the Free."

Free enterprise prevails. The kingdom has a myriad of small family-run businesses and a large proportion of its population is self-employed. There are also close links between the public and private sectors. Retired and occasionally active military and police officers run businesses, while government enterprises enter into joint ventures with private companies.

This environment is favorable to foreign investment. Business opportunities are diverse and they are expanding with economic growth and deregulation. Especially successful are technology transfer, staff training, and the trade of higher-quality consumer goods and of pollution-control equipment.

Changing production and consumption patterns bring Thailand closer to industrialized countries, but they have little effect on traditions. The deeply rooted culture and the regulatory environment produce a distinct approach to business. The following sections show how Thais do business and how regulations affect trade and investment.

8.1 THE BUSINESS COMMUNITY

Diversity is probably the main trait of the business community. Although Thailand has many small enterprises, it is also the home of large conglomerates similar to business empires. The biggest Thai companies have diversified interests both locally and abroad. Prominent Chinese families are key players in many of these conglomerates, but they are not the only ones. The military, government, and foreign investors also have extensive interests in business.

8.1.1 THE CHINESE

The Chinese are among the most important business people in Thailand. They are traders by tradition, but they also engage in financial and industrial activities. While many Chinese run small businesses, some have achieved spectacular results. They built empires with interests in trade, finance, manufacturing, and real estate.

These successful Chinese are influential. They dominate the business community and they head some of the wealthiest families in Thailand. The kingdom's largest agro-industrial group, a conglomerate of over 200 companies, for instance, is controlled by a Thai-Chinese family. The group has operations worldwide and its interests range from agribusiness to retailing and telecommunications. It is so large and diverse that Thais have nicknamed it the "parallel government."

The Chinese are also the biggest minority in Thailand. About 240,000 Chinese nationals, this is almost 90 percent of all foreign residents,[1] and far more Thai-Chinese live in the kingdom. More arrive every year because Thailand remains a favorite destination of illegal Chinese migrants.

The exact size of this community is unknown because many Chinese assume Thai names or intermarry. Centuries of migration and assimilation have produced many families of mixed origin. A story goes that in the early 1900s, when King Vachiravut asked his courtiers who had Chinese ancestry to move to the right of the room, 90 percent did so.

Chinese businesses in Thailand go back a long way. In the thirteenth century, the Chinese already traded at Thai ports and by the nineteenth century, they held a quasi monopoly over the retail, wholesale, import, and export trades. By the early 1900s the Chinese controlled the milling and marketing of rice and they held stakes in other lucrative manufacturing and service industries including saw milling, banking, insurance, and shipping. These people have also been the architects of modern Thai infrastructure. They dug canals, built railroads, and erected buildings and bridges.

From early on, the Chinese have been well accepted. They performed a valuable service in this predominantly agricultural society. In the past, Thai kings often rewarded successful merchants with noble titles, official appointments, and monopoly rights. The monarchy also called on the Chinese to run its businesses, like the royal trading.

However, this policy stopped. In the early 1900s, Thai governments became less favorable to the Chinese and after the 1932 military coup, relations grew hostile. Subsequent administrations nationalized companies, set up state enterprises, and reserved occupations for Thai nationals. They also enacted regulations to control Chinese businesses and force them out of certain industries. Most of these regulations were ineffective or impractical, but they prevented Chinese businesses to operate profitably within the law and they encouraged bribery.

During this period, the Thai government gained a greater control over the economy, but it did not eliminate Chinese businesses. The Chinese protected themselves by taking Thai citizenship and by assuming Thai names. Wealthy Chinese also invited Thai military officials to join the board of directors of their companies.

8.1.2 THE MILITARY

Thailand now has democratic governments, but the military still play an important role in the economy. They hold key positions in both the public and private sectors. A large proportion of top- and middle-ranking managers in state enterprises are retired military officers. High-ranking military officers also sit on the boards of Chinese companies and they run their own businesses.

The armed forces derive their power from their strong, although recent, organization. Until the mid-nineteenth century, the Thai army consisted of only some ten thousand men who were poorly trained, undisciplined, and ill equipped. It became more professional after King Chulalongkorn came to power in 1868. The king reorganized the armed forces along Western lines. He founded the Ministry of Defense, created a king's guard regiment, set up a Military Cadet School, sent military officers abroad for training, and decreed universal conscription. These well-trained people emerged as an elite group and in 1932, they took over the government.

Access to power brought control over lucrative enterprises like gem, timber, and especially drug trades. The military revived the opium industry, which had been a profitable royal monopoly in the nineteenth century. In the late 1930s, they promoted the cultivation of opium and they made contact with drug dealers of the Burmese Shan States. In the 1950s Thailand had become the world's leading distribution center of opium. The armed forces supervised the trade, shipping opium by aircraft and naval vessels.

International pressure, however, ended this official opium monopoly. In 1959, the government prohibited the smoking and distribution of opium in Thailand. Subsequently, the military distanced themselves from the drug trade although they were said to keep extracting informal tributes from opium warlords. The armed forces then turned to other businesses both in the public and private sectors.

This alliance of business and politics was conducive to trade restrictions. Under the military regime, import bans and high customs duties multiplied. The military also secured monopoly rights over some industries. Until 1992, for instance, the Royal Thai Air Force had a monopoly on the chairmanship of the national carrier, Thai Airways International.

The military now have less control over politics, but they still form a close-knit group intent on reaping the spoils of its position. They reward each other through promotions, often being at pain to create new posts. In 1992, the Thai armed forces had about 900 senior-ranking officers, one for every 315 men; there were some 600 generals, 140 air marshals (the highest-ranking officers in the airforce), and 160 admirals.[2] Incidentally, the Navy has more admirals than it has vessels.

8.1.3 THE GOVERNMENT

Decades of centralist ambitions have endowed the Thai government with many businesses. The administration runs major utilities, providing water and electricity; and operating postal services, telephone, telegraph, railroads, ports, and airlines. It also holds stakes in virtually all industries, including rubber, sugar, tobacco, textile, hides, oil and gas, tin, jute, pharmaceutical goods, alcohol, playing cards, arms and ammunitions, paper, matches, leather, timber, cement, glass, refractories, dairy products, batteries, lottery, shipping, trucking, banking, insurance, etc.

The performance of these enterprises is variable. A few companies generate the bulk of the profits, while many others are either barely profitable or debt-ridden. This has encouraged the Thai authorities to privatize part of the public sector. A plan, initiated in 1986, covers about two dozen companies in various industries. The large size of some of these enterprises and extent of vested interests, however, hinder changes. In 1993, for instance, Thai Airways International was still 93 percent state-owned after the government listed it on the stock exchange.

In the meantime, state companies are getting more independent. Successful ones reach the status of first-grade enterprise and they become self-managing. These upgraded enterprises are treated as private companies. They contribute 30 percent of their annual profits to the Finance Ministry and private agencies assess their performance.

This extensive participation in business has strengthened the ties between private and public sectors. Many private companies deal, directly or indirectly, with the government. Selling is, perhaps, the principal activity; the government is Thailand's biggest buyer. Private companies also lease state-owned factories, bid for government contracts, run businesses under government concession, and enter into joint ventures with state enterprises.

Such joint ventures are getting more common. They are opportunities for public enterprises to expand activities. State-owned petroleum companies, for instance, have formed joint ventures with private concerns to set up small gas stations in rural areas and to operate networks of gas stations abroad, especially in China.

Joint ventures also create opportunities for consulting. Since December 1991, any government agency or state firm willing to enter into a joint venture must conduct a feasibility study. In case of large projects, a report by an independent consultant is compulsory.

8.1.4 FOREIGN INVESTORS

Foreign investors are, perhaps, the main driving force in the Thai economy. They are major sources of capital and technology. The large inflow of foreign capital finances plants and infrastructure. Investors are diverse, but two major groups dominate, Westerners and Japanese.

Westerners Westerners have gained a strong foothold in Thailand. They distribute their brands locally, operate factories, run branch offices, and source products. Principal investors are American firms and European companies, especially British, French, and German.

European companies have established some of the biggest trading houses in the country and they are involved in many other activities like manufacturing, construction, and advertising.

American companies also have a large presence in the market. The most visible ones are perhaps the food and beverage companies because leading American food chains have outlets in all major Thai cities and soft drink manufacturers hold a significant share of the beverage market. This is, however, a small part of the American investment in Thailand. American companies hold large interests in mining, manufacturing, and in the financial sector. In addition, some of the biggest direct-selling concerns in Thailand are American.

Both Europeans and Americans have a long history of doing business in Thailand. Their interest in the kingdom dates back to the mid-nineteenth century. Import, export, banking, and shipping were their principal activities then. Some of Thailand's large Western trading houses, which distribute a wide range of imported goods, for instance, were established in the early days of Western trade.

For some time, Westerners were also the most influential people in the kingdom. Until the 1920s, Thai kings appointed teams of foreign advisers to introduce Western knowledge into Thailand. A general adviser, usually American, supervised the teams. Duties extended to most aspects of the economy, including agriculture, trade, education, taxation police, etc. The kings also employed foreigners in various capacities. Danish officers served in the navy; French people drew legal codes; while German and Italian engineers advised on railroads, mail, telegraph, and other public works.

Japanese Japan is the single biggest foreign investor in Thailand. Some 1,000 Japanese companies are said to operate in the kingdom. Japanese firms are prominent in manufacturing, especially for electrical and electronic goods, transportation equipment, and textile. They also hold large interests in construction, financial services, and retailing.

Japanese-owned factories produce mainly for exports, but they also target local people. Producing in Thailand helped them gain access to the domestic market. Locally made Japanese goods bypass import duties and other trade restrictions. Many like cars, electrical items, and electronic equipment have now gained a strong foothold on the market.

These factories have been producing for several decades, but capital keeps flowing in. Thailand remains a favorite destination for Japanese investment. A survey conducted in November 1992 by the ASEAN Center in Tokyo shows that a third of the Japanese companies willing to invest overseas consider Thailand as a potential destination.[3]

Aid features highly in the Japanese investment strategy. Japan is a leading provider of international assistance to Thailand. Between 1987 and 1991, it accounted for 56 percent of the foreign technical cooperation to the kingdom.[4] Japanese aid includes concessionary loans, grants, fellowships, training, and donations of equipment.

Loans, however, are the main form of assistance. They account for about three-quarters of total aid. Terms are attractive, with an interest rate of 3 percent, a repayment period of 25 years, and a grace period of 7 years. Amounts are also substantial. In 1993, the eighteenth low-interest yen loan exceeded US$1 billion.

This assistance is instrumental in developing the Japanese presence in Thailand. Loans often include procurement conditions, requiring that the contractor, equipment, and materials be Japanese. Funds also finance projects beneficial to Japanese companies. Since congested communications impair business, the Japanese assistance focuses on developing infrastructure.

While prominent, Japanese investment is fairly recent. It developed over the past few decades. Although some Japanese, who were mainly Christian refugees, lived in Thailand in the seventeenth century, they became disruptive, and in 1632, the Thai monarchy severed relations with Japan. Formal contacts resumed only toward the end of the nineteenth century. Subsequently, a Japanese community settled in Bangkok, but until the late 1930s, it was small and non-influential.

8.2 BUSINESS PRACTICES

In many ways, doing business in Thailand is similar to doing business in the West, although culture and regulations affect decisions.

8.2.1 DEALING WITH THE ADMINISTRATION

The Thai administration is large and intricate. In 1991, the government employed over 7 percent of the labor force. Each ministry splits administrative duties between a host of agencies, often creating problems of coordination. Over twenty agencies, for instance, administer land transportation. The maintenance of a bridge in Bangkok, alone, needs the intervention of two agencies, the Public Works Department of the Interior Ministry for the bridge and the Bangkok Metropolitan Administration for the bridge ramps.

Cost is also an issue, delaying procedures. Decisions on large projects take years to finalize because of their financial implications. The new deepwater port of Laem Chabang near Bangkok, for instance, opened in 1991, more than forty years after the government launched the idea of building it. Similarly, Thai authorities have been delaying the construction of a second international airport for the past thirty years.

The Thai government is relying increasingly on the private sector to develop its infrastructure, especially through concessions. Utilities such as telephone lines, mass transit, freeways, and port terminals are now in private hands. The most popular financing means are build-operate-transfer contracts. These let a concessionaire build a project and retain exclusive rights to operate it for a specific duration, while transferring its ownership to the government. Throughout the concession, the government earns a share of the returns.

These are potentially lucrative deals, but they are difficult to conclude. Successful tenders often guarantee high returns to the government and arrange for private funding. Money, however, is only part of the success; connections and a thorough understanding of business practices are essential. Foreign companies stand better chances when bidding jointly with a Thai partner.

This strategy helps avoid costly mistakes. Concession holders may have problems enforcing agreements. The most notorious case is, perhaps, the row over the management of an expressway built by a leading Japanese contractor in 1993. The government agency, Expressway and Rapid Transit Authority of Thailand, had granted the contractor the right to build a freeway and operate it for thirty years under a revenue-sharing formula. Upon completion, the agency and the contractor disagreed on the interpretation of the terms of the contract. The dispute lasted over a year and was settled by local investors buying the contractor's stake in the project.

Negotiations on government contracts also require patience as they are often protracted. Infighting is common. Agencies compete for prestigious projects, causing delays and overturns of decisions. An agency may select a winning bid and have its decision overturned by another agency. In 1986, for instance, the Thai government called tenders for the construction and operation of an overhead rail system in Bangkok. Later, it selected two consortia and at various times designated one or the other as the winner before making a final decision in 1989.

Contracting with the private sector is, however, a return to traditional policies. When the administration was small, Thai kings subcontracted the operation of state monopolies to private parties. They licensed the gambling, lottery, opium, and liquor monopolies. They also granted concessions to build and operate public utilities. The government, for instance, granted private businesses the right to operate the now defunct Bangkok trams from their introduction in 1887 until 1950.

8.2.2 TRADING WITH THAILAND

International trade is expanding rapidly. Increasing incomes have brought imported goods within the reach of many more people. Foreign products are more expensive than local goods, but they are prized for their quality. While this growing demand is an essential stimuli for commerce, it is not the only one.

Favorable policies also contribute to the development of international trade. The Thai administration is removing trade barriers gradually. Between 1990 and 1993, it reduced and restructured trade duties on about 2,000 items. Officials say that the objective is to confine import tariffs to six main rates: 0, 1, 5, 10, 20, and 30 percent.[5] The Ministry of Commerce is also dropping licensing requirements on many product categories.

Previous military regimes had restricted trade. They had often relied on legal provisions that allow the Ministry of Commerce to designate classes of goods for import or export controls. The law offered endless possibilities for protectionism, and governments used them generously. They banned imports of certain goods, introduced import licenses, and set prohibitive import duties.

Although declining, restrictions still exist. They apply to items which compete directly with local goods. Controls are especially important on foods and pharmaceutical products. Many products are still subject to licensing. License registration is a lengthy process, taking up to a year. It also requires applicants to provide proprietary information like a detailed list of ingredients and a description of the manufacturing process.

Less obvious, perhaps, are the barriers stemming from customs procedures. Thai customs officers may assess the value of merchandise imported, regardless of the information provided in the invoices. They base their assessments on the highest declared price for similar goods previously imported from the same country.

Other regulations are minor by comparison. They emphasize protection of consumers. Food containers, for example, must meet basic hygiene standards while labels must display the usual information on contents and origin and, occasionally, warnings like "prohibited for feeding infants." Laws also ban certain additives. Meeting trade laws is an essential part of selling goods in Thailand, but success also depends on other attributes, especially packaging and labeling.

Packaging should be sturdy and visually appealing. Boxes must withstand rough transportation and handling. Presentation is also important because of the development of modern retailing methods. Department stores and upmarket shops emphasize display and they prepare elaborate giftwrappings. Elegant packages enhance sales prospects.

Labeling should adhere to local standards. Product descriptions and instructions written in the Thai language help sales. Since Thais use the metric system, labels that indicate measures in these units are more effective.

8.2.3 DISTRIBUTING AND SOURCING

Many agencies specialize in distributing and sourcing products. They range from the large international trading firms to small specialized enterprises.

Distributing The distribution industry is developing rapidly with the demand for imported goods. A host of distributors, both local and foreign, operate in Thailand. They fall into two principal groups: large trading houses and specialized distributors.

Large trading houses are among the oldest and the most renowned distributors in Thailand. This group comprises Western companies, some of which were established in the last century, and local concerns. Both have extensive connections with the retail industry. They distribute a variety of goods ranging from fast-selling consumer items to industrial supplies. Their marketing techniques are sophisticated and they usually provide maintenance and repair services. They are especially efficient at selling well-known brands.

Specialized distributors are usually smaller but effective. They focus on specific products or distribution channels. Some of these companies use modern management techniques, and they develop rapidly, occasionally becoming leaders in their field.

Major brands still dominate the market, but consumers now have access to a wider selection of products. Brand names are important when sales staff have little training. Purchases are then *caveat emptor*, and buyers rely on brand names for quality. Stores are, however, improving customer service, increasing sales potential for less-known products.

Sourcing International trading companies have set up buying offices. They assist foreign importers in sourcing products in Thailand. Agents charge a commission, usually 5 percent, on the items purchased. Orders cover a wide range of goods, but textile and food products figure prominently.

Many companies, however, source products directly. They either organize purchase trips or set up their own buying office. Foreign buyers may seek assistance from Thai government agencies both overseas and in Thailand. Commercial counselors, usually located in Thai embassies and consulates, keep trade directories and information on specific industries. In Thailand, the Department of

Export Promotion provides advisory and other services, while the Board of Investment helps companies source raw materials and components.

Monitoring is often essential when dealing with local enterprises, especially smaller ones. Importers complain of late delivery and of output not meeting specifications. A loose concept of time, the language barrier, and a lack of experience are usually the problems. Buyers may protect themselves by conducting quality controls either directly or through local testing and inspection companies.

8.2.4 THAILAND AS A REGIONAL BASE

Thailand is an attractive base for conducting regional business. The country is part of the agreement between members of the Association of Southeast Asian Nations (ASEAN)[6] to cut tariffs and create a free-trade area. Thailand is also located at the heart of the Indochinese peninsula and it offers the best infrastructure and legal organization in this region. In addition, transportation costs between Thailand and Indochina are lower because the kingdom shares borders with all Indochinese countries except Vietnam.

This regional role has become more potent with the lifting of the American trade embargo on Vietnam in February 1994. Within hours of the official announcement, for example, Bangkok-based executives of leading American manufacturers of soft drinks left for Vietnam to prepare their marketing and distribution campaigns in this country.

The Thai government also encourages the development of trade in the region. This policy began in the late 1980s. Subsequent deregulations paved the way for greater international transactions. Officials say that they aim to establish Thailand as a regional trading and financial center. This may be a long-term goal, but changes are already noticeable.

Border trade is increasing. Since the opening of the Thai-Lao Friendship Bridge across the Mekong River in 1994, goods no longer cross the river on a vehicle ferry. Products from China and Vietnam now transit through Laos and they are sold on the Thai markets. The bridge may soon become a major route for trade because it allows land transportation from Beijing to Singapore. Tourism is already booming in its vicinity.

Companies are also expanding their regional activities. In 1992,

Thai direct investment in China and Indochina combined reached US$36 million, up from US$3 million in 1991.[7] In China, companies invest mainly in real estate and light industries. In Indochina, investment focuses on infrastructure. Companies are especially keen to build industrial estates as Thailand may benefit from close offshore manufacturing bases. Banks also open branches in neighboring countries and in 1994, a state-owned Thai bank arranged Vietnam's first offshore syndicated loan.

Western enterprises take part in these changes. They turn their local offices into regional operations and they join Thai companies in foreign ventures. These multinational consortiums are usually involved in construction projects like roads, housing, and industrial estates.

8.3 LABOR

Thailand has an ample supply of labor. The country's young and rapidly growing population is a valuable resource for the expanding manufacturing industry. The kingdom, however, no longer specializes in cheap labor-intensive productions. Factories are now investing in machinery and they upgrade their output, leaving simple processes to low-cost areas like China and Vietnam.

8.3.1 TRAINING

Training is, perhaps, the single most important issue for Thai labor. Because of its rapid development, Thailand is short of qualified workers. Companies are growing so fast that they run out of people to lead them. Employers are increasing salaries to attract skilled personnel; they offer scholarships to students who agree to work for them later; and they recruit government employees.

Skilled people often hold several jobs. Daytime staff in government hospitals, for instance, do night shifts in private clinics; bank employees work on weekends as accountants; teachers drive school buses; and office clerks work as waiters in the evenings. These multiple activities are especially common for civil-service employees with light workload.

Training programs are in growing demand. Universities are offering new courses and degrees, often in alliance with foreign institutes. Trade associations organize classes and they set up training centers. In 1991, for instance, the Federation of Thai Industries and Keidanren (Japan's Federation of Economic Cooperation) funded an institute of technology to train engineers. Consulting companies organize seminars and training sessions. These are often related to management and marketing although some address technical problems like computing and electronics.

Companies also set up internal training programs. These range from informal workshops and seminars to specialized classes. Larger companies run their own training center and they send their senior staff overseas for training. Staff training is especially common for foreign enterprises. This strategy, for instance, was instrumental in upgrading the quality of output in Japanese-owned factories.

8.3.2 EXPATRIATES

Foreign companies usually dispatch a small managing team from their overseas headquarters. Expatriates are often stationed in Bangkok. The city is especially convenient for families because of its numerous international schools. These include British, American, French, Swiss, and Japanese schools. There are also many nurseries and kindergartens.

Bangkok offers all the conveniences of modern life. Accommodations are up to international standards, with a wide range of serviced apartments and top-quality condominiums and houses. Entertainment is diverse. The many museums, temples, and theaters speak of the cultural life. The city also organizes many exhibitions and festivals. Some, like the kite festival, are international events, attracting foreign participants. There are also golf courses, sports grounds, and parks for outdoor activities.

Life in the provinces is quieter, but attractive. Major cities and business areas have high-quality accommodations and good shopping facilities. Entertainment is less varied, although provinces organize colorful festivals. Outdoor activities also feature highly in these places. Golf courses, beaches, jungle areas, and countless temples and archaeological sites offer endless possibilities for recreation.

The business activities of foreigners are, however, restricted by Thai laws. The kingdom bars foreign nationals from certain occupations. Employment restrictions date back to 1942 when the Thai government reserved 27 activities for Thai nationals. The list underwent various amendments, and lately, it covered 38 occupations (see List A.3.1 in Appendix 3). These regulations, however, do not apply to US citizens. The list may also shorten because the Thai government has indicated its intention to open more professions to foreigners.

8.3.3 SOCIAL COVERAGE

Provident and compensation funds are the principal sources of social coverage for workers. They draw their resources from contributions based on salaries of participants.

Provident funds Provident funds are savings plans for employed people. The funds, which started in 1984, are jointly contributed by employers and employees at rates defined individually by the companies involved. Employees who join their company's fund obtain a pension upon resignation or retirement.

Although recent, pension funds are becoming more common. In 1991, there were over 1,100 registered funds and many non-registered ones. The pending introduction of the Central Pension Fund for government employees is a major step in the development of this system. This new fund is also expected to become a substantial source of liquidity for the capital market.

Compensation funds Compensation funds are insurance packages for working people. Contributions are based on salaries. Principal funds include the Workmen Compensation Fund, the Social Security Fund, and a few specific funds.

The Workmen Compensation Fund provides insurance against work-related injuries. It was set up in 1972 and it applies to companies with 10 or more employees.

The Social Security Fund offers a comprehensive compensation package. It covers sickness, maternity, disability, and death and its benefits are expected to extend to childcare, old age, and unemployment. The plan, set up in 1990, applies to private companies with 10 or more employees and it will later be available to self-employed people who elect to join. In 1994, social security covered some 4.6 million employees in over 55,000 enterprises.[8]

The benefits of this new fund are still controversial. People complain that medical services at designated hospitals are poor.

Officials announced, however, that social security members would soon be able to choose their hospital.

Social security is mandatory, although partial and total exemptions are possible. These apply to companies which provide their own welfare packages. In addition, some professional groups rely on specific funds. The Teachers' Welfare Fund, for example, provides private schoolteachers with a comprehensive social coverage.

8.3.4 RIGHTS OF WORKERS

Thai laws define acceptable working conditions. Regulations cover working hours, leave, pay, women and child labor, and trade unions. Their success is variable. In the Bangkok area, companies usually comply with legal standards, but in the provinces enforcement is more difficult.

Working hours Working hours are often longer in Thailand than in the West. The typical Thai person works eight hours a day, six days a week. Maximum working hours, however, depend on occupation. They range from 42 hours a week for hazardous work to 54 hours for commercial work.

Pay Minimum wage varies across provinces. The administration identifies three groups of locations. The first group, which comprises the Bangkok area and the southern province of Phuket, has the highest minimum wage rate. The next group covers major regional centers: Ranong and Phangna in the South, Chonburi and Saraburi in the Central Region, Nakhon Ratchasima in the Northeast, and Chiang Mai in the North. The last category comprises the remaining sixty provinces.

The Thai government revises minimum wages regularly. New rates for 1995 ranged from US$4.50 per normal working day in low-cost areas to US$6 in Bangkok Metropolis and Phuket. Overtime pay is 50 percent more on weekdays and 200 percent on holidays.[9]

Compensation packages may include fringe benefits like housing and uniforms. In Thailand as in many Asian countries, uniforms are common in offices, especially for front-desk personnel. These people are the companies' first contacts with outsiders. Their uniforms help project a desired image; besides, many workers say that they like wearing uniforms. Housing is a common benefit outside the Bangkok area. Industrial estates, for instance, often allocate space for accommodation. These range from dormitories for workers to high-quality houses for managers.

Leave The law grants little leave time. Employees may take one day leave per week and 13 traditional holidays per year including National Labor Day on May 1. In addition, paid sick leave is up to 30 days per year.

Women and child labor In a typical Thai household, every member contributes to the common revenue. The law, however, restricts the activities of women and children. Women may not be employed in dangerous occupations and they may not work after midnight except for shifts. Children may start working at 15 years of age, but they may take up dangerous occupations only after they are 18 years old.

Trade unions Trade unions are more active in large companies where union members may use their rights to negotiate wages, benefits, and working conditions. State enterprises have the most powerful unions and they lead national labor movements. They oppose privatization, organize costly strikes, and are notorious for disrupting utilities. Conflicts are less frequent in the private sector although problems do occur. In 1993, for instance, unions organized rallies to oppose mass layoffs in the textile industry.

Thai labor unions tread an uneasy path. They have been successively banned and reinstated. Their most recent return was in 1975 when the Labor Relations Act allowed the creation of both employers' associations and trade unions. In 1991, however, the government removed state enterprises from the coverage of the act, dissolving 120 unions. In 1993, it proposed to reinstate them.

8.4 REGULATION OF BUSINESS

Regulations on businesses are getting less stringent because the government encourages free enterprise. Price controls and taxes are declining, while administrative procedures are getting simpler. A sign of modern times, regulations on pollution are increasing.

8.4.1 BUSINESS ORGANIZATIONS

Thailand allows various forms of business organizations. The principal ones include sole proprietorship, partnerships, private and public limited companies, branches, representative offices, regional offices, and non-registered joint ventures.

Joint ventures of various forms are popular with international investors both for temporary and long-term business. Their life span may be as short as the duration of a specific project but many have longer-term objectives. Advantages are significant. Mixed management combines foreign expertise with experience in local cultures and business practices. Besides, joint ventures with majority Thai ownership are free from restrictions on foreign businesses.

Several organizations help investors find a Thai partner. They keep records of Thai enterprises and they introduce foreign companies to potential business partners. Government agencies that provide these services include the Investment Service Center of the Board of Investment and the Investment Advisory Service of the Department of Industrial Promotion. In the private sector, the main sources of information are commercial banks and large accounting companies.

Less common, but also valuable, are the representative offices. These are especially useful for companies which trade with Thai entrepreneurs. Representative offices may not do business, but they may select suppliers, control the quality of goods bought locally, provide information on products sold to Thai distributors, and report to their head office.

Regional offices have similar functions. They are set up to supervise activities of branches and affiliates in the region, but they may not receive income or negotiate business in Thailand. The services that these offices may provide to their branches include management, human resource development, marketing, sales promotion, and product research and development.

8.4.2 RESTRICTIONS ON FOREIGN INVESTMENT

Thai laws control foreign participation in certain industries. A few laws cover specific activities like banking, insurance, and finance. The most important regulations, however, are those of the Alien

Business Law. This law restricts foreign participation in 63 classes of activities which include most of agriculture, commerce, construction, services, and a few manufacturing industries (see List A.3.2 in Appendix 3).

Restrictions depend on activity. The law defines three groups of industries: A, B, and C. Category A is closed to aliens; Category B allows businesses existing before the law was enacted to keep on operating but is closed to new ones; Category C is open to foreign businesses with permit. Investment in industries not listed in any category and not covered by other legislation is unrestricted. This applies to many manufacturing industries.

All categories of business, however, remain open to foreign investment to some extent. The law targets only non-Thai nationals, partnerships in which the managing partner is a foreigner, and companies with majority foreign ownership. Joint ventures with majority Thai ownership may engage in any activity without restriction. This provision has allowed international investors to hold substantial interests in controlled industries like advertising and construction.

The law also provides for a few exemptions. The principal ones concern American companies. Provisions in the 1966 Treaty of Amity and Economic Relations between Thailand and the United States exempts American companies from most restrictions on foreign businesses. The Alien Business Law does not apply either to people and companies working on government contracts. In addition, Thai authorities grant automatic permits to investors sponsored by the Board of Investment.

Restrictions on foreign investment are fairly recent in Thailand. They started after the 1932 military takeover. In the 1940s and 1950s, a spate of regulations barred foreign investors from certain activities. They were often impracticable and seldom effective. Restrictions became systematic only in 1972 with the enactment of the Alien Business Law. Trends are now reversing. In 1994, the Thai government proposed to open up more activities to international investment.

8.4.3 TAXATION

The Thai government derives most of its revenue from taxes. In 1992, these made up 94 percent of the government's income.[10]

Collection, however, remains low, accounting for about 15 percent of the gross domestic product, compared with 35–50 percent in Western countries.

This centralized system of tax collection is fairly new. Until the last century the government operated as a private enterprise earning income from businesses like royal trading. Kings relied on private individuals for the collection of taxes. These people, called tax farmers, bid for the right to collect taxes. Their profit was the difference between the collection and the cost of obtaining and running the farm.

Taxes applied to specific businesses then. Prospective tax farmers, mostly Chinese, scoured the country to identify tax opportunities. They reported to the king on the activity of his subjects and they petitioned for the right to tax profitable ventures.

Modern taxes have broader coverage. They apply mainly to personal and corporate incomes, domestic sales, and international trade. Sales taxes and trade duties are the most important taxes, together accounting for about two-thirds of the government's tax revenue (see Figure 8.1).

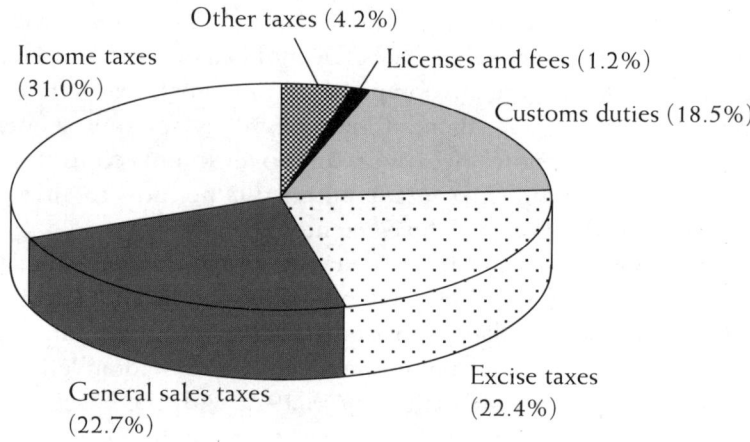

Figure 8.1   Tax Revenue by Source in 1992
(Source: Based on Bank of Thailand, Annual Economic Report 1992, Bangkok, p. 64.)

Sales taxes The principal sales taxes are the excise taxes and the value-added tax (VAT). Excise taxes are levied on a few specific products at variable rates. The VAT, in contrast, has broader coverage. This tax, introduced in 1992, applies at the uniform rate of 7 percent on most transactions. A few industries pay a specific business tax of up to 3 percent instead of the VAT. These include banks, pawnshops, and finance, securities, *credit-foncier*, insurance, and real-estate companies.

Trade duties Trade duties are still high, but they are set to decline. Until recently, most rates were between 25 and 60 percent, while prohibitive tariffs, reaching several hundred percent, applied to goods competing with local productions. Recent deregulations, however, have lowered many of these tariffs. Duties on machinery and capital equipment, for example, have dropped to only 5 percent.

The vast majority of trade duties fall on imports, but a few affect exports. The export tariff includes only seven items: rice, iron scrap, raw hide, rubber, wood, raw silk, and powdered fish.

Income taxes Income taxes apply to individuals and juristic persons at variable rates.

Taxes on juristic persons are moderate by Western standards. Most companies pay a corporate income tax of 30 percent of net profits. Only companies in the oil industry pay higher taxes, with rates reaching 50 percent. Foundations and associations pay between 2 and 10 percent of gross business income and international transportation companies 3 percent of gross receipts.

The personal income tax is progressive. In 1992, rates ranged from 5 to 37 percent. Tax payers may also claim deductions. These include allowances for self, dependents, child's education, contributions to provident funds, and interest payments on housing loans.

8.4.4 PRICE CONTROLS

Price controls are declining. In 1992, controlled items dropped from 111 to 21.[11] Consumer goods, especially basic and fast-selling items are the principal targets of these controls. The latest addition, for instance, is the crash helmet and it coincides with the introduction of compulsory use of helmet for motorcycles.

Profits on controlled products are low. Because manufacturers must petition for the right to increase their prices, margins are minimal and often prevent advertising expenses. Retailers also forego earnings on these products, using them as promotion tools to attract customers.

8.4.5 PROTECTION OF ENVIRONMENT

The environment has suffered extensive damage over the past few decades. Natural resources like rain forests, mangroves, and wildlife are disappearing; garbage piles up, while water, air, and noise pollution plague urban areas. Bangkok is especially affected, but problems are now spreading to the provinces.

This degradation is causing discontent and environment lobbies are developing rapidly, especially in cities. They campaign for greater controls and they oppose projects that affect natural resources. Politicians echo their concern, filling speeches with promises on environmental issues. Businesses also support these ideas. They organize campaigns to raise awareness and they sponsor environmental projects.

Pollution controls are getting more stringent. New regulations emphasize better coordination between government agencies and they impose stiffer penalties on violators. The administration defines quality standards for noise, water, and air and it encourages pollution-causing factories to move to industrial estates equipped for treating waste.

These changes have increased the demand for pollution-control equipment and services. Industries and communities are investing in waste-treatment plants, while government agencies hire consultants to evaluate the environmental impact of projects. Thai authorities also invite tenders to build and operate waste-treatment centers and to run treatment plants on concession basis.

Forest Decades of logging and encroaching have reduced the Thai rain forest dramatically. By 1991, it covered about a quarter of the territory, down from two-thirds in 1950.[12] Wildlife is the principal casualty. Destruction of natural habitats and human presence affect the fauna. Tigers, elephants, and wild water buffalo are now endangered species. The degradation of the rain forest also creates unusually dry conditions, reducing the collection of water in dams.

Mangroves in coastal areas are also largely depleted. Over the past thirty years, the size of mangrove forests has been halved. Various industries have contributed to the degradation. Prawn farms are some of the latest cause of damage. Mangrove forests, which develop in brackish waters, are vital to fisheries, wood-product industries, and wildlife; besides, they protect the coast from erosion.

Attempts to preserve natural resources began some time ago, but they have not always been effective. Early efforts have focused on protecting areas from degradation. Over the past thirty years, the kingdom has developed an extensive network of reserve areas where hunting and logging are prohibited. The system comprises over sixty national parks and many sanctuaries and non-hunting zones, but poaching and illegal logging are still problems.

Enforcing the law is a major concern. In villages, hunting is a means of survival and people do not understand regulations against it. Families who have settled on forest land also resist eviction. The government responds by organizing information campaigns, relocating encroachers, and imposing stiffer penalties on violators.

Efforts also focus on repairing damages. Thai authorities have embarked on a reforestation program, replanting both commercial and regular forests. The private sector also contributes to these efforts through donations and sponsorships. Companies finance goodwill operations like the planting of mangrove saplings by university students.

Some of these programs are controversial. People complain that species selected for reforestation are inadequate. They say that moisture is declining and that the slow-decomposing leaves of the new trees fail to fertilize the soil. Some state agencies are now turning to consultants to assess the impact of reforestation on the environment.

Water Rivers and canals, once the sources of livelihood of the country, have become heavily polluted. Until recently, people have released virtually all wastewater untreated. In the Northeast, for instance, rock-salt farmers discharge wasted brine in waterways and reservoirs, destroying fauna and depriving rice farmers of fresh water. Littering is also an issue, because people often dispose of their garbage in rivers.

The problem is especially acute in Bangkok. Rivers and canals have always been the sewers of the city. This was tolerable when the population was small, but with the demographic expansion, it has become unbearable. The oxygen content of the Chao Phraya River is almost nil; naturally clean water should contain seven milligrams of diluted oxygen per liter. Garbage also clogs smaller canals and it turns their water black and smelly.

The causes of the damage are multiple. Hundreds of pollution-causing factories operate in the Bangkok area. Communities, which include households, restaurants, fresh markets, hotels, and hospitals are also considered a major source of pollution, discharging untreated wastewater along with trash and leftovers.

Although treating waste has been compulsory for some time, laws are seldom enforced. Large hotels and some factories, for instance, have purification systems, but they do not always turn them on to cut costs. Ending wastewater effluents has now become a priority. Some three hundred pollution-causing factories along the river banks are earmarked for relocation in industrial estates, while the Bangkok Metropolitan Administration has invited tenders for the construction of ten wastewater treatment plants.

Pollution-control devices and related equipment like water pumps are in growing demand. They help companies meet regulations and they also facilitate acceptance by the public, especially for controversial projects. Companies even use their treatment facilities to provide benefits to the local communities. Some pulp plants, for instance, treat water and release it to nearby farms.

Garbage Garbage is piling up, especially in cities. Local administrations organize trash collection but they lack resources. Public garbage cans are scarce and poorly maintained, while streets are rarely cleaned. Garbage accumulates on land and in rivers. The problem worsens in densely populated areas. In Chiang Mai, for instance, residents have launched a campaign to end littering and they run small boats to collect garbage.

In Bangkok, the Public Cleansing Department handles the collection and disposal of waste. It cleans major streets and it collects garbage from households, markets, government buildings, and hospitals. The department runs a fleet of side-loading trucks, hydraulic-compressor trucks, container-dump trucks, small trucks (for narrow lanes), and garbage boats and it also manages treatment plants and dumps.

Heavy workload and severe operating conditions, however, impair collection. The Department of Public Cleansing in Bangkok estimates that the average Bangkok resident discards about 1 kilogram (2 pounds) of trash daily.[13] With over five million people living in the city, the task is substantial. Trucks need frequent repairs because they must carry large quantities of garbage and make their way through the congested city.

Garbage disposal is also difficult. Treatment plants have a small capacity. They treat only 7 percent of the collected garbage, leaving the rest piled up in open dumps. Incinerators are often obsolete and they do not handle dangerous wastes properly because they cannot generate high enough temperatures. This is a health hazard because some of the garbage in landfills contain toxic chemicals which may contaminate the underground water.

Equipment for the collection and treatment of waste is in high demand both in the private and public sectors. Thai authorities build and operate waste-treatment centers in association with private enterprises. Factories in industrial areas also pool resources to finance industrial waste-treatment plants.

Air and noise Air pollution is substantial, especially in Bangkok. The air in the capital contains high concentrations of toxic particles including carbon monoxide, lead, benzine, tolane, and pentene. Bangkok has one of the worst ratings for air pollution in the world. In 1993, Japanese scientists who tested the quality of air at major intersections concluded that it was unfit for breathing. They also reported that the risk of carbon monoxide poisoning is worse in Bangkok than in any other city in the world.

The low quality of air has become a health hazard. Doctors claim that the single largest group of patients in hospitals are treated for respiratory diseases, while researchers say that bus drivers who inhale carbon monoxide during long hours suffer from mental disorders and loss of consciousness. Toxic particles also accumulate on homes, endangering the quality of water collected from rooftops.

Vehicles are the principal offenders, although industries contribute to the damage. Fumes are thick along main arteries. The police has published a list of dangerous intersections for pedestrians and passengers of non-air-conditioned vehicles. Oxygen cylinders and masks are now installed at various intersections for traffic policemen.

Noise is also a problem. The principal causes are motorbikes, *tuk-tuks*, and long-tailed boats. Motorcycles and *tuk-tuks* are usually fitted with two-stroke engines. These have been replaced in the West by the quieter and cleaner four-stroke version, but not in Thailand. Many motorcyclists also remove their mufflers, adding to the noise. Worse perhaps are the long-tailed boats, which ply the canals in Bangkok. Because they move at high speed and often use old engines with no noise filter in the exhaust pipe, these boats produce deafening noises.

New laws aim to control emissions and fight noise, but progress is slow. The most significant changes are, perhaps, the introduction of higher-quality fuels and lubricants. Unleaded gasoline became available in 1991, and low-sulfur diesel fuel and low-smoke lubricating oil followed. Since January 1993, catalytic converters have also become compulsory for new cars, but these account for a small proportion of all vehicles.

8.5 FACILITIES FOR INVESTORS

Thailand encourages foreign investment, offering incentives and other facilities. Several agencies assist investors, but the principal ones are the Board of Investment and the Industrial Estates Authority of Thailand.

8.5.1 PROMOTION OF INVESTMENT

The Board of Investment, set up in 1960, is the principal government agency for promoting investment in Thailand. It defines target areas for investment and it grants privileges to selected projects. Between 1987 and 1992, the board received over 6,500 applications for promotion and some 2,000 projects started operation. The average investment is substantial, exceeding US$5 million.[14]

There is no set standard of incentives. The board designs a specific package for each investor. Privileges may include tax holidays (that is, tax breaks) and tax exemptions, permission to bring in foreign technicians and to own land, and guarantees against nationalization and unfair competition. Fiscal advantages usually feature prominently, but recent tax reforms may invite greater emphasis on other benefits.

This promotion program covers a wide range of industries, although the list changes regularly. The board encourages investment in agriculture, mining, manufacturing, and services. It also defines a subset of priority activities for special incentives. In 1993, these covered transportation, public utilities, environmental protection, technological development, and basic industries.

The selection criteria are diverse. The board favors investments which promote exports, use domestic raw material, are labor-intensive, transfer technology, save energy, and operate outside the Bangkok area. It may also stipulate such criteria as capital investment, production capacity, extent of foreign participation, use of local raw material, and destination of production.

While these criteria remain unchanged, emphasis shifts occasionally. Producing for exports used to be the principal selection criteria but developing the provinces is now the main objective. Investors have greater chances of support if they set up their business outside the Bangkok area. Benefits also depend on location. The board divides Thailand into three zones centered on Bangkok. Zone One is the Bangkok area, Zone Two includes the provinces adjacent to Zone One, and Zone Three covers all other provinces. Privileges increase for projects located farther away from Bangkok and they peak in Zone Three.

8.5.2 INDUSTRIAL ESTATES

Industrial estates have become popular. They expanded rapidly in the past few years. In 1991, Thailand had 38 industrial estates nationwide, up from 6 in 1987. The government encouraged these changes, granting privileges to operators of private estates and to companies operating there. It also developed estates through its agency, the Industrial Estates Authority of Thailand (IEAT).

This agency is the prime operator of industrial estates in Thailand. The IEAT, set up in 1972, plans, develops, and manages industrial estates either alone or in association with private enterprises. It also grants privileges like tax exemptions and the right to own land and to bring in foreign technicians to factories located in its premises.

Thai industrial estates are self-contained. They provide utilities, waste-treatment plants, factory space, housing, schools, commercial areas, social and recreational facilities and sports centers. Industrial estates usually fall into two principal categories, export-processing zones for export-oriented factories and general industrial zones for other enterprises. Export-processing zones differ only by the addition of customs offices and bonded warehouses.

Many estates are located in the Bangkok area, but developers are now turning to other sites. Although attractive for its better services like water and electricity the Bangkok area is expensive. More estates are being built in the provinces and especially in fast-growing places like the eastern sea coastal area.

8.5.3 DEVELOPMENT ZONES

Recent economic policies have emphasized the development of industries and decentralization. Development zones epitomize these concerns. One principal such project is the Eastern Seaboard Program launched in 1981. It is a vast development plan for the eastern sea coastal area that involves the construction of industrial estates, ports, railroads, roads, telephone lines, etc.

The Eastern Seaboard comprises two zones, Laem Chabang for light industries and Mab Ta Phud for heavy petrochemical industries. Both areas have attracted many investors. Between 1987 and 1992, over 1,000 factories promoted by the Board of Investment have settled in these places. Developments at Mab Ta Phud are especially ambitious. A gas-separation plant, two olefin complexes, and related factories produce a variety of chemicals for making paint, plastic, textile, etc.

This ambitious program, however, has its detractors. Local observers claim that it is a costly mistake. They say that the large influx of population combined with poor land management, lack of transportation, and uncontrolled development of housing, industrial estates, and golf courses have created problems. They point at the pollution and at the lack of utilities, hospitals, schools, and commercial complexes. Because the issue remains controversial, it has stalled similar development plans for the South.

Developers often envision exploiting the potential of the southern peninsula as a link between the Andaman Sea and the Gulf of Thailand. Their plans usually combine development of industrial estates and transportation links between the two coasts. At its narrowest point, the Isthmus of Kra, the peninsula is only 50 kilometers (30 miles) wide. A canal or land bridge at this place would cut trips between the Indian Ocean and the Gulf ports by 1,600 kilometers (1,000 miles).

8.6 PROTECTION OF INTELLECTUAL PROPERTY

Protection of intellectual property is a problem. Piracy is rife in Thailand. Illegal factories turn copies of designer's items, audio tapes, videotapes, and computer software for the local market. The illegal use of patented processes and foreign trademarks is widespread. The size of the illegal industry is unknown, but in 1993, a survey suggested that Thai vendors sold three times as many pirated international audio tapes as legitimate ones.[15]

Copyright patent and trademark laws have existed for some time, but they do not deter pirates. Until recently, fines have been low and violators viewed them as mere operating costs. Courts were also lenient. Filmmakers complain that between 1986 and 1992, they have not won a single case despite filing nearly 200 law suits.

Enforcement of copyright laws is also lax. The slow prosecution of offenders and the poor timing of factory raids encourage illegal production. This often irritates foreign investors. Thailand has been embroiled in several international disputes over the protection of intellectual property, especially with the United States and the European Community.

This poor legal environment has produced a variety of strategies. Producers, especially American, have set up organizations to support their claims. They have also reduced prices to encourage purchases of legitimate products and undercut the edge of pirates. A few companies have made alliances with powerful local conglomerates which have the means to police local manufacturers. Many companies, however, gave up fighting.

International pressure has, nonetheless, encouraged Thailand to revise its laws on property rights. Main changes affect the coverage of the laws and the penalties. Entrepreneurs welcome these efforts, but they are still concerned about enforcement. While the police is conducting more raids on illegal factories, many judges keep penalties minimal. This may also improve because new laws that come in force in 1995 provide for the creation of special courts to deal with violations of intellectual property rights.

8.6.1 COPYRIGHTS

The copyright law protects literary, scientific, and artistic works. Until recently these covered eight categories of work: literature, dramatic work, artistic work, musical work, audiovisual materials, cinematographic films, disseminated sounds or pictures, and other works in the field of literature, science, or fine arts.

Since this law did not mention computer software, it created much controversy. In 1994, however, following international pressure, the Thai parliament approved revisions to the existing Copyright Act. These are effective starting 1995. The revised act extends protection to computer software and to performances.

The duration of protection depends on the nature of the work. It lasts 25 years for applied artistic work and 50 years for photography, audiovisual materials, disseminated sound and picture, and cinematography. Coverage is much longer for literature, drama, art, and music, extending throughout the lifetime of the creator and for 50 years after his death.

The protection policy also differs by nationality. Creators must be Thai nationals or they must have resided in Thailand during most of the creation time to obtain copyright protection. Otherwise, the protection resorts from international copyright agreements. Thailand protects foreign copyrights only if they are issued by members of the Berne Convention for the Protection of Literary and Artistic Work; the kingdom has been a member of this convention since 1931.

8.6.2 PATENTS

Thai patent law protects inventions and product designs. Inventions are innovations which create new products and processes, or improve known products and processes. Product designs are compositions of lines or colors that give a special appearance to products. To be patentable, inventions must be new, inventive, and have industrial applications while product designs must be new and meant for industrial use.

The law has been amended recently. In 1992, the Thai government extended patent protection to inventions of pharmaceutical products; these had been explicitly excluded before. The government also increased the period of protection on product designs from 7 to 10 years and on inventions from 15 to 20 years.

The revised act remains contentious mainly because it has created a Pharmaceutical Patent Board with sweeping powers. The board has the authority to obtain sensitive technical information from manufacturers. It may also revoke the licenses of patent holders and issue compulsory licenses. Foreign producers lobby to impose strict limits on compulsory licensing and they insist on strong protection of registration data. There is less support in Thailand for improved protection except from some user groups who argue that poor protection reduces the availability of such products as high-quality seeds and medications.

8.6.3 TRADEMARKS

The trademark law is getting more comprehensive. An amendment to the Trademark Act which took effect in 1992 extended protection to more types of marks, tightened the rules for registration, and provided for legal sanctions for violations. The revised act covers trademarks, service marks, certification marks, and collective marks. It grants the exclusive right to use a mark for any class of good in which it is registered.

The principal change is, probably, the introduction of provisions for criminal offense. Penalties vary with the offense. Forgery carries up to four years imprisonment and US$16,000 in fine; imitation, up to two years imprisonment and US$8,000 in fine; and possession one year imprisonment and US$800 in fine.

8.7 TIPS FOR BUSINESS TRAVELERS

Thais are tolerant people who do not expect foreign visitors to be fully aware of the local customs. Showing respect and sensitivity often ensure smooth dealings, although following a few basic rules of behavior may help.

8.7.1 ETIQUETTE

- Thais greet people with a *wai*, that is, joined hands held close to the body and raised slowly toward the forehead. They do not expect foreign visitors to respond. A smile and a nod suffice.
- Address people by their first name preceded by their title (Mr,

Mrs, Dr, General, etc.) Thais address each other by their first names even in formal speech. The press, for instance, refers to government officials by their title and their first name.
- Show respect for the monarchy and for the religion. Thais have a high regard for these two institutions; besides, lèse majesté (showing disrespect for the monarchy) may result in up to 15 years imprisonment.
- Take your shoes off before entering someone's home. If you are invited to a dinner or celebration, bring a small gift for your host.
- Do not open right away the presents that you receive unless you are invited to do so.
- Do not touch people, including children, on the head and avoid pointing your finger. These gestures are rude by Thai standards.
- Do not point your foot at anybody, even by crossing your legs. This is insulting. Thais strive to keep their feet flat on the ground.
- Tip hotel porters, but not taxi drivers whose fares are all-inclusive. Tipping in restaurants is optional because many places include a service charge in the bill.

8.7.2 BUSINESS RELATIONS

- Bring business cards and distribute them generously. They increase your credibility and they help people understand your name.
- Arrange for accommodation near your business meeting place. Traffic in Bangkok may be daunting and you may have to walk to your destination.
- Allow sufficient time between meetings and do not plan a tight schedule. You will probably not be able to manage more than three appointments per day. Trips of two hours between meeting places are routine.
- Clothing should be neat and fairly conservative. Excessively short skirts and bright colors, for instance, may raise a few eyebrows. Thais wear standard office clothes for business, and casual but elegant apparel for social occasions.
- Avoid criticism. Sarcasm and verbal abuse are not regarded favorably. Suggestions on possibilities for improvement are more constructive.

- Be patient. Reckless behavior discredits you and does not speed matters. Smiling is more effective.
- Unless you are invited, be prepared to pay the bill for business lunches and dinners, especially if you are senior.

8.7.3 PRACTICAL INFORMATION

- Tap water is fairly safe, but bottled purified water is recommended. Avoid raw vegetables and cut fruits from stalls.
- Electricity is 220 volts, 50 cycles.
- Currency is the baht divided into 100 satang. Approximate value: US$1 = 25.5 baht.
- Official time is GMT + 7.
- Office hours are Monday to Friday, 8:30 to 12:00 and 13:00 to 17:30. Some offices are also open on Saturdays, 8:30 to 12:00.
- Government office hours are Monday to Friday, 8:30 to 12:00 and 13:00 to 16:30.
- Banking hours are Monday to Friday, 8:30 to 15:00.
- Thais use the metric system although they have kept some traditional measures.
  Land and building space is measured in rais:
  1 rai = 4 ngaan = 400 square wah
  1 rai = 0.395 acre = 0.16 hectare
- Thais drive on the left-hand side. International car rental companies have offices in Thailand. Renting a car with a chauffeur is safer because most signs are in the Thai language and driving style is daring.
- Shops range from street stalls to department stores and boutiques. Department stores and upmarket shops use fixed prices, but elsewhere bargaining is the norm.
- Popular buys include silk, textiles, clothes, handicrafts, gems, and jewelry. Buying may, however, be *caveat emptor*, especially in stalls. It is advisable to check every item selected for defects. Gems and jewelry are better purchased from a reputable dealer.
- Public holidays
  January 1   New Year's Day
  February (full moon)   Maka Puja
  April 6   Chakri Day
  April 13   Songkran (Thai New Year)
  May 1   National Labor Day

May 5   Coronation Day
May (full moon)   Visakha Puja
July (full moon)   Khao Pansa
August 12   Queen's Birthday
October 23   Chulalongkorn Day
December 5   King's Birthday and National Day
December 10   Constitution Day
December 31   New Year's Eve

- The Thai calendar uses the Buddhist Era (BE) as a starting date. It is 543 years ahead of the Christian era. Year 1995 in the Western calendar, for instance, is BE 2538 in the Thai calendar.

8.7.4 SOURCES OF INFORMATION

- The National Statistical Office
  The office produces many surveys, reports, and periodicals. It sells its publications through its Statistical Data Bank and Information Dissemination Division. The principal publications include the Statistical Yearbook, the Quarterly Bulletin of Statistics, and the Annotated Statistical Bibliography. The last is a useful guide to the publications of various government agencies.

- The Bank of Thailand
  The bank produces two main publications, an Annual Economic Report and a Quarterly Bulletin.

- The National Economic and Social Development Board
  The board produces the national accounts that it publishes in the National Income of Thailand.

- The Tourism Authority of Thailand
  This agency records the arrivals, departures, and characteristics of foreign visitors and it surveys their expenses. It also collects information on related matters like international conferences and hotel occupancy.

- The Thai Customs Department
  The department handles customs procedures and it collects customs duties. It also produces the Foreign Trade Statistics of

Thailand monthly. The December issue is especially valuable because it gives the total trade for the year.

- The Port Authority of Thailand
 The Authority supervises shipping at the ports of Klong Toey and Laem Chabang. Its Data Processing Department collects data on the traffic at these ports.

- The State Railway of Thailand
 This agency supervises transportation by train in Thailand and it produces an information booklet annually.

- The Insurance Department
 The department produces the Annual Insurance Report, which provides detailed results of the activities of the industry and its members.

- The Board of Investment
 The board has offices in Thailand and abroad. It provides information on opportunities for investing in Thailand, for sourcing products, and for setting up joint ventures. It also designs incentive packages for companies eligible for promotion.

- The Department of Industrial Promotion
 The department offers translation services and general advice on investing in Thailand. It may also help companies find business partners, especially for joint ventures.

- The Industrial Estates Authority of Thailand
 This agency develops industrial estates in Thailand and it grants privileges to manufacturers which settle in these estates.

- Thai Consulates and Trade Offices
 Thai consulates and trade offices usually keep directories of Thai enterprises and of the Thai administration, along with a few other publications.

- Chambers of Commerce
 Leading trading partners of Thailand like the United States,

France, Germany, Australia, Great Britain, and Japan have chambers of commerce in Thailand. These provide information on legal and business issues.

- Professional Associations
  Thailand has many professional associations, but the principal one is probably the Federation of Thai Industries. Its clubs represent manufacturers in over 20 industries. The federation provides information on regulations and business opportunities in Thailand and it helps business visitors make contacts in local companies.

NOTES

1. Source: National Statistical Office, *Statistical Yearbook Thailand 1993*, OPM, Bangkok, 1993, p. 113.
2. "Strength in numbers for Thai admirals," *South China Morning Post*, 11 April 1992.
3. "Japanese investors focus on Indonesia, Thailand in ASEAN," *Bangkok Post*, 17 May 1993, Business Post section, p. 20.
4. Source: Department of Technical and Economic Cooperation, *Government of Thailand Technical Cooperation under the Seventh National Economic and Social Development Plan (1992–1996)*, Bangkok, 1992, p. 12.
5. Source: Bank of Thailand, *Annual Economic Report 1992*, Bangkok, p. 66.
6. ASEAN countries include Thailand, Singapore, Malaysia, Indonesia, Brunei, and the Philippines.
7. Calculations based on Bank of Thailand, *Annual Economic Report 1992*, Bangkok, p. 92.
8. Potapohn, Manoj, "Social security coverage set to expand," *The Nation*, 14 April 1994, Business section, B1.
9. Sources: AP-Dow Jones, "Thailand decides to raise minimum wages," *The Asian Wall Street Journal*, 29 May 1995, p. 14, and Bank of Thailand, *Annual Economic Report 1992*, Bangkok, p. 126.
10. Supra 7, p. 64.
11. Supra 5, p. 123.
12. Calculations based on National Statistical Office, *Statistical Yearbook Thailand*, OPM, Bangkok, various issues.

13. Kumnuan, Pochana, "4,100 tonnes per day," *Business Review*, May–June 1990, pp. 31–3.
14. Source: Office of the Board of Investment, *BOI Investment Review, A Publication of the Thailand Board of Investment*, various issues.
15. Thapanachai, Somporn, "Pirated audio tapes outsell legitimate ones by three to one," *Bangkok Post*, 21 February 1994.

APPENDIX 1

Table A.1.1   Per Capita GDP

Years	Per capita GDP in US$ (Current)	Per capita GDP in US$ (1991 constant)	Real growth rate in %
1970	199	623	n.a.
1980	689	908	2.9
1981	728	943	3.9
1982	749	974	3.3
1983	809	1,014	4.2
1984	826	1,050	3.5
1985	751	1,073	2.2
1986	814	1,107	3.2
1987	938	1,192	7.7
1988	1,122	1,324	11.0
1989	1,292	1,462	10.4
1990	1,515	1,619	10.8
1991	1,702	1,702	5.1

Source: Based on Office of the National Economic and Social Development Board, *National Income of Thailand,* OPM, Bangkok, various issues, and International Monetary Fund, IFS, various issues.

APPENDIX 2

Table A.2.1 Reasons for Migrating to Bangkok in 1985

Age and sex	Seasonal jobs	Other jobs	Study	Family and other*	Total
Males	52.9	11.1	14.2	21.8	100.0
0–9	0.0	0.0	8.8	91.2	100.0
10–29	64.2	7.1	18.5	10.2	100.0
30+	45.2	36.2	0.0	18.6	100.0
Females	57.3	4.5	9.4	28.8	100.0
0–9	0.0	0.0	3.2	96.8	100.0
10–29	66.5	4.2	11.1	18.2	100.0
30+	28.0	10.2	0.7	61.1	100.0

*Includes move with spouse and move with household head

Source: Based on National Statistical Office, Statistical Handbook of Thailand 1989, OPM, Bangkok, pp. 30–1.

Appendix 3

List A.3.1 Restricted Occupations

1. Labor.
2. Work in agriculture, animal breeding, forestry, fishery, or general farm supervision.
3. Masonry, carpentry, or other construction work.
4. Wood carving.
5. Driving of motor vehicles or non-motorized carriers, except for piloting international aircraft.
6. Shop attendant.
7. Auctioneering.
8. Supervising, auditing, or giving services in accounting except occasional international auditing.
9. Gem cutting and polishing.
10. Haircutting, hairdressing, and beautician work.
11. Hand weaving.
12. Mat weaving or fabrication of wares from reed, rattan, kenaf, straw, or bamboo pulp.
13. Manual fibrous paper fabrication.
14. Lacquerware fabrication.
15. Thai musical instrument fabrication.
16. Nielloware fabrication.
17. Goldsmith, silversmith, and other precious metal work.
18. Bronzeware fabrication.
19. Mattress and padded blanket fabrication.
20. Alms bowl fabrication.
21. Manual silk product fabrication.
22. Buddha image fabrication.
23. Knife fabrication.
24. Paper and cloth umbrella fabrication.
25. Shoemaking.
26. Hat making.
27. Brokerage or agency work except in international business.
28. Dressmaking.
29. Pottery or ceramics.
30. Manual cigarette rolling.
31. Legal or litigation service.

32. Clerical or secretarial work.
33. Manual silk reeling and weaving.
34. Thai character typesetting.
35. Hawking business.
36. Tourist guide or tour organizing agency.
37. Architectural work.
38. Civil engineering work.

Source: Office of the Board of Investment, *A Guide to Investing in Thailand (Including a Guide to the Board of Investment)*, OPM, Bangkok, 1993, p. 22.

List A.3.2 Businesses Falling Under Categories A, B, and C of the Alien Business Law

Category A

Business in agriculture
 1. Rice farming.
 2. Salt farming including manufacture of efflorescent salt but excluding rock-salt mining.

Business in commerce
 1. Internal trade concerning local agricultural products.
 2. Trade in real property.

Business in services
 1. Accountancy.
 2. Attorneyship.
 3. Architecture.
 4. Advertisement.
 5. Brokerage or agency.
 6. Auction.
 7. Haircutting, hairdressing, and beauty treatment.

Other business
 1. Building construction.

Category B

Business in agriculture
1. Farming.
2. Gardening.
3. Livestock farming including cocoon raising.
4. Forestry.
5. Fishery.

Business in industry and handicrafts
1. Rice mill.
2. Manufacture of flour from rice and field crops.
3. Manufacture of sugar.
4. Manufacture of beverage, with and without alcoholic blending.
5. Manufacture of ice.
6. Manufacture of drugs.
7. Cold storage.
8. Wood processing.
9. Manufacture of product from gold, silver, niello, or bronze.
10. Manufacture or casting of images of Buddha and manufacture of alms bowls.
11. Manufacture of wood carvings.
12. Manufacture of lacquerware.
13. Manufacture of all types of matches.
14. Manufacture of lime, cement, or cement by-products.
15. Stone blasting or crushing.
16. Manufacture of plywood, wood veneer, chip-board, or hard board.
17. Manufacture of garment or shoes except for export.
18. Printing press.
19. Newspaper publication.
20. Silk combing, silk weaving, or printing of pattern on silk material.
21. Manufacture of products from silk, silk threads, or silk cocoon.

Business in commerce
1. Retailing of all products except those specified in Category C.
2. Sale of mining products except those specified in Category C.
3. Sale of all types of food and beverage except those specified in Category C.
4. Sale of antiques, period antiques, or works of art.

Business in services
1. Tour agency.
2. Hotel business except hotel management.
3. Business under the law on service-providing establishments.
4. Photography, photographic developing and printing.
5. Laundry.
6. Tailoring and dressmaking.

Other business
1. Internal transportation by land, water, or air.

Category C

Business in commerce
1. Wholesale of all types of products except those specified in Category A.
2. Export of all types of products.
3. Retail of machines, engines, and tools.
4. Sale of food and beverage for the promotion of tourism.

Business in industry and handicrafts
1. Manufacture of animal feeds.
2. Extraction of vegetable oil.
3. Manufacture of embroidered and knitted products including weaving, dyeing, and pattern printing.
4. Manufacture of glass containers including light bulbs.
5. Manufacture of crockery.
6. Manufacture of writing and printing paper.
7. Rock-salt mining.
8. Mining.

Business in services
1. Those not specified in Category A and Category B.

Other business
1. Other constructions except those specified in Category A.

Source: Announcement of the National Executive Council No. 281.

Bibliography

Announcement of the National Executive Council No. 281.
Asia Magazine, various issues.
Asian Advertising and Marketing, various issues.
The Asian Wall Street Journal, various issues.
Bangkok Post, various issues.
Bank of Thailand, *Annual Economic Report 1992*, Bangkok.
Bank of Thailand, *Quarterly Bulletin*, various issues.
Business Review, various issues.
Center for Agricultural Statistics, *Agricultural Statistics of Thailand, Crop Year 1991/92*, MAC, Bangkok, 1992.
Crosby, Sir Josiah, *Siam: The Crossroads*, Hollis & Carter Ltd., London, 1945. Reprinted by AMS Press Inc., New York, N.Y., 1973.
Department of Insurance, *Annual Insurance Report of Thailand 1991*, Bangkok.
Department of Livestock Development, *Yearly Statistic Reports 1991*, MAC, Bangkok.
Department of Mineral Resources, *Mineral Statistics of Thailand 1986–1990*, Bangkok.
Department of Mineral Resources, *Thailand's Metal Statistics 2528–2535 [1985–1992]*, Bangkok, 1993.
Department of Technical and Economic Cooperation, *Government of Thailand Technical Cooperation under the Seventh National Economic and Social Development Plan (1992–1996)*, OPM, Bangkok, 1992.
Division of Health Statistics, *Public Health Statistics A.D. 1990*, MPH, Bangkok, 1992.
Finance and Accounting Department, *Information Booklet*, SRT, Bangkok, various issues.
International Monetary Fund, *IFS*, various issues.
The Nation, various issues.
National Statistical Office, *Key Statistics of Thailand*, OPM, Bangkok, various issues.
National Statistical Office, *Quarterly Bulletin of Statistics*, OPM, Bangkok, various issues.
National Statistical Office, *Report of the 1990 Household Socio-Economic Survey, Whole Kingdom*, OPM, Bangkok, 1993.
National Statistical Office, *Report of the Children and Youth Survey 1987*, OPM, Bangkok.

National Statistical Office, *Report of the Cultural Activity Participation and Time Use Survey 1985*, OPM, Bangkok.
National Statistical Office, *Report of the Cultural Activity Participation and Time Use Survey 1990*, OPM, Bangkok, 1992.
National Statistical Office, *Report of the Labor Force Survey, Whole Kingdom*, OPM, Bangkok, various issues.
National Statistical Office, *Report of the Mass Media Survey, (Radio and Television) 1984*, OPM, Bangkok.
National Statistical Office, *Report of the Newspaper Reading Survey 1989*, OPM, Bangkok.
National Statistical Office, *Statistical Handbook of Thailand*, OPM, Bangkok, various issues.
National Statistical Office, *Statistical Yearbook Thailand*, OPM, Bangkok, various issues.
Newsweek, various issues.
Office of the Board of Investment, *BOI Investment Review, A Publication of the Thailand Board of Investment*, various issues.
Office of the Board of Investment, *A Guide to Investing in Thailand (Including a Guide to the Board of Investment)*, OPM, Bangkok, 1993.
Office of the National Economic and Social Development Board, *National Income of Thailand, New Series 1970–1987*, OPM, Bangkok, 1989.
Office of the National Economic and Social Development Board, *National Income of Thailand, Rebase Series 1980–1991*, OPM, Bangkok, 1993.
Office of the National Economic and Social Development Board, *Population Projections for Thailand 1980–2015*, OPM, Bangkok.
The Port Authority of Thailand, *Annual Report 1992*, Bangkok.
Segaller, Denis, *Thai Ways*, Asia Books, Bangkok, 1989.
South China Morning Post, various issues.
The Stock Exchange of Thailand, *The Stock Market in Thailand*, Bangkok, various issues.
Tourism Authority of Thailand, *Thailand Tourism Statistical Report*, Bangkok, various issues.
US Bureau of the Census, *Statistical Abstract of the United States: 1992*, 112th ed., Washington, D.C., 1992.
Zenith Media Worldwide, *Asia Pacific Market and MediaFact*, London, various issues.

Further Reading

Audric, John, *Siam Kingdom of the Saffron Robe*, Robert Hale, London, 1969.

Carter, Cecil A., ed., *The Kingdom of Siam 1904*, The Siam Society, Bangkok, 1988.

Coughlin, Richard, *Double Identity, the Chinese in Modern Thailand*, Hong Kong University Press, Hong Kong, 1960.

Hong, Lysa, *Thailand in the Nineteenth Century, Evolution of the Economy and Society*, Institute of Southeast Asian Studies, Singapore, 1984.

Lienbach, Thomas R. and Chia Lien Sien, *Southeast Asian Transport, Issues in Development*, East Asian Social Science Monograph, Oxford University Press, Singapore, 1989.

McCoy, Alfred W., *The Politics of Heroin: CIA Complicity in the Global Drug Trade*, Lawrence Hill Books, Brooklyn, New York, 1991.

McKinnon, John and Bhruksasri, Wanat, eds., *Highlanders of Thailand*, Oxford University Press, Kuala Lumpur, 1983.

Moore, Frank J., *Thailand, Its People, Its Society, Its Culture*, Survey of World Cultures, Hraf Press, New Haven, Connecticut, 1974.

Ninth Pacific Science Congress, *Thailand Past and Present*, The Publicity Committee, Ninth Pacific Science Congress, Bangkok, 1957.

Purcell, Victor, *The Chinese in Southeast Asia*, Oxford University Press, Selangor, Malaysia, 2nd ed., 1965, reprinted 1980.

Rimmer, P. J., *Transport in Thailand, The Railway Decision*, Research School of Pacific Studies, Australian National University, Canberra, 1971.

Samudavanija, Chai-Anan, *The Thai Young Turks*, Institute of Southeast Asian Studies, Singapore, 1982.

Skinner, William G., *Leadership and Power in the Chinese Community in Thailand*, Cornell University Press, Ithaca, New York, 1958.

Thompson, J. Jr., "The Thai Military: An Analysis of Its Role in the Thai Nation," Ph.D. Dissertation, Claremont University, 1973.

Toth, Marian Davies, *Tales from Thailand, Folklore, Culture, and History*, Charles E. Tuttle Co., Inc., Rutland, Vermont and Tokyo, Japan, 1971, second printing 1982.

Warren, William and Invernizzi Tettoni, Luca, *Legendary Thailand*, Travel Publishing Asia Ltd., Hong Kong, 1988.

Young, Ernest, *The Kingdom of the Yellow Robe*, Oxford University Press, Kuala Lumpur, 1982.

INDEX

References to illustrations are printed in boldface type

—A—

administration, the, 20–21
　coordination between agencies of, 315
　dealing with, 327, 330–31
　enforcing contracts with, 331
adults, leisure activities of, 77
adults, young, leisure activities of, 77
advertisements
　direct-response, 198
　public-service, 202
advertisers, budgets of, 195
advertising
　in cinemas, 201
　outdoor, 200–1
　in magazines, 199
　messages, 195, 197
　in newspapers, 198–99
　on the radio, 199–200
　regulation of, 203–5, 238
　on television, 197–98
　use of celebrities in, 196
advertising agencies, 161, 201–2
advertising expenses
　evolution of, 161, 195, **196**
　by medium, 195–96, **197**
　per capita, 5, **8**
agriculture, 8–9. *See also* crops
　in the Central Region, 13–14
　composition of agricultural product, 211, **211**
　contract farming, 212

government intervention in, 212
incomes of farmers, 47, **47**, 211
in the North, 12–13
in the Northeast, 13
in the South, 14
as a traditional occupation, 9
aid
　foreign, 212
　Japanese, 329
AIDS. *See* diseases: venereal
air conditioners, 60, 139
airlines
　competition between, 308–9
　helicopter services, 309
　household expenses on local, 147
　national carrier, 308
airports, 307
air transportation, deregulation of, 308–9
Alien Business Law, 340–41
amphetamines, 129
amulets, 83
Andaman Sea
　coastline along, 6, 15
　extractive resources in, 227, 228
animism, 17, 82–83, 125
antibiotics, 127
antivenin, 129
appliances, electrical
　household expenses on, 139
　ownership of, 60, 62
　production of, 244
aquaculture, 224
ASEAN, 266n. 77, 334
aspartame for use in soft drinks, 236

asphalt, 242
automatic teller machines, 273
Ayutthaya, 22

—B—

baht. *See* currency
bakeries, 92
Bangkok, 2, 23, 29, 30, 35–36
  canals in, 313, 315, 345–46
  construction in, 295, 297, 314
  health care in, 126
  living in, 336
  people moving to, 36
  pollution in, 345, 346, 347, 348
  restaurants in, 107
  satellite towns near, 295, 297
  supermarkets in, 157
  traffic control in, 315–16
  traffic in, 141, 144, 314
  transportation in, 314–17
Bangkok Mass Transit Authority, 316
Bangkok Metropolitan Administration, 255, 315, 330, 346
Bangkok Post, 182, 183
Bank for Agriculture and Agricultural Cooperatives, 276
banking
  history of, 272
  offshore, 274
  retail, 273
bank notes, 268
Bank of Thailand
  deregulation implemented by, 270–72
  duties of, 267–68
  monetary activities of, 268–69
  publications of, 356
banks, commercial, 272–74
banks, special-purpose, 274–77
batteries, 136, 256
beds, 60, 136
beef, 92–93
beer
  consumption of, 112, 236
  production of, 237
behavior, 18–19
beliefs, 17–18, 77–83
Berne Convention for the Protection of Literary and Artistic Work, 352
betelnut, 113–14
beverages
  energy drinks, 110
  household expenses on, 109
  household expenses on alcoholic, 111, **112**
  household expenses on ingredients for, 109, **110**
  household expenses on non-alcoholic, 109, **111**
  packaging of, 237
  production of, 236–37
bicycles, 63
billboards, 200–1
bird's nests, 14
birthday parties, 151–52
birth rate, 30
Board of Investment, 348–49, 357
boats, long-tailed, 145, 348
bonds, 268, 283, 288
Border Patrol Police, 56
borders of Thailand, 6
Bowring Treaty, 24–25
boxers, 71–72
Brahmanism, 17, 22, 82

brand names, 333
brandy, 112
bread and pastries, 92
breakfasts, 108
Broadcasting Directing Board, 164–65
brokers
  activities of, 278–79
  monitoring of, 286–87
buckets, 138–39
Buddhism, 17
  expenses on, 151
  influence of, in Thai society, 78
  making merit, 78, 81
  origin of, in Thailand, 18
  philosophy of, 80
  practice of, in cities and villages, 79
  and social work activities, 79, **80**
buffaloes, 220, 221
buses, 144, 312
  in Bangkok, 316
  long-distance, 146
business
  conducting regional, 334–35
  dealing with government, 327
  dressing for, 118, 121, 354
  during Chinese New Year, 69
  environment for, 323
  hierarchy in, 19
  influence of superstitions on, 83
business cards, 354
business community, 324–27
business districts, 297
businesses
  American, 328
  Chinese, 324–25
  European, 328
  Japanese, 329
  limits on foreign ownership of, 285
  military, 325–26
  state-owned, 327
business organizations, types of, 340
business visitors, facilities for, 259

—C—

calendar, Thai, 356
canals, 313–14. *See also under* Bangkok
cancer, 37
candles, 135
Cane and Sugar Board, 218
capital
  raising, 287–90
  repatriating, 271
capital city. *See* Bangkok
care, personal. *See* personal care
cars. *See also* vehicles
  insurance for, 294
  for personal transportation, 63, 147
  renting, 355
cassava, 218
cattle breeding, 222
celebrations
  Buddhist, 67
  household expenses on, 151, **152**
  for New Year, 68–69
cement, production of, 252
Central Region, the, 13–14
  livestock in, 221
  population of, 35–36
ceramic products, manufacturing of, 253–54

cereal products, household
    expenses on, 91–92, **91**
chambers of commerce,
    357–58
Chao Phraya River, 12, 13
    pollution of, 346
cheeses, 103
chemicals, production of,
    242–43
chicken, household expenses
    on, 92
chickens, breeding of, 222
children, leisure activities of,
    74–76
chili peppers, 105
Chinese
    in business, 22, 24, 324–25
    immigration of, 16
Christianity, 18
cigarette smoking, 114–16
    by age and sex, 115, **115**
    evolution of, 115, **116**
cigarettes, production and
    distribution of, 238
cinemas, 192–94
    advertising in, 201
    age of audience in, 193,
        194
    films shown in, 193
    profile of audience in,
        193–94
cities, 29–30
    leisure activities in, 74
clay, ceramic, 232
cleaning and cleaning supplies,
    household expenses on,
    141, **142**
climate, 15
clothing
    household expenses on
        children's, 121
    household expenses on
        female, 118, **120**
    household expenses on male,
        118, **119**
    style of, 118, 121
clothing and footwear
    household expenses on, 116,
        117
    sizes and style of, 117
clubs, 154
coaches, 146
coffee, 109, 111, 219
colonization. *See under* history
Committee on Advertising,
    203
communications, 317–21
    household expenses on, 148,
        150
    in villages, 33
Communications Authority of
    Thailand, 318
computers, 320–21
concessions for building and
    operating infrastructure,
    330–31
condominiums, 57, 297–98
Confederation of Thai
    Traditional Medicine,
    125
conglomerates, 317, 324
constitutions, 20
construction
    production of materials for,
        251–54
    quality of, 251, 297–98
consulting
    on the decoration and
        management of retail
        stores, 88, 157
    on government projects, 327
    on staff training, 53, 336
consumption
    patterns of, 33, 87, **89**
    trends in, 30, 40, 57, 87, **88**
containers for shipping, 302,
    310

contractors, 250–51
convenience stores, 157
conventions, 259
cooking fuels, 65, **68**, 134
cooperatives, 282
copyright law, 352
corner stores, 88
cosmetics, use of, 130
cotton
    imports of, 239
    production of, 220
crafts, 34, 72–74
crawling, public, 19, 25
credit-foncier companies, 279–80
credit rating, 289
crops, 213–20. *See also under specific agricultural product names*
    revenue from, 213, **214**
Crosby, Sir Josiah, 26
Crown Property Bureau, 251
cuisine, 89–90
    fruit and vegetable carving in Thai, 96–97
    international, 107
    in the Northeast, 93
    seasonings used in Thai, 105
    use of meat in Thai, 92
currency, 355
    exchange rate of, 268, **269**
    pegging of, 269
curries, 90, 108
customs duties, 263, 331–32, 343
customs valuation, 263

—D—

Dairy Farming Promotion Organization, 222
dairy products. *See under specific dairy product names*
dams, 255, 256

death, causes of, 37, **38**
De Beers, 48, 249
debentures
    euro-convertible, 288
    golf course, 72
    rating of, 289
democracy, 27
Department of Industrial Promotion, 357
Department of Insurance 290, 357
department stores, 156
diamonds, 249
diesel fuel, 148
diet, 89. *See also* food
diplomacy, 24–25, 26
direct marketing, 202–3
diseases
    cerebrovascular, 37
    control of, 40, 126
    diarrheal, 38–39
    gum, 126
    heart, 37
    respiratory, 347
    venereal, 39
distilleries, 237
domestics, household expenses on, 141, **143**
Don Muang Airport, 307
durians, 99

—E—

Eastern Seaboard, 304, 305, 350
eating out, 89, 107–9
    household expenses on, 108, **108**
economy, 2–5
education. *See also* schools; training
    compulsory, 49, 55
    cost of, 52

education (*continued*)
  in villages, 50
  of workers, 48–49, **50**
  of workers by sex, 50, **51**
eggplants, 99
eggs and dairy products
  in the diet, 100–2
  household expenses on, 100, **102**
Ekachai, Sanitsuda, 264n. 7
electricity
  consumption and production of, 254–56, **254**
  current, 355
  supply of, 134–36
Electricity Generating Authority of Thailand, 240
elephants, 129, 220, 221, 223
energy
  solar, 256
  sources of, 255, **255**
environment, protection of, 344–48
etiquette, 353–54
exchange, foreign, 270
exhibitions, 156, 336
Exim Bank, 271
expatriates, 336–37
  employment of, 336
exports, 5, **6**
  by category, 261, **262**
  by destination, 260, **261**
expressways, 315
expropriation, procedures for, 313

—F—

face powder, 130
factories, Japanese, 329
factoring, 281–82
fairs, 67

fans, electric, 60, 139
farmers, 9, 211
feed, animal, 234–35
fees, membership and entrance, household expenses on, 154, **155**
festivals, 67–68
fibers, production of, 220, 239–40
finance and securities companies, 277–79
finance industry, deregulation of, 270
fire, insurance against, 292–93
fish
  catch of marine, 223, **223**
  household expenses on fresh, 95–96, **95**
  household expenses on prepared, 96, **97**
  preserving processes for, 96
  processing of, 224, 234
fish sauce, 105
floods
  in Bangkok, 122, 315
  fertilization of land during, 13
food
  advertising of, 204–5
  consumption of, 89–109
  household expenses on, 89, **90**
  processing of, 233–35
  storage of, 102–3, 138
  for take away, 108
Food and Drug Administration, 203, 236
  licenser of, 205
food stalls, 92, 94, 96, 107–8
football, 72
footwear. *See also under specific footwear product names*
  household expenses on female, 123–24, **124**

375

footwear (*continued*)
   household expenses on male, 122–23, **123**
   production of, 240
   style of, 121–22
Forest Industry Organization, 129
forestry, 9–10, 225–26
   revenue from, 225, **225**
forests
   depletion of, 9–10, 12
   encroaching, 226
   mangrove, 224, 345
   protection of, 345
   rain, 344
   replanting, 226, 345
   slash and burn, 34
fruits. *See also under specific fruit names*
   household expenses on, 97, **98**
   pickled, 100
   processing of, 235
   production and consumption of, 97–99
funds
   compensation, 337
   mutual, 281
   provident, 337
furnishing, household expenses on, 136, **137**
furniture. *See under* homes
futures market, 212

—G—

gambling, 69–70
garbage, collection and disposal of, 346–47
garlic, 105
gas
   for cooking, 65, 134, 139
   energy produced with natural, 255
   production of natural, 227, 228
gasoline, 148, 241
gas stations, 241–42, **241**
Gemopolis Industrial Estate, 248
gemstones
   cutting and polishing, 248–49
   production and trade of, 230–31
generators, 136
geography, 6–7
gestures, 354
glass, production of, 253
gold, 271
Golden Triangle, the, 10
golf
   insurance for hole-in-one, 294
   playing, 72
Government Housing Bank, 276–77
Government Savings Bank, 275–76
governors, 21
greeting people, 353
grooming. *See* personal care
gross domestic product
   evolution of, 40
   by industrial origin, 209, **210**
   per capita, 4, **4**
Gulf of Thailand
   coastline along, 6, 15
   extractive resources in, 65, 227, 228, 229, 240
gypsum, production of, 231

—H—

hair care products, 132

hairdressing, 129
health care. *See also* medicines
   demand for, 36–37
   facilities for, 40, 125–26
   household expenses on, 126, **127**
   prevention of diseases, 40, 126
   role of herbal medicine in, 125
health-care personnel, 40, 126
health insurance, 294
health patterns, 37
helicopters, use of, 309, 315
hierarchy, 19
highways, 312
hill tribes, 16, 33–34
   crafts of, 73–74
history, 21–27
   of appointing foreign advisers, 55, 328
   of Chinese businesses in Thailand, 23–24, 324–25
   of colonization, 2, 25
   of contracting with government, 55
   of dictatorship, 25–26
   of foreign trade, 22, 23–24
   of Japanese investment, 329–30
   of the military, 325–26
   of restrictions on foreign investment, 341
   of tax farming, 25, 342
   of transportation, 309, 310, 312, 317
hobbies, 74, **76**
holidays, 67–69, 355–56
homes
   construction materials of, 59, **59**
   fire risk in, 59, 293
   furniture and appliances in, 60, **61**
   household expenses on, 133, **133**
   household expenses on housing, 132, **132**
   household expenses on major equipment for, 139, **140**
   household expenses on minor equipment for, 136, **138**
   ownership of, 58, **58**
   radio, television, and videocassette recorders in, 62, **62**
   rental cost of, 58, 133
   style of, 57–60, **57**, 296–97
Hong Kong & Shanghai Banking Corporation, 272
horse racing, 70
hospitals and hospital beds, 125, 126
hotels, 107, 258–59, 309
houseboats, 313
household as a production unit, 42

—I—

ice creams, 100, 102
illiteracy, rate of, 49, **49**
immunization, 40
imports, 5, **7**
   by category, 262, **263**
   by origin, 260, **262**
income
   fringe benefits, 338
   growth of, 4, 40
   home production as a source of, 43
   household, 42–43, **44**
   from salaries, 43–47

income (*continued*)
  taxes on, 343
Indians, 16
industrial estates, 349–50
Industrial Estates Authority of
    Thailand, 304, 349, 357
Industrial Finance Corporation
    of Thailand, 280
infrastructure
  congestion of, 5, 142,
    312–13
  developing, 300
insurance
  companies offering, 290
  growth rate of premiums for,
    292, **293**
  policies in force for life,
    291–92, **291**
  policies issued for non-life,
    292–94, **293**
interest rates, 272
International Banking Facility,
    274
investment, foreign
  American, 341
  incentives for, 232, 348–49
  Japanese, 40–41, 232
  in labor-intensive processes,
    48
  restrictions on, 340–41
investment, Thai, 335
iron, 252
irrigation, 256
Islam
  dress code, 35, 118
  practice of, 18, 35, 81–82

—J—

jewelry, manufacturing of,
    249–50
joint ventures, 289–90, 340,
    341

jungle. *See* forests

—K—

King Bhumipol Adulyadej, 20
King Chulalongkorn, 19, 25,
    220, 326
King Mongkut, 24
King Prachathipok, 26
King Ramakamhaeng, 17, 323
King Taksin, 23
King Vachiravut, 324
kitchen tools, 137
Klong Toey. *See* port of
    Bangkok
Kumnuan, Pochana, 359n. 13

—L—

labeling, 332
labor force, composition of,
    41–42. *See also* workers
labor laws, 338–39
land
  foreign ownership of, 296
  use of, 7, **9**
  use of, by region, 10, **12**,
    13, 14
Land Transport Department,
    315
language
  English, 16
  Thai, 17
lard used for cooking, 103
leisure activities, 74–77, **75**
leprosy, 39
life expectancy, 30
lignite, production of, 229
liquor, consumption and
    production of, 237
Liquor Distillery Organization,
    237

literacy, 48, 49
livestock, production of
   220–23, **221**
logging, 12, 225–26
lottery, 70

—M—

magazines, 181, 184
mail, 321
malaria, 37
Malay, 16
management
  autocracy and paternalism
    in, 19
  of printing companies, 191
  of shopping malls, 157
  in small family-owned
    businesses, 42
managers, scarcity of, 48
manufacturing industries
  in the Central Region, 14
  production of, 40–41, 232,
    233
map of Thailand, 11
mass transit, 144, 316–17
mats, 136
mattresses, 141
meat
  household expenses on
    fresh, 92–93, **93**
  household expenses on
    prepared, 94, **94**
  processing of, 222, 234
media, 161. *See also under specific*
    media names
medicines
  advertising of, 203–4
  availability of, 40, 127–29
  herbal, 129
  household expenses on, 127,
    128

production of, 243–44
  Western, 129
Mekloy, Pongpet, 206n. 12
Mekong River, 13, 255, 314,
    334
military, the
  control over air
    transportation by, 308
  history of, 25, 325–26
  promotions among, 326
milk
  consumption of, 100–2
  production of, 222
Miller, Lee, 206n. 11, 208n. 45
minerals. *See* resources,
    extractive
mining revenue, 226, **227**
monarchy
  absolute, 22, 26
  constitutional, 20
moneychangers, 270
monkhood, 79, 80
monsoon, 15
Moreau, Ron, 159n. 34
mosquito nets, 136
motorcycles
  for hire, 144
  ownership of, 63, 147
  production of, 247–48
movies, 193
music, 178–79

—N—

Nation, The, 182, 183
National Economic and Social
    Development Board,
    356
National Housing Authority,
    297
nationalizations, 325
National Statistical Office, 356

newspapers
  circulation of, 183–84
  format of, 190
newspapers (continued)
  languages of, 182–83
  readership of, 184–85
  sharing, 187
newspapers, reading
  commentaries in, 189, 192
  features in, 189, 191
  by level of education, 184–85, 185
  the news in, 188–89, 190
  by occupation, 185, 187
  patterns of, 189
newsprint, 182
New Years, 68–69
noodles
  household expenses on, 92
  restaurants specialized in selling, 107
  as traditional stall food, 108
North, the, 10–13
  crafts in, 73
  livestock in, 221
  population of, 33–34
Northeast, the, 13
  livestock in, 221
  population of, 34–35

—O—

office hours, 355
oil, crude
  production of, 228
  refining of, 241
oil, lubricating, 242
oil, palm, 104, 219
oil, vegetable, 103–4, 218–19
oils and fats, household expenses on, 103–4, 103

opium
  military control over the trade of, 326
  production of, by hill tribes, 34
oranges, 99

—P—

packaging, 332
paging, 319
painkillers, 127–29
Panyacheewin, Saowarop, 158n. 2, 207n. 42
papayas, 99
parliament, 20
patent law, 352–53
pawnshops, 282–83
pedicabs. See samlors
Pendragon, Victor, 298n. 2
perfumes, 130
personal care
  household expenses on products for, 130–32, 131
  household expenses on services for, 129–30, 130
petroleum
  production of, 226–28
  refining and separation of, 240–43
pets, 152
Pharmaceutical Patent Board, 243
photography, 153
pickup trucks, 63, 246
pigs, breeding of, 222
pineapples
  processing of, 235
  production of, 219
pneumonia, 37

politics, 20–21
pollution
  air, 144, 248, 347
  causes of, 346, 347
  controls on, 344, 346, 348
  noise, 348
  water, 345–46
population
  distribution of, by age, 30, **31**
  internal migrations of, 34, 36
  regional distribution of, 31–36, **32**
  size of, 2–3, **3**
  structure and evolution of, 30–31, **32**
pork, household expenses on, 92
Pornpitagpan, Nilibol, 207n. 36
Port Authority of Thailand, 301, 357
port of Bangkok
  berthing capacity at, 301–2, 303
  cargo throughput at, 302, **302**
  congestion at, 303
  history of, 301
  private wharves at, 303
port of Laem Chabang
  berthing capacity at, 304
  traffic at, 305
port of Mab Ta Phud, 304
port of Phuket, 305
port of Sattahip, 303
port of Si Chang, 305
port of Songkhla, 305
ports, 301–5
Potapohn, Manoj, 358n. 8
prawn farming, 224
prawns, frozen, 234

price controls, 343–44
printers, 191–92
programmers, 321
property, intellectual, 351–53
protectionism, 332
publications. *See also* magazines; newspapers
  distribution of, 187, 190
  household expenses on, 154, **155**
  market for, 181
publications, reading
  by age, 185, **188**
  by area, 186, **189**
  by occupation, 185, **186**
Public Warehouse Organization, 212
publishers, 181, 182, 183
purchasing power. *See* income

—Q—

quality control, 334
Queen Sirikit National Convention Center, 259

—R—

radio
  composition of audience of the, 174–75, **177**
  listening to the, by age, 174, **175**
  listening to the, by occupation, 175, **176**
radio programs
  ratings of commentaries, 179, **181**
  ratings of entertainment programs, 178, **179**
  ratings of features, 179, **180**
  ratings of news, 178, **178**

radio programs (*continued*)
　selecting, 177, **177**
radio sets, ownership of, 62
radio stations, 172–73
radio telephone system, 319
railroads
　cost of train trips, 310
　freight carried on, 310
　network of, 309–10, 310–11
　passenger traffic on, 146–47, 310
　train cars by type, 310, **311**
rais, 355
real estate
　developers of, 133, 295, 296
　financing of, 279, 295–96
　prices of, 295
　market for, 296–98
real-estate-financing companies, 295–96
recreation. *See also under specific recreation names*
　forms of, 66–74
　household expenses on, 149, **150**
　household expenses on electronic equipment for, 153, **154**
　household expenses on equipment for, 152, **153**
　sports played for, 70–72, **71**
Red Cross Snake Farm, 48
refrigerators, 60, 62, 102, 139
regional offices, 340
regions. *See under specific region names*
religion, household expenses on, 151, **151**. *See also* beliefs; Buddhism; Christianity; Islam
representative offices, 340
reservoirs for water, 256

resources, extractive, 10, 226–32
　in the Central Region, 14
　in the North, 13
　in the Northeast, 13
　in the South, 14
restaurants, 107–8. *See also* eating out
rice
　exports of, 213, 215
　household expenses on, 91–92
　production, history of, 9, 214–15
　production of, by region, 213, **215**
　regulations on the trade of, 216
　species of, 215
rivers. *See also* Chao Phraya River; Mekong River
　household use of water from, 63
　in the North, 12
　pollution of, 64, 345–46
roads
　in Bangkok, 314–16
　network of, 312–13
rock salt, 231
rubber, production of, 14, 216–17
rubies, 230, 231

—S—

salaries, distribution of, 44–47, **45**, **46**, **47**
samlors, 144–45
sapphires, 230, 231
satellite, 320
schools
　affiliation of, 55–56

schools (*continued*)
   attendance in, 50, **51**
   curriculum in, 55
   international, 336
   reasons for non-attendance in, 50, **52**
   in remote villages, 56
Securities and Exchange Commission, 212, 286, 288–89
securities companies. *See* brokers
securitization, 281
Segaller, Denis, 83
sewing machines, 60
shipping lines, 305–6
shoe polish and repair, 124
shoes, 121–24
shopping, 156, 355
shopping malls, 87, 156–57
Siam Cement Group, 251–52
silk, 73, 220, 239
slippers, 122, 123
slums, 297
Small Industry Credit Guarantee Corporation, 281
Small Industry Finance Corporation, 280
smile, function of, 18, 355
snacks, 108, 109
snakes, 129
sneakers, 122, 124
soccer, 72
Social Security Fund, 337–38
social work activities, 79, **80**
soft drinks, 110, 236
software, 321
Songkran, 69
sourcing products, 333–34
South, the, 14–15
   development plans for, 350–51

livestock in, 221
population of, 35
soybeans, 219
spices and seasonings, household expenses on, 105, **106**
sports
   interest in, by age group, 76, 77
   playing, 70–72, **71**
State Lottery Bureau, 70
State Railway of Thailand, 310, 311, 357
steel, production of, 252–53
stock exchange
   getting listed on the, 287
   history of the, 283
   securities turnover on the, 283, 284, **284**
   trading hours on the, 284–85
stock trading
   by brokers, 278–79
   monitoring patterns of, 286
   organization of, 284, 285
   regulations on, 286–87
storage, cost of, for supermarkets, 157
stores, chain, 157–58
stoves, 90, 134, 139
strokes, 37
sugar
   consumption of, 104
   production of, 217
sugar and sweets, household expenses on, 104, **104**
sugarcane, production of, 217–18
Sukhothai, 21
supermarkets, 157
superstitions, 29, 82–83, 151. *See also* animism
sweets, 105

—T—

tableware, 90, 137–38
tailoring, household expenses on, 121, **122**
takraw, 71
tapes, audio, 74, 77, 152, 351
tapioca, production of, 218
tattoos, 83
taxes, 341–43
　customs duties, 263, 331–32, 343
　income, 343
　revenue from, 342, **342**
　sales, 343
taxis
　in Bangkok, 316
　collective, 145
teak wood, 225
teenagers, leisure activities of, 76
telephone
　cellular, 319
　lines, 148, 318
Telephone Organization of Thailand, 317, 318
television
　composition of audience of, 168–69, **168**
　viewing, by occupation, 167, **167**
television, cable, 163, 165
television, satellite, 163, 166
television, terrestrial
　channels of, 162–64
　deregulation of, 164–65
　station owners and operators, 164
television programs, 163–64, 165, 166
　ratings of commentaries, 172, **174**
　ratings of entertainment programs, 170, **171**
　ratings of features, 172, **173**
　ratings of news, 170, **170**
　selecting, 169, **169**
television sets
　household expenses on, 153
　ownership of, 62, 63, 162, 166
textile and clothing, production of, 239–40
Thai Airways International Company, 308
Thai Customs Department, 356–57
Thai-Lao Friendship Bridge, 334
Thai National Banking Bureau, 268
Thai Rating and Information Services Company, 289
Thapanachai, Somporn, 359n. 15
Thon Buri, 23
tin, production of, 14–15, 229–30
tipping, 354
tobacco
　consumption of, 114
　production of, 219–20
tobacco products
　distribution and advertising of, 116, 205, 238
　household expenses on, 113, **113**
　manufacturing of, 237–38
toilets, availability of, 64–65, 67
tourism. *See also* visitors, foreign
　and AIDS, 39
　revenue from, 257
　in the South, 35
Tourism Authority of Thailand, 356

tours, 147, 258
trade unions, 339
trade, foreign, 5, 331–32. *See also* exports; imports
  evolution of, 260, **261**
  financial transactions for, 271
  history of, 22–23
  with Indochina, 334
  restrictions on, 262–63, 326, 332
trade, retail, 33
  changes in, 87–88
  convenience stores, 157–58
  department stores, 156
  door-to-door, 141, 158
  mail-order, 158
  shopping malls, 156–57
  supermarkets, 157
trade, wholesale, 333
trademark law, 353
traditions, 2
traffic. *See under* Bangkok
training. *See also under* workers
  programs, 53, **54**
  reasons for, 53, **53**
trains. *See* railroads
trams, 317
transportation
  household expenses on local, 144, **145**
  household expenses on regional, 146, **146**
  personal, 147–48
  public, 144–47
transportation and communications, household expenses on, 142, **143**
transshipment, 303, 304
Treaty of Amity and Economic Relations, 341
Treaty of Friendship and Commerce, 24–25

tuna, 224, 234

—U—

uniform
  for office use, 338–39
  for school, 121
urbanization, 33
utilities. *See also under specific names of utilities*
  availability of, 63–65
  household expenses on, 134–36, **135**

—V—

vaccines, 125
value-added tax, 343
vegetables
  household expenses on, 99–100, **101**
  processing of, 235
vehicles. *See also under specific vehicle names*
  household expenses on personal, 147, **148**
  household expenses on the operation of, 148, **149**
  inspection of, 247
  number of private, 245, **246**
  ownership of, 63, **64**
  production of, 244–48
  registered, composition of, 245, **245**
  suppliers of parts for, 247
videocassette recorders
  household expenses on, 153
  ownership of, 62, 167
villages, 29, 33
  leisure activities in, 74
visitors, foreign
  arrivals of, 257, **257**

visitors, foreign (*continued*)
   country of residence of, 258, **258**
   expenses of, 258, **259**
   length of stay of, 259, **260**

—W—

washing machines, 60
water, 63
   for agricultural and industrial uses, 256
   indoor plumbing, 63, 134
   pricing of, 257
   sources of drinking, 64, **66**, 110
   sources of non-drinking, 63, **65**, 134
water pumps, 134
water tanks, 134
wells, 134

Whiskey, 112, 237
wines, 112–13, 237
workers
   computer training of, 321
   education and skills of, 48
   occupations of, 41, **41**
   occupations of male and female, 42, **43**
   status of, 42, **44**
   training, 48, 52–53, 335–36
   unpaid family, 47
working hours, 338

—Y—

yogurt, 102

—Z—

zinc, production of, 230